Deza and Its Moriscos

Early Modern Cultural Studies

SERIES EDITORS

Carole Levin

Marguerite A. Tassi

Deza and Its Moriscos

Religion and Community in Early Modern Spain

PATRICK J. O'BANION

University of Nebraska Press | Lincoln

Library of Congress Cataloging-in-Publication Data
Names: O'Banion, Patrick J., 1975–author.
Title: Deza and its Moriscos: Religion and community
in early modern Spain / Patrick J. O'Banion.
Description: Lincoln, [NE]: University of Nebraska
Press, [2020] | Series: Early modern cultural studies |
Includes bibliographical references and index.
Identifiers: LCCN 2019037838
ISBN 9781496216724 (hardback)
ISBN 9781496221599 (epub)
ISBN 9781496221605 (mobi)
ISBN 9781496221612 (pdf)
Subjects: LCSH: Inquisition—Spain. | Moriscos—
Spain—History. | Spain—Church history.
Classification: LCC BX1735 .O23 2020 | DDC
3035.6/97094609031—dc23 LC record available at
https://lccn.loc.gov/2019037838

Set in Arno Pro by Mikala R. Kolander.

For Susan Vogt Benes

Contents

List of Illustrations ix

Acknowledgments xi

Editorial Notes xiii

Abbreviations and Conventions xv

Introduction 1

1. Town, Contours, and Kingdoms: Deza and Its People 19

2. Deza Divided: Bernardino Almanzorre's Story 39

3. Getting On With Their Lives: Alexo Gorgoz's Story 63

4. Seeking a Freer Land: Lope Guerrero's Story 81

5. The Guardians of Morisco Culture: María la Jarquina's Story 101

6. Favor and Fame: Román Ramírez el Menor's Story, Part 1 119

7. The Demons of Tajahuerce: Román Ramírez el Menor's Story, Part 2 141

8. The Better Law: Román Ramírez el Menor's Story, Part 3 161

9. Small-Town Dreams: Miguel García Serrano's Story 189

10. As Much Moors Now as Ever: Ana Guerrera's Story   207

11. Cleverer than His Father: Miguel Ramírez's Story   227

   Conclusion   247

   Notes   259

   Bibliography   337

   Index   351

Illustrations

MAPS

1. The Iberian Peninsula in the Early Modern Period   xvi
2. The Aragonese-Castilian Border near Deza   18
3. The Town of Deza, ca.1600   33

FIGURES

1. The Almanzorre-Almoravi Family   51
2. The Guerrero Family   86
3. The Ramírez Family   121
4. The Barnuevo Family   134
5. The Family of the Dukes of Medinaceli   221

Acknowledgments

I found Deza almost a decade and a half ago while doing research in Spain. Breaking from my usual archival patterns, I took the early bus one morning from Madrid to Cuenca, where Marcelino Angulo García provided access to the city's rich diocesan archive. While browsing the catalog I noted the surprising number of inquisitorial documents related to the town of Deza. I was entirely ignorant of the place. As happens, one thing led to another and I wound up writing this book about the people who lived in that town during the so-called Morisco century. Getting to know Deza—both the early modern and twenty-first-century versions—has been a great joy and I am grateful for the providential encounter.

This book would have been impossible to write without the support of archivists and librarians across Spain (and closer to home as well), perhaps none more so than Vicente Alejandre Alcalde, who rescued, organized, and cataloged Deza's own municipal archive. It is also unlikely that I ever would have found the time to complete this book without having been able to step back from a busy teaching schedule. I appreciate the generosity of the Reformation Studies Institute at the University of St Andrews, which awarded me a James K. Cameron Fellowship in the spring of 2013. Some years later a fellowship from the American Council of Learned Societies and a membership at the Institute for Advanced Studies (Princeton, New Jersey) allowed for an extended period of fruitful research and writing.

Over the years I received encouragement for the project and aid from many individuals, among them Gonzalo Díaz Migoyo, Clair Gilbert,

Fabien Montcher, Sabine Schmidtke, Jonathan Israel, Roberto Tottoli, Andrew Pettegree, Bridget Heal, Emily Michelson, Jan Machielsen, Jodi Bilinkoff, and Alison Weber. Damian Smith offered timely advice at a moment when discouragement threatened the project, and Lloyd Jackson saw, long before I did, that this needed to be a book about people. I deeply appreciate the generosity and friendship of Charles Parker. Our many long conversations led me down unexpected paths and caused me to frame questions in new ways that have, I hope, made this a better book; they certainly have made being a historian more enjoyable.

I have incurred many domestic debts as well, and I am aware of the irony involved in taking time away from my own family in order to study the intimate inner workings of a community of people who lived and died four centuries ago. Yet my wife and children have always stood with me in this work and, in both small and great ways, encouraged me to pursue my vocations. A deep and final word of gratitude goes to my mother, Susan Vogt Benes, whose love for Spain inspired my own.

Editorial Notes

NAMES

Early modern Dezanos, like their counterparts elsewhere in Spain, frequently recycled names over the generations and parents often named
sons after fathers and/or grandfathers. (It was not uncommon for daughters to share the name of their mothers or grandmothers but this causes
less confusion since the surnames of women changed over the generations.) To distinguish individuals across generations, they added suffixes—*el menor, el viejo, el mozo,* or *el más mozo.* Suffixes were subsequently
dropped, added, or amended as generations came and went. To avoid
confusion, names have been standardized in this book: Román Ramírez
el menor is never referred to as el viejo, even after the death of his father
and the birth of his son, both of whom were also named Román. Additionally, some Dezanos were distinguished by nicknames. For example,
neighbors knew Lope de Deza by at least two other names: Lope del Sol
and Pascual de la Pituerta—the former for unknown reasons; the latter
because his father was named Pascual and his wife was club footed—
pies tuertos. Íñigo de Hortubia was known as "the Soldier" (*el soldado*),
because he had been one and, although his son Juan followed a different
course, he nevertheless inherited the nickname.

CURRENCY

The basic exchange rates for early modern Spanish currency are, of course,
simple: 1 *real* = 34 *maravedis* (mrs.); 8 *reales* = 1 ducat = 1 Spanish *peso* (or
piece of eight). But describing the buying power of those currencies in
terms of their present value is notoriously difficult. Inflation calculators

offer one way of solving this problem, but early modern people had a very different experience with money than do the vast majority of this book's readers. Consequently, such calculators can be as misleading as they are helpful. The conversion to contemporary equivalents is made all the more treacherous because European prices shifted over time and varied by region. Spain, in particular, experienced wild price fluctuation and inflation (the so-called Price Revolution) during the sixteenth and seventeenth centuries and, even within Spain, different regions felt the effects of those economic trends differently.

Earl Hamilton's classic work *American Treasure and the Price Revolution in Spain, 1501–1650* provides helpful lists of prices and wages in late sixteenth-century Castile. While even this can only generally approximate how the inhabitants of Deza experienced shifts in the financial winds, it does provide meaningful points of reference. He notes that:

> A liter of wheat cost less than six mrs. in the early 1570s but was approaching nine by the end of the century.
> A liter of wine cost about eight mrs. in 1569 but jumped to over twenty mrs. in some years by the end of the century.
> A laborer earned, perhaps, two *reales* (or 68 mrs.) for a day's work in 1568, and wages, if they increased at all, tended to lag well behind rising prices.

INQUISITION SOURCES

Providing helpful citations for the many different types of inquisitorial sources used in this book has proved challenging. The files (*legajos*) that contain individual case files (*expedientes*) are rarely foliated, making it difficult to indicate specific locations within the document. In most cases, then, the most effective system has been to indicate the type of source (e.g., inquisitorial trial of María la Jarquina), followed by the section within the larger document (e.g., first audience of the accused) and the date (June 6, 1608). Fortunately, a handful of *expedientes* are foliated, including that of Román Ramírez el menor, which is one of the most frequently cited sources and examined at length in chapters 6–8. These documents are simply cited with reference to the folio number.

Abbreviations and Conventions

ADC   Archivo Diocesano de Cuenca
ADM   Archivo Ducal de Medinaceli (Toledo)
aft.   after
AGS   Archivo General de Simancas
AHDOS   Archivo Histórico Diocesano de Osma-Soria (El Burgo de Osma)
          APD   Archivo Parroquial de Deza
          LS   Libro Sacramental
AHMD   Archivo Histórico Municipal de Deza
AHN   Archivo Histórico Nacional (Madrid)
AHPS   Archivo Histórico Provincial de Soria
          AMD   Archivo Municipal de Deza
AHPZ   Archivo Histórico Provincial de Zaragoza
ARCV   Archivo de la Real Chancillería de Valladolid
          PC   Pleitos Civiles
          RE   Registros de Ejecutorios
          SH   Sala de Hijos de Algo
BCLM   Biblioteca de Castilla-La Mancha (Toledo)
bef.   before
BNE   Biblioteca Nacional de España (Madrid)
cap.   capítulo
doc.   documento
exp.   expediente
fol.   folio
leg.   legajo
mrs.   maravedis
RAH   Real Academia de la Historia (Madrid)
          SC   Colección Salazar y Castro

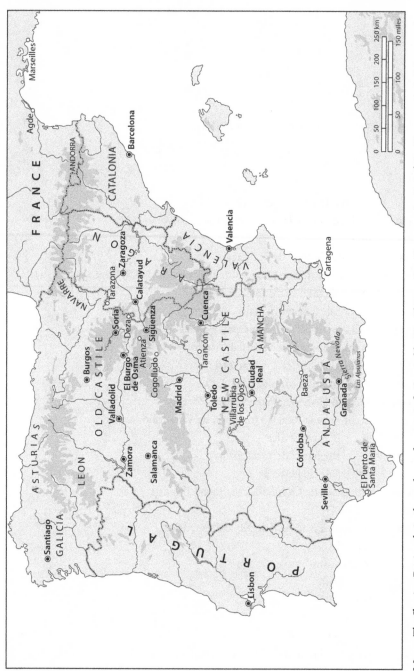

Map 1. The Iberian Peninsula in the early modern period. *Created by David Cox, Cox Cartographic Ltd. (Chadlington, Oxfordshire, UK).*

Introduction

The expulsion from Spain of the Moriscos—the baptized descendants of peninsular Muslims converted en masse and by order of the monarch early in the sixteenth century—was a large-scale event only in a secondary and, for most of those who lived through it, abstract sense. They knew about the royal decree, of course, and that efforts to implement it affected many thousands of people across the peninsula yet, primarily, they experienced all of this locally—in their hometowns, villages, and cities. It played out in distinct ways conditioned by the insular realities of daily life and left a rather different Spain in its wake—or rather multiple wakes. Understanding the specific contours of the communities in which Moriscos participated over the course of the sixteenth and early seventeenth centuries is, therefore, essential to understanding how and why the expulsions unfolded as they did. This point of departure differs significantly from the one historians have traditionally taken. Most scholars, even those sympathetic to the Moriscos' plight, have viewed the Expulsion (and note here the capital "E") as an episode of Spanish history initiated, directed, and more or less successfully conducted between 1609 and 1614 by King Philip III and his ministers with the support of (most of) the Council of State and significant portions of the Spanish ecclesiastical hierarchy.

Historiographically, the stakes here are high because the Expulsion has been the fulcrum of debate in Morisco studies. Supporters as well as opponents of the decision have principally made their case based on whether or not the Moriscos could have been (or perhaps had already been, or were in the process of being) assimilated to Spanish society and its brand of Catholicism.[1] Already in 1978, Carla Rahn Philips noted that "a thorough examination of the Morisco expulsion must move back into the sixteenth century and take account of the regional and local differences among the Morisco communities. If there was one central decision to expel the Moriscos, there were many separate expulsions, and their effects varied considerably."[2] For that reason Moriscos' behavior and beliefs over the entire course of the century come under scrutiny when assessing their relation to other Spaniards, the monarchy, and the church, for that assessment either justifies or condemns the decision to eject them from Spain.

Considering the history of the Moriscos and their expulsion from the perspective of kings, royal councilors, archbishops, and grand inquisitors is not necessarily wrong but stopping there obfuscates a more complicated reality. The experience of Moriscos in, for example, the Campo de Calatrava, differed dramatically from those who dwelt in Granada or Seville, who faced a different set of issues than those from Castilian cities hundreds of miles to the north like Ávila or Valladolid, let alone modest towns like Aragonese Burbáguena. We could go on ad nauseam, but the point is that these differences were not inconsequential. To offer just one obvious point of contrast: those living in the Kingdom of Granada experienced a pre-expulsion exile at the beginning of the 1570s. They were moved north into Castile following the suppression of the rising known as the Second Revolt of the Alpujarras. The history of, for example, the Moriscos in Murcia's Valle del Ricote between conversion and expulsion seem relatively uneventful by comparison.[3]

Yet, much of Morisco historiography casts the whole lot of them in monolithic terms. This approach has its roots in the anti-Morisco propagandists and expulsion apologists who justified their position by denying that any of the *conversos de moros* had undergone true conversions. They were regarded, explains Grace Magnier, as "congenitally incapable of change."[4] *Todos son uno*, explained their detractors.[5] Into the nineteenth and early twentieth century, Spanish historians like Pascual Boronat y Barrachina, Manuel Danvila y Collado, and Marcelino Menéndez y Pelayo contested that Spain's Moriscos were simply incapable of being integrated; rather, "their expulsion was overdue and justifiable for securing the unity and security of church and state."[6] Even modern scholars who are critical of this approach (myself included) often paint the Moriscos of Spain in a similarly broad-brush fashion, as if they were all of a piece (or, at best, as if three or perhaps four different types of Moriscos existed—Valencian, Aragonese, Granadino, and the rest), and speak of the Expulsion as though it affected all in an unmediated and identical way.

This assertion of monolithic homogeneity has resulted in both the depersonalization of Moriscos and their historiographical depiction as passive. Reflecting on the former point, Trevor Dadson comments, "It is rare when reading a standard history of the Moriscos to get any sense of the individuals involved."[7] We don't even know their names. The two most famous Moriscos are certainly the so-called Young Man (or *mancebo*) of Arévalo, who left behind a fascinating literary corpus, and the character Ricote from Miguel de Cervantes's *Don Quixote*. That one is known only by his alias and the other is fictitious drives the point home. Only recently have scholars begun to bring the lives and personalities of towering figures like Francisco Núñez de Muley and Miguel de Luna into focus.[8] Even so, these last two are outliers, albeit important ones—highly educated and socially elite Moriscos from Granada. Of those who lived elsewhere or in obscurity very little is known, and what is known is often communicated in tables, graphs, and lists that describe economic and demographic trends. All of it is of great value, of course, but loses focus on the people who lived through it all. Morisco historiography is frustratingly short on personality.

This depersonalization, combined with a focus on elites (who left behind better records) and impersonal historical forces, has led scholars to depict Moriscos as passive, disempowered, impoverished, and marginalized. If we don't know who they were, they couldn't have been doing much. This is particularly striking in the case of Castilian Moriscos, some of whom are at the heart of this study. When distinguished from their counterparts elsewhere in Spain or discussed at all, historians have regularly dismissed them as historical actors. For instance, John Elliott's classic study of early modern Spain suggests that,

Castilian Moriscos, unlike their Valencian brethren, were rootless and scattered; and where the Valencian Moriscos were largely agricultural labourers, those of Castile had drifted to the towns and taken up a wide variety of fairly menial occupations, as carriers, muleteers, and small craftsmen. Since they were so widely dispersed, they hardly represented a very serious danger, but they were disliked by many Old Christians for spending too little, working too hard, and breeding too fast.[9]

Although industrious, they were "neither wealthy nor economically enterprising members of the community."[10]

Similarly, Mercedes García-Arenal's study of Moriscos under the jurisdiction of the inquisitorial tribunal headquartered in Castilian Cuenca concludes that they occupied "the lowest strata of a peasantry and rural proletariat" and that "one encounters nothing in the documentation that might indicate the existence or the possibility of a middle class, let alone an aristocratic or leading group among the Morisco minority itself. One is dealing with a group that was practically headless and deprived of all possibility of development or social ascent."[11] John Lynch described them as a "poor minority of small traders and artisans."[12] And Luis García-Ballester insinuated that Castile only became important for Morisco history once the more interesting Granadinos showed up: "It is not that there were no Moriscos in Castile before 1570—the date of the Granadino diaspora—but they were in every case very small groups and incorporated into the mass of the population."[13]

Despite pathbreaking studies of Morisco communities by Serafín de Tapia Sánchez and Rafael Benítez Sánchez-Blanco, as well as the important synthetic work of Antonio Domínguez Ortiz and Bernard Vincent, in the 1980s and 1990s, it was in large part Trevor Dadson's research on Villarrubia de Los Ojos and the wider Campo de Calatrava at the beginning of the new millennium that trumpeted the significance of the local context for Morisco history.[14] In a significant set of comments, he noted, "In many ways, the accepted history of the Moriscos is like a house built the wrong way round, with roof put on before the foundations have been dug and the walls erected."[15] Noting the rarity of finding individual

Moriscos mentioned in the books about them, Dadson reminds us to keep in mind that they were "real people, living real lives, integrated into their local communities, well adapted to their environment, respected by their neighbours."[16] To do otherwise risks interpreting all of Morisco history in light of a few red-letter days. Henry Kamen makes the point effectively if in a slightly different context: "A historian whose perspective is dominated by Lepanto, or even more crucially by the expulsions of 1609, may tend to look backward and see only the clouds of a gathering storm."[17] But the storm is only part of the story.

Dadson's study of Villarrubia is a case in point. By mining archives and engaging diverse archival sources, he discovered not only a group of strikingly assimilated Moriscos but also a local community in which bonds between Moriscos and Old Christians remained intact. Thanks to that cohesion and the support of the town's seignior, Villarrubianos effectively resisted the efforts of the king, the Duke of Lerma, and the Count of Salazar, who was responsible for carrying out the royal edict. Even Moriscos who were expelled found their way back home and, in the decades that followed, reestablished ownership of lost property. In other words, with its assimilated Moriscos and failed expulsion, Villarrubia challenged a great deal of what historians thought they knew.

If Dadson provides an important point of departure for this study of the Castilian town of Deza, it should be noted at the outset that Deza was no Villarrubia de Los Ojos, which parallels Deza no more closely than do the older depictions of Castilian Moriscos referenced above. To be sure, at the level of politics, economics, religious practice, social relations, and so forth, Moriscos in both Deza and Villarrubia proved remarkably active and, in both cases, became deeply integrated into the life of the whole community. Moreover, the Dezanos accumulated wealth and power (both formal and informal) and, like the Villarrubianos, negotiated alliances and patronage relationships with those more wealthy and powerful than they, especially their seignior. But when the Count of Salazar came to Deza none of the local Old Christians intervened in order to halt the expulsion of their neighbors. Thereafter, a mere handful of Moriscos remained in town, and none of the exiles returned.

This outcome raises a new question. Given the similarities between the two towns, why were there differences? Rather than finding common cause and crafting a communal identity, Deza's population found itself divided between Old Christians and Moriscos. In other words, there was a failure of neighborliness. But why? And who is to blame? Both sides bear some responsibility for this breakdown of trust—the Moriscos were deceptive in religion and untrustworthy in politics; the Old Christians acted out of bigotry, suspicion, fear, and animosity. And the interventions of external figures and institutions—the Moriscos of Aragon, the Holy Office, the local bishop, even the dukes of Medinaceli—aggravated those divisions.

By the 1590s Villarrubia's Moriscos had "chosen the road of assimilation" and "were not going to abandon it now," especially when they observed the Inquisition launch a ferocious assault against the Granadinos who had recently been settled in their midst.[18] No Granadinos were exiled to Deza, and when the inquisitorial hammer fell in the early seventeenth century, it fell on a Morisco community drifting toward Islam, not away from it. The town's lack of cohesion produced a community too weak to withstand both external pressures and the internal strains of disputes and suspicion. Instead it fractured along geographical, religious, and ethnic lines—all of which divided the Moriscos from their Old Christian neighbors.

Digging deeper for the source of this failure of neighborliness leads to several specific events that arose out of the local context and loomed large. These include the infamous condemnation of one Dezano as a crypto-Muslim diabolist who sought the overthrow of Christian Spain, the collapse of a political alliance among the entire citizenry and, in 1607, both the untimely death of the Moriscos' patron Duke Juan de la Cerda and a vigorous inquisitorial assault, which was itself initiated as a consequence of internal civic disputes. Despite their determination and creative use of law courts, governmental bureaucracy, noble patronage, and their position in local politics and town affairs, Deza's Moriscos eventually lost the fight for their home. The actions and choices of individuals interacting with local realities; with wider geographic, social, economic, and political developments; as well as with people and institutions beyond the town walls combined to create a specific context within which Deza's expulsion played out.

Thus, Villarrubia cannot serve as a new model for the narrative history of the Moriscos, not even merely those of Castile.[19] Instead, in order to build the house right way round, we need to grasp the diversity of the Morisco experience so that we can make sense of the various patterns that emerge. Deza offers only one such pattern, albeit one of strategic importance that caught the attention of the crown, episcopacy, and Inquisition. If local study of Moriscos promises profitable yields, studying those communities is easier said than done, and trying to bring individual Moriscos into historical focus offers a real challenge, for the archival sources that allow for a granular approach remain difficult to access and time-consuming to evaluate.

One important source for Morisco history—one that is both tantalizing and treacherous—are the records of Spain's Holy Office of the Inquisition. For Deza, these sources are particularly rich. Some documents have been lost or destroyed, so a complete tally is impossible, but certainly inquisitorial representatives operating under the authority of the tribunal at Cuenca examined or pursued more than three hundred of Deza's Moriscos between 1523 and 1611. Many of these evolved into full-fledged trials; others were abandoned for (among other reasons) lack of evidence; still others were abbreviated trials related to an Edict of Grace granted to Deza's Moriscos in 1570, which allowed them to avoid arrest and most punishments by making preemptive confessions. In addition to the many trials and potential trials, each of which contains its own complicated series of documents—sometimes running to several hundred folio pages—inquisitorial archives also contain records of visitations to Deza and its environs, notebooks, administrative documents, and correspondence between local agents, the regional tribunal, and the Supreme and General Council of the Inquisition (*Suprema*) in Madrid.

Much of the most detailed and, frankly, colorful information about Deza's Moriscos comes from these sources—and not merely about their religious activities. They offer valuable glimpses into the complexities of daily and private life, social relations, economic transactions, material culture, and the emotional and physical states of individuals. But inquisitorial documents, especially trial records (*procesos*), are notoriously troublesome. One scholar memorably commented that "building a picture of rural Catholicism from [inquisitorial] archives would be like trying to get a sense of everyday American political life from FBI files."[20] Point taken, but is it so hard to believe that four centuries from now even FBI files might offer valuable information to historians of twentieth-century American political life? Certainly from this distance, and given the limited sources otherwise available, the records of the Holy Office are an invaluable resource for studying the lives of early modern Spaniards. The richly detailed glimpses of life recorded in procesos should not be dismissed precipitously.

Instead, inquisitorial documents, especially trial records, need to be read carefully, comparatively, against the grain, and alongside other contemporary sources, especially other types of archival materials. For Deza, this has meant reading through not just individual procesos of particular interest but all of them along with any related documents, coordinating the various data they contain. This includes tens of thousands of folio pages spanning a period of just over a century—from the first decade of the 1500s when the Holy Office investigated Deza's Jewish New Christians until 1616 when it passed through town while conducting a regional visitation. The chronological scope of these documents and the large pool of individual but interconnected trials means that they can be compared in meaningful ways and to profitable ends. For example, the same event may be described by multiple witnesses within a single trial or even multiple trials. These accounts can be critically examined. Moreover, since inquisitors often assumed that heresy spread among relatives, it was common for many members of the same family to be investigated. In Deza it was not unusual for three or even four generations of a family to have firsthand encounters with the Holy Office. Records provide not just a snapshot of life but rather a vivid catalog of images depicting change over time.

Furthermore, the information contained in inquisitorial sources does not bear merely on the (suspected) Islamic activities of the accused. Although inquisitors were primarily interested in reconciling heretics to the church, their records offer a bonanza of details about genealogical ties, social interactions, material and folk culture, the use of space, education, gender relations, and much more. For example, scholars have profitably mined the proceso of one of Deza's most remarkable native sons for information about early modern medical practices, oral performances, and the magical arts.[21] That is to say, one way that historians can profitably use these sources is by asking questions of them that differ from the ones that drove inquisitors, or by asking the same questions inquisitors did but getting to the answers by analyzing the evidence in different ways.

Inquisitorial sources are crucial for studying the Moriscos of Deza and, despite their inherent difficulties, often supply critical information to the overall narrative. Yet they are only one thread in a much larger tapestry. Students of Deza's history are fortunate not only to have the inquisitorial section of the Archivo Diocesano de Cuenca but also to be able to compare its documents with those in other archival collections. Notably, the town's municipal records survive largely intact in its own Archivo Municipal and in the Archivo Histórico Provincial de Soria. The Archivo Ducal de Medinaceli details interactions between the townsfolk and their seigniors over the centuries. Deza's parish archive and its sacramental books, which proved invaluable for establishing chronology and genealogies, have been incorporated into the episcopal archive in El Burgo de Osma. Like many early modern Spaniards, the Dezanos were a litigious lot and left their mark in the records of the Royal Appellate Court of Valladolid. To this list can be added Zaragoza's Archivo Histórico Provincial, the Archivo Histórico Nacional and Real Academia de la Historia in Madrid, and the Archivo General in Simancas. By coordinating episcopal, seigniorial, municipal, legal, royal, and private archives it has frequently been possible to substantiate, controvert, or shed additional light on details that appear in inquisitorial records as well as to get a broader perspective on the lay of the historical land.

Take, for example, the witness who claimed that Román Ramírez el menor, one of Deza's Moriscos, had told him that he and his grandfather used the incantation *bon y varón* to ride a horse fifteen leagues in an instant to Zaragoza and then, having concluded their business in town, magically returned home in the same fashion.[22] The witness indicated that he found the story preposterous, and Ramírez agreed. Standing before an inquisitor in 1599, he denied outright having ever made the claim, although he did recall a Franciscan from Medinaceli mentioning, some fourteen or fifteen years previously, a friend in Rome who knew of a similar incantation.[23]

What are we to do with this, besides simply dismissing it? How can we even begin to untangle who said what to whom and when and what it might matter? The story of the flying horse, for all of its specific implausibility, is characteristic of the frustrating complexity involved in piecing together the past using sources that contain deliberate obfuscations, scandalous rumors, and faded memories intermixed with more judicious accounts. While certainty about the past is always elusive, despair is not the way forward. Instead of allowing episodes like this one to produce narrative incoherency, various strategies can move us toward likely, if always tentative, interpretations. In this case, if we avoid being distracted by the outlandish and focus upon the long history of the relationships involved, we can make some progress.

The witness who testified about the magic steed before inquisitorial agents, an Old Christian named Licentiate Bernardino Bonifacio (ca. 1567–aft. 1629), was a longtime acquaintance of Ramírez. They had eaten and traveled together many times, and Bonifacio, at least, framed their relationship in terms of cordiality, if not outright friendship. In a statement before the Holy Office, he emphasized Ramírez's above average Christian devotion (for a Morisco) and his successes as an herbalist healer. Bonifacio also indicated that, in conversation, Ramírez had denied a rumor that he had inherited a familiar spirit from his grandfather. This too would appear to be a point in the Morisco's favor.

Yet, the Licentiate, a lawyer (*abogado*) in Soria, was the grandson of Domingo Diez de Soria, whose son (Bonifacio's father?) Ramírez had assaulted in the 1560s.[24] Bonifacio was also the son-in-law of Pedro de Barnuevo, Deza's castellan (*alcaide*) and chief magistrate (*alcalde mayor*) between 1584 and 1595.[25] Barnuevo and Ramírez had a rocky relationship that came to a head in 1592 while the latter was serving on the town council. They ended up *mano a mano*, and Ramírez was subsequently arrested and transported to Medinaceli, where the matter was set before the duke.[26] He was soon released even though, as Bonifacio told the Inquisition, a case investigating Ramírez's medical practices was still pending in the ducal court.[27] What Bonifacio did not mention was that, although his father-in-law continued to play an active role in town politics, Barnuevo had already fallen from seigniorial favor.[28] Within a few months of this testimony, the duke relieved him of his offices and replaced him.

Working only with the proceso, L. P. Harvey suggested, "Román cited [Bonifacio], as he was entitled to do by Inquisition procedure, as an enemy, and so as a possible hostile witness." Yet Harvey contended that Bonifacio was "not significantly more hostile than many others who gave testimony," was "in all likelihood telling the unvarnished truth," and at least some of what he said "counted in Román's favour."[29] This excursus into their family history, however, suggests that the Morisco knew what he was doing when he named the Licentiate as his enemy. While Bonifacio's testimony made few direct charges against Ramírez, he introduced into the record several matters that became central to the inquisitorial case.[30] It also turns out that Bonifacio kept company with several other men who harbored similarly deep animosity for Ramírez and who played key roles in his inquisitorial denunciation in fall 1595. Thus, a surprising amount of local context lies behind Licentiate Bonifacio's casual mention and flippant dismissal of *bon y varón*. While his testimony appears to offer positive statements about the accused, the relational context indicates that he acted out of animosity.

Of course inquisitors made all sorts of presumptions about the guilt of Deza's Moriscos, and we dare not simply accept their conclusions at face value. They may well have been wrong to believe that specific individuals were crypto-Muslims and, contrariwise, they may have erred in determining others to have been faithful Christians. Nevertheless, using such sources to piece together the lives of townsfolk sheds light on their beliefs and practices. Placing them within a specific context and tracking their actions and interactions over time makes clear that Deza's Moriscos were hardly monolithic; they were a diverse lot. The same approach also demonstrates the limits to their diversity, for while everyone was different in some ways no one was completely unlike his or her neighbors.

We cannot know for certain what was going on in the heart or mind of any one of the Moriscos at any given moment. Yet, despite my initial expectations, I have grown increasingly convinced that many of Deza's Moriscos were to a greater or lesser extent crypto-Muslims. They did not merely hold onto certain cultural elements of their Islamic past such as songs or dances or foodways, which may or may not have been religiously significant to those who partook. Nor did they merely act out of ignorance about the differences between Christianity and Islam. Rather, in spite of their baptisms and continued participation in the rites and rituals of Christianity, many wanted to be and regarded themselves as Muslims. Evidential ground zero for this claim is their ownership of Islamic texts, the widespread ability to recite Islamic prayers, and knowledge of how to perform Islamic rituals. Beyond this are the vast number of actions and statements attested by multiple witnesses (both Morisco and Old Christian, allies and enemies) that can often be comparatively assessed with one another. I have found the cumulative effect of it all to be both overwhelming and compelling.

But if many of Deza's Moriscos held to Islamic beliefs and performed Islamic rituals, this claim must be nuanced, for their religious identity was often in motion. At times, especially perhaps in the 1570s and 1580s, we can locate only a small core of active practitioners. At other times, in the 1560s, the late 1590s, and the first decade of the seventeenth century, Islamic activity became more pronounced. Note that at this point I speak in terms of activity and practice, since many *moriscos dezanos* tried to guard their true (Islamic) convictions in their hearts while performing Christianity with their bodies.[31] Yet the wise, old dictum *lex orandi, lex credendi* suggests that the way people pray (that is, the external form of religiosity) shapes their beliefs over time. And Deza's crypto-Muslims frequently alluded to the discomfort they experienced on account of divorcing their beliefs from their actions. They longed for heart and body to be integrated, and when opportunity presented itself they broke out of the constraints imposed upon them by Catholic Spain. Their bodies mattered to them.

When Román Ramírez told inquisitors that, for nearly two decades of his adult life, he "performed not a single Moorish ceremony," even though "his heart always inclined toward being a Moor" and that "he vacillated within himself over which was the better law, that of the Moors or the Christians and in which he would be saved," we need not read this as a ham-fisted effort to convince them that he was innocent.[32] Ramírez, a veteran and renowned teller of tales, knew what he was doing. He was not claiming innocence but rather offering a plausible description of what it felt like to juggle competing claims to religious identity. Note that his statement reflects entirely upon the internal conflict he experienced without reference to any external activities. Inquisitors had no evidence that he had taken part in Islamic rituals; he offered none. Yet he could speak movingly about his heart, something otherwise inaccessible to them. For my part, I find it entirely plausible that Dezanos like Ramírez gravitated toward Christianity at times but sometimes found Islam the more compelling option.

While the Moriscos of Villarrubia followed a trajectory of assimilation that was accelerated by the arrival of Granadinos in the Campo de Calatrava, Deza's dynamic was different. At times the town's Moriscos appear to have been moving toward assimilation, and they formed a solid alliance with their Old Christian neighbors in the last third of the sixteenth century. But they seem never to have resolved the conflict between the intentions of the heart and external practices. Instead, the disjuncture was aggravated by frequent interaction with the Morisco communities in the region around the Aragonese frontier. They reminded the Dezanos of their shared Islamic heritage and emphasized their distinctiveness. That same process of differentiation was reinforced from the opposite direction by the efforts of the episcopacy and, especially, the Inquisition, which frequently reinforced the idea that Moriscos and Old Christians were essentially dissimilar. Whether Villarrubia, Deza, or some other local model was more typical of the Morisco experience in Castile and elsewhere remains as yet unclear. More work has to be done in building that house the right way round.

This book attempts to recover something of the lost lives of Deza's Moriscos, so it emphasizes the complexity of individual personalities and relationships. Each chapter is framed around a specific individual and uses his or her life as a window onto the larger story of the Moriscos and their interactions with one another, other townsfolk, and outsiders with the goal of providing a coherent narrative from conversion to expulsion. The partial exception to this rule is the first chapter, which focuses on the town of Deza itself. It surveys the town's medieval history, geography, and demography, its social and political order, and its ties to external authorities and institutions—episcopal, inquisitorial, seigniorial, legal, and royal. Yet, even here, it may be helpful to think of the town as another character in the story, one that changed over time and that shaped and was shaped by those living within its walls.

Chapter 2 focuses on the life of Bernardino Almanzorre, the great-grandson of Deza's pre-conversion Islamic religious instructor (*alfaquí*), and his efforts to fortify the town's crypto-Muslims by strengthening their ties to the more knowledgeable Moriscos of nearby Aragon. These efforts not only provoked conflict between Moriscos and Old Christians but also between various groups within the larger Morisco community. In 1569 these tensions came to a head when a regional inquisitorial visitation revealed the extent to which Islam had been reestablished in town. Many of the ringleaders were arrested and confined to galley service or executed, causing local Islamic activities to retreat further underground or cease all together.

In the wake of the 1569 visitation and the 1570–71 Edict of Grace that followed, Deza's Moriscos developed three distinct strategies for getting on with their lives. Chapter 3 describes the efforts of those who attempted to separate their internal convictions from outward religious observance. Rather than risk being arrested as relapsed heretics, subject to the harshest penalties, many of Deza's Moriscos opted to dissimulate and conform outwardly to Christianity. Among others, Alexo Gorgoz, a wealthy Morisco leader, pioneered a strategy that responded to the pressure placed upon Deza's Moriscos to become good Christians by conforming.

Others, however, saw Gorgoz's approach as a failure to live as a faithful Muslim and, instead, attempted to enact their Islamic identity by seeking temporary safe haven outside of town and away from prying eyes. Muleteers, for example, played an important economic role by transporting goods across Iberia, but their itinerancy also allowed them to follow their consciences in matters of religion and to reestablish ties with the crypto-Muslim communities of the Aragonese-Castilian frontier and beyond. Lope Guerrero, the focus of chapter 4, took advantage of opportunities both abroad and closer to home to convert his crypto-Islamic convictions into actions. Yet even those who followed this course continued to long for a better land where they could freely practice Islam.

Moriscas can claim a relatively minor position in the relevant historiography, in part because even fewer sources describe their activities than their male counterparts, and yet evidence suggests that they played a key role in the communal life of Spain's secret Muslims. Chapter 5 considers Deza's crypto-Islamic women, who guarded religious knowledge and passed it on to their children, other women, and sometimes even to men. An active group of older Moriscas, prominent among them María la Jarquina, presided over rituals and ceremonies that occurred during pivotal moments of community life—births, marriages, illnesses, and deaths. This domestication of religiosity in the hands of Moriscas not only safeguarded and incubated crypto-Islam in Deza during years of intense scrutiny but also facilitated the restoration of its more communal elements as the sixteenth century drew to a close.

Chapters 6–8 focus the narrative on the most infamous of early modern Dezanos, Román Ramírez el menor, whom the Holy Office tried in 1599 and posthumously condemned as a relapsed Muslim heretic, diabolist, and enemy of Christian Spain. His complex and contested life and death became a major catalyst for the deterioration of relations between Deza's Moriscos and Old Christians. Chapter 6 considers Ramírez's rise to prominence as a master storyteller and healer. These activities drew him into the orbit of powerful nobles, government officials, some of the wealthiest men in Spain, and even King Philip II. His celebrity also brought him into contact with Deza's seignior, the Duke of Medinaceli, who became the Morisco's patron.

As a member of the town faction that owed its loyalty to the duke, Ramírez became a contentious figure in local politics. He opposed, sometimes violently, those whose agenda favored the town. Chapter 7 describes how his successful healing of a woman plagued by a bizarre malady provided Ramírez's enemies with fodder for an arrest on trumped-up charges of diabolism. His transportation to the inquisitorial jails of Cuenca precipitated a major crisis, for the Morisco's greatest secret was not that he kept a demonic familiar but that he had taken on the role of alfaquí in Deza. If enough leverage could be brought to bear, he might reveal the identity of the town's crypto-Muslims and describe the Islamic networks operating throughout the region.

Ramírez's own inquisitorial trial comes into focus in chapter 8. Over the course of several months in 1599, and despite deteriorating health, Ramírez the veteran performer wove a narrative in which he cast himself as a repentant former diabolist, rather than a crypto-Muslim, and as an illiterate simpleton, rather than a well-read (if informally educated) alfaquí. His strategy diverted the inquisitors' attention from Deza's Morisco community and he died before the instruments of torture could be brought to bear. But Ramírez's death did not save his reputation and, in an astonishing moment of staged political theater, his bones and effigy were posthumously consigned to the flames at a celebrated auto de fé in Toledo that shaped royal policy and paved the way for the expulsion decree.

While Ramírez was meeting his end, back in Deza Old Christians and Moriscos had joined forces to pursue a high-profile legal case to limit seigniorial privileges in town. When the latter group withdrew unilaterally and unexpectedly, a faction of Old Christians led by Miguel García Serrano, the subject of chapter 9, determined that the Moriscos (and the duke as well) had finally revealed themselves as the town's dangerous enemies. The result was violence and armed riots on the streets of Deza. Further efforts to bar Moriscos from holding civic office led to a new series of legal battles, which eventually came before the Royal Appellate Court. In that venue the Moriscos secured a stunning victory. Stymied in the secular courts, Old Christians opened up a second front to the attack by denouncing their neighbors to the Holy Office.

One of those denounced was Ana Guerrera, a twelve-year old Morisca, whose arrest in July 1607 triggered a final inquisitorial onslaught in Deza. Chapter 10 describes the efforts of the girl's family, friends, and community to secure her release and protect the town against further investigations. They failed, and perhaps a fifth of all the town's Moriscos were subsequently transported to the inquisitorial jails of Cuenca or fled abroad to avoid capture. The arrests converged with news of the royal expulsion decree, for which the remaining Moriscos in Deza sought remedy. But absent the protection of noble patrons or the support of Old Christian neighbors, their efforts proved fruitless and the expulsion was carried out in town on July 8, 1611.

Even after the expulsion, however, dozens of Dezanos languished in inquisitorial custody, among them Miguel Ramírez, the son of Román and heir to his father's role as Deza's alfaquí. Chapter 11 describes the efforts of a group of Moriscos condemned to the royal galleys to gain their freedom. By cunningly pitting the interests of the Royal Council and the Suprema against those of regional inquisitorial agents, Miguel and three others avoided the galleys and secured their release along with orders to follow the rest of their nation into exile. Although the documentary evidence of the *moriscos dezanos* comes to an abrupt end here, their legacy continues, especially in the appropriation of the memory of Román Ramírez in the seventeenth century and beyond.

As this overview suggests, this book engages the history of the Moriscos by viewing it primarily as a matter of local history. Yet, what follows is not intended to be a work of antiquarianism but rather part of an ongoing scholarly discussion about how best to understand the various Morisco communities and their place within the larger Spanish world. The words, actions, and ends of those who lived in Deza had a direct and meaningful impact on Spanish monarchs, nobles, and high ecclesiastical officeholders as they grappled with the so-called *problema morisco*, which occupied so many minds in the sixteenth and early seventeenth centuries. The experience of the Dezanos also tells us a great deal about how Moriscos and Old Christians interacted with one another. Above all, however, the goal is to recover some part of the lives of those whose worth and dignity (along with their counterparts elsewhere) were dismissed in the early modern period and who, even today, remain mysterious and largely forgotten.

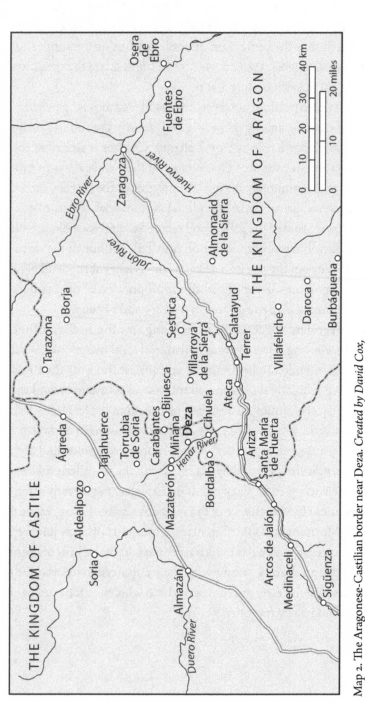

Map 2. The Aragonese-Castilian border near Deza. *Created by David Cox,*
Cox Cartographic Ltd. (Chadlington, Oxfordshire, UK).

1

Town, Contours, and Kingdoms

Deza and Its People

The small Castilian town of Deza is located in the Henar Valley, set against the Sierra de Miñana mountain range. The hilly terrain is characteristic of Aragon (just a few miles away) rather than inland Castile with its mesas and plateaus. At nearly three thousand feet above sea level Deza is one of the lowest lying towns in the region. From its headwaters south of Gómara, the Henar River flows southeasterly just to the west of town toward its confluence with the Jalón about fourteen miles downstream. A pair of springs northwest of town form the Argadil, a creek that flows into Deza. In the sixteenth and seventeenth centuries it powered mills, provided drinking water, and removed waste. The waters nourished the land, which produced wheat, barley, and oats; hemp and flax; saffron, grapes, melons, cherries, cabbage, garlic, garbanzos, and string beans. Sheep, goats, and pigs grazed, and the hinterland was rich with game, but the ground produced little of value beside clay and ochre.

Two Royal Roads framed the town. The first, an alternate route for the thoroughfare that connected Toledo to Zaragoza, was rougher and less frequently traveled than the main artery. It passed south of Deza, through Sigüenza and Medinaceli in Castile, on its way to Calatayud in Aragon. The second ran north of town and joined Madrid to Pamplona, then wound through the Pyrenees via Roncesvalles on its way to France. Other regionally significant byways bisected the town connecting Ariza to Borja (and on to Catalonia), Calatayud to Almazán, and Ateca to Soria.[1]

Deza also reflected the peculiar political geography of the Iberian Middle Ages. Muslim conquerors had pushed northward from Africa in the eighth century and, in 714, the Henar Valley fell under the control of the Berber Banu Mada. Between the late eighth and mid-ninth century, they founded Deza as part of a system of towers and castles that comprised a defensive and communications network. Positioned on the frontier between the so-called Upper and Middle Marches—Deza belonged to the latter—the network formed along a triangle of frontier cities: Medinaceli, Ágreda, and Calatayud.[2] Early in the eleventh century, the town passed into the possession of the *taifa* of Zaragoza and around 1120 King Alfonso I, known as the Battler (r. 1104–34), claimed Deza for Christendom and Aragon. But kingdoms continued to coalesce, shift, and stabilize into the late fifteenth century and by 1136, if not before, Deza came under Castilian control despite being surrounded on three sides by Aragon—two Christian realms with distinct traditions, legal systems, and political settlements.[3]

Between the thirteenth and fifteenth centuries, Deza frequently participated in dynastic conflicts within and between Castile and Aragon. It played a part in the War of the Two Peters (1356–66).[4] And in the 1360s, while much of Soria declared for the upstart Enrique II of Castile, first of the Trastámaras, Deza probably remained loyal to Pedro I (d. 1369).[5] In 1429, King Alfonso V of Aragon entered Castile, conquered Deza, sacked it, and took the entire population—*asi cristianos como moros*—captive. According to the royal chronicler, the Christians were soon freed so long as they did not return to Deza; the Muslims he purportedly sold into slavery.[6] By the fifteenth century, powerful kingdoms having defeated and swallowed up weaker ones, three major players remained: Portugal in the west looking toward Africa and the Atlantic; an ambitious Castile dominating the northwest and center; and the Crown of Aragon in the east and northeast with its Mediterranean empire. To the south lay the faltering Kingdom of Granada, the last of the Muslim dominions in Iberia, which finally surrendered to the Catholic Monarchs in January 1492.

Deza's military importance declined significantly when the future King Ferdinand of Aragon married the future Queen Isabella of Castile in 1469, but the town's frontier position left it bound to the people and economy of both kingdoms. It became an official inland customs post or dry port (*puerto seco*) where goods could be legally transported across the border, registered, and taxed. Many Dezanos, especially Moriscos, were active in trade around the region, and others worked as muleteers (*arrieros* or *trajineros*), packing goods across the peninsula. They married into, visited with, and farmed their children out to families in both kingdoms. They frequently received visitors from Aragon and enjoyed reciprocal hospitality. So, despite its isolation, the political geography of Deza placed it at the intersection of two related but distinct societies and, during the sixteenth century, in large part because of its frontier mentality, Deza's small *republica* drew upon this dual heritage.

The general demographic trend during the late Middle Ages was slow growth through the fifteenth century, which accelerated in the sixteenth century before slowing again in the seventeenth. The town's medieval population was somewhere around five hundred to six hundred inhabitants in approximately one hundred and twenty-five households.[7] By 1530 the town boasted one hundred and ninety-five taxpaying householders (*vecinos pecheros*), which corresponded to a slightly larger number of total households since some citizens were exempt from paying taxes. A reasonable estimate is two hundred to two hundred and ten households and some eight to nine hundred inhabitants. In the mid to late sixteenth century Deza experienced striking population growth, virtually doubling by 1591 to include three hundred and ninety households—three hundred and seventy *vecinos pecheros*, a dozen *hidalgos*, and eight male religious.[8] In 1606 the pecheros numbered three hundred and fifty-nine and the hidalgos twenty-one, suggesting that the population had leveled off at about sixteen hundred residents.[9] In addition, some individuals and families lived in Deza without citizenship—visiting relatives, traveling merchants, migrant or itinerant laborers, Aragonese who had settled in Deza but without formal permission, representatives of the town's duke—perhaps another hundred at any given time.

As in much of Spain three religions had been practiced in late medieval Deza—Christianity, Judaism, and Islam. Perhaps ten percent of the town was Jewish, but after Judaism was proscribed in 1492 they had to choose between conversion and expulsion.[10] No evidence reveals how many of Deza's Jews remained in town, but many who did were wealthy, socially influential, or both.[11] During the sixteenth century many of them entered the ranks of the gentry as Old Christians. Many more Muslims than Jews lived in late-medieval Deza, which boasted perhaps the second-largest community (after Ágreda) of practicing Muslims living under Christian dominion (or *mudéjares*) in the diocese of Sigüenza.[12] Tax records indicate that in 1495 there were forty-seven Mudéjar households in Deza, suggesting a community of around two hundred members.[13]

The 1492 Treaty of Granada granted Muslims religious tolerance but, in 1502, subsequent to a rising of Granadan Mudéjares, the situation changed. Like the Jews in 1492, Castile's Muslims were now given a choice between baptism and exile. A handful of Deza's Muslims had converted prior to 1502 and a small number, refusing baptism, emigrated to Aragon.[14] But most remained in town as New Moorish Converts (*nuevos conversos de moros* or *moriscos*) and, consequently, the royal decree of 1502 opened the way for growth. The Morisco population increased during the century and did so at a pace that outstripped the Old Christians, some of whom began to fret at the fecundity and local influence of New Christians.[15] By 1594 Deza's Moriscos were a thriving community of one hundred and twelve households.

It was no metropolis but, on a per capita basis, Deza could claim the densest population of converted Muslims anywhere in the Castilian provinces of Cuenca, Toledo, Ciudad Real, Guadalajara, and Soria. Here Deza followed the pattern of Aragon, where Moriscos comprised about one-fifth of the population, rather than Castile where they tended to be more dispersed amongst Old Christian populations. In Aragon (and Deza), Moriscos also frequently lived and worked alongside Old Christians. Forced to convert or leave in 1526, a generation after their Castilian counterparts, Aragonese Moriscos retained many elements of their religious and cultural heritage. Yet, they generally assimilated, at least to the point of adopting Christian names, giving up traditional garb, using the Christian calendar, baptizing their children, and abandoning Arabic. In the Kingdom of Valencia, by contrast, Moriscos, who comprised about one-third of the population, often lived apart from

Old Christians in villages on the lands of great nobles where they continued to use Arabic.

When discussing the domains of Castilian monarchs, historians sometimes speak broadly of two groups of Moriscos. In the Andalusian south, a dense population of *moriscos granadinos* maintained Muslim traditions and identity largely intact while the smaller enclaves further north began to lose touch with their Islamic past.[16] But the War (or sometimes Rebellion) of the Alpujarras, which saw Granadinos respond to aggressive Christianization efforts by rising up in the late 1560s, marked a watershed. After the revolt was subdued the government exiled most of the region's surviving Moriscos into Castile proper. Rather than diffusing rebelliousness and heresy, newly arrived Granadinos (or *moriscos nuevos* as they were often known) became influencers, teaching the Moriscos of Castile (*moriscos antiguos*) amongst whom they settled the ceremonies, prayers, and pillars of the faith.

More recently, Dadson's work on the Moriscos of Villarrubia and the Campo de Calatrava has complicated this dichotomy with its picture of a largely assimilated community of Antiguos whose ties to their Old Christian neighbors was stronger than any temptation to return to Islam offered by the Granadino exiles. Villarrubia's Antiguos lost their local alfaquí at the beginning of the century and, with him, a sense of Islamic identity. The appearance of the Granadinos in March 1571 emphasized how much they had in common with the town's Old Christians. This drove them toward even greater assimilation, seen especially in the Moriscos' 1577 petition asking the king to confirm a 1502 privilege that recognized their parity with the town's Old Christians.[17] Ultimately, the communal bond in Villarrubia proved so strong that Old Christians, Moriscos, local priests, the municipal council, and the town's seignior collaborated to defend the town's Antiguos against expulsion.

Deza's experience was different. Because it was relatively northerly and authorities already viewed the town's dense indigenous Morisco community with suspicion, no Granadinos were settled there. Instead, Deza's lifeline to the Islamic world came from the east. Although Castilian, Deza's Moriscos interacted with and learned about Islam primarily from their Aragonese cousins. As a result, Deza's Morisco community acquired a sharp Islamic edge and became a source of concern for various Christian authorities in Spain, especially as Islamic belief and practice were transmitted from generation to generation.

From a bureaucratic and legal perspective, the fundamental unit of social organization in Deza was the household, which usually comprised a nuclear family. The taxpaying male head of household (*pechero*) was the legal representative of the family and, in Deza, his citizenship was predicated upon owning a house and vineyard plot. The householder's citizenship was communicated, in turn, to wife and children, entailing privileges and obligations determined by local custom and via negotiation with the town's seignior.[18]

A wife, then, held a subordinate legal role to her husband and moralists fixed her position within the domestic sphere.[19] Yet as religious, economic, and social actors, Spanish women regularly engaged the world beyond their front door.[20] Dezanas were tied more closely to the home—rearing children, cooking, keeping house—than their men, and long-distance travel was unusual. But some labored outside of the home, performed work not directly related to housewifery, or worked alongside their husbands and children in a family trade. Traveling regionally was not unusual, especially to visit relatives or attend social events like weddings or funerals. A few women lived without male oversight or pushed the boundaries of conventional expectations about feminine sexuality.

While women's identities were typically framed in terms of their relationships to male relatives—as daughters, wives, or mothers—the reality was often more complex. As widows, for example, some women commanded considerable personal freedom and economic power.[21] In the 1540s several widows rented orchards and farmland directly from the duke of Medinaceli.[22] Old Christian widows doña Petronilla de Luna and doña Beatriz Pérez owned substantial holdings and managed their own estates.[23] And even lesser women could control property, as in the case of the Morisca Ana de Deza (d. ca. 1594), who owned the home in which her family lived and, despite predeceasing her husband, willed it directly to their children.[24] Younger widows tended to remarry and older ones often moved in with children, but at the death of their husbands some women simply took possession of the household, which became identified, for example, as the house of Isabel Navarra, the widow of Luis de Liñán.

A small minority of Dezanas lived independently, apparently without male oversight as widows, spinsters, lay holy women (*beatas*), or prostitutes. While the lives of women were more circumscribed than those of men, they often exhibited striking resolve and self-determination. Relatives, especially male ones, might move around, abandon, or lock women into undesirable marriages as necessity or convenience demanded. Yet, like Carcayona, the handless maiden of Morisco lore who suffered indignities and family betrayal, Deza's Moriscas often proved resourceful at marshaling their limited resources to take advantage of the opportunities available to them.[25]

Predictably, Deza's society was ordered hierarchically, and not only along gender lines. The highest echelons of the social pyramid were occupied largely in absentia. Kings and queens, for instance, passed through town only a handful of times.[26] The dukes of Medinaceli visited intermittently and maintained a fortress and arsenal in town. These were placed under the control of an *alcaide* (castellan or warden). Appointed by and representing the duke, the alcaide wielded military power as well as political and social influence. The office holder was usually a local hidalgo, frequently a member of either the Fernández Abarca or Barnuevo families.

The town's hidalgos were a growing contingent in Deza. In the mid-sixteenth century a number of leading families filed legal suits in the Royal Appellate Court to confirm their status as members of the lower nobility.[27] In addition to enjoying social rank, hidalgos were exempted from paying many taxes, granted the privilege of bearing arms and establishing a coat of arms, and permitted to use the honorific *don* or *doña*. Deza's hidalgo families intermarried with one another and with other regional elites, sent their children to schools, even to universities, and joined military orders. By 1591 twelve hidalgo families lived in Deza. There were twenty-one in 1606, although the town's total population had already leveled out.[28]

Most Dezanos were pecheros, or *buenos hombres de pecheros*—the "good men." Their taxes maintained the town and paid feudal and royal dues. They owned their own homes and often owned or rented additional land as well, usually for agricultural purposes. Unlike hidalgos, they expected and were expected by others to earn their livelihoods by the sweat of their brows. Every citizen—Old Christian, Morisco, or Judeoconverso; pechero or hidalgo—was a voting member of the town commune.

A number of variables determined status among the pecheros. A poor pechero might fall into arrears on taxes or debts, threatening his good standing, but a wealthy one could rent and sometimes even purchase land, thereby increasing estate and honor. Moriscos and Judeoconversos could be maligned, especially if they had a family history of inquisitorial trouble. And while it was possible to overcome the taint of bad blood, doing so was a complex and lengthy process. Performing work that neighbors considered vile reduced honor and could hinder access to civic office. Conversely, a pechero could increase status by serving on the town council, as a churchwarden, or in the local *santa hermandad*. He could also join one of Deza's religious confraternities or even become an inquisitorial familiar. The rising and falling of hidalgos and pecheros was also tied to female relatives, whose propriety and piety, or lack thereof, could aid or inhibit. For a few fortunate pechero families, honor and wealth was parlayed into strategic marriages that eventually provided access to the lower ranks of nobility.

The Barnuevo family, for example, claimed descent from the "twelve lines" of the city of Soria, which suggested they had, in a sense, always been noble—that, after all, was the whole point. Yet one can chart the growth of power and influence of this family. In 1511 a Francisco de Barnuevo founded a chapel and benefice in the parish church, and in the 1520s and 1530s one Alonso de Barnuevo acquired land and married well when he received the hand of the sister of Almazán's castellan.[29] The family built one of the finest homes in town and, in the 1560s, petitioned the Sala de Hijosdalgo at the Royal Appellate Court in Valladolid to recognize the family's gentry status. That suit was met with some opposition.[30] Nevertheless, their accumulation of wealth and land continued, they became literate, and eventually they gained their petition.[31] In 1584 the duke named Pedro de Barnuevo the town's castellan and chief magistrate.

Beside and often below the pecheros were noncitizens, some of whom lived in Deza for long periods of time. Diego Rodríguez, a carpenter from Cogolludo hired by the duke, worked in Deza for at least a decade without becoming a citizen.[32] Aragonese Moriscos Mateo Romero and his wife Ana de Almoravi lived in town for a dozen years, merely as inhabitants.[33] The status of these *forasteros* or *estantes* did not derive from the typical constellation of local factors, and they could not exercise the privileges due to *vecinos*.[34] Poverty, however, did not exclude one from citizenship. Although the penury of Juan Corazón was a byword in town, it made him no less a vecino.[35]

One useful way to differentiate the townsfolk is by considering how they earned their daily bread. As Ruth MacKay notes, however, career trajectories were not clear-cut life choices, closing off other options, but tended to be "multiple and transient."[36] Many Dezanos engaged in a plurality of occupations, and nearly everyone participated in agricultural labor to some extent, whether on their own plots and fields or on their neighbors'. Thus most vecinos identified themselves as *labradores* (farmers) or *trabajadores* (here, meaning agricultural laborers). Deza, like many Castilian towns, had no craft guilds in the sixteenth century; municipal authorities oversaw admission to crafts and their administration, while the artisans themselves wielded only limited political bargaining power.[37]

Deza's industrial heart, such as it was, consisted of three grinding and one fulling mill, at least one pottery works located north of town, and a tile works west of the Henar.[38] Municipal bakers operated the town's two public wood fire ovens, one in each of the town's principal neighborhoods.[39] Dezanos worked as bricklayers, plasterers, carpenters, and painters.[40] They were copper smiths, blacksmiths, and locksmiths.[41] They made rope, saddles, wineskins, and baskets.[42] They wove hemp and linen, and engaged in cobblery, needlework, and tailory.[43] In accord with its status as a dry port, Deza had five *mesones* (public houses offering food, drink, and lodging) in addition to several *tavernas* (taverns) and *posadas* (inns).[44] There was a grocer, one butcher, a fishmonger (who also sold oil), and a Morisco-owned dairy that peddled goat milk, cheese, curds, and whey. Juan Ruiz traded in jewelry.[45] The coppersmith Gerónimo de

Leonis ran a shop on the main plaza.[46] The Mellas family owned a dry goods store and the Morisca María la Jarquina kept a small shop that sold "fruit and other things."[47]

Small towns struggled to secure and maintain the services of qualified medical practitioners and sometimes skirted purity of blood statutes to do so.[48] Such was the case in Deza during much of the sixteenth century, when the town retained Licentiate Antonio Páez (ca. 1510–77), a Judeoconverso physician. He worked alongside local midwifes, barber-surgeons, and apothecaries.[49] Dezanos also relied upon herbalists, folk healers (*curanderos*), witches (*brujas*), and the keepers of familiar spirits for their medical needs.[50] New Christians were sometimes excluded from the orthodox medical establishment and pushed to the margins of medical theory and practice. In Deza this was less the case for Judeoconversos than for Moriscos, who lacked formal medical training or licensing.[51]

Many members of the leading families learned to read, write, or both and sometimes sent their sons to universities; even a significant number of pecheros achieved basic literacy.[52] Those intended for the professional ranks of merchants, scribes, healers, educators, clerics, and so forth needed the appropriate levels of literacy or numeracy. But most of the town's pedagogical energies focused on teaching trades, domestic skills, and religion. From the late 1530s, at least, local clerics ran a parish school that drew regionally—one of, perhaps, four thousand *escuelas de gramática* operating in Castile by the early seventeenth century.[53] Its original purpose may, in fact, have been the Christianization of young Morisco males, who appear with surprising frequency as alumni in later documents. The priest Gonzalo de Santa Clara (d. bef. 1568–70) exposed his pupils to various literary genres. One former student remembered that instruction began with a primer but advanced to the reading of *coplas y bulas* (poetry and crusade indulgences).[54] Another Morisco scholar from the same era recalled Santa Clara using books of chivalry, which appear to have captured the imagination of several of his contemporaries.[55] Unlike elsewhere, none of Deza's Moriscos acquired a formal university education.[56] By the late sixteenth century, the town employed a layman as schoolmaster and his pupils included both Moriscos and Old Christians.[57]

A theatrical Deza existed as well. Troops of performers passed through town regularly and sometimes the council footed the bill. Townsfolk also produced their own versions of morality tales and pastoral dramas with biblical themes on feast days. Local Moriscos were surprisingly active in Deza's theater scene. They not only performed in feast-day productions but also independently rehearsed and subsequently staged *farsas*, perhaps during intermissions.[58] There must have been lengthier local productions as well, for a few lines from an original *comedia* written by one Dezano have fortuitously been preserved on the back side of a recycled scrap of paper.[59]

Governmental bureaucracy proliferated in Deza, as it did elsewhere in Spain, and the bailiwicks of political and civil officers must have overlapped with one another. In addition to the members of the town council, these included granary superintendents, tax and tithe collectors, an overseer of weights and measures, various collectors of revenues, an administrator of estates and rents, an appraiser, a fishing and hunting warden, and so forth.[60] Deza supported *escribanos*, who served both private and public functions. They were "scribes," certainly, but also notaries royal and public, recorders of documents, executers of deeds, and clerks for the town council and sometimes for the local inquisitorial commissioner (*comisario*).[61] A customs official, a dedicated scribe, and at least two guards managed traffic at Deza's dry port, assessing goods, imposing customs, and monitoring movement.[62]

The enforcement of laws also required human resources. An annually installed constable or bailiff (*alguacil*) served on the town council.[63] As part of a royal effort to assert control over salt production, in 1570 Philip II took possession of several salt flats owned by the dukes of Medinaceli, who, in exchange, received possession of the "Four Places of the Recompense" (that is, Deza's villages: Miñana, La Almeda, Almazul, and Mazaterón). Dukes appointed chief magistrates (*alcaldes mayores*) with legal jurisdiction over the villages as well as *alguaciles mayores*. Occasionally, royal soldiers billeted there, at the town's expense, and a local branch of the *santa hermandad* (Holy Brotherhood), a rural police force that operated under royal authority, was stationed in town.[64] Furthermore, citizens might be drafted as peacekeepers when necessary. A town jail (and an accompanying jailor) existed, but homes and *mesones* were often used to secure prisoners, especially on a short-term basis until transportation to the ducal or inquisitorial court could be arranged. Episcopal authorities even endorsed the appointment of a local layman to encourage Morisco attendance at Mass on Sundays and obligatory feast days, a task he "sometimes" accomplished with the use of "force."[65]

Deza had many servants (*criados*) and a few slaves (*esclavos*). An African slave was baptized in 1544 and Hernando de Torres, a retainer of the duke, kept a Native American boy as a slave. An unbaptized Turk lived in Deza in the 1580s and 1590s, the property of one Captain Cabrera.[66] Most *criados*, by contrast, were local youths whose parents put them into service to learn a skill or trade, because they were of no use at home, or out of financial need. Some continued in service for relatively short periods before establishing their own households; others made a career of it.

Most jobs in town were equally the purview of both Old and New Christians. Among men, the most common occupations were *trabajador* and *labrador*. Most people engaged in agricultural work throughout the year and kept bees, chickens, goats, horses, donkeys, cows, and sheep. (Keeping pigs, of course, indicated a dramatic cultural choice for a Morisco, but many Old Christians had them.) Moriscos often farmed, but if they kept grape vines, which they were obliged to do according to local requirements for citizenship, they did not ferment their fruit (which was prohibited in Islam) like Old Christians.[67] They also worked in many of the same trades as Old Christians, engaged in commerce together, and shared the same offices. Moriscos worked for Old Christians and vice versa. They lodged with one another and formed relationships, even friendships. Sometimes they ate together, gathered to celebrate births and marriages, attended church together, and visited each other's homes.[68] Very occasionally, Moriscos and Old Christians married or engaged in illicit sexual relationships. On the whole, relations between the two groups tended to be peaceful and cordial.[69] At times, however, the distinctiveness of the two communities became more pronounced.

Moriscos, for example, dominated two occupations: those of muleteer and potter. Old Christians held these positions in far fewer numbers or not at all. Muleteers (*arrieros*) transported goods both regionally and over long distances, sometimes on a part-time or seasonal basis. By the later sixteenth century Morisco men recognized that being a muleteer provided an income as well as exceptional freedom.[70] They traveled to big cities and commercial centers, interacting with other Moriscos (especially in Aragon) who had a stronger grasp of Islamic belief and practice than they did. Sometimes they coordinated trips with the lunar month of Ramadan, which allowed them to fast without being discovered by local authorities. Moriscos also dominated pottery production in Deza. They extracted clay and added ochre for coloration. While this remained a local affair, business was good enough to support several extended Morisco families as potters and miners. When the Moriscos were expelled from Deza, they took this craft knowledge with them. The pottery industry collapsed and lay dormant for more than two decades.[71]

Sometimes Moorish descent complicated life and limited vocational horizons.[72] Few in Deza were clamoring for admittance, but most religious orders refused to accept Moriscos—the Jesuits were the last to bow to pressure in 1593—and, formally at least, New Christians could not be hidalgos. The descendants of Conversos (whether Jewish or Moorish) convicted by the Holy Office found their vocational options further restricted. Yet the enforcement (or not) and implications of these rules often had to be worked out and applied at the local level. And while the Holy Office tried several Dezanos for Judaizing early on, by the second half of the sixteenth century inquisitorial interest shifted toward the town's Moriscos as its Jews embraced Christianity, passed into the ranks of Old Christians, and became hidalgos and secular clerics.

The Morisco experience was rather different. In 1502 Deza's Mudéjares were baptized, took Christian names, and saw the local mosque closed. But the critical mass of now-Moriscos meant that the community remained intact, making it more difficult for others to forget their origins. Their cultural and religious identity tied them to Iberia's Islamic past, which many refused to abandon despite passing through the baptismal waters. Throughout the sixteenth and early seventeenth centuries many of Deza's Moriscos lived as crypto-Muslims and even celebrated that lineage. Francisco de Gonzalo, for example, could declaim, "I am of Moorish descent and it doesn't bother me in the least."[73]

The distinction between Moriscos and Old Christians was most clearly expressed in the urban geography of Deza and especially in the principal division of neighborhoods. The Morisco *barrio de arriba* (Upper Neighborhood) or *barrio nuevo* (New Neighborhood) occupied the heights on the northeastern side of town. By the early 1530s, at least, Moriscos owned and occupied the houses around the *plaza de la calle nueva* (later known as the *Corillo*), and in the late 1550s the Morisca María de Molina noted that Islamic activities were a regular facet of life there.[74] A few Old Christians lived in the *arriba* and a few Moriscos dwelt in the *barrio de abajo* (Lower Neighborhood), so segregation, while real, was never absolute. Through it all, Deza's Old and New Christians continued to interact, crossing from one neighborhood to the other as they went about their business. And if the ranks of the nobility and clergy were closed to Deza's Moriscos, they nevertheless took a leading role in many of the town's affairs not only *in spite* of their ancestry but even *because of* it.

The highest political authority residing in Deza was the alcaide. He was the region's chief military figure and the representative of the duke of Medinaceli, who appointed him directly. He took the foremost position during processions, at meetings, and at church; he spoke first at gatherings of the town commune. The alcaide controlled Deza's medieval castle and its arsenal, which had been militarily important in previous centuries but by the sixteenth century was largely symbolic of ducal power.[75] His family was, by extension, the most important in town and among the wealthiest. Beginning in 1570, the duke appointed his alcaide to the office of alcalde mayor, chief civil magistrate of the *cuatro lugares de la recompensa*. In that capacity he dispensed justice and claimed authority in Deza and its hinterland to try all cases in the court of first instance.[76] In practice, however, management of most municipal affairs devolved upon the town council (*consejo* or *ayuntamiento*), although the jurisdictional claims of the alcalde mayor-alcaide and consejo increasingly overlapped or came into direct conflict.

The council consisted of two annually elected *alcaldes ordinarios* (magistrates); two to three *regidores* (aldermen), who managed the budget and income, and oversaw municipal property; a *procurador general* (solicitor general), who set the council's agenda; and a bailiff (*alguacil*), who acted

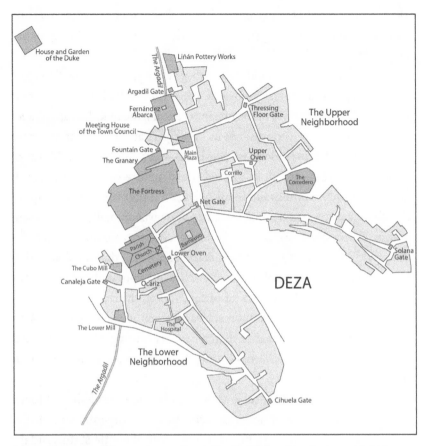

Map 3. The town of Deza, ca. 1600. *Created by David Cox, Cox Cartographic Ltd.* *(Chadlington, Oxfordshire, UK).*

as the executive arm. All offices were tenable for one year and elections (such as they were) ordinarily occurred in late December in the parish church at a gathering of the town commune, which was comprised of all male citizen heads of household.[77] Each outgoing officer nominated someone for his council seat after which other commune members were allowed to submit additional names. The town forwarded these to the duke of Medinaceli, who, by tradition, chose from among them the subsequent year's office holders and granted their titles. They were usually installed with staves of office at the beginning of the year.[78] After the installation, with the approval of the remaining council members, the aldermen selected as many as four or five *diputados* (deputies), usually from among the outgoing officers, in order to advise the sitting members of the council.[79]

Who, precisely, could hold these offices changed over time.[80] In 1566 the septuagenarian priest Juanes de Altopica recalled that, in former times, probably at the end of the fifteenth century, the duke had appointed one hidalgo and one commoner as co-magistrates each year and had done likewise for the aldermen. But later—certainly after the Morisco baptisms of 1502—the duke altered the structure of the council and appointed only commoners to all offices.[81] Either immediately upon this change or soon thereafter, one magistrate was annually chosen from among Deza's Old Christians and one was chosen from the Moriscos.[82] Thus, within less than a generation of the baptism of the Mudéjares, the town had formalized a political system that incorporated both Old and New Christians.[83] The former far outnumbered the latter in Deza, and Moriscos sometimes found themselves on their heels, working to safeguard privileges. Yet for more than a century, during one of the most prosperous phases of the town's history, they shared political power and did so effectively.

In the late sixteenth century, as hidalgo families reestablished their credentials, a further refinement occurred in the organization of the council. Having acquired official recognition of gentle status, hidalgos reasserted a claim to seats on the town council and, in 1590, they petitioned for *mitad de oficios* (half of the offices), which privilege they gained, despite opposition, beginning in 1592. Thereafter, two hidalgos served each year, as a co-magistrate and an alderman.[84] The second magistrate and alderman were commoners—typically an Old Christian in odd-numbered years and a Morisco in even.[85]

As the role played by the town's duke in conciliar appointments suggests, Deza's political life combined local and extra-local elements. While the duke himself rarely visited, all political authority was legitimated by his approval, and the alcaide in particular functioned as his executive agent. The duke also appointed the council's scribe, although the council itself had to pay his salary.[86] The town found this arrangement undesirable but grudgingly accepted it. Even more disagreeable was his practice of sending judges of inquiry (with retinues) to town to be maintained at local expense in order to investigate and adjudicate on civil, criminal, and executive legal matters.[87] At other times, the duke dispatched judges of residency, commission, and accounts to investigate and oversee local affairs, much to the annoyance of Deza's council, which believed that it could manage without them.

Governance of Deza's religious affairs mirrored the secular in combining local and extra-local components. The parish church operated as part of a hierarchical religious network that stretched across Spain and the Roman Catholic world. As Christ's earthly vicar, the pope claimed spiritual authority from God and, in turn, delegated jurisdiction to regional authorities, especially archbishops and bishops. Although Deza might easily have fallen within the diocese of Osma, as it does today, twelfth-century papal mandates placed it under the authority of the bishop of Sigüenza, whose cathedral was located about fifty-five miles southwest.[88] Many of the diocese's parishes, including Deza, were divided among archpresbyteries, creating an extra layer of bureaucracy and oversight. Deza's archpresbyteral see, located in Aragonese Ariza, exercised authority over several other towns and villages in both Castile and Aragon.[89]

Deza's parish church, which presided over much of the town from its location just below the fortress, was dedicated to Our Lady of the Assumption and was something of a work in progress. In the mid-sixteenth century the old church (probably a twelfth-century Romanesque building or, less likely, a converted mosque) was demolished and construction began on a larger edifice built in late Gothic style and modeled after the collegiate church of Berlanga de Duero. Eventually it contained chapels endowed by local notables and devoted to Saints James and John, and the Souls in Purgatory.[90] The parish church's large crucifix (known as *Santo Cristo*) performed miracles over the years and was processed through town in times of serious dearth or hardship.[91] The building was completed in three phases over sixty-five years: from 1548–58 the main body of the church; from 1574–79 the roof and ceiling; and from 1599–1612 the tower.[92]

During the sixteenth and early seventeenth centuries, no parish priest (*cura*) resided in Deza.[93] It seems likely that the curacy was in the gift of the dukes of Medinaceli and absentee officeholders appointed representatives to serve in their stead. Thus, in practice, the preeminent local priest was the vicar (*vicario*). Sometimes a *teniente de vicario* or *de cura* served as the vicar's lieutenant. Various other clerics—sacristans, chaplains, beneficed clergy, and priest clerics (*clérigos presbíteros*)—also participated in the religious life of the parish. Some were sons of important families for whom perpetual chaplaincies or benefices had been endowed. Most used the title *bachiller, maestro,* or *licenciado,* which suggests that they had a university education. Clerics were exempt from taxation, could only be tried by ecclesiastical courts, and received a stipend, which was sometimes supplemented by saying Masses for the dead, officiating at marriages or burials, and performing various other rites and ceremonies. Many, but not all, of Deza's clerics had spent their entire lives in town.

Although no religious houses or regular clerics were based in Deza, the Franciscan friars from Almazán (about thirty miles west), as well as others in the region, frequently visited to serve as confessors during the holy seasons, especially Lent, and to run short-term missions. Nor was a community of female religious located in Deza. Nevertheless, women who felt called to the religious life had a local option: they could embark upon the path of the lay holy woman. These *beatas,* of whom only one or two seem to have been active at any given time, took informal vows of poverty and chastity, living on their own or with family rather than communally in a *beaterio.*[94] Although the post-Tridentine Church expected beatas to spend their time withdrawn from the world in prayer, they were also supposed to pursue works of charity.[95]

Despite its lone church and lack of monasteries, Deza claimed multiple sites of religious significance beyond the parish. At least three shrines were active during the town's Morisco century: the first shared by San Roque and Santiago (built in 1533), the second shared by San Sebastián and (probably) San Antón, and the third dedicated to San Miguel.[96] The earliest evidence of a shrine for Santa Ana dates to 1625, but it may have been erected earlier, since a confraternity with that devotion was founded in the 1590s.[97] A *humilladero,* which consisted of an elevated cross or religious image enclosed by a low wall, was established on the heights to the southeast of Deza. Located along the roads entering or leaving towns in the region, humilladeros served as sites of prayer and local pilgrimage, as did the shrines. San Roque, for example, was incorporated into an annual two-day procession—the Litanies (*Letanías*)—that visited regional shrines and culminated in a communal meal.[98] Dezanos celebrated the annual cycle of holy days, both moveable and fixed, and focused special attention on the feasts of the Trinity and Corpus Christi (both celebrated during the eighth week following Easter, usually in June or early July) as well as on the feast days of important local saints such as James (Santiago) and Roque.

Many of these chapels, shrines, and processions were linked to local confraternities and communal organizations. Santa Catalina, active from the 1560s, was probably the first of the town's confraternities, and its membership was limited to hidalgos.[99] In 1570, Deza's clerics formed their own fraternal organization: the *cabildo* of Saint Peter.[100] The Confraternity of the Holy Cross was active by 1571 and included both Moriscos and Old Christians.[101] The confraternities of Our Lady of the Rosary and San Antonio had formed by the early 1580s, at least, and Santa Ana was founded in June 1591.[102] The Most Holy Sacrament, Holy Name of Jesus, and Saints Sebastian and Roque were active by 1600.[103]

Extant confraternal records shed little light on the activities of members or the function of the organizations. Elsewhere, in the absence of trade guilds, confraternities sometimes provided oversight for craftsmen, but no evidence exists of this in Deza. Some Spanish confraternities included female members and, unusually for early modern Europe, single-sex organizations were as likely to have been formed by women for women as by men.[104] By the seventeenth century active participation of female *cofrades* in public processions was being reined in, although the confraternities themselves continued. Yet no evidence exists of female confraters in Deza, let alone of an exclusively female confraternity. Nevertheless, local confraternities were certainly social clubs with religious elements. The exclusivity of Santa Catalina or San Pedro reflected and reified existing divisions, but the openness of Holy Cross and (albeit, briefly) Santa Ana to Moriscos as well as Old Christians hints at varying levels of diversity.

Deza, idiosyncratic as it was at times, conforms to many of the regional norms for small towns, and it played a relatively minor role during Spain's *siglo de oro*. In only one way did it truly distinguish itself: the remarkable number of inquisitorial trials that proceeded against the town's Moriscos. Between the 1520s and 1610s, hundreds of them came under various forms of inquisitorial scrutiny. Although a relatively small number of individuals underwent torture or died—whether by succumbing during their imprisonment or being relaxed to the secular arm for execution—as a consequence of their run-ins with the Holy Office, over a hundred procesos worked their ways through the inquisitorial tribunal at Cuenca. This is an astonishing number of cases for any town, the more so for one as small as Deza. This peculiarity reflects the reality of the town's historical trajectory during the early modern period. But understanding the significance of those trials and the inquisitorial activities to which they were connected requires familiarity with the Dezanos and their associates, and how their lives and relationships changed over time.

2

Deza Divided

Bernardino Almanzorre's Story

By the early seventeenth century differences among Dezanos usually formed around whether they were Moriscos or Old Christians. The primary point of tension within town, the one that tended to devour all others, was the confrontation between those who viewed themselves as good and faithful Christians and those who were convinced that Islam was the "better Law for the salvation of their souls."[1] The process by which this religious conflict came to dominate life in Deza was hardly straightforward or inevitable. The primary agent driving the change was the Holy Office of the Inquisition, specifically the tribunal headquartered at Cuenca, which, in an effort to enforce religious discipline, conducted a major assault on the town's New Christians about once every generation, thereby engineering a legacy of religious stigmatization.[2] Yet other forces, both internal and external, also contributed. Although less aggressive than the Inquisition, episcopal disciplinary efforts differentiated between Old Christians and Moriscos, especially by barring the latter from the Eucharist toward the end of the century. The dukes of Medinaceli fostered dissention by favoring and protecting the Moriscos. And, significantly, increased interaction with Aragonese New Christians stimulated local Islamic activity and provoked concerns about the extent to which heterodoxy had spread among Deza's Moriscos. Rather than binding the town together, these factors heightened divisions and stiffened Morisco resolve to embrace Islam.

The story of this divided Deza was also an internal one, the legacy of a transformation that occurred in relations between local Old and New Christians over the course of the sixteenth century. Following the baptism of most of the town's Moriscos in 1502, the local mosque was closed and Islam formally extinguished. Yet without any serious effort to Christianize or internal inclination to convert, many of the newly baptized remained committed Muslims. They continued to participate in both Islamic cultural practices and religious ceremonies. Between 1523 and 1533 the Holy Office initiated about twenty-five trials against Islamizing New Christians, as much as 10 percent of the town's entire Morisco population at the time.[3] Subsequently, the overt practice of Islam in Deza substantially diminished. And, to judge from the evidence that exists, even covert Islamic activities went into retreat over the next few decades. A general decline in Islamic knowledge took place: the young did not learn Arabic, Muslim literature disappeared, the practice of daily prayers appears to have ceased, and no one knew how to determine the start of Ramadan or, if they did, they kept silent about it. At certain moments and for certain people Christianity and Islam came into conflict in Deza, and Dezanos did not demonstrate the same drive to assimilate and integrate that Trevor Dadson has found in his studies.[4] Nevertheless, in the wake of that early crackdown, little evidence suggested that the town would eventually divide primarily along a Morisco-Old Christian fault line.

Thus, although Ruy Diaz de Mendoza, the alfaquí of Deza's Mudéjares at the beginning of the sixteenth century, had lamented the conversions of 1502, suggesting that, instead of accepting baptism, they all "should have died as Moors that day, like men," his children and grandchildren conformed to Christianity.[5] Only in the fourth generation did his great-grandson Bernardino Almanzorre (1546–ca. 1571) lead the family back to the Law of Mohammed after spending two years in Aragon studying with "a man of great authority."[6] In or soon after 1502, another unnamed religious leader in Deza, who must have been a rough contemporary of Ruy Diaz, left Castile for Aragon, where Islam was not proscribed until 1526.[7] He and his family put down roots in Villafeliche (Zaragoza), but they maintained intermittent contact with Deza and, in the 1560s, local Moriscos turned to them for instruction in *cosas de moros*.[8]

Mid-sixteenth-century Deza was certainly no utopia; divisions and conflicts abounded. Yet, tension predicated upon opposition between religious practice or belief was only one potential source of conflict and, moreover, was not necessarily the controlling element in a conflict.[9] That is, when confrontations arose in town, even over matters that pitted Christianity against Islam, Old Christians did not necessarily muster in support of other Old Christians against Morisco neighbors. Nor did Moriscos necessarily oppose Old Christians to support their own. Instead, a less binary system of alliances and networks evolved, creating unexpected alignments among Deza's citizenry. The trial of Morisca María de Hortubia (ca. 1526–92) provides a case in point that also adumbrates some ways in which inquisitorial activities undermined communal bonds. The trial, which became a pivotal moment in Deza's religious history, did not manifest the expected pattern of cultural confrontation, with Old Christians and Moriscos forming ranks and facing off.

In early 1557, Licentiate Moral, an inquisitor from the tribunal at Cuenca, arrived in Deza as part of a regional visitation. Only four cases against Moriscos developed as a result of his efforts—far fewer than the twenty-five cases from the 1520s and early 1530s—but among them was that of Hortubia, a native Dezana. Unusually, the Holy Office initiated a formal trial based on a single denunciation, made by Old Christian Mari Gil (b. ca. 1536) in February 1557. Gil claimed that Hortubia had denied the Virgin Birth, shunned pork and wine, and wore clean clothes on Fridays.[10] The Morisca was arrested a year later, in spring 1558, separated from her family, and transported to the secret jails of Cuenca, where her case wound its way to a conclusion in July 1559.

In April 1558, at her first inquisitorial audience before Licentiate Moral and Dr. Diego García, and for more than a year thereafter, Hortubia maintained her innocence and defended herself against all charges. Despite repeated warnings and admonitions to scour her conscience and speak the truth, she consistently avowed that Mari Gil's denunciation was a matter of personal rancor. Formerly a servant in Hortubia's household, but dismissed for frequent drunkenness, Gil was merely being vindictive. To prove it, in early June, the accused requested that inquisitors confirm her innocence and Gil's dishonesty by interviewing neighbors of good reputation who knew the women and could speak to their characters and activities.[11]

The results came back strongly in María de Hortubia's favor. A series of local worthies rallied to her cause: three of Deza's priests, the castellan, and members of several hidalgo families—all of them Old Christians. María de Hortubia, they asserted, was a "virtuous and good Christian" and an "honorable woman." She attended Mass and vespers regularly, gave alms, performed other pious works, and received the sacraments. One witness even recalled seeing Hortubia's children eat pork. The vicar Francisco Navarro, then inquisitorial *juez de comisión*, was especially effusive in his support. He noted that he had confessed the accused often over the course of his twenty-six years in the parish and that, as a result, they had developed a rapport.[12] He specifically noted her custom of fulfilling the Easter Duty at the *beginning* of Lent rather than waiting until the last minute. To Navarro, this practice smacked of real Christian devotion.[13]

Gil, by contrast, was universally dismissed as untrustworthy, a liar, and drunkard. In an interesting inversion of the common Moriscos-as-dogs trope, respondents hammered on the fact that María de Hortubia's Old Christian accuser was the daughter of "crazy" and "vile" Miguel Gil, whose chief occupations were catching dogs and eating them. Hidalga Ana de Torres y de Rebolledo took Mari Gil into service after her dismissal from Hortubia's household, which gave her firsthand experience of what Gil's former mistress must have endured. Torres described the young woman as "stupid and crazy," "lacking judgment," "a friend of prattling and gossip," and an "incautious girl who almost never tells the truth." To emphasize her point, she recounted an episode that had occurred the previous Easter Sunday, when she had sent Gil to the cellar to fetch wine "and other things" for the meal. The serving girl, who had received the Eucharist earlier that day, eventually returned from her errand so thoroughly drunk that she could not speak coherently.[14] In short, Hortubia had the right of it, and the case, which for lack of evidence should never have proceeded to a formal trial, was baseless.

This strong support from Old Christian worthies for María de Hortubia challenges the paradigm of confrontation and only makes sense in light of Deza's broader social context. The accused had personal relationships with several of the people who testified on her behalf. Some of those relationships—like the one with her confessor—she established independently, but her husband, Luis de Cebea (ca. 1524–1609), played a key role in facilitating others. Cebea was a native Dezano orphaned at a young age who became an apprentice cobbler. He abandoned that profession for soldiery in the early 1540s and, when he returned to Deza, married Hortubia and went into service with the Fernández Abarca family, one of the most influential hidalgo families in town. Cebea worked for the house of Fernández for twenty-nine years and became majordomo of the estate. In this capacity, a patron-client relationship developed, especially between Cebea and Martín Fernández (ca. 1498–ca. 1572), a commander in the military order of the Knights Hospitaller, a local cleric, and the first Old Christian to testify on behalf of María de Hortubia.[15] The commander's elder brother, Rodrigo (ca. 1490–ca. 1558), who had served as the duke's castellan in Deza for two and a half decades, also testified. Cebea even became a member (and later an office holder) in the confraternities of the Holy Cross and Santa Ana, thereby forming additional connections that facilitated the support of local notables for his wife.[16]

Unfortunately for María de Hortubia, by the time the documents attesting to her good Christian standing arrived in Cuenca, she had already been put to the question under torture. In that and subsequent audiences she finally acknowledged her guilt, after a fashion. She confessed that, following the birth of her daughter Isabel in 1556, she had experienced a period of "diminished judgment" and had been "out of her senses." During that time an aunt led her to reject Mary's perpetual virginity.[17] After about six months the afflicted woman was bled by a physician from Ariza and, subsequently much improved, returned to her senses. But, growing concerned about the spiritual element of her illness, the Morisca made a confession to the vicar Navarro. According to Hortubia, Navarro had viewed her heterodoxy as a function of the malady she suffered and not a matter of willful sin. He read to her from the gospels before an image of the Virgin and she was returned to the "Law of Jesus Christ and Our Lady."[18]

Hortubia's claim to have confessed her denial of Mary's perpetual virginity to Navarro may well have been true. The priest, who was very near the end of his life, referred in his interview to an experience in which a confessant—unnamed because of the confessional seal but, certainly, Hortubia—had been "illuminated by the Holy Spirit" (*alumbrada por el Espíritu Santo*) while kneeling at his feet. Independently, the accused described her reconversion using the same verb.[19] Yet, the inquisitors remained skeptical about the whole thing, even as the accused held firm, blaming her theological errors on a temporary postpartum loss of sound judgment. Once, she insisted, she even ventured out of the house wearing only a shirt. She urged the inquisitors to interview her neighbors, for they would confirm her statements. Thus, on July 11, three Moriscos from the Trascastillas neighborhood in Deza (as well as a local barber-surgeon and Gil, the serving girl) were asked whether they remembered Hortubia experiencing a period of temporary insanity some three years previously. None of them did; as far as they knew, she had always been in her right mind.[20]

Later that month, María de Hortubia was reconciled to the church. She was sentenced to wear the *sanbenito* and to penitential confinement in Cuenca for one and a half years. In January 1561 she requested and gained her release, then returned to Deza to care for her husband and seven children, who had suffered "great weariness and toil in her absence."[21] She spent the remainder of her days there, outwardly (at least) conforming to Christianity, although many of her children and grandchildren lived as crypto-Muslims and, years after her death in 1592, one local Morisco denounced her again, claiming that she had "lived and died in the Law of Mohammed."[22] Whether she did or not, the alignment of witnesses in her 1558 trial, with Old Christian worthies strongly supporting her cause and Morisco neighbors failing to back her insanity defense, emphasizes that, at least in the late 1550s, Deza had not yet become a place where being a Morisco or an Old Christian immediately determined whose side one was on.

If, however, María de Hortubia and Luis de Cebea could receive support from staunch Old Christians priests and hidalgos, then Hortubia's subsequent confessions and reconciliation signaled that local notables might do well to exercise greater caution before entering into relationships with, extending trust toward, or vouching for Moriscos in the future, particularly in religious matters. The result, not only of Hortubia's trial but also of the others that took place in the late 1550s, was an undermining of trust between Old and New Christians. Three other local Moriscos—Luis de Liñán el viejo (ca. 1521–92), Juan de Contreras (ca. 1530–72), and his wife María de Molina (ca. 1532–72)—were tried and reconciled at the same time as Hortubia.[23] And although Hortubia lived quietly in Deza after her release, the other three were denounced again in the 1560s, arrested, retried, and sentenced to death.[24] In fact, the trajectory of their religious lives after being reconciled to the church in the late 1550s indicates that they moved further away from Christianity rather than toward it. All three had strong ties to the Moriscos of Aragon and, in the years following their first trials, those ties tempted them to return to the Law of Mohammed.[25]

Deza's Old Christians, its priests, and certainly the Holy Office, believed that Aragonese Moriscos were the heart of the problem. Their contact with the town's indigenous Morisco population allowed for the reinvigoration of a waning Islamic identity. It was a concern about which Deza's vicar Juanes de Altopica, in his capacity as inquisitorial *juez de comisión*, had sounded a warning as early as 1533. "During the year," he wrote to his superiors at Cuenca, "many of the newly converted from Aragon come to this town and refuse to eat the meat slaughtered at the butcher shop, but instead they slaughter it at home."[26] This in apparent contrast to homegrown Moriscos. And although the presence and influence of Islamizing Aragonese in Deza diminished in the 1530s and 1540s, perhaps as a result of the 1523–33 inquisitorial crackdown, the late 1550s and the 1560s saw new waves of immigrants. Their individual motives are rarely clear, but risings tension between Moriscos, the Holy Office, and the Crown probably pushed some New Christians out of Aragon while opportunities abroad drew them to Castile.[27] Deza, for its part, encouraged immigration by basing citizenship merely on "making a house and planting vines."[28]

Educational opportunities drew some. Several Moriscos who settled in town in the 1550s, often with families in tow, had their first contact with Deza as boys a decade or two earlier, when they attended the parish school run by local priest Gonzalo de Santa Clara.[29] Many more came for economic reasons. They became part of a broader migratory pattern that saw rural laborers relocating from small villages and flooding into towns and cities during the boom years of the sixteenth century.[30] Many of them, like migrant farm worker Gerónimo de Villaverde of Terrer who stayed for a single harvest, had no intention of remaining, but others put down deep roots in town. Ana de Almoravi (b. 1521) and her family also came to Deza from Terrer, but they were looking to escape creditors and start over. They arrived in 1558 and worked hard breeding goats, growing saffron, and selling dairy products. Eventually they became "rich."[31] Yet despite her own immigrant past and the opportunities she had found in Deza, Almoravi expressed exasperation when she learned about yet another Aragonese laborer's arrival in town.[32] For Moriscos in western Aragon looking for a place that reminded them of home, Deza's own population of Moriscos, one of the largest in the region, was another important consideration.

This influx invigorated and extended the network of relations between the Moriscos of western Aragon and eastern Soria, with Deza at a key point of confluence. The result was cross-border marriages, apprenticeships, and the farming out of children in both directions. Examples abound. Locksmith Juan de Ropiñón (b. 1529) of Daroca (Zaragoza) immigrated (by way of Zaragoza and Calatayud) and married Dezana María de Hortubia (b. 1540) in about 1555. Alonso Ropiñón (ca. 1515–ca. 1575) of Deza married Ana de Liñán of Ariza in ca. 1563. Dezano Alonso Aliger (b. ca. 1540) was apprenticed at a pottery works in Brea (Zaragoza). The blacksmith Francisco de Arcos (b. 1544), born in Ágreda (Soria), moved to Deza with his family when he was a boy but learned his trade in Aragonese Ariza, where he worked alongside another Morisco apprentice from Brea. Juan de Cieli (1539–1607) was a journeyman bricklayer in Torrellas (Zaragoza). Lope de Obezar (b. 1546) learned cobblery in Villafeliche. Gerónima la Cándida (ca. 1528–72) and María la Carnicera (ca. 1552–1611), both born in Ariza, went into service in Deza and eventually married local men.

Other Moriscos engaged in short-term regional travel between Deza, its environs, and western Aragon during these decades for social or economic reasons. María de Almanzorre (b. ca. 1525) spent time in Bordalba (Zaragoza) in the 1560s while her son was apprenticed there. Diamira de Medina (ca. 1501–88) visited Daroca, Morata de Jalón (Zaragoza), and Sestrica (Zaragoza). Ana de Cieli (1543–ca. 1604) sought a cure to a lingering illness in Gotor (Zaragoza). Román Ramírez el menor (1540–99) spent time as a youth with his maternal grandfather in Burbáguena. Gerónimo de Molina (b. ca. 1550) apprenticed in Zaragoza with an Old Christian tailor before working his way through jobs in Soria, Almazán, Ariza, Tarazona, Tudela, Terrer, Villarroya de la Sierra, and Calatayud. The men described as *tratantes, camineros,* or *trajineros* traveled even more frequently, trading goods and bearing loads over mountain passes and byways to the villages, towns, and cities of the region and beyond. They talked with fellow travelers along the way and stayed at inns and taverns or the homes of relatives, friends, and business associates. And these networks expanded beyond western Aragon and Soria later in the century as more of the town's Moriscos turned, at least seasonally, to muleteering.

These exchanges poured fresh life into Deza's Islamic community. Immigrants from Aragon brought with them a strong Muslim identity and a clearer understanding of the accompanying ceremonies, traditions, and beliefs. Most of those whom Deza's Moriscos named in inquisitorial trials as having introduced them to Islam were Aragonese. And while many of those so named may have been fictions—"Miguel from Almonacid de la Sierra," "two Aragonese Moriscos, Zúñiga and Poyo," "Bengala, the wife of a farmer in Plasencia de Jalón," "Orosia from Sestrica, who once lived in Deza"—others can be shown to have been real people who lived in or were connected to the town and whose influence is established by multiple sources.

Many of the fiercest Muslim proselytizers and apologists living in Deza during this period were women. One of them, Catalina Pérez (ca. 1526–aft. 1574) of Ariza, moved to Deza with her husband Francisco de la Huerta in ca. 1555. Huerta was among those who had introduced Luis de Liñán, one of the quartet of Moriscos tried by the Holy Office in 1557–58, to Islam. After her husband's death, Catalina remained in (or perhaps returned to) town.[33] Notoriously, she wore distinctively Morisco clothing and taught *cosas de moros* not only to the adolescent daughters of Francisco de Gonzalo (alias, de Baptista) and Gerónimo de Molina but also to Luis de Cebea, the husband of María de Hortubia (another member of the quartet).[34] Rumor had it that Cebea was carrying on an affair with Pérez in the late 1560s, that he performed guadoc and azala (i.e., ritual ablutions and Islamic prayers) in her home, and that she taught him an Islamic prayer in Castilian. Purportedly, she also told him that if he could not fast during Ramadan, he could give alms instead.[35]

One Teresa of Ágreda (d. ca. 1568), whom everyone called Aunt Teresa, had been reconciled by the inquisitorial tribunal of Calahorra (La Rioja) sometime prior to 1565. Subsequently exiled from Ágreda, the widow somehow found her way to Deza. Teresa's story is largely unknown and, given the date of her death, which was just prior to the arrival of an inquisitorial visitation and an accompanying series of arrests and trials, she may merely have been a convenient scapegoat. Yet several Dezanos, mostly women but some men, claimed that she taught them Islamic prayers and ceremonies. Ana de Almoravi asserted that Teresa had convinced Juan de Ropiñón and Francisco de Gonzalo to observe Ramadan and perform guadoc and azala.[36] Among Teresa's many other purported disciples were María la Carnicera (ca. 1551–1611), Francisca la Ollera (b. ca. 1520), Ana de Arellano (1549–1607), Gonzalo el Burgueño (b. 1537), Ana de Cieli (1543–ca.1604), María la Gallega (1539–aft. 1609), Velasco de Medrano (b. ca. 1535), and quartet member María de Molina, who blamed Teresa for leading her back to Islam in the 1560s after her 1557 reconciliation.

Ana de Almoravi, who came to Deza in ca. 1558 from Terrer with her second husband, Mateo Romero el mayor (b. ca. 1530), briefly denounced Aunt Teresa as her Islamic tutor in ca. 1565, but later acknowledged having learned from her own stepmother in ca. 1540. Several Dezanos, some credibly and others less so, denounced Almoravi herself as an Islamic instructor. As far back as summer 1563, claimed local Morisco Luis Martínez (b. ca. 1545), she had "taught him Moorish things [cosas moriegas]," including how to fast for Ramadan and two Arabic prayers.[37] Román Ramírez el menor spun a spurious tale in 1571 about Almoravi pressuring him and his wife to fast for Ramadan after her son, Mateo Romero el menor (b. ca. 1545), introduced him to Islam.[38] Nevertheless, while she staunchly maintained (even under torture) that she had not "taught anyone," she (contradictorily) admitted to telling two local men how to perform azala correctly.[39] She also provided an important service during Ramadan by making curds, whey, cheese, and milk available to Moriscos who were without food after sunset but dared not reveal themselves by cooking over a hearth fire or at the communal ovens.[40]

Religious instruction during this period was by no means solely the purview of Aragonese women. Male Moriscos from Aragon also played important roles, and sometimes they did so from a distance. Just as Aragonese boys had come to Deza in the 1540s to learn to read from Santa Clara the priest, so in later decades Dezanos went east, to the cities and lugares de moriscos of Aragon. There they came under the influence of those who could provide a foundation in Islamic belief and practice. In August 1559, for example, the vicar of Montón (Zaragoza) reported that one Mendoza from Deza, since deceased, was known to have come to neighboring Villafeliche to study there. Every day "they taught him a lot of prayers and how to live like a Moor." And although "he knew nothing about cosas de moros" when he arrived, local alfaquíes "instructed him."[41]

Similarly, Gerónimo Martínez (ca. 1534–ca.1603) received instruction from Francisco Calemón in Torrellas in ca. 1565.[42] His brother Luis (b. ca. 1545), who had already learned about Ramadan and azala from Almoravi, was taught to perform ritual ablutions by Juan Gallego in Ariza in ca. 1563–64. Luis de Mendoza (1538–71) learned from Luis Azan of Almonacid de la Sierra, a notorious center for the production of Aljamiado texts. Lope de Obezar (1546–bef. 1594), who was apprenticed to cobbler Alonso Zapatero of Villafeliche in ca. 1564, admitted that, after nine months, he knew little of shoes but a lot about Islam. Their religious educations in these venues were hardly formal, but these young men (and others as well) returned home, passionate in their convictions and intent not only to continue practicing in Deza but also to share their knowledge with family and friends.

One such young man, a key figure in Deza's Islamic renewal and part of that same pivotal generation born in the decade around the year 1540, was Bernardino Almanzorre (alias, González). Born, probably in 1546, and raised in Deza, Bernardino was the son of cobbler Francisco Almanzorre

(d. ca. 1555) and María de Almanzorre (alias, de Navarra; b. ca. 1525), the granddaughter of Ruy Diaz de Mendoza, the town's former alfaquí.[43] The boy was literate and probably learned to read from Santa Clara. He spent time in Aragon during his teens, ostensibly to learn shoemaking but, like Lope de Obezar, his energies were primarily directed toward acquiring a solid foundation of Islamic knowledge.

Between 1564 and 1566 Bernardino lived in Torrellas and nearby Trasmoz, where he sat under the teaching of a "man of great authority."[44] That man, probably the person whom Bernardino elsewhere identified as Alexos Maestro, taught the young Dezano "everything about Ramadan and doing azala and guadoc."[45] When he returned home, he was able to determine (and informed others of) the start of Ramadan and felt himself competent to announce the end of the fast and the start of the three-day feast of Eid al-fitr.[46] Bernardino also learned a fair number of Arabic prayers and surahs by heart—more than anyone else in Deza is known to have memorized—and recited at least some of them before inquisitors during his 1570 trial.[47] More significantly, perhaps, he learned to read Aljamiado and maybe also some Arabic while abroad, collected a small library of texts, and began to copy out selections of material that he saw as useful or significant.

The full contents of his library are unknown, but it was not inconsequential. In addition to several sheets containing azoras (surahs), some written with "Arabic words but using Christian letters," and others in Arabic script (moriego), he also owned the "gospels in the vernacular" and a copy of Bernardo Pérez de Chinchón's Antialcoran (Valencia, 1532), which he had received from Alexos Maestro.[48] He also had "una escritura de Sansón," which has not been identified.[49] Other works were more firmly part of the milieu of Morisco Aljamiado literature such as the Regla de las lunas, various manuscript versions of which survive and provide instructions for following the Islamic calendar. He owned Los consejos al hijo de Ādam,[50] two copies of the Sueño del çalhe de Túnez,[51] and "un auto de Jacob que se dize Josephina," probably the Recontamiento de Yaçub y de su fifo Yuçof.[52] Presumably the inquisitorial scribe became confused when recording this last title.[53]

1. The Almanzorre-Almoravi family tree.

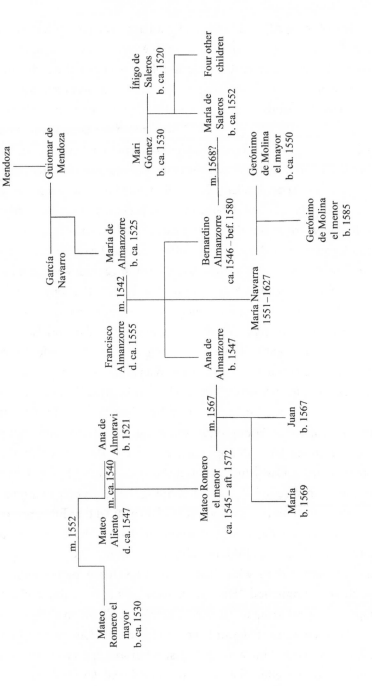

Any of these Aljamiado titles might have been part of longer manuscripts containing additional writings. The various extant copies of books about the Islamic calendar, for example, the length of which varies in manuscript versions from a couple to tens of folios, were often adjoined to condensed versions of the Quran and to other instructions for "practical religion" to make a longer work.[54] Bernardino did not comment on the size of his copy of the *Regla de las lunas* except to note that it was "about as big as a hand," which must refer to the size of the sheets rather than the length of the work. Similarly, Bernardino noted that his two copies of the *Sueño del çalhe de Túnez* differed in size substantially—one was recognizably "bigger" than the other. His wife described the smaller one, which he had "brought from Aragon," as a "little book with just a few pages" and he confirmed it was just "ten pages" long.[55] This suggests it was a stand-alone copy of the *Sueño*, which spans only nine folios in the copy included in the Biblioteca Nacional's *Breviario Çunní*. If Bernardino's second copy was "bigger," it may be that it was bound with additional materials.

Bernardino kept these writings, along with what his wife described as "*coplas* and other things," at home in an *arquimesa*, an escritoire with a chest or compartments.[56] Precisely how he used these various writings is not always clear, but some of them became tools for proselytizing and educating. For example, sometime after Bernardino's return to Deza, he interacted with Lope Guerrero (b. 1547), a Morisco blacksmith apprenticing in Castilian Torrubia de Soria but visiting home at the time of their conversation.[57] Lope, describing the encounter to inquisitors in 1610 at the end of his own long trial, explained that Bernardino had told him about living in Aragon, where "they knew about *cosas de moros*" and claimed that he also knew about such things.[58] Contrasting what he had learned there with what he and Lope had experienced in their youth, he commented, "Here in Deza they are in error about what they [specifically referring to Moriscos] profess as Christians."

With these and similar words, he convinced Lope Guerrero to "become a Moor" and gave him "a paper, half-sheet in size, upon which were written in Castilian letters the Arabic prayers *alhanduliley* and *colua*," along with instructions for performing guadoc and azala.[59] Lope took that paper with him when he returned to Torrubia but, uncomfortable about possessing such a dangerous object, "after a few days" he was back in Deza to return it. Sometime thereafter, on another visit home, Lope asked to see the document again, but it had been "hidden with other papers" and was not easily accessible.[60] Likewise, in around 1568, Bernardino loaned his copy of *Los consejos al hijo de Ādam* to cobbler Francisco el Romo (ca. 1533–ca. 1572), who could only read the bits in Latin script.[61]

Beyond loaning books and written instructions to the literate, Bernardino also acted more generally as a source of religious information and guidance, especially to the younger generation of male Moriscos who were his contemporaries. Many of them had already been introduced to Islam either in Aragon or through interactions with visiting Aragonese Moriscos, but Bernardino became a permanent local point of contact. He made sure that blacksmith Francisco de Arcos, who was introduced to *cosas de moros* while apprenticing in Ariza in the mid-1560s, fulfilled his obligation to keep the Ramadan fast.[62] At the end of the decade, cobbler Luis de Mendoza looked to Bernardino to know when Ramadan began and ended, and asked him to critique his recitation of the azoras he had previously learned.[63] Alonso Aliger (b. ca. 1540), a potter and healer, learned both when and how to fast in the Moorish style from Bernardino.[64] Mateo Romero el mayor claimed him as the source of his Islamic knowledge, and although this was probably untrue, it suggests that local crypto-Muslims saw Bernardino as an alfaquí.[65] Other young men of his generation— Juan de San Juan, Juan Ramírez (b. 1544), Mateo Romero el menor, Luis Martínez, Hernán Mancebo (b. ca. 1535), Diego Martínez, Lope de Obezar, and Gerónimo de Molina—discussed and engaged in *cosas de moros* with him, sometimes as pupils and other times as peers.[66]

These Morisco males of Bernardino's generation were not the only ones whom he encouraged to embrace the Law of Mohammed. Strong evidence suggests that he also proselytized among his extended family. Initially he focused on close relations, especially his widowed mother, María de Almanzorre, and his sister Ana (b. 1547).[67] In her own inquisitorial trial, Ana indicated that when she and Bernardino learned their mother had fasted for Ramadan they could hardly believe it, since they had always "considered her so very Christian and very pious."[68] When Bernardino shared what he had learned with his mother and Ana, they "said that they believed it and that they were good things." His mother pronounced herself "very amazed that, in all these years, she had never heard such a thing as what he told her." Neither woman, however, mastered the "backward"-sounding Arabic prayers he tried to teach them.[69]

Following his engagement to Morisca María de Saleros (b. ca. 1552), probably in 1568, Bernardino extended his proselytizing activities to her family as well. In late 1568 or early 1569 he told the family they needed to fast for Ramadan and celebrate the subsequent feast.[70] He captured their attention with a reading of the *Sueño del çalhe de Túnez* and taught them about guadoc, azala, the various festivals, giving alms, dietary restrictions, and wearing clean clothes on Fridays.[71] Although his mother-in-law did not "know a thing about the ceremonies of Moors" before interacting with him, when Bernardino told them they were "good things," the whole family agreed "they were good things for serving God" and "for being saved and going to heaven."[72] His wife, her older brother Francisco (b. 1547), mother, Mari Gómez (b. ca. 1530), and father, Íñigo de Saleros (b. ca. 1520), all became converts.[73]

Bernardino never called himself as an alfaquí, nor did anyone else, but, in spite of his relative youth, he frequently wore the mantel of religious authority after his return from Aragon. He had been taught "everything" while he was there. His ability to locate Islamic feasts and fasts over the course of the year, his library of religious texts, and his ability to supply either verbal or written instructions to those interested in performing Moorish ceremonies were powerful tools in their own right. Yet, whatever his pretensions or hopes, Bernardino was not the only Islamic authority in town. The death or departure of religious instructors earlier in the century, and the disruptive effects (to local Islam) of the inquisitorial trials of 1523–33, created space for multiple authorities to operate within the community. As the town's Moriscos reasserted their religious heritage and reclaimed a position in the broader Islamic community, individuals found themselves drawn toward or moving between various purveyors of Islamic knowledge. Among these were the previously mentioned women—Aunt Teresa, Catalina Pérez, and Ana de Almoravi—who provided religious instruction, at times, to men as well as to women.

Various members of the Deza-Cañamenero family acted as another important source of local Islamic authority. They were (or claimed to be) the descendants of an unnamed alfaquí who had left Deza, presumably at the time of the conversions.[74] The family settled in Aragonese Villafeliche and perhaps took up the trade of rope making (hence, *cañamenero*). Certainly by the mid-1560s three men—Juan, Pedro, and Francisco de Deza (alias, el Cañamenero)—probably all brothers and born in the 1510s or 1520s, had reestablished ties with Deza and were, in various ways, involved in proselytizing. Each of them was described as "from Villafeliche," yet Juan apparently lived in Deza for long periods of time. Between 1540 and 1555 he and his wife María Fernández saw five children baptized (but none confirmed) in Deza. Juan was probably acting as an alfaquí during this period. In the 1550s he must have moved (back?) to Villafeliche, since several people later described him coming to Deza from there in late 1567 to arrange the sale of a house he owned in town.[75] By that point, if not before, he certainly knew Aljamiado, owned Islamic books, and was actively proselytizing.

All three Cañameneros married Dezanas, and the family was related to Morisco brothers-in-law Juan de Contreras (reconciled in 1558) and Leonis de Saleros (b. ca. 1525), both of whom reckoned Juan de Deza their "cousin," a broad term of familial relation.[76] In or before 1564, Francisco and his wife settled in Deza and remained there through the birth of two children (in 1567 and 1569) before returning to Villafeliche, probably in 1569.[77] No evidence paints Francisco as an alfaquí, but he did facilitate the arrival from Aragon in winter 1564–65 of his brother Pedro, whose primary activity in town during the sojourn was Islamic instruction. Although Pedro never lived permanently in Deza, he had married local Morisca Inés Fernández (b. 1537), the sister of his brother Juan's wife. His stay in town, a closely guarded secret, was sponsored by a group of six literate Moriscos: Gerónimo Gorgoz (ca. 1520–78), potter Francisco de Baptista,[78] Francisco de Gonzalo,[79] farmer Diego Montero, Francisco Mancebo, and Román Ramírez el mayor (d. 1592).[80] They organized funds, food, and lodging to bring Pedro to town for a period of about six months.

Pedro el Cañamenero's primary objective was to teach these men to read the *letras de moros* (Aljamiado), but he interacted with many other locals in significant ways during his extended visit. Juan de Contreras; potters Bernardino el Burgueño, Velasco de Medrano (b. ca. 1530), and Juan de Amador Fernández (ca. 1541–ca. 1604);[81] weaver Lope de Cieli; locksmith Juan de Hortubia Ropiñón (b. 1529); painter Francisco de Medrano (b. 1520); and Román Ramírez el menor (1540–99) sat at his feet along with a number of Moriscas who attended clandestine mixed-gender gatherings of small groups in houses that lasted into the early hours of the morning. Among his female disciples were María Romera (b. ca. 1550[?]; wife of Agustín de Cieli), Gracia la Valenciana (b. ca. 1545 in Brea; wife of Rodrigo de Obezar), Luisa la Viscaina (b. ca. 1534; wife of Francisco de Gonzalo [ca. 1530–ca. 1571]), Ana Mancebo (b. ca. 1525; wife of Gerónimo Gorgoz), Francisca de Baptista (b. ca. 1552; Ana Mancebo's niece), and Cándida de Deza (d. ca. 1582; Bernardino el Burgueño's wife). Quartet member Luis de Liñán (reconciled in 1558) provided the alfaquí with a house and the artist Francisco de Miranda el viejo (ca. 1521–ca. 1570) negotiated with him for the sale or loan of a book at his departure.[82]

Whatever other services he provided, Cañamenero read to his students from two "very good and very excellent books," presumably written in Aljamiado, that he brought with him. Ana de Almoravi, who described the books to inquisitors during her own trial, explained that one of them was about "how to wash" but obscurely explained the other book's purpose as "teaching them what comes there [*lo que viene alli*]." When asked to elaborate, she explained with little more clarity that "six prayers and azalas came there."[83] At least one of these volumes remained in town after the alfaquí's departure in 1565 in order to be copied. Subsequently, Francisco de Miranda and Román Ramírez el menor used it to instruct Morisco youths.[84] In fact, the visit appears to have renewed enthusiasm for Islam. The upper floors of Miranda's home, which he also used as an art studio and rehearsal space for the town's thespians, provided several Moriscos with a line of sight to await the appearance of the Ramadan moon.[85] And rooms in several private homes were now regularly given over for prayer and fellowship meals.[86] Pedro el Cañamenero may have made return trips to Deza after this sojourn, for one of his disciples, Juan de Amador Fernández, recalled him leaving town in the days before inquisitor Licentiate Reynoso arrived in autumn 1569 as part of a regional visitation.[87]

Pedro's brother Juan also visited town at least once to offer religious instruction. In December 1567, a clandestine group congregated north of town at the pottery works of Luis de Liñán. The host, Juan de Contreras, along with Leonis de Saleros, Lope de Obezar, Gerónimo de Obezar, and Francisco el Romo gathered to witness an ordeal of Islamic knowledge that pitted the Dezano Lope del Sol (alias, de Deza) against Juan de Deza (el Cañamenero). When Juan remarked upon "how badly the Old Christians in this place treat you, like Moorish dogs," Saleros resignedly commented, "What else can we do but give thanks to God and accept it all with patience?" But Lope del Sol (1539–1611) responded, "Let no one lose heart on that account or give himself over to evil. It is not so great a dishonor to be treated as Moorish dogs; the greater part of the world is [made up] of Moors and, in the end, the Moors think that they serve God as do the Christians."[88]

Juan de Deza now suggested that they "let that be" and called upon Lope del Sol to "tell us something about times past" in order to test his knowledge of *cosas de moros*. The group was obliged with the story of Abraham's near sacrifice of his son, who went unnamed in the telling as in the Quran (37.102). As Lope's narrative neared its end, Juan de Deza urged him to continue until, finally, the storyteller arrived at the moment when "the angel seized [Abraham's] arm and told him, 'Sacrifice that ram that you will find behind you.' And so, he did." Juan de Deza responded, "Many thanks to you, friend [*tío*]. You have spoken this to us also."[89] The whole episode is obscure, but the rationale behind the alfaquí's testing of Lope del Sol's knowledge about Abraham appears to have been to emphasize, in the face of Old Christian mistreatment, the importance of submission to God's will and of obedient sacrifice. And, although Lope moved on to discuss the story of Jonah and other topics, Juan de Deza won the night's contest, having demonstrated his superior grasp of Islam.[90]

In the aftermath of the showdown, Contreras and Saleros prevailed upon their cousin to stay in town a few days longer in order to provide them with a "rule and order with which to serve our Lord." He gave some time over to instructing Francisco el Romo (ca. 1533–ca. 1572) and Luis de Mendoza, and taught at least Juan de Contreras to read Aljamiado.[91] He even gave the latter a book about one hundred pages in length that discussed punishments, the Day of Judgment, and the "great terrors" that would accompany it.[92] Contreras read this aloud several times to his wife, his sister Ana, and his brother-in-law Leonis de Saleros. Juan de Deza's death in 1569 or 1570 put an end to this collaboration, but a man in Villafeliche who was probably his son continued to exert influence from a distance into the 1580s.[93]

While participants in the Almanzorre and Deza-Cañamenero circles overlapped or collaborated occasionally, on the whole the two groups operated independently throughout much of the 1560s. Yet, when Ana de Almoravi's son Mateo Romero married Bernardino Almanzorre's sister Ana in 1569, the result was the formation of an alliance with a potential for substantial influence, especially in light of the deaths of Aunt Teresa (ca. 1568) and Juan de Deza (ca. 1569). Some of the latter's disciples, like Luis de Mendoza and Francisco el Romo, now turned to Bernardino for guidance.[94] Deza's crypto-Muslims never divided into factions organized around gurus, but a certain amount of tension did develop. For instance, in her inquisitorial trial, Ana de Almoravi denounced Aunt Teresa and many members of the Cañamenero circle but avoided mentioning anyone associated with herself or Bernardino. She showed particular disdain for Román Ramírez el menor, one of Pedro el Cañamenero's disciples.[95] Ramírez's 1571 confession for an Edict of Grace responded in kind, casting Almoravi and her son as the primary peddlers of Islam in Deza.[96]

These tensions between crypto-Muslim factions are significant but risk diverting attention away from what was a more important development, namely that the 1560s witnessed an Islamic revival in Deza. This was all the easier to accomplish because of the growing differentiation, even animosity, between the town's Moriscos and Old Christians. That animosity manifested in distinct ways for each group. For Old Christians it originated with the knowledge that something was amiss with local Moriscos. They felt threatened by suspicious behavior and the presence of visitors from Aragon. Moriscos, by contrast, expressed a sense of being confined and oppressed, of being treated like second-class citizens in their own town.[97] Thus, the lines between the groups solidified and reified in distinct religious identities. The town was not yet at a breaking point, but by 1569 communal bonds were being stretched.

The Old Christian sense of being threatened by the Moriscos was not completely delusional. During his December 1567 visit, Juan de Deza Cañamenero had raised the question of how to react to Old Christians who treated the town's Moriscos like Moorish dogs. Leonis de Saleros advocated resignation and the alfaquí stressed submission to God's will. But Lope del Sol's answer was more ambiguous and emphasized the relative global strength of Islam as compared to Christianity. Late one night during Lent 1569 that same Lope del Sol and his companion Lope Guerrero met with several older Moriscos at the home of Agustín de Baptista (b. 1504) to discuss events unfolding in Granada. Since December of the previous year the Moriscos there had been in revolt, and the two Lopes "wanted to go to the Sierra Nevada and die with their friends." Less zealous and more inclined to resign themselves to the will of God, the older men said that they "did not dare so much."[98]

The virtually eschatological hope that the Granada revolt would succeed or the Ottoman Turks would invade Iberia and sweep over the land boiled to the surface in Deza, at least among some Moriscos. Ana de Almoravi claimed that in ca. 1565 Aunt Teresa had prophesied the coming of the Granadinos: "some Moors who are in the Sierra Nevada will come and demand of [the unfaithful Moriscos] why they don't know *cosas de moros*. And they will burn and kill those who don't know them." Their coming would be "like the sea spread out. And they would overwhelm the whole of Christendom. And everything would be under one King," who would slaughter "the Christians and the *convertidos* [i.e., Moriscos] who did not know the Law of the Moors."[99] Mateo Romero el mayor and Velasco de Medrano rejoiced when an entire contingent of soldiers from Soria perished in Granada.[100] A militant slant to local Islam during this period tended to be popular among Deza's younger Moriscos and those associated with the Almanzorre-Almoravi circle, but it was real, and Old Christians projected it upon the entire community.

Old Christians responded to whispered threats and perceived danger with violence of their own. The fear of a peninsular-wide Morisco uprising, paired with the reinvigoration of Islam in Deza, provoked renewed efforts, especially inquisitorial efforts, to expose heresy and root out local crypto-Muslims. And when Licentiate Alonso Jiménez de Reynoso, inquisitor for the tribunal of the Holy Office in Cuenca, announced his impending arrival in town as part of a regional visitation, Aragonese Moriscos like Pedro el Cañamenero, Ana de Almoravi, and Mateo Romero packed their bags, proof to some Old Christians that they had been up to no good all along. The inquisitor's arrival in late September 1569 elicited denunciations by thirty-three members of the community.[101] Some came forward eagerly with much to say, while others acted more reluctantly or only appeared at Reynoso's summons. Neighbors denounced local Judeoconversos, Old Christians, and Moriscos to the inquisitor, but he was only seriously interested in the latter.

He left town in August and continued with his regional visitation, but his time in Deza bore fruit. Beginning in late 1569, about forty-five of Deza's Moriscos were transported to Cuenca for trial.[102] Luis de Liñán and Juan de Contreras, two of the quartet reconciled in 1557–58, chose the better part of valor and fled for Aragon in February 1570, but they too were eventually captured. The tribunal sentenced them, along with María de Molina (Contreras's wife), to death as relapsed heretics. The impoverished widow Catalina la Rabia (alias de Aranda; ca. 1520[?]– 71) died in the secret jails and was posthumously reconciled. The other detainees abjured and were released. For penance, in addition to the confiscation of their goods, they were confined in Cuenca's perpetual prison and ordered to wear the penitential habit "irremissibly"—in practice, about three years.

Many of the men's sentences were commuted to three or four years in the galleys. For most of them—Francisco el Romo, Alonso Aliger, Luis Martínez, Francisco de Gonzalo, Luis de Mendoza, Bernardino Almanzorre, and others—it was a death sentence. Lope de Obezar, Francisco de Arcos, Luis de Cebea, and Juan de Cieli survived the ordeal and returned home with stories of Lepanto and the Ottoman fleet. Nearly four decades later, Cebea's son was still telling the story and lamenting the Turk's failure to raise a new armada "to attack Spain, so that we might all be made one and freed from this subjugation."[103]

The twin frustrations of the collapse of the Granada revolt and the Turkish defeat at Lepanto were accompanied by the death or disappearance of local religious leaders like Almanzorre, Pedro el Cañamenero, Juan de Deza, Aunt Teresa, and Ana de Almoravi, who was arrested in Sestrica in September 1570 and appears to have died while doing penance in the perpetual prison.[104] Many of the local men who could read Aljamiado were also lost—Contreras, Almanzorre, Francisco de Gonzalo, Francisco de Miranda (d. ca. 1570)—undermining the town's Islamic revival.

Moriscos who had inclined toward the Law of Mohammed now veered back toward Christianity. Almanzorre's own sister, María Navarra, presented herself as a witness against Mateo Romero. In the years that followed, she became a true convert and increasingly gravitated toward Old Christian society.[105] Those who would not abandon Islam found themselves struggling to reconcile their internal convictions with external conformity to Christianity. They vacillated between religions, sought to blend them together, made Islam merely a matter of the heart, or found ways to avoid the watchful gaze of the church and Old Christian neighbors. Eschatological hopes for the reconstitution of the Islamic community (*ummah*) in Spain under Muslim temporal authority had been frustrated and Islam driven out or forced more deeply underground. In the wake of Reynoso's visit, Deza's remaining Moriscos now had to chart a course forward that would avoid the destruction of their community. But the short term brought more pressing matters: in 1570 the Holy Office offered the town's Moriscos an Edict of Grace. To accept meant admitting the extent to which Islam had proliferated in Deza. To refuse would risk opening the community up to a spreading epidemic of denunciations, arrests, and trials.

3

Getting On With Their Lives

Alexo Gorgoz's Story

The arrival in Deza of the inquisitor Dr. Diego Gómez de la Madriz on December 15, 1570, proved less dramatic than the Holy Office might have wished. The Edict of Grace that he peddled offered a relatively pain-less resolution to the problem of a potential inquisitorial trial. Crypto-Muslims who confessed their errors would avoid arrest and a full trial, and they could expect leniency in their reconciliation to the church. Yet Moriscos felt ambivalent, especially since more than forty of their num-ber had already been arrested and transported to Cuenca. What would happen to them? And if those who were in custody accused relatives and neighbors back home of specific activities that were unmentioned in confessions for the Edict, would reconciled sinners be subject to new trials as relapsed heretics? Other concerns surfaced as well. In particular, willingness to take the Edict was hampered by fears about the potential confiscation of property and the fact that reconciled Moriscos would be barred from holding civic office. As a result, initially only nine people took advantage of the opportunity.[1]

The foot dragging of the rest was, in fact, part of a broader strategy to negotiate a revised version of the Edict. But doing so required the coordination not only of resources and actions at the local level but also the interests of some of Europe's most powerful figures. Locally, a trio of respected men masterminded the effort: Luis de Cebea el viejo (ca. 1524–1609), Román Ramírez el mayor (d. 1592), and Alexo Gorgoz (ca. 1534–99). For support, they turned to the town's lord, Duke Juan de la

Cerda (r. 1552–75), who agreed to travel to Madrid on their behalf. While his willingness to support the Moriscos may have stemmed in part from economic interests in Deza, Duke Juan was a religious moderate willing to endorse toleration for those with whom he disagreed.[2] Accompanied by an unnamed papal nuncio, the duke pursued the Moriscos' cause before King Philip II, the Royal Council, and the Suprema.

Ramírez served as the Moriscos' go-between with the duke, and his son, also named Román, was involved at some level as well.[3] The older man left Deza soon after the inquisitor's arrival, rendezvoused with the duke, traveled to Madrid in his entourage, and corresponded with Gorgoz, who managed the situation back home. When Ramírez returned to Deza on January 21, 1571, he announced that a deal had been struck. The floodgates opened, and over the next few months 173 Moriscos took the Edict. Ramírez also carried a letter from the duke addressed to the inquisitor himself. It urged leniency and emphasized that Deza's seignior had always known his Moriscos to be "good Christians."[4] In early March, the full harvest of Ramírez's labors arrived in town: a revised Edict of Grace from the inquisitor general accompanied by a royal decree signed by Philip II. Meant to remove any impediments that might otherwise have hindered the Moriscos from confessing, these documents waived property confiscation as a punishment along with the office-holding restriction implicit in the original Edict.

The confessions made by the Moriscos were often formulaic, but none were mere repetitions and some were strikingly creative.[5] The inquisitor expressed disappointment at the quality (if not the quantity) of the bounty, yet on March 30 and April 1 he received the confessants' formal abjurations and reconciled them to the church. Despite the appeals of the duke, king, and inquisitor general for moderation in the imposition of any financial penalties, Madriz eventually levied fines of between three and fourteen ducats upon the wealthier Moriscos who took the Edict. They responded with frustration, disappointment, and claims of poverty.[6] Yet what was there to do but pay up? In addition to the financial burden, he imposed spiritual penalties for the good of their souls, compelling them to confess thrice annually—at Lent, Pentecost, and Advent—in perpetuity and to keep receipts for those confessions on hand.[7]

Madriz had spent four months in Deza—an extraordinary amount of time for so small a town—but his work was done and he continued on his way, visiting the region's towns and cities and offering their Moriscos access to the church's grace. He doubted the insincere, general, and incomplete confessions the Dezanos had made would bear much fruit, but in at least one important respect he was successful. He had deliberately and carefully gathered as much information about the town's Moriscos as possible, even recording the full genealogy of each confessant. These records formed a foundation for the inquisitorial investigations that unfolded over the next forty years. And although the town was largely free from inquisitorial activity for the next decade, many of its secrets had been exposed. During the intermission, as Deza grew and its population increased, and as some of its inhabitants became wealthy and influential, everyone got on with their lives, working, marrying, burying, and raising families.

Among them was Alexo Gorgoz, one of those who had masterminded the effort to secure the revised Edict of Grace. Gorgoz became Deza's most important Morisco leader during the era and helped to establish a tradition of accommodating dissimulation among its crypto-Muslims. Born in about 1534, Alexo was native to the town. Little is known of his parents, but they were presumably first generation converts from Islam. His father, Gerónimo Gorgoz (d. 1557), was a cobbler and sat on the town council in the 1530s and 1540s. He and his wife Catalina Ropiñón (d. 1563) raised at least four children. Two boys survived into adulthood, Alexo and his elder brother Gerónimo (b. ca. 1520). According to their own admission and the testimony of others, the brothers actively engaged in Islamic practices for much of their lives.

In his December 1570 confession for the Edict of Grace, for example, the elder sibling, Gerónimo, confessed having been exposed to Islam in ca. 1565 when he and his wife had traveled to Aragonese Sestrica to inspect some beehives they owned. They had lodged for seven or eight days with one *mosén* Sancho, a local Morisco. Sancho and his wife Juana had informed their guests that Ramadan (of which, purportedly, they had never heard) was upon them and that they could "earn many pardons" by fasting. The Dezanos took up the fast that year and Sancho encouraged them to practice almsgiving as well. Particularly on days when Gorgoz was unable to fast or in years when he could not fix the precise dates for Ramadan, he made it a practice to give alms to needy Moriscos.[8]

Yet this was probably an incomplete confession on Gerónimo's part. Other, more substantive, evidence surfaced against both brothers in Ana de Almoravi's trial. Arrested in 1570, Ana's testimony carefully deflected blame from the members of her circle, but she proved willing to denounce others. She made the February 1571 denunciations primarily in view here about a month after her one and only experience of inquisitorial torture. Although doubtlessly fashioned to suit her needs, the specificity of her statements and their correspondence with independently verifiable information nevertheless suggests they were not mere fabrications.

Among other things, she spoke at length about Pedro el Cañamenero, the alfaquí from Villafeliche, and his 1565 visit to town. According to Almoravi, the local men who paid for Cañamenero's maintenance during his "five or six" months of teaching in Deza learned Aljamiado and were instructed about "what they needed to do."[9] But knowledge of the alfaquí spread and others—both men and women—took advantage of the opportunity to sit at his feet. One of the groups subsequently organized for recitation of prayers and meals convened in Alexo Gorgoz's home.[10] The extent to which these groups remained in place after Cañamenero's departure is unclear, but Ana de Almoravi claimed that Gorgoz himself continued to practice regular prayers in an Islamic style, even if he was doing so alone. In June 1567 she entered his house without announcing herself and found him in an upper room kneeling on a cloth and "doing azalas, lowering and raising himself." She heard him saying *Al-hamdu lillahi*, a portion of the Quran's first surah, which is recited during daily prayers.[11]

Despite their ties to the Law of Mohammed, the brothers cut quite a figure about town. Rather than becoming a cobbler like his father, the elder brother Gerónimo moved into farming, bought property, and became an adept local politician. He acquired a variety of fields and properties in and around Deza, but his business interests extended beyond the merely local for by the 1560s he and his wife Ana la Manceba had business interests in Aragon, among them the aforementioned beehives.[12] The honey they produced was transported northward to Biescas, near the French border, where it was used in poultices.[13] The transportation of agricultural goods was probably the major source of Gerónimo's wealth, which in 1571 was reckoned the greatest among Deza's Moriscos.[14]

Gerónimo's growing wealth and status in the community provided new opportunities and he began to appear regularly among the members of the town council. He held various offices in 1560, 1565 (around the time of Cañamenero's visit), 1572, and 1577. In 1570 (the year of the Edict of Grace) and 1575 he served as co-magistrate and would have done so again in 1579 but for his death in October of the preceding year. Although his wife gave birth to multiple children, they all died "very young," so, having no heirs of his body, Gerónimo established a pious work (*obra pía*) that provided dowries for poor and orphaned Moriscas of "his lineage."[15]

Alexo was cut from the same cloth as his elder brother. As a younger man, at least, he played a role in Deza's Morisco-run pottery works located north of town just outside the walls. The endeavor began in the mid-1540s by permission of the duke, to whom the operators paid 104 *reales* in rent per annum, and was initially operated by Francisco de Baptista, a frequent associate of the Gorgoz brothers.[16] By midcentury, the works had passed onto the Liñán family, close relatives to Alexo and Gerónimo on their father's side.[17] Alexo himself was described as a potter into the early 1570s and may have continued his involvement in that industry, but after successfully brokering the revised Edict of Grace in 1571 his standing in Deza rose to new heights.

Immediately afterward, he began to sit frequently on the town council—in 1572, 1575, 1577, 1578, 1581, 1583, 1593, and 1598—and three times held the office of magistrate. His status among the Moriscos was such that one local Old Christian described him posthumously as "the head and governor of them all, whatever their station, such that they did nothing, no matter what it was, without giving him notice of it." He claimed, "they did" whatever Gorgoz ordered "with such humility and simplicity that it was as if the King were commanding it."[18] Even Old Christians addressed him with respect.[19] He joined at least one confraternity, Our Lady of the Rosary, and in about 1579 became churchwarden (*mayordomo de la iglesia*). He continued in that post until the end of his life, at which point he generously forgave a 200-ducat loan to the church building fund.[20]

To social prestige and pious activities Alexo added financial muscle. Some wealth, especially real property, came to him at his brother's death, but his own efforts were also profitable. Mostly located in and around Deza, his assets included houses, farmlands, several apiaries, corrals, stables, and cave warehouses, in which he stored goods, especially linen cloth.[21] He acquired quality household furnishings and substantial coin. Alexo also invested in the town itself. Because Deza's council controlled little rentable municipal property—the duke owned most of it personally—the council had to devise alternative revenue streams to pay for extraordinary expenses. One such expediency was to pay out annuities in exchange for lump sum investments. In 1585 Alexo and the council agreed to terms for a redeemable annuity, which drew upon the revenue produced by some of his agricultural land.[22] The land, valued at 800 ducats, returned 50 ducats per year during his life and continued after his death.

Despite marrying twice, first to Inés de Deza (alias la Montera; d. 1578) and then to the much younger Ana López (b. ca. 1568), Alexo's domestic life mirrored his brother's, for none of his children survived infancy.[23] Nevertheless, he cultivated paternal relationships with young relatives. He lodged and employed his grandnephew Juan Corazón (1579–aft. 1616) from the time he was a boy until Gorgoz's death. Ana de Hortubia (ca. 1577–aft.1608), his first wife's cousin, lodged and served in Gorgoz's home for seven or eight years. Her father had died when she was young and, although Ana's mother still lived, Alexo took it upon himself to act in loco parentis. In about 1596 he saw the young woman married from his own home and almost certainly provided for her dowry.[24]

Even his death in November 1599 did not stop his generosity. Juan Corazón was provided for, and most of Gorgoz's moveable property and household goods were entailed upon a sister.[25] His "nephews" (actually cousins once removed) Luis and Gerónimo de Liñán, who by then were operating the family pottery works, received some of their uncle's real property outright, but the bulk of his wealth was put to other uses.[26] In the final disposition of his worldly goods, Alexo arranged for a novena and anniversary Mass, burial by the town's clerical chapter, and four hundred Masses to be said for his soul (half at the parish church and half at a monastery in nearby Almazán) over a span of two years. He gave three hundred *reales* to fund annual Masses on his saint's day, thirty *reales* to a local confraternity, and two hundred ducats for the fabrication of new church doors. Finally, he gave over the proceeds from his lucrative redeemable annuity to help establish poor and orphaned Moriscas in matrimony.[27]

That annuity was joined with the pious work established by his brother two decades earlier.[28] Gerónimo's endowment drew upon the income from land that produced eighteen *fanegas* of wheat and nine of barley annually.[29] The charity was established through the local parish and over-seen by a trio of patrons: the presiding town magistrate, the vicar, and Alexo's cousin Luis de Liñán (ca. 1547–aft. 1609). The latter collected the funds and dispersed them in accordance with decisions made jointly.[30] Whatever the formal role of the other patrons, Deza's Moriscos took it as a matter of course that Liñán could direct the funds as he saw fit.[31] Likewise, although the obra pía was founded to provide for girls of the Gorgoz "lineage," that was interpreted broadly to mean whomever the patrons (or at least Liñán) deemed appropriate, since most of the town's Moriscas were related in some fashion or other.

The minutiae of Alexo Gorgoz's life and legacy go some way toward evoking the atmosphere in Deza in the decades following the 1571 Edict of Grace. They were heady times of growth. North of town, the construc-tion of the duke's house and garden, a project that had begun in the 1550s, was completed in the 1570s. In the heart of Deza, 1579 saw the addition of a roof and vaulted ceiling to the striking new parish church, a build-ing suited to the town's growing population. Major renovations were undertaken on the fortress as well. The local economy was buoyed by the influx of rural laborers and also saw internal growth. But Deza benefitted additionally from an increased share of the trade between Aragon and Castile during this period. Briefly in the 1560s it even displaced Ágreda as the second busiest dry port in Soria.[32] Opportunities abounded for local merchants and Morisco muleteers and drovers, who increasingly conveyed goods not only regionally but also to fairs and markets in Catalonia, the Basque Lands, Valencia, and across Castile and Aragon.

These years also saw a significant reorganization of Deza's political life. In one important example, late 1570 saw the duke appoint a new chief magistrate (alcalde mayor) over the Four Places of the Recompense, local hidalgo Francisco López de Rebolledo. Previously, that title had been reserved for men whom the duke had dispatched to exercise judicial power in his name in order to address specific crises or concerns. Now, for the first time, the nominee was not only a local but also the recently appointed alcaide of Deza's fortress and arsenal.[33] Although the chief magistracy gave him oversight of the four hamlets near town, López de Rebolledo understood the title to entail judicial authority within Deza and without reference or regard to the jurisdiction of the town's own magistrates. Unsurprisingly, alcaldes mayores became controversial figures, often perceived as heavy-handed and oppressive. Twice during the late sixteenth century, the town agitated for the removal of its chief magistrate.

The first of these efforts saw petitioners seek the dismissal of that same Francisco López de Rebolledo in 1571–72—not from being castellan but from the chief magistracy—claiming that his appointment created jurisdictional conflicts in town. Deza's co-magistrates (alcaldes ordinarios) asserted their privilege to act as judges of first instance in any civic disputes and resented the infringement of their judicial authority. The petitioners furthermore "humbly" asserted that it was justly contrary to Castilian law for the same man to be both castellan and chief magistrate of a place, since "the two are considered incompatible."[34] Ultimately, rejected by the citizenry, López de Rebolledo was removed and the duke named another local hidalgo, Gonzalo Fernández Abarca, to replace him in 1572. At his appointment, the new man was installed only as alcaide, the other title being noticeably absent, but within a few years it was restored.[35]

The removal of López de Rebolledo was a pyrrhic victory for his opponents but it demonstrates an important feature of Deza's political life during the period. The affair united Old and New Christians, especially the men who sat on the council. All felt threatened by what they perceived as a seigniorial attempt to restrict local privileges. Townsfolk responded with a united voice to that challenge in respectful but assertive language. The entire council—including Moriscos Francisco de Baptista (magistrate), Lope Guerrero (alderman), and Luis de Cebea (deputy)—signed the petition requesting that the duke redress their grievances. Time and time again during the 1570s, 1580s, and into the 1590s New and Old Christians collaborated on the council and elsewhere in the best interests (as they understood them) of the town and its citizenry.

Thus, if Deza experienced dramatic change toward the end of the century, those same years also witnessed collaboration between Moriscos and Old Christians. And that collaboration was more than merely political. Old Christians attended Morisco weddings and marriage suppers (although no evidence exists of the reverse). They visited one another's homes, joined many of the same confraternities, formed friendships, occasionally intermarried, ate and traveled together, and worked for and with one another. At significant moments of crisis—during times of plague, famine, drought, financial crisis, and in defense of their legal rights and privileges—the whole citizenry could unite in pursuit of common goals. Indeed, little evidence of division between Moriscos and Old Christians exists in the town's municipal or legal records. Instead, the tense years of the 1560s and early 1570s appear to have given way to a period of substantially diminished religious contentiousness.

Sometimes shared experience even helped to align the religious outlook of the citizenry. In Deza's sacramental register, for example, the priest Juan de Ozuel recorded a striking account of a freak storm that gathered at the edge of town on July 14, 1575 and struck the parish church with lightning. It damaged the building, and many of those inside were rendered senseless by the blast. Afterward, the people gave thanks to God for preserving them. The town's priests, "all" of the members of the town council, and "everyone" in Deza resolved henceforth to set July 15 aside in commemoration of the miracle.[36] Several Moriscos sat on the council that year, among them Gerónimo and Alexo Gorgoz. Four years previously they had confessed to Islamizing and received the Edict of Grace but, in the wake of this miraculous intervention, the brothers, together with everyone else in town, corporately expressed their thanks for divine mercy.[37]

If, however, unity could be fostered by shared experiences and forged in crises, those same crises could also expose weaknesses and cause fractures. To his Old Christian neighbors and local religious authorities, Alexo Gorgoz was the model of a Morisco who had sincerely embraced Christianity. Despite dallying with Islam as a young man, he had repented, abjured his errors in 1571, and spent the remainder of his life serving the town on the council and the parish as churchwarden. He and the local vicar became friends.[38] He dutifully confessed thrice annually, and when the inquisitor Dr. Francisco de Arganda passed through town as part of regional visitation in 1581, Gorgoz's Christian bona fides went unquestioned.[39] Even as he prepared for death, he went to great lengths to demonstrate his devotion by endowing Masses and novenas, making donations to a confraternity and the clerical chapter, establishing his obra pía, and funding construction of the doors for the parish church. Throughout most of the sixteenth century, this was sufficient to maintain his good reputation among Deza's Old Christians.

Yet the period immediately preceding Alexo's death again saw rising religious tensions in Deza, and a town that had been characterized by substantial cooperation between Moriscos and Old Christians become increasingly divided. After his death, as those divisions became even more pronounced, doubts emerged about his true allegiance. The memory of Alexo became a matter of dispute. His bequests to, and association with, the parish and various religious institutions made it difficult for anyone to denounce him as a heretic, and the parish vicar spoke of their "great friendship" and the mutual "confidence" they enjoyed.[40] Nevertheless, many Moriscos believed Gorgoz had lived as a secret Muslim who played a game of "caution and deception" so adroitly that he fooled the Christians into thinking he was one of them.[41]

During the same period, other seemingly Christianized Moriscos also had their sincerity questioned—not by local Christians but rather by Moriscos who inclined toward crypto-Islam. The brothers Agustín Carnicero (b. 1542) and Juan Agustín (b. 1550), for example, were the children of a Morisco father and an Old Christian mother. They wedded Old Christian women and married their own children to Old Christians. Although the Bishop of Sigüenza forbade the town's Moriscos from receiving the Eucharist beginning in the mid-1580s, Agustín and Carnicero were notable exceptions.[42] They and their children were omitted from a 1594 census of the town's Moriscos.[43] Yet, other Moriscos believed they knew these "wealthy" and "circumspect" men better than the bishop, local priests, and inquisitors.

One claimed to have seen Juan Agustín fasting for Ramadan on "some years" but noted that the brothers proceeded with such wariness (*recato*) and displays of Christian piety that they were regarded as "the safest in the world." They separated themselves from the rest of the Moriscos socially and, probably, geographically as well by living in the Lower Neighborhood. They were reported to have refused to hold civic offices specifically afforded either to Moriscos or Old Christians. Instead, they labored to be seen as "neutral" in local politics in order to avoid calling attention to their ancestry. In 1607, however, when the Holy Office unexpectedly arrested a young Morisca named Ana Guerrera, the brothers contributed money for her room and board, and when inquisitorial pressure heated up in Deza a few years later, Carnicero purportedly agreed to hide some goods belonging to one Morisco couple.[44] For Moriscos Antón Guerrero el viejo and Gabriel de Medina, this was incontrovertible proof that the brothers were themselves crypto-Muslims, although others were less certain. When inquisitors pressed Antón's brother Juan to denounce Agustín and Carnicero, he claimed he "didn't know anything about them," although he had long since denounced dozens of relatives, friends, and other neighbors.[45]

Yet Alexo Gorgoz, not Agustín or Carnicero, proved to be the most contentious figure among Christianizing Moriscos, for his wealth continued to play an important role in Deza after his death and his activities had linked him so firmly to local civic and religious institutions. Thus, by the early seventeenth century, with many Moriscos and some Old Christians expressing doubts about the Gorgoz brothers' religiosity, inquisitorial officials became keen to accumulate evidence of their crypto-Islamic activities. As local inquisitorial familiar Pedro de Cisneros explained to the tribunal at Cuenca in 1608, Alexo had been the "richest of them all," and his estate could "supplement the shortfalls" of poor Moriscos, whose incarceration and trials were costing the Holy Office dearly but whose confiscated goods were insufficient to recoup expenses.[46]

The problem was Cisneros had no actual evidence of Islamic activities to offer; he merely emphasized Gorgoz's role as leader of the Moriscos until his death in 1599. And, in fact, evidence that the Gorgozes were secret Muslims was difficult to come by, for both men took pains to avoid behavior that might be perceived as Islamic after taking the Edict of Grace in 1570 and 1571. When, at the end of the sixteenth and in the early seventeenth centuries, Old Christians in Deza began to offer denunciations of local Moriscos, they often drew upon memories of events that had occurred while Alexo was alive, but his reputation remained unscathed. Although he lived in the Upper Neighborhood, no one remembered him being present at meetings for Islamic prayer and instruction, Moriscos weddings, or naming ceremonies, not even those attended by his own relatives and associates.

Yet, inquisitors in Cuenca, eager to make up financial shortfalls, found it expedient to press defendants on their knowledge of the brothers and were especially eager for details about Alexo's estate.[47] Some, like Ana de Hortubia, the young relative who had lived in his home for years, refused to denounce him. After more than two years in the secret jails, she was asked about Alexo and his wealth. She briefly described his obra pía and donations to the parish but claimed, "She does not know that he was a Moor, but rather [she considered him] a good Christian, nor did she ever see him do or say anything that she should reveal."[48] The closest she came to speaking against him, nearly three years into her trial and long after she had denounced a host of Deza's other Moriscos, was when she admitted that, while living in Alexo's house, she had told him she was fasting as a Muslim. He had scolded her for it but told her, "Since she was fasting in his house, she must keep it a secret in such a way that no one knows." As for the master of the house, "She never saw Alexo Gorgoz fast or declare himself to be a Moor."[49]

Juan Corazón, another young relative with close ties, was even more guarded. Queried about the Gorgoz brothers by inquisitors on two occasions, both times he was unequivocal. He admitted they had endowed the pious work and claimed the Liñán brothers had control of Alexo's goods but categorically denied any Islamic activities.[50] Faced with heavy torture, Corazón refused to denounce either man or implicate his benefactor in any way. Other Moriscos proved more pliable.

By autumn 1607, for example, Juan Guerrero (b. ca. 1555) knew he was in trouble. His daughter Ana had been denounced by local Old Christians and arrested in July of that year by the Holy Office. He doubted she would keep silent for long under the pressure she would face in Cuenca. Sure enough, in early November, her parents and seven others were arrested and transported to Cuenca primarily on the basis of the girl's testimony. Believing that the only way forward for him was to come clean, Juan confessed his own Islamic activities and began denouncing others almost as soon as he arrived in the secret jails.

Yet, he was slow to denounce the Gorgoz brothers formally. Perhaps Guerrero felt indebted to them, since he and his wife Francisca de Hortubia had married in ca. 1585 thanks to Gerónimo's obra pía. In March 1608 one of Guerrero's cellmates reported that Guerrero did not want to mention the brothers Gorgoz to the inquisitors lest they appropriate the endowments.[51] But in mid-May 1608 he told another cellmate (a Morisco from Deza named Francisco de Cebea) that he wanted to denounce Alexo Gorgoz. He was convinced that Ana de Hortubia, his sister-in-law, had already done so, which left him appearing to be withholding information.[52] Since Guerrero was intent upon making the denunciation, Cebea advised him to say no more than that Gorgoz was "a Moor" and to avoid any elaboration. Old Christians, explained Cebea, believed Alexo Gorgoz had died a Christian and "if you reveal the cautions and deceptions [cautelas y engaños] we have practiced to make them believe we are Christians, we will lose everything, and after we've been released from here, however much we dissimulate, they will know our hearts."[53]

Although Cebea promised his cellmate fifty ducats from the endowment if he would keep quiet, Guerrero requested an audience and, on June 18, informed the inquisitors that he had known Gorgoz to be a Muslim since at least 1592. That was when they had mutually declared themselves "to be Moors" and followers of the "Law of Mohammed." Guerrero had seen Gorgoz and his first wife fasting for Ramadan on multiple years, and once, when Guerrero was helping him bring in a harvest of wheat on a Christian fast day, Gorgoz provided the laborers with a meal of sausage and other meat. The couple, he claimed, were the "finest Moors" (más *fino moros*) in Deza. He went on to describe Alexo's estate and named other witnesses who could corroborate his testimony.[54]

The potential corroborators, however, turn out to be dead ends. Juan Corazón and Ana de Hortubia had little to offer (or at least refused to offer much) despite knowing Alexo well. Cecilia la Montera (Inés de Deza's aunt) might have cast light on the situation, but she had died in her cell several months before. Francisco de Cebea's trial has been lost. Guerrero also offered his two brothers Antón and Lope as potential witnesses. Antón (like Juan) immediately denounced anyone and everyone who came to mind. Yet, more than three years into his trial, when inquisitors asked him about the Gorgoz brothers, he eagerly described their estates but otherwise claimed to know "nothing about them."[55]

The other brother, Lope, initially proved even more reluctant than Antón or Juan to offer denunciations and, when queried about Gorgoz, would only say that he knew nothing about him but had seen him "live in a very Christian way."[56] Nine months later, however, having been delivered to the torture chamber, Lope broke down and provided a stream of denunciations, the last of which was against Alexo Gorgoz. Reversing his previous statement, Guerrero now claimed that eighteen or twenty years previously (ca. 1592), Gorgoz had approached him and privately confided that the moon had appeared, signaling the start of Ramadan. Subsequently Gorgoz had fasted and "declared himself to be a Moor." Thenceforth they had "treated each other as Moors and talked to one another as such." Why, the inquisitor asked, had Lope withheld this information when asked about Gorgoz nine months previously? "Because," he explained, "at that time he was denying everything he knew about him and all the rest."[57]

It is impossible to know for certain whether Alexo Gorgoz continued to perform Islamic rites after receiving the Edict of Grace in 1571. Given his high profile both in life and in death, remarkably little dirt was found to sully his reputation. Despite the efforts of the Holy Office, only Juan and Lope Guerrero denounced Gorgoz; their testimonies went unverified and might have been fabricated. Since the inquisitors at Cuenca never attempted to appropriate the Gorgoz wealth, we must assume they judged the evidence insufficient. Even the town's Old Christians had trouble mounting an attack against him. If he did continue to perform

Islamic rites, then he followed an even more circumspect course than Deza's other crypto-Muslims. As a result, most Old Christians simply regarded him as a true convert.

Perhaps a more nuanced way of viewing Alexo Gorgoz's religious life is to see him as a crypto-Muslim who eschewed outward conformity to Islam in favor of internal devotion. The baptism of Castile's Moriscos in 1502 was followed two years later by a *fatwa* delivered by the so-called Mufti of Oran. Islam had long endorsed the notion that permissible acts of dissimulation existed (*taqiyya*), and the Mufti's ruling, which circulated in manuscript copies in Castile and later in Aragon, provided Moriscos with legal justification to conform externally to Christianity when their lives or livelihoods were in danger.[58] In offering this defense, the Mufti signaled that Moriscos could separate intentions (*niyya*) from external actions (*a'mal*). Normally the two needed to be aligned, but when this proved impossible it was understood that intentions took priority.[59] As long as one guarded the truth in one's heart, the body could perform actions otherwise forbidden.

This was meant to be a temporary solution, for the Mufti expected the Turks to recapture Iberia soon and for the Moriscos to be reincorporated into *dar al-Islam*. Instead, for roughly a century, many of Spain's Moriscos lived as Muslims who baptized their children, recited the Lord's Prayer, and joined Christian confraternities. This dissociation between intentions and actions became the status quo for those Moriscos who remained committed to Islam. Rather than becoming martyrs, they became dissimulators. According to the Mufti, Spain's crypto-Muslims were permitted to use double *entendres*, verbal ambiguities, and mental reservation in their speech, and their actions could be couched in similar ways. When performing the ritual ablutions that preceded prayer, for example, they were permitted to "do it under the appearance that you are taking a bath, 'swimming' in the sea or river." When even that was impossible, he advised his reader, "Rub your hands against the walls, or tree or stone, or sand." If the daily prayers could not be performed at the normal time, "do it at nighttime, in this manner you will fulfill your obligation." If almsgiving drew attention, then give "to the poor as a present" or "waste it among the people to create fame of being beneficent and liberal."[60]

Whether they had direct knowledge of the Mufti's *fatwa* or not, Deza's Moriscos followed the course he charted. In 1569 local Morisco Diego Martínez, for example, purportedly taught two other men to wash and pray during Ramadan, explaining that if they only performed the rituals once, "they could fulfill their duty for all the times they had missed," and when they wore clean clothes during Ramadan they could put them on "underneath" the dirty ones. If it was impossible to fast in Deza without being discovered, they could "stop fasting" and "make up the days they missed later."[61] Or, as *mosén* Sancho purportedly instructed Gerónimo Gorgoz, if unable to fast, then give alms instead.[62] Similarly, when Román Ramírez el mayor decided to perform ritual ablutions, he did so in the local river at night, and when Luis de Cebea el menor could not perform the physical motions associated with guadoc while in the jails of the Holy Office, he enacted the ceremony "by word" alone.[63]

Not all Muslims condoned this sort of dissimulation. In 1491, the North African Muslim jurist Aḥmad al-Wansharīsī penned an influential *fatwa* that explained, "Emigration from the land of unbelief to the land of Islam is an obligation until the Day of Judgment."[64] Failure to keep intention and action integrated would, he feared, mean the slow acculturation of Spanish Moriscos to Christianity.[65] Thus, early in the sixteenth century Yuce Banegas, an esteemed Islamic scholar from Granada, had warned the mysterious Castilian Morisco known as the Young Man from Arévalo,

Son, I do not weep for the past, for there is no way back, but I do weep for what you have yet to see if you are spared, and you live in this land, in this peninsula of Spain. . . . For anybody with feelings it will all seem bitter and cruel. What troubles me most is that Muslims will be indistinguishable from Christians, accepting their dress, and not avoiding their food. May God grant that at least they avoid their actions and that they do not allow the [Christian] religion to lodge in their hearts.[66]

Despite the inherent dangers, Moriscos like the Gorgoz brothers attempted to guard Islam in their hearts while conforming externally to Christianity. If they performed Islamic obligations and rites at all, they did so in the most circumspect of ways.[67]

Or, at least, this is what their Morisco neighbors believed about the brothers. Whatever their actual intentions, soon after Alexo's death, Deza's crypto-Muslims viewed the siblings as dissimulators who had merely accommodated their external behavior to Christian standards, thereby preserving their lives and livelihoods, and passing their legacy on to the next generation. Certainly Francisco de Cebea and Juan Guerrero believed this to be the case. The pious work of the Gorgozes was an important local element in the network of dissimulation that had been and was being constructed in Deza, the region, and across Spain. But if the brothers worked (or were believed to have been working) toward the viability of crypto-Islam in Iberia, they did not seek to do so by overthrowing the state, challenging civil or religious laws, or in any way directly pursuing the public acceptance of Islam. Rather than following the lead of Lope del Sol and Aunt Teresa, they embraced the Deza-Cañamenero school's emphasis on submission to the will of God and obedient sacrifice. The fact that they had wealth and status to protect only made this option more attractive.

Their accommodation to the dominant religious culture enabled them to collaborate with the Old Christian elite as virtual equals even as they gained the respect of other Moriscos. But their version of Islam (such as it was) privileged privacy and individual religiosity while altogether lacking a communal element *except* perhaps in its posthumous outworking. Presumably this was the reason why the Gorgoz endowment continued to operate in Deza into the nineteenth century, long after the brothers were dead and their questionable origins forgotten.[68]

If Alexo Gorgoz was a crypto-Muslim, his success belies the dangers of taking this approach. Of the other Moriscos who accommodated— Agustín Carnicero, Juan Agustín, and their children, but also Alonso de Paciencia (who purportedly ate pork and drank wine on a regular basis to avoid scrutiny), María Navarra (the sister of Bernardino Almanzorre), and her son Gerónimo de Molina el menor (who became a swineherd)[69]—at least some remained in Deza after the expulsion, yet no evidence exists that they maintained any sort of allegiance to Islam in the years that followed, or that they wanted to do so. When the Inquisition visited town again in 1616, no one said anything about the lingering presence of a few Moriscos; now it was all about witches in the nearby village of Cihuela.[70] For the Moriscos who accommodated, the disassociation between belief and action appears to have moved them toward the appropriation of Christianity.

This long-term trajectory of their accommodating was not only a function of the tendency for liturgical action to spawn conviction and belief—heart and body are not so easily disentangled—but also of the fact that by the end of the sixteenth century in Deza the period of collaboration and cooperation between Old Christians and Moriscos was drawing to a close. This rupture revealed a number of strategies beyond complete external conformity. But, more alarmingly, it shone a light on a thriving crypto-Islamic community that had grown up in Deza since the Edict of Grace and that was tied into Morisco networks spanning nearly the entire Iberian Peninsula.

4

Seeking a Freer Land

Lope Guerrero's Story

The decade following the Edict of Grace in Deza was a quiet one, at least as far as inquisitorial activity was concerned. Those Moriscos who had been reconciled to the church found themselves responsible for making three annual confessions; most attempted to fulfill that duty. Some took this as a time to reevaluate their religious lives, and many drifted toward Christianity, even if only for the sake of external compliance and to avoid condemnation as relapsed heretics. Like Gerónimo and Alexo Gorgoz, they found it possible to accommodate their lives to the expectations of Christianity and to conform—merely externally or internally as well. They learned the prayers of the church, joined confraternities, and saw their children baptized and confirmed.

For Old Christians, however, fears and concerns lingered about the Moriscos' religious sincerity, and not without reason. Although the events of 1569 and 1571 had set Muslim Deza on its heels and frustrated aspirations, a core of adherents had been driven underground but not defeated. What was more, in the final decades of the sixteenth century the church signaled its unwillingness either to settle for mere external conformity or turn a blind eye when the mask of conformity slipped. In Deza this became clear in summer 1581 when the inquisitor Dr. Francisco de Arganda passed through town during a regional visitation. Arganda had previously served as the prosecuting attorney (*fiscal*) for the tribunal in Seville before being named inquisitor at Cuenca in the 1570s. Like most of his counterparts at that tribunal, he was a hardliner on the Morisco question and his interactions with the New Christians in Deza did nothing to moderate this impulse. Within two years of his visit, Arganda was actively advocating for more intense persecution of crypto-Muslims, including capital punishment for first offenses.[1]

His arrival in Deza on Thursday, June 15 was followed on Sunday by the reading of a formal Edict of Faith from the pulpit. It urged and commanded audience members to scour their consciences and denounce anyone whom they knew or believed to have rejected the faith or committed a sin over which the Holy Office exercised jurisdiction.[2] Come Monday morning Dezanos responded by appearing before the inquisitor to denounce neighbors. But, evidence that relations between Moriscos and Old Christians in Deza had improved over the last decade and that tensions were at a low ebb, denunciations against the town's New Christians were slow to materialize and restrained when they did.

To judge from the denunciations, by the early 1580s the most contentious Morisco-related issue was the ongoing presence of Aragonese troublemakers. The burial practices of Deza's own Moriscos, which differed from those of Old Christians, worried some, but those concerns were muted by comparison with the accusations made during the 1569 visitation. Even less controversial than the burials were Morisco marriages. They regularly participated in formalized marriage negotiations and betrothal celebrations, which occurred prior to the sacramental solemnization of the union by the church and were often attended by Old Christians, including members of the clergy. But such festivities, which had been a cause for concern during the 1569 visitation, went unmentioned in 1581, although accusers now spoke more specifically about the "Moorish" nature of certain activities.[3] And while local Moriscos' idiosyncratic death and burial practices were troubling, their religious significance was unclear. A foursome of Old Christian youths, for example, reported that on Christmas night 1580 a group of Moriscos had carried the body of a dead Morisco child from house to house in a shroud, wailing and lamenting as they went. But no one knew quite what to make of this. The youths imagined it was either "a Moorish ceremony or some foolishness," and Inquisitor Arganda dismissed it out of hand.[4]

The only other matter of consequence laid against Deza's Moriscos was the claim that some of the families living in the Upper Neighborhood around the *Corrillo* plaza cooked meat empanadas and stews late on Thursday nights, presumably with the intention of consuming them on Fridays and, thereby, breaking the church's prohibition against eating meat. The meals were cooked at the neighborhood's communal oven, which was operated during most of the 1570s by Old Christian Martín Blasco, an immigrant from Villarroya de la Sierra in Aragon. Blasco had told a neighbor that he had proof of Islamic activity among Deza's Moriscos. Unfortunately, in early 1580 he had returned to Villarroya following a row with Lope de Deza (alias, del Sol), who may even have threatened the baker's life.[5]

This loose end intrigued Arganda but, before pursuing it, he focused on the opportunities at hand. On Saturday, June 21 he initiated a second phase to his visitation by calling in the confessional receipts for the Moriscos who had taken the Edict of Grace a decade earlier. Arganda determined that in sixty-one cases the documents failed to demonstrate that their owners had successfully complied with the terms of their reconciliation. He summoned these individuals for further examination.

Among them was that same Lope de Deza who may have threatened Martín the baker. Lope (1539–1611) was a native Dezano muleteer who had narrowly avoided inquisitorial arrest a decade earlier. According to the testimony of an eleven-year-old Old Christian boy, when news of the Alpujarras Revolt had reached town in 1569, Lope de Deza and Lope Guerrero (b. 1547) had urged their companions to join the uprising: "Let's go to Sierra Nevada and die with our friends."[6] Although the boy's testimony was suspect, the Holy Office ordered the arrest of both men.[7] They evaded capture, however, and in early 1571 ended up back in Deza where they offered unremarkable confessions to Inquisitor Madriz, took the Edict of Grace, and were reconciled to the church.[8]

A decade later, during Dr. Arganda's visitation, Lope de Deza presented his confessional receipts according to the inquisitor's order. Subsequently summoned to appear before Arganda, Lope did so believing that his affairs were in order. He admitted that six years earlier he had missed a confession while traveling to Medina del Campo and Zaragoza during Advent, but he had confessed belatedly and performed the penance assigned by his confessor. Lope was, therefore, surprised when the inquisitor accused him of failing to confess and of having presented false confessional receipts. As it happened, rather than writing out a receipt for each confessant after each confession over the previous decade, most local priests had produced them in bulk at the time of Arganda's arrival. In their haste mistakes were made.

The inquisitor saw this as inherently dishonest and incongruous with the terms of Lope's reconciliation. He even considered initiating cases against two local confessors.[9] Yet, if Lope and the sixty other Moriscos who were called to account were guilty, their crime was more a matter of carelessness than willful disobedience or deception. Arganda recognized that using confessional slip-ups as a pretext for retrying the Dezanos as relapsed heretics was a waste of resources.[10] In the end, as happened to all of the Moriscos examined in late June and early July, Arganda merely fined Lope (3,000 mrs.—about 88 *reales* or 11 ducats) to cover "extraordinary expenses" and admonished him to do better.[11]

Arganda completed his examinations of the recalcitrant confessants on July 12 with little to show for it. Yet he remained convinced that Deza's Moriscos were truly crypto-Muslims whose compliance with the church was mere show, so he pursued the one avenue that remained unexplored: the possibility that Martín Blasco the baker, now living in Aragon, might supply hard evidence. Following a morning audience on the twelfth, Arganda's entourage traveled a day's ride due west into Aragon (and outside of his jurisdiction) to meet with Blasco. But the baker had little to offer beyond unsubstantiated rumors of meetings at the Liñán pottery works, stews and empanadas cooked on Thursday nights, and Moriscos who looked faint during Advent (and must, therefore, have been fasting for Ramadan). Asked directly whether Lope de Deza had threatened to murder him if he denounced the Moriscos, the baker acknowledged leaving town for fear of the man but maintained their quarrel had been about a broken window in the oven.[12] He had nothing more to offer. Arganda returned to Deza, finished his work, and left town four days later, presumably disappointed at the harvest.

Either because his confessional behavior had been faultless or because he was not in Deza at the time, Arganda did not examine Lope Guerrero, the man who, along with Lope de Deza, had urged their companions to join the Granada uprising in 1569.[13] Yet Guerrero, no less than the other Lope, played a key role in establishing a pattern of practice for Deza's crypto-Muslims and in passing on Islamic rites, ceremonies, and beliefs to the generation reared in the wake of the Edict of Grace. Alexo Gorgoz's Islamic identity (to the degree that it existed outside the memories of those who survived him) was divorced from external performance except perhaps of the most profoundly cryptic sort. By contrast, Lope Guerrero and others simulated conformity to Christianity much of the time but also sought opportunities to practice Islam by enacting it with their bodies as well as by guarding it in their hearts.

The Guerreros were one of Deza's largest Morisco families. Lope's parents, Lope (d. ca. 1582) and María de Sepúlveda (d. ca. 1597), raised six sons, all of whom survived into adulthood, married, and raised children of their own. María and Lope were an odd couple, for while he indoctrinated his sons into crypto-Islam she was an Old Christian on her mother's side and, Lope claimed, a sincere believer.[14] Her son Antón likewise asserted she was as devout "as any Old Christian."[15] Yet, their brother Juan purportedly told his cellmates in Cuenca that she had been persuaded to follow the Law of Mohammed by María de Luna (d. bef. 1569), the mother of Román Ramírez el menor.[16]

When inquisitors accused Juan of making the preceding statement, he acknowledged it but offered an emendation: he did not know "with certainty" that she was a Muslim. His point, he asserted, was rather that his mother had gone to great pains to see that her sons were viewed as Christians even though she "knew" they were secret Muslims.[17] Thus, she forbade her three youngest sons to take the Edict of Grace in 1571. And in 1584, when the bishop of Sigüenza withheld the Eucharist from Deza's Moriscos, he "ordered" the town's parish priest to give it to María de Sepúlveda. Yet she refused to receive the sacrament unless the same privilege was extended to the rest of her family. The request was granted and thereafter she and her sons communed annually.[18]

2. The Guerrero family tree.

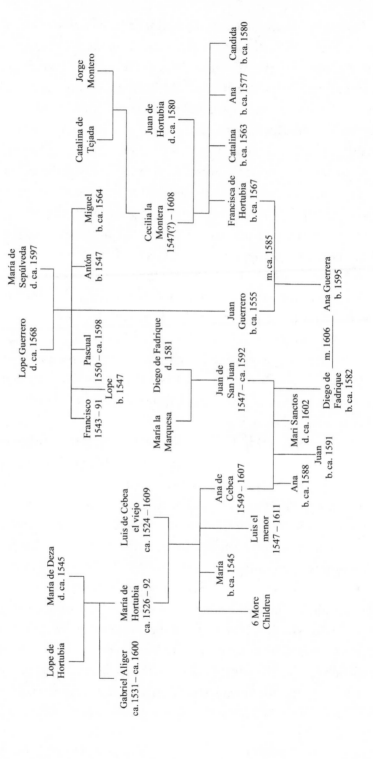

As for Lope, despite his participation in the Eucharist, he considered himself a Muslim and tried to live as one both internally and, whenever possible, externally. At around age sixteen, he left home to apprentice with blacksmith Miguel de Deza (his mother's half-brother) in Torrubia de Soria, about a dozen miles north of town. He spent most of the 1560s there but returned home at the end of the decade to marry Margarita de Truillo (alias de Vera) from Ariza (Zaragoza), who died just a few years later. After her death, Lope went back to Torrubia, where he remained as a journeyman, working with his uncle for some years before returning to Deza in the early 1580s. There, he established his own forge and married a second wife, Ana de Deza (d. ca. 1594).

The canonical prohibition against consanguineous unions kept the marriage from being solemnized by the church for a time. The trouble was not in securing a dispensation from Rome—Lope simply had to pay the price. Rather, he was slow to collect and present it to the episcopal provisor so that the ceremony could be performed in the parish. In fact, he and Ana had already been married "in the Moorish fashion" by a Morisco from Ariza and were living as husband and wife.[19] By the time he finally collected the dispensation, Ana was two months pregnant and, lacking a provision for dispensing with the sin of fornication, the document no longer sufficed. Ana was prevailed upon to swear a false oath before the vicar, deny the pregnancy, and claim that she and Lope had lived chastely.[20]

Chastity, however, whether inside of marriage or outside of it, was not one of Lope's virtues. Even before the death of his second wife in ca. 1594, he was widely known in Deza to have had affairs with María la Jarquina (b. ca. 1568), the widow of Luis de Hortubia el mayor (d. ca. 1592), and Isabel del Valdelagua, his wife's sister-in-law.[21] His affair with Isabel continued into the seventeenth century.[22] María de Cebea (b. ca. 1546) was another of his conquests. This so upset her father Luis de Cebea el viejo (ca. 1524–1609) that he thereafter blocked Lope's appointment to any posts on the town council.[23] In fact, the blacksmith's reputation as a womanizer was so bad that in 1606 he was made the convenient scapegoat for a sexual indiscretion of which he was entirely innocent.[24]

These intimate details of daily life played out alongside the drama of Lope's religious journey.[25] He was exposed to Islam in the mid- to late-1560s, probably through the influence of Bernardino Almanzorre, who had recently returned to Deza from his Aragonese apprenticeship. During one of Lope's visits home from Torrubia, Bernardino told him about having lived abroad and receiving religious instruction from a "very learned" man.[26] Lope indicated to his friend that he was curious about Islam and was obliged with a copy of instructions that outlined the method for performing guadoc and azala, along with four Arabic prayers written out in Latin script.[27] These he returned after a short time, but subsequently, back in Torrubia, an otherwise unknown Morisco named Hernando Mexo provided him with a similar set of instructions (regla) for Islamic ceremonies.[28] It was probably on a later visit to Deza, during Lent 1569, that Lope Guerrero encouraged his companions to make common cause with the Moriscos rising in Granada.[29] By that point, then, he considered himself a Muslim as he continued to do after 1571, despite having abjured his errors and received the Edict of Grace.

Lope's solution to the dilemma of post-1571 Morisco religiosity differed markedly from Alexo Gorgoz's, for Lope pretended to be a Christian only when he believed himself in danger of discovery. By contrast, however much Gorgoz may have remained a Muslim in his heart, the evidence suggests he set aside external observance of Islam after taking the Edict. The difference between the two approaches was subtle but real, and contemporary Moriscos acknowledged the distinction.

Consider the following anecdote told by the imprisoned Morisco Gabriel de Medina (ca. 1575–aft. 1610) and recounted by one of his cellmates to inquisitors. Once, Medina was traveling with the Dezano Alonso de Paciencia and his son whom he knew to be "Moors who keep the Law of Mohammed." As they went, Paciencia took out a bit of pork to eat and offered some to Medina. But when Paciencia's son saw the exchange he rebuked his father and wondered, "How could he not be ashamed to eat that?" For his part, Medina responded to the offer by claiming that he did not "want to deceive the world but rather to serve God."[30] Paciencia, who was regarded by other Moriscos as a Gorgoz-like crypto-Muslim who pretended to be Christian, is described here as having a different primary purpose than Gabriel de Medina, at least as the latter understood it.[31] Deception and dissimulation so permeated Paciencia's life that he felt no shame about eating pork even when no Old Christians were around to see him do it. Medina, by contrast, saw dissimulation as a tool to be used only when necessary. So did Lope Guerrero.

While Paciencia's and Gorgoz's religiosity had turned inward, severing intention from action, heart and mind from body, Guerrero frequently enacted his beliefs physically and in the presence of others. Over the course of his life, he regularly performed guadoc and azala, praying the same Arabic prayers that he had learned from Bernardino Almanzorre in the 1560s. He gave alms and fasted for Ramadan when he could do so discreetly and, when he could not, he fasted only a single day.[32] To facilitate fasting, in 1600 he even coordinated a trip to Calatayud in Aragon (to get iron for his forge) with the arrival of Ramadan. Lope traveled with his brothers Juan and Antón, his nephew Lope el menor, and Gabriel de Medina. After sunset, they gathered at the inn of local Morisco Juan Mayor to break their fast with Islamizing New Christians from various Aragonese towns: Sestrica, Belchite, Villafeliche, Brea, and Calanda, among others.[33] Even a pair of confused Old Christians joined the party and called for wine.[34] Both the fasting and the travel took their toll on Lope el viejo; on the return trip he was so exhausted that he had to ride, recalled his brother Juan.[35]

Travel of this type proved essential for many of Deza's Morisco men, and it was no coincidence that so many of them took up as muleteers, drovers, transporters, traders, and carriers at least seasonally. By the late sixteenth century, in addition to a busy local trade, they regularly trekked east into Catalonia and Valencia, north to the Basque Lands and Navarre, west to Zamora and Salamanca near the Portuguese border, and south as far as Ciudad Real, a few dozen miles from Andalusia. Moving at a pace of about twenty miles a day, muleteers often spent weeks on the road, primarily in the company of other Moriscos. As they traveled, they discussed Islam, fasted and broke their fasts together, performed ablutions, and recited prayers.

Sometimes they behaved daringly on the road, interacting with the Christian culture that permeated the physical landscape in ways that would have been unsafe at home. For example, on a trip to Soria, the brothers-in-law Hernando Martínez de la Castellana and Antón de Deza came upon one of the many shrines that dotted the landscape. They decided to move the statue out of its enclosure and leave it sitting in the open, joking that the saint was probably cold and would be warmed by the sunshine. Purportedly they performed similar stunts in their travels whenever the opportunity presented itself. Likewise, on one of his trips, Francisco de Cebea traveled past a hermitage. A boy begged alms for a candle to set before the Virgin, but Francisco boldly suggested, "if she were to go to bed early, she wouldn't need a light."[36]

Away from home, the risk of discovery diminished and Moriscos felt freer to behave like Muslims. "We can't be good Moors," explained one of them, "in a narrow (corta), Christian land like this one," where neighbors kept constant watch. Life on the road provided the men of Deza with sufficient latitude to bring actions into alignment with intentions.[37] It even offered sociability as they formed caravans with New Christians from Aragon or elsewhere in Castile. These and similar links strengthened and expanded networks that crisscrossed Iberia and of which Deza was a part.[38] Travelers lodged and traded with, worked for, and married Moriscos of like mind, and they treated the New Christians who visited Deza with similar hospitality. They encouraged one another to persevere, shared their knowledge of Islam, and proselytized those who were as yet unconverted.

The best documented of these excursions occurred in early 1604 when a group of Dezanos spent the entire month of Ramadan traveling from Reus (Tarragona) in Catalonia, some two hundred miles due east of town, through Aragon, and into and around Castile. Eight travelers, including Lope Guerrero's brothers Antón and Juan, left Deza in January loaded with wool.[39] When they arrived in Reus they rendezvoused with two or three more Dezanos who were staying at the same inn: Luis de Cebea (b. ca. 1580), his brother Francisco (b. ca. 1583), and perhaps another brother, Juan (b. ca. 1588).[40] Luis de Arride Lumán, a Morisco muleteer from Brea (Zaragoza), who was also something of a traveling alfaquí, joined the caravan there as well.[41]

On the return trip, which began at the end of January, Francisco de Cebea found himself the odd-man out. Nicknamed the Friar, he was the only one who had not yet been won over to Islam. At the end of the second day out from Reus, the travelers stopped for the evening in Falset. It was there on February 2 that the Ramadan moon appeared and the company began to fast—at least most of them. The next night, at an inn in Batea near the Catalonian border, an unknown and unnamed Morisco from Belchite purportedly approached Francisco, informed him of his error, and urged the young man to follow the Law of Mohammed "as all your companions are doing." Francisco demurred. The following morning the nameless Morisco joined their caravan and, again, approached Francisco, who was walking apart from the rest. He told him, "All of them over there, even his own brother, were fasting according to the Law and that [Francisco] was in error." If he wanted, the man would direct (*encaminar*) him in what he had to do and teach him some prayers. Francisco may have wavered at this point and fasted for half a day—although he denied it—but if he did, he soon refused to continue.[42] Thereafter, his companions "looked askance" at him, "mocked him, and murmured amongst themselves."[43]

Other members of the caravan took full advantage of the opportunity afforded by travel. They arrived in Jatiel on the evening of February 5, and when they found the inn full they lodged in houses instead. One of these was located in a large garden on the bank of the Martín River, and from there everyone but Francisco and the company's youths undressed, waded into the water, and performed ritual ablutions—"everyone declaring themselves to be Moors one to another."[44] They continued in this fashion until the party began to break up. The unnamed Morisco ended his journey when they got to Belchite, while Francisco and Luis de Cebea and Arride Lumán parted company with the rest at Viver de la Sierra (Zaragoza) half a day from the Castilian border.[45]

When the remaining travelers arrived at Deza, not yet halfway through Ramadan, several decided to continue on into Castile while the rest broke their fast early.[46] Those who continued loaded their train with almonds and went as far as Medina del Rioseco (Valladolid). On the return, they traveled the royal road to Valdenebro (Soria) on the banks of the Sequillo River, arriving there on March 2—the last day of Ramadan and, coincidentally, Shrove Tuesday. On the morning of the third and despite a heavy frost, Antón Guerrero and most of his companions braved the Sequillo's icy waters to perform ablutions and afterward celebrated the breaking of their fast "for the honor and joy of the festival of Ramadan" on Ash Wednesday, just as Christians were beginning theirs.[47]

These trips were important social experiences for participants and also times of religious devotion and proselytizing. And however ineffective had been the initial efforts to convert Francisco de Cebea while on the road from Reus, they eventually bore fruit. A little more than a year later, social pressure of another sort drew him toward the Law of Mohammed, for in 1605 his parents contracted a marriage with local Morisca María Martínez (b. ca. 1584). Having arrived in Deza from another trip the previous night, he was awakened in the morning and ushered into an upper room in his family's house where he was meant to wed María in a Moorish ceremony performed with Arabic prayers. Afterward, the officiant—none other than Luis de Arride Lumán—assured the couple they were truly married and could live as husband and wife. Marriage in the church, which Arride dismissed as a "joke and deception," would, of course, be necessary but merely for the sake of appearances.[48]

A parish wedding, however, was easier said than done in this case, for Francisco and María were second cousins and needed papal permission to dispense with the impediment. By April 1606, when the dispensation arrived from Rome, María was already visibly pregnant. To legitimize the marriage she delegitimized their child. Accompanied by her mother and mother-in-law, she appeared before the vicar and swore the child was not Francisco's but rather Lope Guerrero's.[49] In view of María's oath and the dispensation, the episcopal provisor approved the union and the vicar finally performed the ceremony in late May. None too soon, for a daughter was born the following month.[50]

Lope had not fathered the child, but in the years surrounding his 1600 Ramadan trip to Calatayud he was guilty of other things. Principally, he attended numerous semi-public events in Deza that allowed him to perform and participate as a member of the local Islamic community. In about 1605, for example, he attended the naming ceremony for

"Mohammed," the son of Gerónimo de Leonis, a Morisco smith from Ariza (Zaragoza) who married into the Guerrero family and kept shop on Deza's main plaza. Here Lope was merely an observer, but at weddings he frequently took a more active role.[51] In late 1606, for instance, he presided over the Moorish marriage of his niece Ana Guerrera (b. 1595) to Diego de Fadrique el mozo (b. ca. 1582), and a few months later, in early 1607, he officiated at the marriage of his own son Juan to María de Cebea. Both Diego and María were grandchildren of Luis de Cebea el viejo, whose daughter Lope had seduced some years earlier.[52] That the serial philanderer now found himself presiding over a pair of ceremonies uniting his family with los Cebea is an unexpected twist probably best accounted for by Lope's own religious maturation and his willingness to support the Cebea family during a time of crisis.

Over the previous decade, Lope had become a significant figure amongst Deza's crypto-Muslims. By the late 1590s he was participating in a group that gathered regularly to hear lectures about Islam organized around local gadfly Román Ramírez el menor. Other attendees included the heads and scions of several important Morisco families. The venue for their meetings, a house and gardens north of town owned by the dukes of Medinaceli but perpetually rented out to Ramírez, was a key center for Islamic confluence in Deza and regionally. Not only did the town's Muslims find it easier, as one inquisitorial familiar put it, to "practice their wickedness" within the confines of the property and away from prying eyes, but Aragonese New Christians also frequently visited and lodged there.[53]

The duke's garden provided Lope and his cohorts with an analog to what his muleteer brothers regularly experienced on the road. They could learn from the better informed and practice as Muslims in external conformity to the demands of Islam. Among the attendees of the gatherings, none of those whose names are known traveled regularly or were primarily occupied as farmers. Instead, they practiced a craft or trade in town: Lope Guerrero (blacksmith), Francisco de Miranda (painter), Lope de Arcos (blacksmith and politician), Francisco de Hortubia el Calistro (blacksmith), Juan de Amador (blacksmith), and Román Ramírez (gardener, among other things). Several of Ramírez's close male relatives attended as well, and it was his son Francisco (b. bef. 1570) who was responsible for turning Lope Guerrero into a "very firm Moor."[54]

Literacy also played an important role in Lope Guerrero's growing prestige amongst Deza's crypto-Muslims. His ability to read had facilitated his initial introduction to Islam in the 1560s, when Bernardino Almanzorre loaned him a set of written instructions.[55] Lope did not indicate from whom he learned to read and write, but like several generations of Moriscos, he probably studied with parish priest Gonzalo de Santa Clara.[56] Santa Clara taught his students using a primer, then set them to practice on a literary diet that included poetry, vernacular papal bulls, and chivalric tales.[57] Old Christian teachers continued to welcome Morisco students after Santa Clara's death. A sacristan took up the task for a time and later the town paid a layman to instruct the youths.[58]

Deza's literate Moriscos went on to read (and sometimes write) chivalric tales, Christian devotional works, medical treatises, poetry, farces, letters, the more pedestrian documents of local business, legal, and civic affairs, and various writings of Islamic interest. For the Muslims of Deza, men like Lope Guerrero who could interact with that last group of documents were important; they did not have the status or learning of an alfaquí and could not manage Aljamiado (let alone Arabic), but they received written instructions in Castilian translation or Latin script from more learned Aragonese Moriscos that, in turn, enriched local practice. Women in particular, because they rarely knew how to read, relied on literate men to provide them with Arabic prayers and phrases, which they memorized and shared amongst themselves.[59]

Lope's literacy and maturing conviction as a Muslim helps explain why friends and family came to view him as an appropriate figure to officiate at weddings but gaining the approval of the Cebea clan demanded more. Prudently, he joined his family in providing unwavering support for los Cebea as they weathered a series of lawsuits and feuds. Although traditionally Moriscos have been seen as socially monolithic, driven by a single interest (namely crypto-Islam), Deza's Moriscos could be remarkably fractious. In the early 1530s, for instance, the friendship between the Moriscas Isabel Rebolledo and Ana López soured after a falling out that saw Isabel call Ana a "bitch" and use "other injurious words" as well.[60]

The feud festered for decades and drew in not only the families of the two young women but also the sons of the town's castellan, each of whom took the side of their respective *enamorada*. The brothers behaved badly, fought often, and refused to speak to one another.[61]

The first decade of the seventeenth century saw Dezanos engage in several noteworthy internal conflicts. Sometimes Old Christians aligned against Moriscos and sometimes Moriscos formed up against factions within the larger body of Old Christians. But one of the period's most contentious and infamous feuds was that between the Cebea and Romo families, all Moriscos. On February 23, 1605, four days after the end of Ramadan and one week into Lent, Luis de Cebea el menor (1547–1611), already in poor health, was set upon in Deza's main plaza and publicly beaten by Juan el Romo, a man twenty years his junior. Martín Fernández Abarca, the town magistrate, immediately initiated an investigation and summoned witnesses, but the aggressor refused to appear.[62]

What drove Juan (who normally used the surname Mancebo)[63] to attack Cebea is unclear but may have to do with a failed bid on the part of the Cebea family to trade their Morisco identity for deeper integration into Old Christian society. In July 1592, Luis de Cebea el viejo was elected to hold office in the recently established confraternity of Santa Ana. The following year, his son Luis el menor was chosen to serve.[64] Santa Ana's members were among the most influential citizens in Deza and, except for the Cebeas, they were all Old Christians. By the mid-1590s the Cebeas disappear from confraternal records and no other Moriscos ever held office. Presumably, rebuffed by the Old Christians, the Cebeas were now thrown back upon the Morisco community.[65] If so, most welcomed them and even acclaimed the family as among the "the best" of the Upper Neighborhood.[66] The Romo clan, by contrast, supported several initiatives that suggest that, rather than pursuing rapprochement or intermixing, they championed a more distinct separation of Deza's Moriscos from its Old Christians. One of Juan Mancebo's elder brothers, for instance, served as the Moriscos' solicitor at the Royal Appellate Court for a series of trials pitting the inhabitants of the Lower Neighborhood against the Upper. Whatever his reasons for assaulting Luis el menor,

Mancebo subsequently celebrated his actions, and Deza's Moriscos lined up to support one side or the other as the crisis unfolded.[67]

Juan Guerrero and his kin immediately threw in their lot with the Cebea family, lamenting the offense, especially in light of the victim's age and poor health. The circumstances made retribution all the more appropriate and the Guerreros suggested appealing to the duke if the magistrates failed to provide satisfaction.[68] The wheels of justice turned slowly, however, and the situation devolved into a feud that spread amongst the two men's families, friends, and associates. Around this same time, Juan Guerrero verbally assaulted Mancebo's brother, Román el Romo. Recalling the fate of their father Francisco el Romo, who had died at the oars of a royal galley after his inquisitorial reconciliation, Guerrero creatively cursed Román as the "scoundrel son of a waste of a vile father."[69]

This strong support for the Cebea cause found purchase in the marriages that joined the clans together. In late 1606 the town celebrated the betrothal of Ana Guerrera to Diego de Fadrique el mozo, favorite grandson of Luis el viejo. At the party, Lope Guerrero let slip to an Old Christian attendee his intention to marry his own son to one of Luis's granddaughters, thereby forming an advantageous connection with the upper crust of the Upper Neighborhood.[70] Later that night, after most attendees had gone home, Lope and the Morisca María la Jarquina jointly presided over a small marriage ceremony "in the Moorish style." And in early 1607 Lope made good his boast, officiating at the marriage of his son Juan to María de Cebea.[71]

The strength of the union formed between the Guerrero and Cebea families was soon put to the test. For, although the investigation into the beating of Luis de Cebea eventually returned a guilty verdict and the magistrates settled on "a certain exile and pecuniary punishments," the sentence was not enforced.[72] If the duke was approached, in accordance with Juan Guerrero's suggestion, he failed to provide satisfaction. Outraged by the miscarriage of justice, two of the victim's sons, Luis el más mozo and Juan, fell upon Mancebo in the countryside on April 16, 1607, beating him very badly and cutting off an ear. The attack occurred the Monday after Easter, when, for the first time in more than two decades, the bishop had granted the town's Moriscos permission to receive the Eucharist.[73]

Left for dead and covered in blood, Juan Mancebo staggered back to town where he lingered on the verge of death for some time. His wife María feared his demise was imminent and set matters in order, borrowing a neighbor's bull of crusade and placing it on her husband's chest so that the vicar would grant absolution.[74] Bedridden for weeks, the injured man finally recovered and, on May 18, appeared before the town's notary public to initiate a lawsuit. The Cebea brothers had already been arrested and were being held in the town jail, in addition to Luis and Juan, Mancebo's suit named their father, mother, and brother (Francisco "the Friar"), along with three others: Hernando Martínez de la Castellana, Juan de Deza, and Lope Guerrero.[75]

Extant sources provide no details about the involvement in the attack of anyone other than the brothers Luis and Juan de Cebea, but Juan Mancebo named those who to him "seemed most guilty."[76] They were, in any case, all closely related to the Cebeas by marriage. Hernando Martínez de la Castellana was the father-in-law of Francisco de Cebea and Juan de Deza was the widower of Luis el viejo's daughter, Inés (d. ca. 1588[?]). Whatever their actual involvement, neither Lope nor the other in-laws were found guilty in the magistrates' final verdict.[77] No one was particularly satisfied with this resolution and the feud continued to escalate. Francisco de Cebea carried a sword and gun with him and moved about only at night. Román el Romo fixed a blade into his cane, hoping to kill Luis de Cebea el menor the next time their paths crossed.[78]

Belatedly, on October 12, 1607, Juan Mancebo appeared before Morisco Lope de Arcos and Old Christian Antonio de Ucedo Salazar, Deza's co-magistrates. The fine and exile that had been determined two and a half years earlier were now formally applied to him.[79] If the Cebeas and Guerreros saw this as a victory their joy was muted, for young Ana Guerrera was already in inquisitorial custody. Her parents and uncles would soon join her. In early March 1608, the inquisitors of Cuenca ordered the arrest and transportation to Cuenca of Luis el viejo and Francisco de Cebea, as well as Juan Mancebo's wife and brother, among others. As for Mancebo and his assailants, local civic authorities arrested all three of them on March 22, purportedly on account of the ongoing quarrel but in fact at the request of the Holy Office. They remained in Deza's public jails for the better part of two years, until the order arrived for them to be remanded to inquisitorial custody.[80]

In the wake of the Edict of Grace, Lope Guerrero and his associates had charted a course for following the Law of Mohammed in Deza. While some of the town's Moriscos may have inclined toward Christianity after their 1571 abjurations, and others took greater care to conform externally to Christian expectations, thanks to local efforts and renewed ties with Aragon, many of Deza's New Moorish Christians were once again gravitating toward Islam as the sixteenth century gave way to the seventeenth. Unlike the individualistic and internalized crypto-Islam practiced by or attributed to Alexo Gorgoz, Agustín Carnicero, and Alonso Paciencia, Morisco families such as the Guerreros, Cebeas, Fadriques, Romos, and many others embraced an approach that allowed them to share their religious lives with one another in more robust ways.

While traveling, they took advantage of opportunities to bring heart and body into alignment and fostered connections with Moriscos from Aragon and elsewhere. These social networks drew visitors into town and likewise bore fruit as a result of the literacy of Deza's Morisco men, who could thereby recall and circulate at home knowledge from abroad. Alongside family, friends, and neighbors, they enacted Islam locally in naming ceremonies, weddings, and meetings at the duke's garden as well as in the corporate performance of fasting, ritual ablutions, daily prayers, almsgiving, and in opposing or mocking Christian beliefs and practices.

This communalizing trajectory expressed the desire to be part of the broader Islamic community (*ummah*) and, more specifically, a hope that Spain's Muslims would be reincorporated into *dar al-Islam*. But that desire was tinged with regret, since Christianity remained triumphant in Iberia. Thus, Francisco de Cebea longed to see a Turkish invasion "so we might all be one."[81] And, from his inquisitorial jail cell, Juan Guerrero lamented that the Moriscos could not be "perfect Moors" in Spain since "they don't let us serve God." He proposed, "If we get out of here, we have to go to Algiers, where we can live freely (*en nuestras anchuras*)."[82]

The Moriscos' awareness of the contrast between the confining experience of living as Muslims in a narrowly Christian land and the breadth of a life lived openly among fellow believers was striking and often verbalized. More than a few hoped that the Ottoman Empire would conquer Spain but, barring that resolution, they considered Algiers or Istanbul potential venues for relocation. Some even saw France as a likely home. For a time Francisco de Cebea and Luis de Hortubia el Jarquino considered moving to Bayonne after the wheat harvest. They had it on good authority that many Moriscos from Granada were already there and that they would be able to live among them, *en sus anchuras*, since the French king had established a mosque and the Muslims of Bayonne practiced Islam openly in exchange for a tribute.[83]

Probably in the 1530s the Mancebo de Arévalo had visited Zaragoza where an Islamic scholar proclaimed that, even though they were currently experiencing a "period of terror," Allah would not "fail to punish" Iberian Muslims who "neglect[ed] the service of his kingdom insofar as [their] legal obligations were concerned." Yet, the scholar conceded, dissimulation was a legitimate approach and he permitted crypto-Muslims to join the "singing of the foreigners whereby the Christians seek salvation."[84] In making this pronouncement he endorsed the notion that Spain's Moriscos could live in such a way as to separate the intentions of their hearts from bodily practice and privileged the former over the latter.[85] Whether or not the scholar correctly interpreted Islamic law, the lived reality of Deza's Moriscos suggests how difficult a path it was to follow. Over the decades those who did so were troubled at their inability to be "perfect Moors" and longed for the full realignment of body and soul, whether through the overthrow of the Christian state, flight from Spain, or pursuit of martyrdom.

5

The Guardians of Morisco Culture

María la Jarquina's Story

Late one night in December 1596, María la Jarquina, a Morisca of Deza, was called to the home of Román Ramírez el menor. There, along with Román, his young second wife Ana de Ucedo, and the Morisco Francisco el Romo, la Jarquina participated in a secret Muslim naming ceremony (*fadas*) for the couple's infant daughter, who had recently been baptized María in the parish church. The mother was still recovering from what had been a difficult birth, so la Jarquina took the infant in her own arms and removed her swaddling clothes. An ornate gold and white bowl was filled with warm water and, in the water, the child's father placed several Spanish *pesos*, some coral, and a handful of wheat berries. The older woman took up the child, washed her, and probably recited a short Arabic prayer from the Quran. She also blessed the baby, saying, "May you be as abundant in worldly goods as this vessel," then gave her a Moorish name—Marien—and adorned her with bracelets and necklaces of coral and gold.[1]

Drawing upon medieval rites that had once included animal sacrifice, feasts, and dancing, less-acculturated and Islamizing Moriscos practiced variations on the fadas ceremony across Iberia.[2] Ostentation diminished in the years after the baptisms of the Mudéjares, especially from midcentury, as increasing pressure was placed upon Moriscos in many areas to conform to the expectations of their new religion and to abandon Islamic activities and their cultural accoutrements. Subsequently, women like María la Jarquina replaced fathers and alfaquíes, who had been key figures in the ceremony. Other elements of the religious life of Morisco infants and children evolved as well: boys were rarely circumcised on the eighth day, elders kept children in the dark about Islam until they understood discretion, and Moriscas took a more active role in transmitting the legacy of Islam to the next generation through ritual, instruction, and practice. They became, as Trevor Dadson explains, "the route through which the Muslim system of beliefs and values was transmitted to new generations" or, in Bernard Vincent's pithy phrase, "the guardians of Muslim culture."[3]

Historians have noted that increased efforts to eliminate Spanish Islam drove it underground and into the domestic space. Some level of cultural and religious practice continued in isolated Morisco villages or in exclusively Moorish quarters of towns, but these were fragile ecosystems, and the appearance of outsiders demanded a retreat to secrecy and silence. In towns like Deza, where Moriscos and Old Christians regularly interacted, Moorish activities might be expected to have disappeared from communal spaces and retreated behind closed doors. This strategy offered some hope of avoiding persecution while allowing Islam to be practiced after a fashion, even if under less than ideal conditions. Yet, in some regions, even this domestic retreat was threatened as the church deputized Old Christians to inspect Morisco homes for evidence of Moorish activity and ensure they were attending Mass and raising their children in the true faith.[4] In the face of such efforts, concludes one scholar, survival demanded "conforming on the surface to obscure a deeper resistance and subversion of the dominant order."[5] Few options remained viable for those eager to practice Islam or partake of Islamic traditions.

Deza's Moriscos experienced many of these pressures and struggled to find satisfying responses. Priests catechized their children and many boys attended parish schools. By 1604 (and perhaps even earlier) layman Juan de Peñafiel el mayor was given the job of patrolling the Morisco neighborhood and "making them go to Mass," a task that he sometimes carried out "by force."[6] No evidence exists of deputized laymen making home inspections, but the Holy Office was eager to receive reports of misdeeds from Old Christian neighbors, or servants of Deza's Moriscos, and acted upon credible evidence. Yet, in spite of this challenge to domestic

Islam, the religious lives of many of Deza's crypto-Muslims—and especially its Moriscas—were manifest not only at home in private but also in communal interactions with family, friends, and neighbors.

For men, communal religiosity of this type could be experienced by abandoning the confines of Deza and finding freedom on the road, if only for a time, or by attending gatherings at the duke's house and garden, or the Liñán pottery works just outside of the town walls. But these options excluded most women. In the 1560s men and women gathered together for daily Islamic prayers in dedicated spaces, but nothing indicates that these continued after the 1571 Edict of Grace. Muslim moralists located females within the home, encouraged a division of the sexes in non-domestic settings, and "encased women in marriages in which husbands would maintain and provide for them, while wives would bear children and care for their families."[7] The men in their lives, who exercised authority over them, restrained the freedom of women. Yet power is not a zero sum game. Despite many constraints, Deza's Moriscas made decisions and exerted influence over the course of their lives in tangible ways. Some exercised a remarkable degree of economic, social, and religious agency.[8]

An autobiographical account given in 1607 by the Morisca Catalina Zamorano (b. ca. 1585) during the early stages of her inquisitorial trial offer some sense of these limitations and opportunities. She explained,

> She was born in Cuenca where she lived with her mother. Later, when [Catalina's family] moved to Deza, her mother carried her because she was so small. She does not know how many years ago it was. And she remained with her mother until she died, which was about ten years ago, more or less.
>
> She stayed in the same house in Deza, living with her father, for about two more years but then he left for Arcos de Jalón. She and her younger sister were taken in by Pedro de Hortubia, a maternal uncle. And when Catalina was around fourteen years old, her uncle arranged for her marriage to Gabriel de Medina [b. 1571], very much against her wishes, and they were united [in marriage] by a priest. Thus married, she remained in Deza for about six months, living in

her uncle's house. While there, distressed by the marriage, she fell ill. During this entire time her husband never initiated sexual relations with her [*nunca se juntó con ella*].

Catalina sent a message to her father, and he took her with him to Arcos, where she stayed for about two and a half years, but then he left and she returned to Deza to her uncle's house. She and her husband participated in the veiling ceremony and established their own separate household. Since then they have always lived together in the town of Deza as husband and wife.[9]

Relatives, especially male ones, controlled Catalina, first as a girl and then as a woman. They moved her around, abandoned, and disposed of her as convenience, necessity, or advantage dictated. Yet, Catalina's resolve and determination are also on display as she navigated (from Cuenca, to Deza, to Arcos, to Deza, to Arcos again, and finally back to Deza) between various family members, neighbors, and religious figures. She was able to influence the course of her life by making specific choices from the limited number of options available to her and accommodating herself to those realities.

As a young bride, she resisted an undesirable husband for three years and orchestrated a move to Arcos de Jalón. When her father left her a second time, she returned to Deza as a married woman with her own home. The story echoes the legend of Carcayona, the handless maiden who became part of Morisco lore. Like Carcayona, Catalina suffered indignities and betrayals from family members and parlayed her limited options into a kind of success.[10] While the activities of Moriscas were constrained, Catalina and others utilized the opportunities available to them. Some, especially those reckoned knowledgeable about Islam and Moorish customs, moved beyond the domestic space to exert influence on the larger community.

María la Jarquina, who performed the fadas ceremony for Román Ramírez's daughter, was such a one. Born in Deza around 1568, she was the daughter of Juan Jarquino, an Aragonese Morisco, and Francisca de Deza, a native Dezana. The couple married in Deza, where they had two children: a son who died young and María. Little is known about

Juan, but he came from Morata de Jalón (Zaragoza), worked as a hemp weaver, and died ca. 1588. María's mother was one of ten children born to Pascual de Deza (d. ca. 1562), a farmer and muleteer—three with a first wife and seven with María's grandmother, Ana Ramírez (d. ca. 1586). Thus Ana was a member of one of the most solidly Muslim families in town and her brother, Román Ramírez el mayor (d. 1592), was the grandfather of María/Marien, whom la Jarquina inducted into the world of crypto-Islam late in 1596. Pascual's first wife, by contrast, was an Old Christian from Layna (Soria), faithful to the church and, eventually, grandmother to Lope Guerrero and his five brothers.[11]

At, perhaps, thirteen years of age la Jarquina married Luis de Hortubia, a locksmith who, later in life, also became a muleteer.[12] They lived in Morata for a time but returned to Deza in the early 1580s.[13] Luis was twenty years the senior but the marriage produced three children: Luis (ca. 1581), María (ca. 1585), and Ana (ca. 1589). Although only in her mid-twenties when her husband died in 1593, la Jarquina never remarried. Shortly after his death, now a self-proclaimed "old widow," she became involved with Lope Guerrero. Local gossips whispered that the relationship did not end well.[14] With no husband or adult children, she became the family breadwinner and proved industrious, supporting herself and her children. She kept a shop in Deza, where she sold "fruit and other things" and traveled frequently "to various places in Aragon and Castile" to gather wares, an unusual display of mobility for a woman.[15] María passed on this entrepreneurial spirit to her son Luis, known as el Jarquino, who acquired a degree of literacy and went into business raising and trading goats. He must have done well, for the Holy Office purportedly collected one thousand ducats from him in the early seventeenth century.[16]

In addition to her work in trade, la Jarquina performed various other important roles in and around Deza, many of which were directly connected to her own Islamic identity. She performed the fadas and weddings, prayed over the sick, attended to the dying, and prepared bodies for burial. She shared these responsibilities with several other Moriscas, typically widows, who together formed the inner core of the town's Islamic community and propagated Muslim devotion and practice from one generation to the next. At the end of the sixteenth century this group included María de Medrano (ca. 1547–aft.1608), María la Roma (ca. 1531–ca. 1605), María la Carnicera (ca. 1551–1600), Cecilia la Montera (1547–1608), María de Cebea (1546–aft. 1610), Francisca de Baptista (1554–aft. 1611), and Luisa la Viscaina (ca. 1534–aft. 1609). La Jarquina was the youngest and most energetic member of the group; the range of her activities outstripped all others.

In different circumstances, male religious authorities would have performed many of the ceremonies and activities undertaken by these women, but precisely because Islam was proscribed they often became women's work amongst Spain's crypto-Islamic communities, which recognized the home as the safest space for such events. The fadas had once been presided over by an alfaquí and included animal sacrifice and feasting. But the mass baptisms of the early sixteenth century and the midcentury inquisitorial attacks against Islamic activities led to more circumspect practices. The ceremony became less overtly religious and the Quran, which had previously been present both physically and aurally during the ritual, disappeared, although recitation of Arabic prayers continued. Modern scholarship emphasizes that the ritual happened soon after baptism and was believed to neutralize the sacrament, a notion familiar to Deza's Moriscos.[17] In at least one case, however, the ceremony purportedly took place on the day before baptism rather than immediately following it, suggesting that locally the ritual's significance was malleable.[18]

When available, an alfaquí (or someone like an alfaquí) usually performed the ceremony. While Gerónimo de Leonis lived in town, for example, he was a popular choice. A coppersmith from Ariza (Zaragoza), Leonis married a Dezana in ca. 1600, moved to town, and set up a shop on the Plaza. Only a few years passed before unpaid debts and a reputation for dishonesty drove him from town, but while in Deza some regarded him as an Islamic expert.[19] He could determine the start of Ramadan, had some knowledge of Arabic, and eclipsed locals in his performance of the naming ceremony; he was even called upon to perform the ritual for María la Jarquina's own grandson.[20] But alfaquíes were often in short supply so, much of the time, others took the lead, frequently women.

Juan Guerrero suggested that by the late sixteenth century *only* women performed the fadas. Following the birth of his daughter Ana in 1595, he claimed, his wife had invited Cecilia la Montera and la Jarquina to perform the ritual while he was away, but Guerrero explained that even if he had been in town he would not have been invited: "the women never call any men for these things."[21] Whatever the truth behind this specific story, however, Guerrero's broader claim was false, for men, especially fathers, did participate in and sometimes even preside over the ceremony.

Francisco el Romo, for example, who attended the fadas ceremony for María/Marien Ramírez, performed the ritual for the girl's younger brother the following year and for "Ali," the son of Pascual de Deza, in ca. 1599, perhaps mimicking the words and actions he had heard la Jarquina use a few years earlier.[22] Yet, while Francisco, who was wealthy and one of Deza's "chief" Moriscos, was probably not regarded in any specific sense as an alfaquí, he did have some expert knowledge that distinguished him.[23] Even so, his participation in the ceremony was anomalous. Both Román Ramírez and, a few years later, his son Miguel, relied upon la Jarquina for the fadas rather than performing it themselves, although they were among the most active and knowledgeable Muslims in town.[24] The ceremony had, by and large, become a specialized duty for those viewed as qualified to officiate, and these were usually women.

By contrast, men were more likely to be involved in presiding over the Moorish weddings of Deza's Moriscos, a ceremony that sometimes also included a Morisca co-officiant. And while men might perform these weddings without a female counterpart, women seem never to have done so without a man. As with the fadas, when a religious expert from Aragon could be had, his services were retained.[25] But usually some local figure (or figures) who "knew the most" about Islam presided.[26] In the early seventeenth century, Miguel and Francisco Ramírez, who had been regular participants at the Islamic lectures convened in the duke's garden, often performed weddings for Deza's Moriscos "according to the Law of Mohammed."[27] And at the 1606 wedding of Ana Guerrera and Diego de Fadrique, María la Jarquina played opposite her erstwhile lover Lope Guerrero.

In what was a typical ceremony of the sort, a large number of Old and New Christians, and among them both hidalgos and members of the clergy, gathered at the house of Juan Guerrero, the bride's father, to celebrate the couple's engagement. But as the evening wore on, most of the Moriscos and all of the Old Christians went home, even as dancing and singing continued in the street in front of the Guerrero home. Late in the evening, perhaps fifty friends and relatives crowded into the upper floor of the house and stood while María la Jarquina took Ana's right hand and Lope Guerrero took Diego's. They joined them together and "mumbled" Arabic prayers. La Jarquina, whose stock of memorized Arabic outstripped Lope's by all accounts, spoke "more words" than him. Diego produced six or seven silver bracelets and a long coral necklace adorned with small silver apples and a silver ornament at the end.[28] These he handed to la Jarquina, who placed them on the bride's arms and neck. At this, the audience called out blessings: "God grant you good fortune and good concord!" and "God make you well married!"[29] Although Ana was not yet twelve years old, they were man and wife even without a parish wedding.

In addition to naming ceremonies and marriages, Moriscas also prepared the dead for burial. Francisca de Baptista, Cecilia la Montera, Luisa la Viscaina, María la Carnicera, and la Jarquina were frequently named as those who "enshroud the Moriscos who die and do so in the fashion of the Moors, according to their sect."[30] They washed the body, reciting the prayers associated with guadoc as they did so, and clothed the deceased in clean garments, before wrapping the body in a new linen sheet.[31] Men also performed at least portions of this office, as when one Bernardo was summoned to help Francisco Guerrero die well. In the dying man's last moments, Bernardo undressed and washed him, spoke Arabic words over him, put him in a clean shirt, and laid him out on the bed.[32] In this case, the women present—María la Jarquina among them—took a supporting role, at least while Guerrero lived. After his death, the body was released into their care. For their part, those who performed the enshrouding were quick to deny wrongdoing and emphasized that they also prepared the bodies of Old Christians.[33]

La Jarquina and her cohorts were also called to the side of the sick or the dying, not merely to nurse them but to perform ceremonies and rituals, which often drew as much upon superstition and magic as orthodox Islam. Thus, in ca. 1602, la Jarquina was summoned to the sickbed of Ana Guerrera, the same girl whose naming ceremony she had attended in 1595 and whose marriage she would perform a few years later.[34] She took the girl in her arms, recited an Arabic prayer, and assured her that if she entrusted herself to God she would be cured.[35] La Jarquina and Cecilia la Montera both claimed the ability to foretell the outcome of certain events, particularly the course of serious illnesses, by observing the shape of molten lead poured into a mortar while they recited Arabic prayer.[36] Early in the seventeenth century, when the Holy Office began arresting Deza's Moriscos, la Jarquina used a similar divinatory method in order to determine whose trial would quickly be resolved and whose would drag on.[37] Such practices were part of the Mediterranean milieu and not confined to a Muslim context, but in Spain they were particularly associated with Moriscos.[38]

Deza also boasted several Moriscas regarded as witches and, predictably, these included the likes of la Jarquina, Francisca de Baptista, María la Carnicera, and la Carnicera's daughter María la Burgueña (b. 1575). Juan Guerrero, who showed little hesitation about denouncing la Jarquina as a crypto-Muslim, nevertheless was reluctant to reveal that she "performed tricks, spells, and other things."[39] Earlier in the sixteenth century, such Moriscas had been regarded merely as cunning women or as healers who operated within a medically pluralistic context that permitted orthodox and alternative practices to coexist.[40] By the end of the sixteenth century, however, amidst souring relations between the town's Old and New Christians, increasing pressure exerted by the Holy Office, and a rising medical professionalism, grave concerns were raised about the relationship between Morisco healing, witchcraft, Islam, and the demonic. In Deza, the watershed moment was the 1599 inquisitorial trial of Román Ramírez el menor, whom the Holy Office condemned as an Islamizing sorcerer and a healer who relied upon demonic aid. Subsequently, Morisca healers were much more readily denounced as witches and associates of the devil.

Ramírez's own mother, for example, had been highly regarded for her skills as a healer and midwife at her death, sometime in the early 1560s. By the end of the century, however, María de Luna's reputation was transformed as a result of her son's trial. As it culminated, one of Deza's hidalgos dredged up (or concocted) a story and reported to the Holy Office that she had conversed with the devil every Sunday.[41] According to the town's Moriscos, nothing about María de Luna was particularly demonic. By century's end they remembered her primarily as a proselytizer for Islam and a religious instructor of women.[42] But to others, such connections had become obvious. Local inquisitorial familiar Pedro de Cisneros, for instance, could neatly tie together the town's Moriscas, their witchcraft, and diabolism in a 1607 letter to the tribunal in Cuenca that was preserved in the inquisitorial dossier of María's grandson, Miguel Ramírez. Recalling a number of strange occurrences in his home over the previous years, Cisneros explained, "In addition to being Moors, I have great suspicions that these people have among them witches [brujas] . . . for such things could not happen except by means of diabolical art."[43]

Similarly, the late 1560s found María la Carnicera embroiled in controversy when she was accused of disinterring the body of a recently deceased woman in order to extract her teeth. The Morisco Pascual Guerrero and Old Christian Juan de Cisneros, who happened upon the scene late one night, believed they saw la Carnicera performing the grisly deed, although it was too dark for them to be certain. The matter went before the town magistrates, was investigated, and another woman was found guilty. While some neighbors continued to believe that la Carnicera had been involved, the uproar faded.[44] Four decades later, in the wake of the Ramírez trial and with Deza's Moriscos under intense inquisitorial scrutiny, neighbors recalled the to-do but this time, despite the old woman's protestations of innocence, put a more disturbing spin on the whole affair.[45] By contrast, when the so-called Old Woman of Leonis, a Morisca, cursed the daughter of Juan de Baptista in 1565, leading ultimately to the girl's death, Old Christian María Pecina denounced her to the Holy Office. Yet Pecina gave no indication that diabolism was involved and the matter was forgotten.[46] In Deza it was only in the new century that magic, even malicious magic, was identified by locals as diabolical or demonic. The infamous 1599 trial of Román Ramírez became the pivot upon which attitudes shifted both for the inquisitorial tribunal at Cuenca and for many Dezanos back home.

Moriscas, who had previously been seen as practicing a relatively benign form of divination or folk magic, became Muslim witches who consorted with the devil. Other activities in which they participated became altogether suspicious by extension. But Ramírez—because of his personality, education, experience, and even his gender—was unusual. The women of Deza who performed the fadas, enshrouded the dead, divined molten lead, and cast spells both preceded Ramírez and continued to practice their craft after his death. Neighbors and local authorities viewed their activities as more sinister and dangerous after the conclusion of his trial, but for the women themselves little had changed. Many of these activities had always been connected to an Islamic identity and they were often zealous about learning more and passing along what they knew to others.

In fact, for all of its secrecy and absence from the public square, for all of its external accommodation and prioritization of intention over action, the religion of Deza's Moriscos could sometimes become remarkably communal. This was true for exceptional ceremonies and rituals that saw family, friends, and neighbors join together in semi-private spaces, but it was also true of the more mundane moments of religious life. Women, for instance, managed certain elements of family religion by necessity, especially those related to food.[47] When possible, they planned meals and cooked in accordance with the requirements of Islamic feasts and fasts, especially by preparing meals early in the morning and late at night during Ramadan, and all but the most Christianized avoided pork and wine. They also cooked meat stews and empanadas on Thursday nights at the communal ovens so they could serve them on Fridays, when Spanish Catholics fasted from meat.[48] But the sociable nature of Morisca religiosity went beyond mere management of the family diet. As Juan Guerrero explained, echoing a recurring refrain, women "talk to each other about things more often" than men.[49]

Such discussions occurred, naturally enough, in the home as mothers, grandmothers, and aunts taught the elements of their religion to children who were old enough to be discreet about such things. The family fasted together and memorized prayers along with the elements of performing guadoc and azala. And once they had been learned, mothers and daughters performed the rituals whether men were present or not. Thus, Juan Guerrero described coming upon his wife and daughter multiple times as they were performing guadoc and azala. In fact, although Juan sometimes carried out the ritual ablutions along with his wife, he repeatedly claimed he was unable to perform guadoc without help, since he could not memorize the Arabic prayers.[50] If this was true, then in his household the women necessarily directed key elements of religious observance. His wife Francisca de Hortubia had learned the rituals and recitations from her mother, Cecilia la Montera, whom Juan Guerrero claimed was responsible for teaching his own daughter several Islamic prayers when she was only eight years old. A widow since the death of her husband in ca. 1580, la Montera oversaw the religious life and education of her five daughters. Even after they married she continued to exert a strong influence on them until her arrest by the Holy Office in 1607.[51]

Yet the communal crypto-Islamic lives of Moriscas were not restricted to interactions occurring in homes and between family members, as María la Jarquina's own experiences suggest. When she was, perhaps, ten years old her mother had pointed her in the direction of Islam, teaching her to fast for Ramadan. But because her mother "did not know" anything more, that was all she did.[52] Although her understanding of Islam was impoverished during these years, la Jarquina kept Ramadan and in the 1590s went so far as to mock the Host one Sunday afternoon as it was being conducted through the streets to the sickbed of a Morisco neighbor.[53] Only at the beginning of the seventeenth century was her perspective on religion expanded thanks to the influence of María la Flamenca (alias González) of Arcos, the widow of Francisco el Bueno (d. ca. 1591), himself a Dezano.[54]

In 1609 and 1610, la Jarquina dated her interactions with la Flamenca to around 1600, but unless her depiction of the relationship was entirely fictitious they must have occurred in the mid-1590s, not long after the death of la Jarquina's husband (in about 1593) and probably after her affair with Lope Guerrero had come to a messy end. Whatever the precise timing, she maintained that in their mutual widowhood the two women became friends and la Flamenca instructed her in the details of proper fasting and of performing guadoc and azala. La Jarquina's precision in describing those ceremonies was unique among Deza's Moriscos. She related that the daily prayers (*salat*) occurred in the morning, at noon, in the afternoon, evening, and night, and she assigned them names that were similar, if not always identical, to their Arabic designations.[55] She also learned various prayers from la Flamenca, both in Arabic and Castilian, and probably was introduced to Islamic fasts other than Ramadan.[56] In subsequent years she gained a reputation for collecting Islamic prayers and Arabic phrases.[57]

María la Flamenca was not la Jarquina's only conversation partner. The core group of devout Moriscas interacted regularly, shared knowledge amongst themselves, and taught children, men, and women, who in turn called upon them to perform Islamic rituals and ceremonies. Young Ana Guerrera, for example, remembered her grandmother Cecilia la Montera and la Jarquina frequently discussing when fasts were supposed to occur. Their discussions were probably less a matter of figuring the date for Ramadan than working out the timing for the fasts known among Moriscos as Jora, Carnero, and the White Days.[58] This information they disseminated among other members of the community. No doubt these determinations also drew upon the knowledge of outsiders, especially Aragonese Moriscos, who often lodged with Morisca widows when they visited Deza.[59]

Learned visitors also read to Dezanas from Islamic books, answered questions, and offered tutorials—at least in the days before the Edict of Grace. A teenage Francisca de Baptista, for example, sat at the feet of Pedro el Cañamenero of Villafeliche in 1565 when he came to teach a group of men to read the *letras de moros*; so did María la Jarquina's aunt Cándida de Deza (d. ca. 1582) and María Romera, Luisa la Viscaina's mother.[60] By the end of the sixteenth century, that younger generation of women was performing Islamic rituals and neighbors reckoned them as those who "knew the most about the Law of Mohammed."[61] And the process of transmission continued to the generations that followed. When Gabriel de Huerta, a Morisco from Ariza, visited Deza in 1607, he was impressed by eleven-year-old Ana Guerrera's precocious grasp of Islam and offered to take her to Aragon where she could learn "prayers and things pertaining to the Law of Mohammed."[62]

Yet, often as not, the visitors who brought knowledge of Islam to Deza were themselves Moriscas who had married locally or had relatives in town. In the generation before la Jarquina rose to prominence, women such as Catalina de Aranda, María la Flamenca, Aunt Teresa, and Ana de Almoravi acted as aggressive proselytizers and apologists for Islam in Deza, especially among women. The widow Catalina Pérez of Ariza moved to Deza in the 1560s and taught Luis de Cebea el viejo Islamic prayers in Castilian and about Ramadan and almsgiving.[63] María de Luna, the Aragonese mother of Román Ramírez el menor, "preached and taught" Islam to the women of Deza and purportedly persuaded María de Sepúlveda (whose mother was an Old Christian) to embrace Islam, or at least to accept with equanimity that her husband and son would be adherents.[64]

The efforts of these women, who flourished in midcentury, bore fruit among those with whom they engaged. María la Carnicera, who claimed to have learned the basics of Islam from Aunt Teresa and received charity from Ana de Almoravi in the 1560s, taught her husband and at least one other man Arabic prayers and helped them perform azala.[65] In the 1590s and 1600s she performed the fadas, attended weddings, and enshrouded the dead. Cecilia la Montera influenced not only her five daughters but also their husbands.[66] And if Gabriel de Huerta was impressed by Ana Guerrera's ability to recite Arabic prayers, it was largely a consequence of the instruction given to the girl by la Montera, her grandmother.[67] Passing along Islamic traditions to the next generation of women was not left to chance, or even merely to individuals and families, thanks to the efforts of the blacksmith Francisco de Arcos and his wife Juana López.[68] By the early seventeenth century they organized regular gatherings for young Moriscas at their home on feast days, where the girls "danced and performed guadoc and azala."[69]

Moriscas in Deza, then, hardly conformed to the images of reclusive domesticity and cultural isolation often applied to them. Where the women of Granada, Valencia, and some of the more isolated villages of Aragon resisted giving up Arabic for vernaculars, all of the town's Moriscas spoke Castilian. If they wore clothes that differed from those worn by Old Christians, these were not as dramatically distinct as the wide hose (*zaragüelas*) or large tunic (*almalafa*) that covered the head and were drawn across the face as a veil, the clothing in which Moriscas are invariably portrayed.[70] And while Deza's Moriscas frequently described themselves as "always in their house with their mothers" before marriage, in practice, few (if any) of them were confined to the house, the church, and the garden.[71] Instead, the sources describe them appearing out of doors frequently and interacting with men outside of both their immediate family and their domestic space. When the woman in question was one of those who "knew the most" about Islam, her interactions with men could be casual, jocular, and even authoritative.

Just days before her arrest by the Inquisition, for example, María la Jarquina was washing clothes in the creek. As she finished her work, Francisco de Cebea happened upon her. "Now I've got clean clothes for when the Holy Office comes to arrest me!" she announced in an effusion of gallows humor. Then, becoming more serious, she offered Cebea a providential interpretation of the events unfolding around them: "It's because we're bad Moors that God sent such a scourge and punishment upon us."[72] Francisco and la Jarquina were both arrested in March 1608, along with María la Carnicera and several others. As they departed town, la Carnicera advised Francisco and another Morisco to resist the temptation to confess or denounce others: "Gird your thighs, son, for the love of God, so that you can keep your youth and we are not lost. Act like a man, for I'll do what I can!"[73] A few years later, when la Carnicera's daughter María la Burgueña found herself squaring off against Gerónimo de Molina, a Morisco who had embraced Christianity, she questioned his manhood and berated him as "ill begotten" and a "scoundrel."[74]

In November 1607, when Juan Guerrero and his Old Christian cellmate Gabriel de León discussed Guerrero's son-in-law Diego de Fadrique, de León asked who had taught the young man about the Law of Mohammed. "The women," he replied, referring in particular to his own wife and Cecilia la Montera, his mother-in-law. "You're lying," the other man retorted, "A woman can't teach a man!" But clearly, in Deza, sometimes they could and did. This is not to suggest that gender relations among early modern Moriscos anticipated feminist ideals. Men exercised authority over their daughters and wives. Sometimes they did so in ways that strike us as unsavory—witness the number of girls aged twelve or thirteen whose fathers arranged marriages, often against their wishes, to men who were their elders by a decade or more. As Mateo Romero el mozo told his wife soon after their marriage, "Women must do what their husbands tell them."[75] And in what was probably a concocted story—but one that reflects cultural expectations—Román Ramírez threatened to "break" his wife's "head" if he caught her fasting when he told her not to.[76]

Yet if women were expected to obey the men who held authority over them, they did not do so as chattel or slaves. The relationships between husbands and wives, parents and children, were complex then as they are now. And if some marriages or families tended toward patriarchal oppression, others hint at sincere affection. Antón Guerrero refused to join in a plot to flee the inquisitorial jails for Algiers because he could not abide the thought of abandoning his children. Román Ramírez and Diego de Fadrique expressed deep regard for their spouses. And if Diego Zamorano denounced his own daughter Catalina to the Holy Office, at least he wept bitterly when he did it.[77]

The activities of those women who "knew the most" about Islam suggest that some Moriscas could wield a certain amount of religious gravitas. Their greatest legacy, certainly, was the key role they played in perpetuating Islamic identity from one generation to the next. They were in large part responsible for the continuity of Islamic activity in Deza subsequent to the 1570–71 inquisitorial arrests and Edict of Grace. Thanks to them, the town's community of crypto-Muslim Moriscos were not merely surviving at the end of the sixteenth century but flourishing. Despite proscription and persecution, they had become integrated into regional and trans-regional Morisco networks, found expression in communal events such as marriage festivals and naming ceremonies, and had a foundation of practice and knowledge upon which to build. If local Islam remained impoverished by the standards of the greater Muslim world, it was nevertheless making full use of available resources. What the consequences of this trajectory would have been over the course of another generation is difficult to chart, for that next generation of Moriscos never reached maturity, at least not in Deza.

6

Favor and Fame

Román Ramírez el Menor's Story, Part 1

Román Ramírez el menor was probably born in late April 1540. He was baptized on May 3 of that year. His father, also Román, was a native Dezano (son of Juan Ramírez and María de Deza) and a farmer.[1] His birth date is unknown but his hair was gray by 1567, and if he was about twenty-five when his first child was born, we arrive at a date of ca. 1515.[2] His parents, our Román's grandparents, were first generation "new converts," but their son was presumably baptized as an infant and grew up professing the faith. As an adult, he knew how to read well and how to write; perhaps he learned from a local priest as part of a Christianization effort.[3] He served several times on Deza's town council, first in 1559 as bailiff, then as alderman in 1562 (and again in 1589), and as co-magistrate in 1566.

In 1569, during Arganda's visitation in Deza, two neighbors reported that they thought (but could not be certain) they had seen Ramírez the elder performing guadoc in the stream.[4] The following year, he was part of the group that negotiated the Edict of Grace on favorable terms for the town's Moriscos. As part of that endeavor, he liaised with Deza's feudal lord, Duke Juan de la Cerda, with whom Ramírez traveled to Madrid. There, the duke and an unnamed papal nuncio negotiated on behalf of Deza's Moriscos with King Philip II.[5] Román el mayor returned to Deza a hero, at least among the Moriscos. However, he appears never to have taken the Edict himself despite having been summoned personally by the inquisitor just before his departure and asked "if he had anything to declare."[6] While he probably inclined toward Islam, he must have been more circumspect about it than some of his contemporaries—perhaps more like Gorgoz than Guerrero—for he remained untarnished by further inquisitorial scrutiny to the end of his life in 1592.

His wife, Román the younger's mother, María de Luna (d. bet. 1565–69), was born to Juan de Luna (d. ca. 1551) and Isabel la Ferrara. Both of her parents were citizens of Burbáguena, south of Daroca in Aragon.[7] María's dates are uncertain, but unless she married very young she was probably born in the early 1520s and may even have remembered her own baptism in 1526. Both she and her father were reputed skilled medical practitioners. Juan de Luna was a "great herbalist and physician." María was "very learned in medical matters and the knowledge of herbs and a very good midwife," drawing clients from fifty leagues away.[8] Decades after her death, María was also remembered as an adept Islamic proselytizer who "preached to and taught" the women of Deza.[9]

No sources describe how Román the elder and María came to be married, but they probably wed in the late 1530s. She moved to Deza, practiced her craft, and bore five sons and a daughter, the last in 1556.[10] But she maintained contact with her family fifty-five miles away in the Kingdom of Aragon, for Román the younger was sent there to live "in Juan de Luna's house" as a boy (*muchacho*) and he himself claimed that he "grew up with" his grandfather.[11] The boy was probably still in Deza when he was "six or seven" (ca. 1546–47), so this Burbáguena sojourn probably occurred between then and his grandfather's death in ca. 1551.[12]

That sojourn appears to have coincided or overlapped with a critical period of formation and mental exertion for young Ramírez. This was initiated by his father (or, according to one witness, his grandfather),[13] who administered to the boy a draught of "camphor juice," which had the "virtue of drying out his brain so that he would have a great memory," although he "almost died" as a result.[14] His father read chivalric tales aloud frequently when the boy was young and these became part of his mental furniture. Later in life, after learning to read, he reviewed the books as necessary to be able to recite and "embellish" them by memory.[15] He boasted that he had enough material to "read" four hours a day for four years without repeating anything of what was in his head.[16] In

3. The Ramírez family tree.

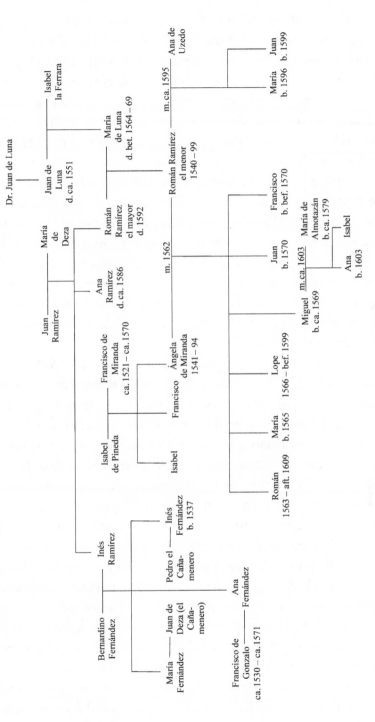

1593 Ramírez purportedly told the camphor juice story to an alguacil in Soria named Francisco de Ávila.[17] And, several years later, he mentioned it to inquisitors, so presumably it was a piece of family lore and perhaps one that he believed to be true, rather than a story concocted on the fly.

Ramírez had a prodigious memory and could recall long passages of books on cue. And whether he imbibed camphor juice or not, it is believable that, around the age of six, he became aware of his ability to recall and began to improve it, especially under the influence of his grandfather. Later in life he purportedly memorized the "entire Mass and all the sermons that they do in the whole year, and all of the Gospels that they preach."[18] Ramírez began to acquire this stock of knowledge of sacred literature as a lad, when (according to a hostile witness who had known him for many years) he memorized *divinas historias*, probably meaning sections of the Bible but perhaps saints' lives as well.[19] Unsurprisingly, he could also recite the Santiguado, Creed, Our Father, Hail Mary, Salve Regina, Ten Commandments, and the fourteen Articles of the Faith without error.[20]

Ramírez also learned a great deal about medicine. Although he acknowledged his grandfather's fame as a "great physician," he identified his mother as the chief source of his medical knowledge and the one who taught him "everything he knew about herblore and curing diseases."[21] Furthermore, he claimed that she had learned her craft not from her father but rather from her grandfather, "Doctor" Juan de Luna, a citizen of Daroca.[22] So, perhaps his medical education only began in earnest in the early 1550s, after he returned to his father's home in Deza. According to Román el menor, his mother was illiterate and he described her medical knowledge as entirely un-bookish. He told inquisitors that she did not possess "books of secrets," or of medicine in any language, nor did she have recipes of herbal remedies and cures written down. Instead, María had simply memorized what she needed to know and Román had done likewise.[23] In 1599 he gave inquisitors a command performance, reciting herbal cures and remedies, often couched in humoral language, one after another.[24]

Sometime around 1551, then, Juan de Luna's death saw young Román return to Deza. Almost half a century later, he claimed that it was shortly after this, in May 1553, that he had a critical interaction with a migrant farmhand, the Morisco Gerónimo de Villaverde from Aragonese Terrer. Purportedly, Villaverde was "the first one to teach him to be a Moor."[25] This may or may not have been true, for the evidence suggests that both Román the elder and María de Luna were secret Muslims.[26] Juan de Luna had been reconciled by the Holy Office in Zaragoza, presumably also for Islamizing.[27] Yet Morisco parents often waited until children reached their teens before revealing the world of crypto-Islam to them, so it is possible that the son was unaware of his parents' religious convictions.[28] Further complicating the details is Román the younger's claim (before inquisitors in 1599) that when Villaverde introduced him to Ramadan in 1553 neither of his parents were in the habit of keeping the fast. Villaverde supposedly described them as "burning in hell even now, while they live" on account of their unfaithfulness.[29] Thus, Román described his early movement toward Islam as a turn away from his family.

Perhaps Villaverde, who returned to Terrer after the harvest, was unaware that his employer was a crypto-Muslim. More likely, Román el menor was trying to deflect inquisitorial interest from his family and Deza's Morisco community by writing locals out of the story he told inquisitors in 1599. In any case, Villaverde purportedly invited the youth to accompany him to Aragon and spend "twelve or fifteen days" there, learning "all the things that the Moors do."[30] Román refused the offer, but he did learn how to fast properly for Ramadan, and Villaverde promised to send word annually so the young Dezano would know when the lunar month was about to begin. As a result, he kept the fast for the next "four or five" years and, rejecting the divine trinity, believed in "one single god."[31]

At the end of this period, in ca. 1557, Villaverde moved from Terrer (twenty-three miles south of Deza) to the city of Teruel (another eighty-five miles further on), stretching the lines of communication.[32] Not until the mid- to late-1560s, claimed Román, did he observe Ramadan again, principally because he had no one to tell him when to fast. In any case, domestic matters soon distracted him. By the early 1560s he had set his eye on Ángela de Miranda (1541–94), the daughter of Francisco de Miranda (ca. 1521–ca. 1571) of Deza, a local Morisco painter and poet.

The marriage of Román and Ángela is usually dated to immediately after Villaverde's departure, for the groom linked the two events in 1599, claiming that, "at the end of that time, Villaverde went to live in the city of Teruel and he [Román] married his first wife, Ángela de Miranda."[33] While it is possible that he married at eighteen or nineteen (i.e., in 1558 or 1559), this would be unusually young for a Morisco male. More likely, his pursuit of Ángela began in earnest only in 1562.

That was the year, Román claimed, that he first summoned the demon Liarde. Decades later, he told the Holy Office that Liarde "was a demon with which his grandfather had entered into a pact. At night, when he lay near his grandfather in bed, he heard them speaking. His grandfather had asked [the demon] about some things that were happening in the world and it told him about them."[34] According to the 1595 testimony of Licentiate Bernardino Bonifacio, one of Román's enemies, Juan de Luna reputedly kept multiple familiar spirits, but when, on several occasions, Bonifacio asked Román whether he did likewise, the Morisco denied having even one.[35] Yet, in 1599 Román himself testified that, on his deathbed, Juan de Luna had bequeathed Liarde to him. If the grandson "found himself in some need, he might call upon and say, 'Liarde', between eleven and twelve o'clock at night." Juan de Luna explained that he had ordered the demon to come to his aid.[36] Although some have proposed that Liarde was an echo of the African *djinn* tradition drawn into Morisco medical practice, Román confessed unequivocally that he knew it was a demon and not a neutral spirit.[37] Their relationship was rocky from first to last; Liarde often mocked Román's ignorance and refused obedience.[38]

That Román summoned Liarde in 1562 is chronologically significant for two reasons. First, it helps to date his marriage to Ángela de Miranda. Román claimed to have summoned Liarde, in part, in order to learn whether anyone else was in love with her. Although the demon refused to provide that information, within six weeks of the summoning, the couple married in Deza.[39] Second, it provides a window into Román's financial situation in his early adulthood. When Román called upon Liarde in his twenty-second year, it was to learn whether the demon could help him locate "lost things," especially "treasure," and not, as the demon presumed, in order to learn how to perform cures, at least not initially.[40] A treasure, Román imagined, would put him on stable financial footing to support not only a wife but also a brood of children.[41] Lacking the treasure, which Liarde refused to help him locate, Román may have initially supported his family by the sweat of his brow, for he reported traveling along the Ebro River in Aragon as a migrant farm laborer.[42] Soon he developed other sources of income.

Certainly by about 1566 he was practicing the family business of healing. He initially built his reputation upon that of his grandfather, for it was on account of Román laying claim to "some part of the great amount" known by Juan de Luna that he was called upon to attend to a knight named Carlos López in Aragonese Calatayud.[43] López was "crazy" and unfortunately the cure was beyond Román's ability. Unsure of how to proceed, he turned to Liarde for help with healing for the first time. The capricious spirit was amenable, and Román concocted an herbal remedy, which he gave the knight to drink to heal him. Consequently, the Morisco "began to acquire fame" for his cures, since "the whole city knew about it because it was a very public matter."[44] In the wake of this success, various notables called upon him to perform healings. Sometimes he summoned Liarde and, when he did so, sometimes the familiar responded, but not always.

According to the 1597 testimony of Pedro Martínez, a blacksmith from the village of Tajahuerce (Soria), the Morisco mentioned in passing that he had once healed the "lord of Cabezuelos," which earned him three hundred *reales*, as well as "the daughter of the duke of Medinaceli."[45] Beyond the *terminus ad quem* of 1593, when the conversation occurred, these events cannot be dated, but the duke in question was probably Juan Luis de la Cerda, Marquis of Cogolludo from 1552–75 and then Duke of Medinaceli until his death in 1594.[46] The healing of that daughter probably fostered a burgeoning relationship between Román and the ducal family and, perhaps, helps explain why, in the late 1560s, Román's relationship with Deza's seigneur took on elements of clientage and patronage.

Around the same time, Juan Luis gave the Morisco control over a house and garden north of town and located outside the medieval walls. The marquis's father, Duke Juan de la Cerda (r. 1552–75), had initiated this building project in the 1550s when his son inherited the family's cadet title.[47] No one from the noble line ever occupied the property, but the ducal family committed substantial money and attention to its construction and beautification. By early 1566 Román was working as a gardener (*hortelano*) at the site and was vying with Martín de Milla, a particularly talented rival, for a permanent appointment.[48] The duke's man on site, Gonzalo Martínez, wrote to his lord (that is, not to Marquis Juan Luis) on March 28, trumpeting Milla's brilliance but worrying that the town's Moriscos had told Milla that, in a year or two, Román would take possession of the garden and enjoy all the fruits of his labor. Martínez assured Milla they were lying. If he continued to show the same "care and diligence" he had in the past, he would have the garden "for his whole life."[49]

Milla, however, remained doubtful. He wrote to the duke—not the marquis—in a state of agitation, explaining, "since you left this place, Román Ramírez has been constantly persecuting me, seeking to cast me from Your Excellency's service and from the garden." Duke Juan's note, scrawled at the top of the original letter, makes clear his opinion on the matter. He forwarded the missive to his son, Marquis Juan Luis, urging him to forbid Milla's removal and prevent any grievance to him. "By no means," he wrote, "is it convenient that [the garden] be given to the son of Román Ramírez [the elder], for reasons of which I am very well informed." If the marquis desired peace in "that garden," he needed to disillusion Román the younger of the possibility that he would ever possess it. "Let it be done thus resolutely," he concluded, "because it proceeds from my will." Unfortunately, he lamented, "They do not understand these words in Deza."[50]

Perhaps his son also failed to understand. At least, he did not comply with his father's wishes. Although the land technically remained a ducal property, by 1567 or 1568 Román had the run of it.[51] The healing of Juan Luis's daughter may have had something to do with the marquis favoring Ramírez in this way but, in his letter to the duke, Milla claimed the Morisco was feeding Juan Luis "false information" and providing him with "favors."[52] Whatever the specific reason, the house and garden were the Morisco's for life.

Ramírez enjoyed his fair share of success during these years. A highly sought-after healer, he could be selective about his clientele and avoid traveling, at least while he was flush. Reminiscing in 1599, he claimed, "He never went out to perform cures nor earned his living from them except when he was requested or besought by persons of quality." Instead, he usually wrote out his curatives and sent the instructions by messenger.[53] When, in 1593, he agreed to travel to Tajahuerce in order to heal one Ana Sanz, a decision that caused him much grief, he accepted the job because he could not pay rent.

Román developed another source of income (and reputation) at roughly the same time. In 1599 he claimed that "twenty-eight or twenty-nine years ago" one Alonso la Fuente de Andrada visited Deza and heard him "read" several times.[54] La Fuente "marveled" at the Morisco's memory and wondered whether or not he had been given *anarcardina*, a confection made of cashews, which were believed to improve memory. At this point, claimed Román the younger, his father told the story of the camphor juice.[55] As it happened, Alonso la Fuente was a client (*deudo*) of the royal financier Gerónimo de Salamanca, then one of the richest men in Spain. Salamanca had fingers in every pie, but among them was the governance of Iberia's dry ports, official points of transit between kingdoms that allowed for control of immigration, transportation of goods, and imposition of duties.

Presumably, la Fuente brought Román's gifted memory to the attention of Salamanca and piqued his interest. Beginning in 1567, and for the eight years that followed, Román worked for Salamanca. He explained in January 1571, "Four years ago this coming Lent . . . Gerónimo de Salamanca sent for [him], and he was with him in Medina for 12 or 13 weeks."[56] He spent the first six years of employment "at court and in the dry ports that [Salamanca] had leased and on the customs tariff." Román traveled constantly during these years: "He would spend sixteen or eighteen months away from Deza at a time. And during those six years he did not reside in the town of Deza for two weeks at a time."[57] What, exactly, was he doing for Salamanca?

From at least 1569 until at least 1571 (and perhaps for the entire eight-year period from 1567–75) he was serving as guard at the dry port in

Deza. How this squares with his claim to have been in town only rarely during that period is unclear. Perhaps the post was a sinecure to facilitate the performance of other duties. In 1569, however, Old Christian Martín Rodríguez, another of the town's port guards, gave no indication that Román was absentee. Rather, he emphasized that Román worked *in Deza* and recounted a conversation they had had in which the Morisco filled him in on some local gossip.[58] And in April 1570 Román testified in his capacity as a local port guard about Mateo Romero el menor's flight from inquisitorial custody.[59] Román's further comment that he worked "on the customs tariff [*en el almojarifazgo*]" as well as at court and in the dry ports might suggest direct involvement in the collection of import tariffs, but even this is ambiguous.

Whatever else Ramírez was doing, Salamanca certainly had him "reading" chivalric tales and other works to nobles and notables. Román surely referred to this period when, in 1599, he claimed to have memorized such stories "in order to recite them by memory to lords and knights. And he read the books of chivalry from memory many times at Aranjuez and El Pardo to the king himself, don Philip [II] our lord, who is in heaven."[60] Performances of this sort account for what Román was doing "at court" in these years.[61] His time there appropriately coincides with the period of Salamanca's ascendancy as a royal financier up to the bankruptcy of 1575.[62] His last trip to Madrid, Román claimed in 1581, occurred in November 1575 and he returned to Deza in May 1576.[63]

If his service to Salamanca came to an end, his celebrity as a storyteller did not. Román probably continued to perform through the 1570s and into the 1580s. He earned a reputation "as a man of great memory and [began] to have a place [*tener cabida*] among knights and lords on account of entertaining them with his readings. And they paid him or granted him favors [*mercedes*] and took him to ladies' balls [*saraos de damas*] and other entertainments." This led him to devote more attention than he had previously to perfecting his method of recitation.[64] In 1595, Alonso de Roa, *alguacil mayor* (chief bailiff) of Soria, confirmed this, recalling that the Morisco had performed before "many people," including "many lords of these realms, like the deceased duke of Medinaceli, and others."[65] He was certainly a prized entertainer in Soria, where he performed in the winter of 1592–93 at the house of the town's *corregidor* (royal district magistrate) before an audience. In October 1595, Pedro Ramírez, then governor of the dry ports, lured Román back to Soria to recite before his guests, among them a judge at Valladolid's Royal Appellate Court and his wife.[66] After 1595 Román largely abandoned the business of amazing crowds with feats of memory, but occasionally he still "read from the head" for Juan de la Cerda (r. 1594–1607), the son of his old patron and now duke of Medinaceli in his own right.[67]

The subject matter and method of these performances has occupied several scholars but some new light may be shed. Román's repertoire was larger than is often assumed, although it certainly did include many chivalric tales. He and others specifically mentioned his recitations of both "sacred writings [*escrituras*]" and any section of the Bible they wished to hear.[68] He could probably recite saints' lives and draw upon non-canonical retellings of biblical stories since he owned several books that contained them. Among these were Villegas's *Flos sanctorum* (first published in Toledo in 1578) with its accounts of the lives of Christ, the Virgin, apostles, and other saints, as well as a book by Fray Juan de Dueñas, presumably his *Mirror of Consolation* (first published in Burgos in 1540).[69] Perhaps this also explains why his library included *Carro de las donas*, the 1542 Castilian translation of Francesc Eiximenis's *Book of Women*: it contained biographies of saints as well as of contemporary figures like Cardinal Cisneros, Hernando de Talavera, and Queen Isabella.[70] Román also owned a book described as *Vidas de los emperadores*, perhaps Pedro Mexía's *Historia imperial y cesárea* (first published in Seville in 1545), and he had at least a passing knowledge of Alexander the Great and the Persian kings Darius and Xerxes.[71] Finally, he had some exposure to popular stories. By the mid-1560s, if not before, he knew a version of the Marquis de Mantua—*coplas del Marques de Mantua*—a popular Spanish *chanson* set in the Carolingian era.[72]

To these can be added a long list of chivalric tales from which Román drew and that belonged to the print genre dubbed "Romances of Chivalry."[73] He certainly knew Beatriz Bernal's *Don Cristalián de España* (first published in Valladolid in 1545) by heart, for in 1599 he recited a chapter for an inquisitor when called upon to demonstrate his memory.

(Either the amanuensis or the inquisitor drily noted that the Morisco made reference to "some battles" in his recitation and "it seemed to be chivalric tales.")[74] In addition to *Don Cristalián*, Ramírez's repertoire presumably included the stories of Florambel, the twelve books of the Amadís of Gaul cycle, don Olivante de Laura, Primaleón y don Duardo,[75] don Clarián de Landanís, el caballero del Febo, don Rogel de Grecia, and Felix Magno.[76] He claimed to have had copies of all these as well as "others which he does not remember at present."[77] These are merely bits and pieces that can be reconstructed of what must have been an impressive repertoire.

Román's performances have been studied at some length by L. P. Harvey, who describes them as "improvised narrations of known stories in a known style, but not in a fixed form."[78] As Alonso de Roa reported, when Román performed, he "took a blank piece of paper out of his satchel and, looking at it as though he were reading that writing, spoke a large part of the book or chapter that they [his audience] indicated to him. And he did the same if they indicated a part of the Bible or holy writing."[79] Román himself described his performances thus:

> Whenever he read from memory, he held in his hand a piece of paper or a book—not the same one that he was reading—and he went on looking at it, keeping his eyes on it without turning the pages. He did this so that he would not distract his memory and to keep his attention fixed on what he was reading and saying but not because he needed to have the book or paper in his hands.[80]

Asked by the inquisitor if he had ever recited without using the prop, Román explained, "He never read from memory without having the paper or book in his hand." And, in a curious comment that emphasized the relation of the word written to the word recited, he admitted, "It seemed wrong to read from the head without having some book or paper in one's hands."[81]

At his height as a performer, he claimed, he had aimed to amaze audiences with his total recall. "He used to read a whole book continuously, according to each line and chapter, using the same phrasing and language, as if [the book] were present and he were reading from it."[82] In fact, however, he never truly memorized word for word. As he explained to the Holy Office in 1599, just prior to his extemporaneous recitation from *Don Cristalián*:

> He wants to tell and reveal the secret of this matter and the manner in which he read, something that he has never told to a living soul or ever thought to tell. And if there is anything else in this other than what he says, may he burn in hellfire. What happens is that he took into his memory the number of books and chapters in the book *Don Cristalián* along with the substance of the adventures and the names of the cities, kingdoms, knights, and princesses that are contained in the said books, and committed it all very well to memory. And then, when he was reciting it, he expanded or abbreviated the phrasing as much as he wanted, always taking care to conclude with the substance of the adventures, such that it would seem to everyone who was listening to him recite that he was very precise and did not alter any of the phrases or language from the books themselves. But the truth is, in effect, that if someone were looking at the actual book from which he was reciting, he would see that although he erred neither in the substance of the adventures nor in the names, yet he erred in many of the phrases and added others that were not written there. Anybody who has good understanding, ability, and memory can do it. There's no more mystery to it than that.[83]

Román then began his recitation of *Don Cristalián* and explained as he went that he could draw out the battle scenes to take up "four hours" in the telling. The trick, he explained, was more about "design" (*traza*) and "inventiveness" (*inventiva*) than "what he had memorized of the books." He encouraged the inquisitor to call for a copy of *Don Cristalián* so he could compare the words in the book with what was "recited from memory" and thus verify that while Román recited "the substance of the adventures" he was "adding and removing phrases as he liked."[84]

Ramírez's audiences were impressed. Those who described his performances often expressed amazement at the feat of memory but also commented upon the *certeza* (sureness or, perhaps in this case, confidence) with which he spoke. Alonso de Roa reflected on a performance he had witnessed in winter 1592–93, indicating that Román's recitation was "apparently so true to the story" he had requested that, "if he had had the original in front of him, he wouldn't have been able to read it with more precision and *certeza*."[85] Even Licentiate Bonifacio, who attended "many performances" acknowledged his "great memory."[86]

Román Ramírez's ability to memorize was remarkable. The fact that he was able to integrate creativeness—*traza* and *inventiva*—into his performances makes them more, not less, impressive. If he had merely recited what he had formerly read or heard in a rote manner, he could be dismissed as a savant. But that he was able to fashion and mold those stories on the fly, while simultaneously holding his audiences' attention and delivering material with *certeza*, in addition to retaining a massive stock of memorized material from various genres, suggests a remarkable constellation of talents. Yet, these virtues were balanced by rather serious vices.

Some found Ramírez insufferable and he made many enemies. Ana de Almoravi described him as "a great knave [*bellaco*]."[87] Licentiate Bonifacio pegged him as "braggart," "talker," and a habitual liar.[88] He was confrontational, often to the point of belligerence. From his late twenties into his fifties he repeatedly found himself involved in physical altercations with those who did not share his opinion or opposed him.[89] The first known incident occurred in August 1567, about the same time that Alonso la Fuente discovered Román for Gerónimo de Salamanca and not long after he healed the knight Carlos López in Calatayud. Details are fuzzy, but the Morisco was accused of assaulting one Domingo de Soria of Ciheula with a knife and wounding him badly. The suit, brought against Ramírez (and his father) by Domingo (and his father), went before Deza's magistrates and eventually found its way to the Royal Appellate Court in Valladolid before being settled in favor of the plaintiffs in 1570.[90] The father of the wounded man was probably one Licentiate Domingo de Soria, who appears intermittently in Deza's municipal archive, sometimes providing legal opinions to the town.[91] He was, therefore, doubly tied to Deza's castellan Pedro de Barnuevo, both as second cousin and as the grandfather of Licentiate Bonifacio, who married doña Francisca de Barnuevo, Pedro's daughter.[92] Such were the origins of a feud between Román and Barnuevo that lingered for years and caused both men trouble.

Probably subsequent to the attack on Domingo de Soria, but before the end of 1570, Román was at it again. As he explained in 1599, "eleven or twelve" years after he lost contact with Gerónimo de Villaverde and stopped fasting for Ramadan, he got into a "knife fight in Deza with Licentiate Páez." Thirty years Román's senior, Licentiate Antonio Páez was one of early modern Deza's most intriguing characters and one of the few in town equally at ease amongst Old Christians and Moriscos. He attended, for example, many Morisco weddings "in order to honor them" and attempted to deflect inquisitorial attention from Morisco Lope del Sol during Inquisitor Reynoso's 1569 visitation.[93] Unfortunately, all that is known is that he and Ramírez disagreed "about a cure," both men survived the duel, and the younger man "was forced" to leave town temporarily, which prompted another Aragonese sojourn, this time as an agricultural laborer.[94]

Yet more evidence exists of an anger management problem. In 1581, more than a decade after the Páez incident, Ramírez and his wife were summoned before Inquisitor Arganda during his visitation to account for discrepancies in the record of their sacramental confessions. During his interview, Román lost his temper again. The details of what he said or did have not been preserved, but the Morisco sent a letter of apology to Arganda after cooling down. "If I have been at all rude or impolite with your lordship," he begged, "pardon me. For I might have acted out of some slight anger or with insufficient understanding, like a weak man."[95]

Finally, in 1592 Román found himself going fisticuffs with Pedro de Barnuevo himself, the region's chief magistrate and Deza's alcaide. Evidence suggests many people struggled to get along with Barnuevo—he was "easily angered, vengeful, and generally bad natured with everyone who approache[d] him seeking the administration of justice"—yet many of those adjectives could also have been applied to Ramírez.[96] Again, the specific events that triggered the skirmish are unknown, but this was a period of intense conflict between Barnuevo and the town council, on

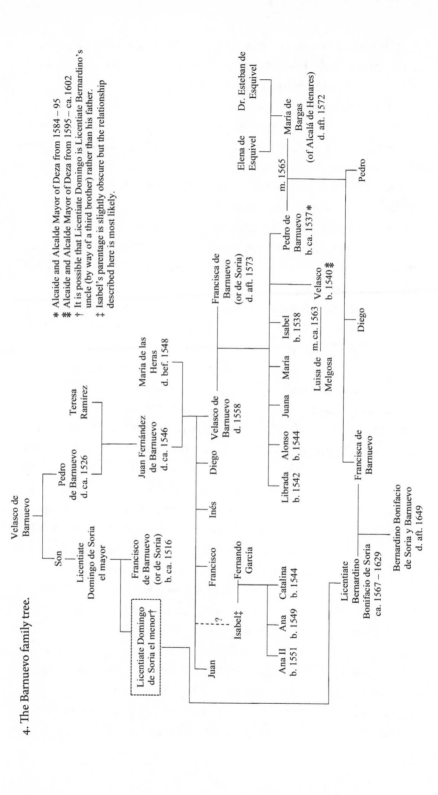

4. The Barnuevo family tree.

* Alcaide and Alcalde Mayor of Deza from 1584 – 95
⁑ Alcaide and Alcalde Mayor of Deza from 1595 – ca. 1602
† It is possible that Licentiate Domingo is Licentiate Bernardino's uncle (by way of a third brother) rather than his father.
‡ Isabel's parentage is slightly obscure but the relationship described here is most likely.

which Román was serving.[97] The dustup culminated in the Morisco's arrest and transportation to Medinaceli for trial by the duke, who must have pardoned or only lightly punished him, since he was soon at large.

Ramírez apparently avoided serious punishment for the twin assaults with deadly weapons in the late 1560s—except perhaps temporary exile for the Páez incident—so it is ironic that he served his first real jail time for a crime he did not commit, or so he claimed. In May 1576, at the end of his employment with Gerónimo de Salamanca, Román left Madrid and returned to Deza to rejoin Ángela de Miranda and their children. But if he expected to slip into quiet domesticity he was mistaken, for within five months he was arrested for horse smuggling. A judge in Soria, one Dr. Camargo, declared Román de Deza (d. ca. 1588) guilty and ordered his arrest.[98] When agents arrived in Deza to arrest him, they somehow ended up with Román Ramírez, his first cousin and brother-in-law. Ramírez was transported "under heavy guard" to Molina where he languished for fifteen months. On Christmas Eve 1577, "some of the prisoners" organized a jailbreak, and Román was either among their number or took advantage of the situation to make good his escape. He eventually sorted matters out with Camargo—so he claimed—and was set at liberty, while the guilty Román was arrested in ca. 1579.[99]

While Román Ramírez never entirely abandoned medicine or story-telling (or fighting), as he entered his forties he became more focused on local affairs and, especially, town politics. Deza's commune, its assembly of citizens, gathered "every year around Christmas, time out of mind . . . in the town's parish church of Santa María to elect and name" several potential officeholders, who were then submitted to the duke for his approval and final decision.[100] Free of the law and settled back home, Román Ramírez slipped into this system. Like his father, he was repeatedly tapped for office and held various seats on the council in 1582, 1585, 1589, 1592 (the year of his quarrel with Barnuevo), 1595, and 1597. While the duke could certainly exert some pressure upon the commune to put forward the names of the right men, especially by way of his castellan, who traditionally made the first nomination, he was hard pressed to get truly objectionable candidates on the council.[101] So, while Román's personal ties to Duke Juan Luis may have been advantageous, he also needed friends in Deza. Despite his hotheadedness and braggadocio, Román's leadership was endorsed by some of the Moriscos with whom he had grown up and who were now, in their thirties and forties, coming into their own.

Nevertheless, Ramírez cast himself as a member of the duke's faction, which made him unpopular with anyone who championed the town's interests over those of the seignior. This was a problem because, in the late sixteenth century, the town was increasingly divided about its future. Some favored casting off the shackles of feudal oppression. They wanted to use law courts to minimize ducal interference in municipal affairs and secure Deza's future as an independent urban center with regional influence. Many hidalgos and Old Christians were committed to this option. And in the early 1590s most of the town's Moriscos cast their lot with the town faction as well. Later in the decade, Román noted that the "citizens of Deza were spiteful toward him in part because he belonged to the duke of Medinaceli's party."[102] So, while friends and family supported him, even among Moriscos his was usually the minority position.

Ramírez's actions on the council are rarely distinguishable from those of the other officers. In November 1582, toward the end of his first year on the council, he was certainly involved in establishing a precedent that caused Deza trouble for years to come. While serving as the town's solicitor general, he wrote on the council's behalf to Duke Juan Luis explaining that "the harvest had been of a much lower quantity" than expected. After having paid out taxes, feudal dues, and other obligations, they now feared that in coming months many would find themselves in dire need. The council, therefore, requested permission to withhold an upcoming payment of grain to the duke but promised future compensation. If the duke refused this scheme, the council explained, their only other option was to float, with his permission, a bond of one thousand ducats to provide for the needs of the poor.[103]

The duke, unwilling to forgo income, responded that Deza's council could float the bond, provided the citizenry agreed and the council kept a record of that approval. If the commune, aware of the potential hazards, endorsed the action, then the council could proceed.[104] Since

Deza had little in the way of municipal property with which to generate revenue, bonds of this sort were one of the few options available to the council. They paid out annuities to bondholders at a fixed rate and could be effective as long as debt was managed well. This first dip into public finance, however, signaled the beginning of bad habits. By century's end the debt had doubled and Deza found itself in difficult financial straits. Back in 1582, however, when the town had turned to Ramírez to present their request to the duke and gain his support, the Morisco had delivered.

In August 1585, during his second stint on the council, this time as an alderman, the council determined, in accordance with best practices, to standardize the measure of wheat (*maquila*) for the town's mills. To that end, it commissioned Ramírez and the miller Juan Donoso el mayor to travel to the city of Soria where the measure that Deza's millers were meant to use was kept. Having established the standard, they were to return home so that it could be applied. The millers opposed the innovation.[105] Deza had never needed a standardized measure in town before, they fussed, so why now?[106] The response of Juan de Deza, solicitor general, was uncompromising and, presumably, the two men made the trip to Soria.

Ramírez's second term as alderman in 1589 passed without serious incident, but by 1592 his feud with Pedro de Barnuevo had reached a boiling point. It was a conflict that ought not to have happened, for both men's interests should have been aligned in support of the duke. Juan Luis de la Cerda was the Morisco's patron; Barnuevo was appointed by the duke and functioned as his most immediate representative in town. Before their disagreements erupted into violence, Licentiate Bonifacio, Barnuevo, and Ramírez interacted cordially. Bonifacio, Barnuevo's son-in-law, had eaten meals and traveled with the Morisco, who had even been a guest in his home.[107] By the early 1590s, this relationship had clearly soured along with Barnuevo's relationship to many of Deza's chief citizens.

When council members complained to the duke about Barnuevo, as they repeatedly did, they emphasized his claims to autonomy. For example, when he presumed to arrest the local chief bailiff, he took the man's staff of office and broke it with his own hands, saying that since he was the one who had presented the staff, he could retract it.[108] He had forgotten, wrote the council to the duke, "that he is, as are we all, Your Excellency's vassals."[109] From Barnuevo's perspective, however, his challenges to the council's authority—and the clergy's, for that matter—were in service to the assertion of ducal authority. The primary objects of his attacks were the "principal and most honorable men of the town"—probably those Old Christians who opposed the party of the duke and championed town autonomy.[110] Yet his approach and methods proved so universally unpopular that, unexpectedly, Román and several other Morisco councilmen sided with the Old Christian citizenry against Barnuevo despite the ducal party's natural alignment.

Conditions should have thrust Pedro de Barnuevo and Román Ramírez into one another's arms but, instead, they were at each other's throats. Ultimately, the duke could not countenance his representative being attacked by a member of the council, even if that council member was his own client. He ordered Román's arrest and transportation to Medinaceli to face justice.[111] In fact, the council may have paid for his maintenance while he was under arrest, as its accounts record two payments made to him during this time for trips to Medinaceli on council business.[112] How the case was settled is a mystery, but the Morisco had been released by the second half of 1592, when he is known to have traveled to Soria, Almazán, and Calatayud.[113]

Following his quarrel with Barnuevo and detainment in Medinaceli, Román may have lost some of the duke's confidence. In fact, the relationship may already have been cooling, for although the Morisco's name had been proposed occasionally for a council seat, the duke had not chosen him since 1589. In 1592 Román served as one of the deputies, but these were selected by other members of the council, not the duke. He may also have begun charging Román for the house and garden around this time, for although previously discriminating about his clientele, the Morisco now claimed to be anxious about paying rent.[114] Lacking a seat at the table and short on funds, he spent more time on the road to perform both healings and readings in the region. Thus, he recited at the house of don Diego de Orozco, the corregidor of Soria, in the winter of 1592–93, and in early 1594 at an inn in Torrubia.[115] Later that year he traveled to Gómara (Soria) to cure one Dr. Villegas de Guevara, a *juez de sacas* who suffered from "retention of urine."[116] And twice he visited Tajahuerce, twenty-six miles north of Deza, to heal Ana Sanz, a young woman suffering from melancholy and fainting spells. No doubt there were other performances and consultations, but it was the complicated and convoluted affair in Tajahuerce that proved to be his downfall.

7

The Demons of Tajahuerce

Román Ramírez el Menor's Story, Part 2

Early in 1593 Ana Sanz (b. ca. 1578) was married in the village of Aldealpozo, just a few miles beyond Tajahuerce, to Bartolomé de Ortega el mozo (b. ca. 1575). The groom's father, Bartolomé el mayor (b. ca. 1551), was married to Petronila Hernández (b. ca. 1546), Ana Sanz's mother, making Bartolomé el mozo both the bride's husband and her stepbrother.[1] Ana opposed the union and claimed to have taken a vow of celibacy.[2] Román Ramírez, who noted her remarkable beauty, believed rather that she was in love with another man. She "wasn't content with the marriage," he opined, because the groom was "undersized [*de mal talle*], a pee-wee [*pequeñuelo*]." "What do you want?" she once demanded of him, "For them to marry me off against my will to this little man [*hombrecillo*]?"[3]

In spite of Ana's wishes and the canonical prohibitions against consanguineous unions, the deal was struck and the ceremony performed. The wedding party traveled thence to Tajahuerce and, according to Bartolomé el mozo, the marriage was consummated that night.[4] When Ana awoke the next morning all seemed well and breakfast was brought to the bridal bed, where they ate together. But she soon developed a fever and "nearly lost her mind."[5] A flow of blood began—perhaps menstrual or hymeneal—that caused her "great embarrassment." She arose, cursing her husband, and the other women in the house pronounced her unable to attend church that morning.[6]

Ana's malady manifested both physically and mentally, and her condition deteriorated the longer she stayed in Tajahuerce, so she was removed to Aldealpozo where she improved briefly. But upon seeing her husband again she went into a sharp decline, claiming that she "detested" him and refusing thereafter to sleep or even eat with him.[7] Moreover, "she did not know her mother, or her father-in-law, or her husband, not even to name them." Instead, she called her mother "woman" and her father-in-law/stepfather "man."[8] She reacted hysterically whenever strangers appeared, cried uncontrollably, suffered fainting spells, and shouted a lot. So grave was the situation that Ana even contemplated throwing herself under a waterwheel; concern for the fate of her soul restrained her.[9]

The family tried various remedies, both medical and religious. Initially they probably turned to *bachiller* Pedro de Rueda, the cura of Tajahuerce, but to no avail. The first person drawn into the affair from the outside was Juan Gómez, chaplain at the Chapel of Souls in Alconaba a few miles away. He gave Ana a rosary and said Mass for her at the altar of Our Lady in Aldealpozo. He found her reactions disturbing and probably feared possession, for she refused to "adore" the rosary and responded hysterically to his presence. Unsuccessful, he gave up but suggested taking her to a "house of prayer" to be "healed by God."[10] Instead, her family sent for Román Ramírez.

Bartolomé el viejo had been soliciting advice and word spread. Miguel de Deza, Román's cousin and a blacksmith in Torrubia de Soria (about eleven miles south of Tajahuerce), mentioned his nephew's skills, perhaps to Francisco de Ávila (one of Soria's alguaciles).[11] Ávila, who had previously met Ramírez at an inn in Torrubia and heard him perform, told Juan Arias de Villacorta (an hidalgo and soldier associated with the Ortega family) about "a Morisco in Deza named Román Ramírez who cured illnesses."[12] This information was communicated to the family, who determined to pursue the option.[13]

Probably in mid-1593 Miguel de Deza and one of Ortega's servants traveled to Deza to enlist the aid of his cousin with promise of a good reward.[14] But Román could not leave for Tajahuerce immediately; he had plans to travel to Alfaro to care for a sick son.[15] Later, Diego Labajao, one of Ortega's servants, was dispatched to Deza and found the Morisco absent. Ángela de Miranda assured him that her husband "already knew" about the woman's illness and would travel to Tajahuerce upon his return.[16] Another two weeks passed before Bartolomé el viejo impatiently sent another messenger, local blacksmith Pedro Martínez, to hurry matters along, and this time Román accompanied the blacksmith to Tajahuerce.[17] There, the Morisco lodged in the young couple's house because Ana, who was staying in Aldealpozo, was discomfited by strangers, whom she abused on sight.[18]

Nevertheless, the following day Román examined his patient and pronounced her cure to be within his powers, "if it pleased God." He tried first to make Ana ingest a concoction he had brought with him— "powder that he had in an egg," said Petronila—but the sick woman refused, knocking it to the ground. He determined incense was a better delivery system for the cure.[19] The healer lacked the necessary ingredients for the pungent mixture of oriental sweetgum, asafetida, juniper, and sulfur, but promised to send them from Deza. He suggested administering the incense to her whenever she "would not do what they commanded." Whoever performed the incensing, he advised, should be "strong" and "of good spirits," and they were to place a cloth over Ana's head to keep the fumes from escaping.[20] For the consultation and cure, he received forty *reales*.[21] The mixture, which Román, Ángela, and one of their sons brewed and sent back with Juan de Llorente (a farmer from Tajahuerce), was foul to smell and "no one could stand it."[22] Pedro Martínez administered it to Ana whenever she refused to eat or sleep with her husband, but it only proved partially successful since she never consented to the latter.[23]

A few days later, Ana's condition worsened. While Petronila was leading her by the hand from the hearth to the stable, Ana "hit the back of her head on the doorframe," convulsed, and sunk into a stupor with her head wrenched to one side and fixed in position. Even more troubling, her jaw was locked shut and the catatonic Ana took no food or water for days.[24] The family fixed upon the only solution that came to mind: Román Ramírez. Bartolomé el mozo was dispatched immediately and traveled eleven miles south to Gómara where, rumor had it, the Morisco physician was working as a healer, but he could not find him there. Initially uncertain of how to proceed, the young man eventually decided to continue on another sixteen miles to Deza.[25]

That night the young man dined and slept in Román's home before they departed together the following morning.[26] Although Bartolomé was certain that his wife would die, the Morisco doubted the situation was so dire, and when they arrived in Tajahuerce, Román claimed, he immediately suggested that *bachiller* Rueda read "the Gospels to her," which he did. He also sent one of Ortega's servants to Gómara for the materials he would need to concoct more incense.[27] Others remembered Román immediately going to Ana to rub her throat with oils "twice boiled with lily roots," then taking her head in his hands—one on the back and one on the forehead—and twisting, returning it to its natural position.[28] "Now then," said the healer, "let's just be still so we don't have to get out the incense." Ana uttered not a word of complaint but sat quietly on a bed next to the hearth.[29]

Her father-in-law, however, began to chide the young woman, telling her to be content and grateful. She got up from the bed and announced that she was going to the stable. Her mother followed and they began arguing in the doorway. Román called for the incense, telling the men in the room to lay hold of Ana. He dosed her with it, which somewhat restored her docility, and they led her back to the bed. Shaking his head at her, the healer said, "You don't want the incense to have to come."[30] Ana began to speak, then indicated she wanted to be alone. Román first sent everyone except the groom away and, later, stayed alone with her in the room for more than a quarter hour. When he finally left, he said her condition had improved. Later that night, however, the young woman confided to Bartolomé el viejo that she had heard Román carrying on a conversation with some third party in the room.[31]

The various accounts of witnesses are confused, but while only the young couple and healer remained in the room—making Bartolomé el mozo the only witness able to testify—several curious things happened. The most troubling was that Román asked whether the Turk was coming against the king. Bartolomé heard a voice coming from Ana's mouth respond affirmatively.[32] Román also wondered whether he would be paid well for his work as a healer.[33] Primarily, however, the discussion focused on the couple's relationship. Román asked Ana why she did not want to sleep with her husband, and she responded, "It wasn't time."

The Morisco probed further, and she explained she first had to make a pilgrimage to the Sanctuary of Our Lady of the Sierra, "whereto she was promised [*a donde estaba prometida*]." Only then would she "lie with her husband and live with him in his house."[34] Later, the groom's father and mother-in-law convinced him that Román had carried on this conversation with a demon speaking through Ana's mouth.

Román's second visit to Tajahuerce was brief, but long enough for his relationship with the family to deteriorate. It coincided with a feast day on which he attended Mass and heard a sermon preached by *bachiller* Rueda. Bartolomé el viejo claimed that later in the day he overheard the Morisco criticize Rueda's effort to his demonic familiar: "What did you think? How did that jackass do? I'd do a lot better if I were to preach!"[35] Soon Ana's father-in-law concluded that Román was not proceeding "in a Christian fashion" and consulted with Rueda about whether to seek his arrest. Rueda urged him to be rid of the man as soon as possible.[36] He dismissed the healer with a payment of only thirty *reales*. Román, disappointed and "very upset," had hoped for one or two hundred *reales* to pay his rent.[37] "I promise you," he threatened, "you'll come looking for me again!"[38]

Yet Román did more than solve Ana's immediate health crisis; he also provided her family with a critical piece of information. Recalling Ana's desire to visit the Sanctuary of Our Lady of the Sierra in Villarroya de la Sierra (Zaragoza), he encouraged the family to take her there as well as to the shrine of the Virgin at the hermitage of Our Lady of the Fountain near Gómara.[39] They scorned his advice for the moment, perhaps because they found themselves facing a new phase of the drama: the younger Bartolomé also began to exhibit signs of illness. Even before Ramírez's departure, the young man's physical and mental state began to deteriorate. Increasingly, he felt "anxious and afflicted," and would go missing for hours.[40]

By summer 1593 the decision was made to engage another healer; this time they sought a "spiritual remedy." Bartolomé el viejo dispatched his son to Madruédano, sixty miles away, to secure the help of that town's cura, *bachiller* Juan de Ortigosa, who was reputed to "have the grace and the knack for curing such illnesses."[41] He soon diagnosed the malady suffered by both husband and wife as demon possession and marshaled all of the powers at his command.[42] He used "the prayers of the church," drew "signs of the cross on their eyes, cheeks, and mouths," gave them holy water to drink, and performed exorcisms according to both the "old and new ecclesiastical manual" to cast out the spirits.[43]

Years later, in the autumn of 1597, Bartolomé el mozo described his experience during the illness. He explained that Ortigosa recited "certain prayers and conjured [*conjuró*] at him. And while conjuring at him, [Bartolomé el mozo] fainted and remained completely senseless. *Bachiller* Ortigosa made some crosses on his face, eyes, and mouth, and he became anxious and disquieted." Petronila called it a "paroxysm."[44] In that state, "there appeared in his imagination [*se le representaban*] some shadows that frightened him and he could not comprehend their meaning. Meanwhile *Bachiller* Ortigosa, conjuring at Bartolomé, said, 'On behalf of God, I command that you depart from this human body and let it go free!'" This continued for some time, and the priest even placed the cord of his clerical robe on the patient, again commanding the spirit to depart. The young man recalled experiencing great "fatigue" thereafter and seeing many frightening "illusions, figures, and shadows," although he could recall few details. Finally, "he sensed a great cry being given out," but could not tell who made the noise. Subsequently, he felt much improved.[45]

Other witnesses filled in the gaps, describing the exorcism and, especially, the signs of demonic possession. While the young man was in his stupor, the priest ordered holy water to be brought, but Bartolomé bit through the jug with his teeth.[46] He smiled at Ortigosa and told him, "The devil has brought you here. The devil has got you already." When the priest commanded the spirit to depart, it used the young man's mouth to respond, saying, "he didn't want to" and refused to do so for "six days or more," no matter what Ortigosa did.[47] But Ortigosa would not let up and eventually wrung from the body the truth that Bartolomé el mozo was possessed not by one but rather three demons: "Satan, Barabbas, and Beelzebub."[48]

Finally, on the "sixth or seventh day," Ortigosa cast out the demons.[49] Using his cord to whip the young man's body, he reduced them to obedience. One of them explained that it had possessed Bartolomé on his wedding night, when Ana had cursed him. She gave the demon a small coin, a *cuartillo*, as a token (*prenda*). Later, on the feast day of St. Mark, while visiting the church bazaar, Bartolomé had bought several aiguillettes, one of which broke. "To the devil with you," he cursed and cast it away, but the devil took it and kept it as a pledge. The third spirit found entry when Ana's mother threw away a pin, saying likewise, "To the devil with you." Each of these admissions was accompanied by the emergence of the related token from Bartolomé's mouth.[50] At the last he gave out a "great cry" and lay as though dead. According to Rueda, the cura of Tajahuerce, the demons had departed; the young man had been "well, whole, and free" ever since.[51]

In spite of Ortigosa's best efforts, however, Ana Sanz showed no improvement, and in August 1593 he departed.[52] Like Román Ramírez, he had only half-resolved the problem, but although Ana's melancholy continued and the family remained convinced she was possessed, they must have found the situation tolerable, for they waited perhaps half a year before pursuing another round of cures.[53] This time, rather than bringing the solution to them, they went to it. A series of pilgrimages and "spiritual errands" ensued. Ana traveled to the Benedictine Monastery of Our Lady of Valvanera (seventy miles away in La Rioja), which boasted a demon-expelling chasuble, and completed a novena there. They visited while an indulgence was being offered and even convinced Ana to make a confession, but when the priest asked her to name her sins she claimed ignorance and "returned as she had gone."[54] Another seven or eight days were spent in Lardero (outside of Logroño), where she was conjured at by a priest, "who they said had grace to cure such infirmities." But despite performing "thirteen *diligencias*," he could not restore her. They even heeded Román's advice and took Ana to the hermitage of Our Lady of the Sierra for a novena and to Our Lady of the Fountain outside of Gómara, in addition to "other hermitages and houses of devotion."[55] Even if multiple sites were visited on each journey, the company traveled more than two hundred and fifty miles during spring 1594 with no results.

They were running short on options. In June of that year, Bartolomé el viejo recalled *bachiller* Ortigosa from Madruédano. Ana was moved to the church where he recited prayers, made signs of the cross, and put holy water on her.[56] He conjured at her for the span of two novenas but made no progress.[57] By this time Ana's father-in-law was ready to try anything and the widow Francisca Hernández, a local witch with a "bad reputation," suggested to Petronila that her daughter needed to return to the site of the original affliction. Thus, the afflicted woman, Francisca the witch, Bartolomé el viejo, the priests Rueda and Ortigosa, and several others spent some days together at the house in Tajahuerce.[58] Ortigosa blessed the building, room by room, and conjured at Ana, who screamed the entire first day and night. Her mother, unwilling to endure Ana's behavior, refused to remain.[59]

Ortigosa ordered Ana bound with his cord and, when she refused to eat or even open her mouth, he tightened the ligaments on her thigh until she opened her mouth "a little," then shoved a cross (or a key, according to Bartolomé el viejo) into her mouth. He damaged her teeth but they were able to force some broth into her.[60] Ortigosa kept at it for several days and nights, despite threats from the demon. After a particularly trying phase of the ordeal, during which Ana suffered much and cried continuously, he finally made a breakthrough. Speaking through Ana's mouth, the demon Barabbas admitted that, although it was alone at present, 101 spirits dwelt inside her. At that very moment, its fellows were in Deza, visiting Román Ramírez. None of them would leave her body without his permission, for they were under the Morisco's control.[61]

Ortigosa's reintroduction of Ramírez to the possession narrative here is jarring and was, presumably, part of the exorcist's effort to discredit his rivals. This interpretation is supported by a parallel narrative spun by Ortigosa to implicate Francisca Hernández, the witch who wielded the "evil eye."[62] He claimed to have learned from Barabbas that the demons, in fact, had not been responsible for most of Ana's physical distress. Rather, Francisca and her coven of witches were "roasting" his patient alive.[63] Thus, Ortigosa offered two distinct but related explanations for Ana's condition, one pertaining to the Morisco (a long term, underlying problem) and the other (more acute problem) to the witch. This information he passed onto his employer.[64]

Presumably Ortigosa believed in his ability to expel the demons and heal Ana. To triumph in the face of Barabbas's refusal to depart without Román's permission would be to go beyond implicating his rival to demonstrating his (and the church's) superiority. Ana was transferred to the parish church on Friday, June 9, 1594, and there Ortigosa continued to conjure at her. He read the gospels aloud that day and the next, until sometime around midnight. Despite his best efforts, however, the exorcist "could not cast out the demons," and he finally confided to Juan Arias de Villacorta, who was with him in the church, "This woman is killing me."[65] If anything, her condition was declining, and they again feared death was imminent. Ana's mother, father-in-law, and husband consulted with *bachiller* Rueda and collectively decided "among themselves" to pay Román off.[66] Since the rest of the company was too frightened to go, Villacorta departed alone for Deza on June 12.

When he arrived, he spoke first with an acquaintance, Román's brother-in-law Francisco de Miranda, and asked him to mediate. Miranda confessed that the healer had been very "upset" when he left Tajahuerce the last time and might refuse to help. Nevertheless, the Moriscos closeted together for some time and Román eventually assented. He took Villacorta to an upper room in the duke's house and asked for a full account of what had happened in Tajahuerce.[67] Learning of Ana's continued "infirmity and fatigue," as well as "the danger in which she remained," Ramírez told Villacorta "not to worry," for "she was already improving when he left her and by now is up and about and recognizes her parents, husband, and neighbors." He assured Villacorta he would find her "content and well" and would "dance with her."

That evening, by appointment, Villacorta called at Ramírez's home to collect the incense.[68] He also received written instructions:

> Take a pot and toss in a good amount of coals and on top of them two or three pieces of [the incense] and put them so close to her nose and mouth that that smoke gets right into her mouth and nose. Take hold of her very firmly and really threaten her, telling her not to let that evil [*mal*] come again or, if it does, that they will always give that smoke to her. And tell her to call her husband by his name, to eat and drink, and to listen to what she is told and that if she doesn't they'll give her the smoke.[69]

Román reported that he was paid "twenty *reales* for the consult and another twenty for the medicine."[70]

Upon his return, Villacorta found the situation to be just as the Morisco had described it. A crowd had gathered, and "everyone was dancing and they were all very happy to see [Ana] well," It turned out that, about noon the previous day, not long after he had left for Deza, she had "stood up and called to her mother and embraced her, calling her 'mother,' which she hadn't done since becoming ill." Shortly thereafter, when her father-in-law, her husband, and *bachiller* Rueda returned from church, "she called each one of them by his name and embraced him, very contentedly, which she hadn't done up to that point. And then she went to Juan Llorente's house to dance." Villacorta came upon the party in process, and "danced with her and she embraced him."[71]

Unfortunately, the drama was not quite at an end. That night, at the home of Bartolomé el viejo, *bachiller* Ortigosa suggested that Ana should sleep with her husband. She started to resist, but Villacorta was summoned and he brought the incense. Ana told them she knew Bartolomé el mozo "was her husband, but she didn't have to lay with him. She didn't want to be married, but since they had married her off, she didn't want to sleep with anyone." Villacorta, Juan Llorente, and Bartolomé el viejo laid hold of her and forced her face toward the smoke. Villacorta read the words Román had given him: "Get out of here for Román commands it! And if you don't watch out I'll send for him and he will come, for he promised he would!" After receiving a dose of the smoke, she called out, "Sir, let me be! Do me no more evil [*mal*]. I will do whatever you want." They carried Ana to her bed, and Villacorta ordered her to undress and lay with her husband, which she did. The next morning, she awoke, commended her mother to God, and asked for the keys to her own house. She immediately went there and established herself with her husband. Three and a half years later Ana and Bartolomé were living "together and very content."[72]

No one could deny that Ramírez had healed Ana Sanz, and even Juan de Ortigosa acknowledged that his rival succeeded where he had failed.[73] As though coordinated, this success in early June 1594 coincided with a larger shift in the Morisco's fortunes. At the end of May, in Madrid, just as the tempest surrounding the Barnuevo affair was reaching its culmination, the old duke died. The news must still have been fresh in Deza when Villacorta arrived there on the twelfth. One week later, from June 19 to 20, an elaborate ceremony took place in town that saw local hidalgo Gerónimo de Ocáriz stand in for the new duke, Juan de la Cerda (1569–1607), theretofore merely Marquis of Cogolludo. This ceremony formally enacted his possession of Deza and raised the question of his relationship with Román Ramírez, and Deza's Moriscos generally.

Román was not a member of the town council in 1594, but he was present for the possession ceremony. According to tradition, the ceremony afforded an opportunity for the new duke (or, in this case, his representative) to address grievances, especially related to the execution of justice. And, at the appropriate moment in the proceedings, Pedro de Barnuevo expressed concern that, while serving as chief bailiff, one Juan Ramírez, had allowed a prisoner to escape confinement.[74] This Ramírez remained at liberty despite Barnuevo having ordered his arrest for dereliction of duty. He urged Ocáriz to correct this lapse lest absence of discipline encourage others to commit "similar offenses."[75] The former bailiff feebly defended himself by claiming the jailbreak had occurred despite his efforts, and Ocáriz ordered his incarceration until proven innocent.[76]

Using possession ceremonies to enforce order and resolve local disputes was not unusual. These were moments of supreme power for the duke (either in his own person or through a proxy) during which all other officer holders, including the alcaide and councilmen, were symbolically stripped of their authority and reduced to being mere citizens. At times they were used strategically to address points of major tension between the townsfolk and their lord, or between factions within the town. In 1594, for no obvious reason, Román Ramírez was chosen to act as witness to the order commanding Juan Ramírez's detention. Perhaps it was a signal that he would begin playing a more active role in town affairs than he had in recent years. In any case, in late December he was selected for the town council but now for the first time as co-magistrate, administering justice in the municipal court of first instance. Around the same time the duke named Román's son Miguel (b. ca. 1569) alguacil mayor, an office he certainly held until after 1599 and perhaps as late as 1605.[77] The Ramírez family, it seemed, would enjoy particular favor under the new regime.

Román's position on the council and his ties to Deza's new seignior also facilitated an attack, this time political and bureaucratic rather than physical, against his nemesis Pedro de Barnuevo. Barnuevo had been the town's chief magistrate and castellan since 1584 and had so successfully alienated much of the citizenry that he united the hidalgos, Old Christians, and Moriscos on the town council against him. As co-magistrate in 1595, Ramírez presumably played an important role in organizing the factions, gathering legal consultations, and formulating the "memorial concerning some of the things that Pedro de Barnuevo, chief magistrate of the town of Deza, has done against the vassals" of the duke. The document listed his many offenses and described his efforts to undermine ducal authority by claiming power to make and break local officeholders.[78]

If the new duke wanted an excuse to remove the incumbent castellan, a remnant of his father's regime, then the memorial and related documents provided good grounds. Ramírez probably encouraged him in this. He had personal access to the new duke before and after his accession; although he was no longer performing many recitations, the Morisco made an exception for his patron.[79] Barnuevo was out before the end of 1595. Temporarily, he was succeeded, in turn, by a pair of local hidalgos and then, more permanently, in 1596 by Velasco de Barnuevo (b. 1540), Pedro's younger brother.[80] These maneuvers, combined with the bad blood already present, did nothing to lessen the animosity of Licentiate Bonifacio, the former castellan's son-in-law.

Charting a course through the choppy waters of local politics was not the only call upon Román's attention. In April 1594, a month before the death of Duke Juan Luis, two months before the possession ceremony, and after three decades of marriage, Ángela de Miranda died.[81] No account of her death or how her loss affected him exists, but he was not without the comfort of family. Two of his youngest and as yet unmarried sons, Miguel and Francisco, still lived at home, and a boy, perhaps a nephew, accompanied him when he traveled in order to learn healing from the master.[82] Whatever affection Román felt toward Ángela, he remarried quickly, probably in 1595. Precious little is known about his new wife, Ana de Ucedo, but in 1599 Román noted that her father was "so and so" de Ucedo, a "*capitán* who was a citizen of Montuenga"—probably Montuenga de Soria (about twenty-three miles southwest of Deza).[83]

This "so and so" may have been Juan de Ucedo of Montuenga, a man of some wealth. In July 1594 Duke Juan tapped a group of investors, many of them Moriscos from Deza, to provide financial backing for one Dr. Diego López de Rebolledo, whom the new duke had appointed to the potentially lucrative position of *receptor general* for El Puerto de Santa María.[84] Ucedo was among those who contributed to this semi-forced loan. His sizeable estate, valued at three thousand ducats, included goods and property located in Deza as well as in Montuenga.[85] Román was not asked to contribute funds—his estate was probably insufficient to warrant inclusion—but his family's involvement in the affair is attested by his son Miguel, who acted as witness for the signing of documents in Deza and signed on behalf of those who could not write their names.[86] Perhaps this new endeavor drew Ucedo into closer contact with Deza's Moriscos and facilitated an arrangement between Román Ramírez and Ucedo.[87]

The same year that Román gained the magistracy, removed his nemesis from power, healed Ana Sanz, and remarried was also the beginning of his downfall. The affair began innocently enough, with an invitation from Pedro Ramírez, governor of the dry ports, to entertain guests at his home in Soria, especially the guests of honor don Gil Ramírez de Arellano, a judge at the Royal Appellate Court in Valladolid, and his wife doña Catalina.[88] Román performed at Pedro Ramírez's house for three or four days in a row in October 1595, probably the fourteenth through the seventeenth. Then, probably for the evening of the eighteenth, don Diego de Orozco, Soria's corregidor, requested his services. Orozco, who had previously retained Román for a performance in winter 1592–93, approached Arellano (not Pedro Ramírez) directly. Orozco was playing host to a group of knights from Guadalajara and wanted Román to entertain them, but Arellano, the region's royal judge, saw an opportunity to assert his authority over the city's royal district magistrate. He refused to allow Orozco to enter with his staff of office in hand. And when the corregidor made his request empty handed, Arellano refused, alleging his wife had already invited several ladies to attend the evening's performance.[89]

Infuriated by the slight, Orozco grew vindictive and urged a local inquisitorial commissioner, one Francisco González de Rueda, to arrest the Morisco. According to Román, Orozco offered to provide the Holy Office with "sufficient evidence" to prove he had "cured with the help of the devil and kept a familiar and that the demon in Tajahuerce had refused to leave [Ana's] body unless Román from Deza ordered it and that the devil told [Román] what to read [from memory]." That very night "three or four knaves [bellacos]" were dispatched to arrest the performer, but word reached Arellano first. He, along with Pedro Ramírez and one don Antonio de Río, urged Román to depart immediately for Deza. They suggested that, "if they came to arrest him there in Soria, half the town would be lost."[90] The rationale is obscure but may refer to the performer's fame in that city, or maybe they feared an arrest would escalate into a larger showdown between local factions. Román claimed he would have preferred to stay and be arrested but allowed himself to be persuaded.

As he fled east along Calle el Collado, Alonso de Roa, Soria's alguacil mayor, spotted but did not try to detain him. Instead, he hailed a passing group of students traveling in the company of the priest Pedro Díaz de Carabantes. In the manner of one "speaking about something remarkable," Roa pointed out a man in a brown cape thirty or forty paces away and said, "Come, your honors! That one down there is called Román, a citizen of the town of Deza, Morisco by nation." He explained that, the previous night, Román had been at the house of Antonio de Río [sic], where several knights had gathered, "playing and enjoying themselves." "Hey!" some of the attendees had shouted, "Tell us a bit of such and such a book of chivalry!" and named the book. Román pulled a blank piece of paper from his satchel, looked at it, and began to "read." He recited a large section of the requested book, "as though he were reading something written."[91]

With his audience hooked, Roa declared, "I'll tell your honors another story about that man that will amaze you even more." He proceeded to offer a version of the events that occurred in Tajahuerce, emphasizing Román's control over the demons. The priest Díaz de Carabantes, who claimed to have had no previous knowledge of the Morisco, told Roa that what he had described was an inquisitorial matter, "and if it is as you say, that man deserves to be burned." Roa urged the priest to bring it to the Holy Office's attention and, for his own part, promised to supply a written account of the events signed by those who had been directly involved.[92]

Four denunciations against Ramírez followed, all of them made in Soria in the presence of commissioner González de Rueda and his apostolic notary Jusepe Zapata. They give every indication, as the Morisco later claimed, of having been concocted to satisfy Orozco's vindictiveness. The only question is how far the conspiracy extended. On October 18, Díaz de Carabantes and Roa offered their denunciations, but the priest's entire testimony was hearsay, fed to him during the encounter with Roa. Perhaps, then, he was innocent of collusion. Roa could not claim first-hand knowledge either. Instead, he based his statement on an account of the Tajahuerce affair that he claimed to have been shown by Francisco de Ávila, the alguacil for the sexmo de Arciel, part of Soria's hinterland.

That very same day, despite the weak evidence, the commissioner dispatched an inquisitorial familiar to arrest Ramírez, and Alonso de Roa, presumably in his capacity as alguacil mayor, witnessed the order. All of this is contained in the inquisitorial dossier, but the documents are intentionally out of order. Instead of being arranged chronologically, the arrest order of October 18 follows the deposition of a third Soria witness, Licentiate Bonifacio, whose testimony occurred only on the nineteenth. This may have been done to obscure the fact that sufficient evidence to warrant an arrest was lacking.[93] Bonifacio's deposition asserted that at nine or ten o'clock at night on the eighteenth, González de Rueda had come to his door with questions about Román Ramírez. Although the licentiate spoke "without knowing that [the caller] was an [inquisitorial] commissioner," he nevertheless recounted "what he knew about [the Morisco] and where he thought he was and where he was staying." Only at the end of the nocturnal interview, the record claims, did González de Rueda reveal his identity. It being too late to accomplish the business that night, Bonifacio made plans to present himself for a formal denunciation the following morning.[94] No explanation was offered as to how, precisely, the commissioner knew to show up at Bonifacio's door that night.

Receipt by the commissioner of the written record of events in Taja-huerce, to which Roa had referred on the eighteenth, occurred even later, on October 26, pursuant to the deposition of a fourth and final Soria witness, Francisco de Ávila.[95] The puzzling document that he presented recounts events that occurred in "the month of June, the year 1594" but is itself undated and bears the name of no author or scribe. One and a half folios in length, it is witnessed and signed at the end by three key figures from the Tajahuerce affair: the priest Pedro de Rueda, the elder Bar-tolomé de Ortega, and Juan Arias de Villacorta. In his testimony, Licen-tiate Bonifacio claimed to have seen the document on October 15 or 16, 1595, while Alonso de Roa claimed Francisco de Ávila had shown it about "eight years" previously.[96] "Eight years" is clearly an error, for the events of Tajahuerce had not even begun. Perhaps the scribe meant "eight months" (i.e., February 1595), "eight days" (i.e., ca. October 10), or perhaps Roa misspoke. In any case, none of these dates is likely to have been true.

When he submitted the document on October 26, Ávila also offered testimony and some of what he said helps make sense of the written record. He noted that "about a month previously," while he was on his way to the sexmo de Arciel, Ávila passed through Tajahuerce and there spoke with Bartolomé the younger and Ana Sanz. Astonished by their story, he asked *bachiller* Rueda to confirm it. Rueda "told [Ávila] what had happened, which is that which this present notary [i.e., Zapata] wrote in the presence of his honor, the lord commissioner [i.e., González de Rueda], the whole thing written in this notary's own letter and hand on three pages of paper."[97] This suggests that, despite what Bonifacio and Roa claimed, the document was newly minted, not eight years or months old. Instead, it was probably written out on October 18 in Soria by Zapata in the presence of González de Rueda and based on a state-ment made by Ávila soon after Ramírez de Arellano spurned Orozco. Only after the account had been composed did the alguacil take it to Tajahuerce to secure signatures from the three witnesses.

Alonso de Roa, Francisco de Ávila, and Licentiate Bonifacio presented themselves as disinterested parties who only learned of the Tajahuerce affair when Ávila passed through that village in September 1595—a half-truth at best. When first approached about going to Tajahuerce in mid-

1593, the Morisco secured "permission from the corregidor" of Soria, Diego de Orozco. Without it, he claimed, he would "not have dared to enter the region" and perform cures.[98] For their part, Ávila and Bonifacio had acted as go-betweens to acquire that permission. Román knew Bonifacio through Pedro de Barnuevo, and Bonifacio declared himself Bartolomé el viejo's "best friend."[99] Ávila, who had shared a meal with Román and seen him perform at an inn in Torrubia, was responsible for telling Bartolomé about him, by mentioning him to Villacorta. Alonso de Roa had heard the Morisco perform in Soria at the corregidor's home in winter 1592–93. In short, all three key witnesses had preexisting relationships with Román and were connected to Diego de Orozco's circle.

Additional layers of conspiracy are possible but less certain. The surnames of inquisitorial commissioner Francisco González de Rueda and Pedro de Rueda, cura of Tajahuerce, might indicate a relation. Pedro de Rueda, whose sermon Román mocked, had reason to dislike the Morisco, even apart from concerns about diabolism. Furthermore, Francisco González de Rueda and Jusepe Zapata were not the commissioner and notary who would normally have received the denunciation against Ramírez. In addition to being the cura of the parish of San Salvador in Soria, González de Rueda was, indeed, a *comisario*, but his jurisdiction was limited to the Archpresbyterate of Rabanera, part of the city's hinterland.[100] Dr. Juan de Vinuesa Solera was the man who should have received the denunciations but, on October 18, he and his notary, Juan de Paredes, were away from Soria.

Although González de Rueda lacked jurisdictional authority, he not only gathered testimonies and evidence but also ordered Ramírez's arrest. When Vinuesa and Paredes returned, probably within a day or two of the first denunciations, they immediately demanded all materials related to the case. When Zapata complied, they found that virtually all of the evidence against Román was hearsay, for the purported record of the events that transpired in Tajahuerce had not yet been manufactured. Perhaps an inclination to see the case die—either because of pressure from Román's allies or out of animosity for the other commissioner— explains why Vinuesa decided to send the documents to the inquisitors at Valladolid, who had jurisdiction over Soria and Tajahuerce (but not

Deza). He did so "without having finished [the inquiry] or giving a copy of it" to González de Rueda. The latter complained and was informed by Vinuesa that he ought not to have been involved in the first place in this or "any other [business] in this city," but should rather have stayed within his own jurisdiction.[101] As the case stood, it was an embarrassment and Valladolid showed no interest in pursuing it.

Despite having been waved off, González de Rueda continued to pursue the case. On October 26, he and Zapata received Francisco de Ávila's denunciation along with the account of events in Tajahuerce, signed by witnesses. Lacking the original depositions or arrest order, however, González de Rueda was in an awkward position. Since Román had already slipped out of Soria, González de Rueda wrote and requested help from Deza's own inquisitorial commissioner, Licentiate Miguel Benito.[102] He justified this move on the basis that "tardiness or delay" was dangerous since the accused, in addition to having passed beyond the jurisdiction of the tribunal at Valladolid, was "a Morisco by nation, and for that reason very suspect."[103] González de Rueda also sent Ávila's denunciation and written account of the Tajahuerce affair to Valladolid with various explanations in the hope of justifying his hasty actions and buttressing what was, until then, a very weak case.

If Arellano, Antonio de Río, and Pedro Ramírez had hoped to protect Román from the Holy Office by sending him back to Deza and beyond the jurisdiction of the Valladolid tribunal, they underestimated their opponents' commitment. The Morisco's return home could not have long preceded the arrival of González de Rueda's letter asking his counterpart in Deza to arrest Ramírez. Certainly, Pedro de Barnuevo, who was in his final days as chief magistrate, must have relished the moment.[104] Román was in custody before October 26, placed in fetters, and kept under guard in the home of a local inquisitorial familiar.[105] Perhaps Barnuevo's harsh treatment of the duke's Morisco was the final straw precipitating his removal. Several years later, Román indicated that he had only spent "two or three" days in this condition, but this cannot be correct. On November 1, Licentiate Benito wrote to his inquisitorial superiors at Cuenca, advising them of the arrest and placing the matter in their hands, so he was certainly still in custody at that point.[106]

How long Ramírez remained so is unclear but probably for a relatively brief period; he was certainly released before January 21, 1596. On that date, a letter (unsigned but probably from Benito) was written from Deza to Cuenca providing an update on the local situation. It advised that the denunciations and evidence related to the Ramírez case, which ought to have already arrived in Cuenca, were delayed, having been sent first to Valladolid. The letter's author, nevertheless, was confident they would soon arrive, allowing justice to proceed in the new jurisdiction. The accused remained under arrest but his situation had changed. Although it was "not very appropriate given his flight from Soria . . . and the force of commissioner [González de Rueda's] warning," in view of the fact that Román was one of Deza's magistrates, he had been granted "the town for his jail." The parolee promised to present himself "each and every time the castellan summoned him" and as security a bond of two thousand ducats was posted.[107]

Now free from close confinement, Román suffered another tragedy. Soon after his release "he discovered one of his sons stabbed to death in the countryside around Deza." He provided no additional details except internal and psychological ones: he claimed to have been "altered" on account of "these pains" and to have "lost" his remarkable memory. Although somehow still able to "read from the head," he had only done so a few times thereafter ("for the duke of Medinaceli") and he could no longer "embellish books" as he once had.[108] Román offered no indication of his suspicion as to the guilty party or parties, but likely suspects must include Pedro de Barnuevo, Diego de Orozco, or their lackeys.[109]

Despite the privations he suffered at the hands of enemies, the years immediately following his release suggest a return to normalcy or at least something close to it. His new wife bore two children, María (b. 1596) and Juan (b. 1597), and he remained active at the duke's garden and about town. His movements were more restricted—both by virtue of his confinement to Deza and on account of his enemies. In spring 1597, for instance, one María de Neyla of Hinojosa del Campo (Soria) sent for his help in curing her son. Román refused to travel, not because of his arrest but because he had vowed "not to enter the region of Soria while [Orozco] held the staff of office."[110] Nevertheless, his involvement in local affairs continued and, in 1597, he served on the town council, as a deputy.[111] In March 1596 and September 1597 he testified in a trial related to the town's finances, and he signed the council's account books in 1596, 1597, and 1598.[112] His name was even proposed for the co-magistracy in both 1598 and 1599, but it was disallowed in both cases.[113] Román may have, with some reason, concluded that the troubles of 1595 had blown over. In fact, this lull was the calm before the storm.

8

The Better Law

Román Ramírez el Menor's Story, Part 3

Ramírez secured his freedom from close confinement in 1595 with a bond of 2,000 ducats, an enormous amount for a man who had trouble scraping together 200 *reales* (about 18 ducats) just a few years earlier. Even if he only posted 100 ducats as surety, as a comment he made two years later may indicate, this remains an unexpectedly large sum of money for him to have accessed.[1] His relations with the duke remained largely intact during this second half of the 1590s and even saw his son Miguel named the chief bailiff over Deza's hamlets. So, perhaps Duke Juan de la Cerda provided security for the bond or, if not him, then maybe the men from Soria—Ramírez de Arellano, Pedro Ramírez, and Antonio de Río—played a role.

One source of extra income during this period that may have contributed was a payment he received for the composition of an original chivalric romance. In his trial, Román made tantalizing reference to "a book of chivalry entitled *Florisdoro de Grecia*" and noted that "they" had given him "300 *reales* for what he has written."[2] Unfortunately, the inquisitors did not take the bait, and no one mentioned the book again. Which "they" paid the money? A publisher, perhaps, but more likely, some patron or patrons, who found Román interesting primarily because of his storytelling. The duke is the most likely candidate, especially given his family's interest in chivalric tales.[3] Even more intriguing is the question of *Florisdoro*'s contents. No copy of the book has (or is likely ever) to come to light, but serendipitously a brief extract survives that raises and answers questions about Román Ramírez's literacy and his Islamic identity. In fact, the two were deeply intertwined.

Back in 1594, Román provided Juan Arias de Villacorta with instructions for using the incense to heal Ana Sanz. They were written down on the back of a recycled scrap of paper taken from the Morisco's rooms upstairs in the duke's house. Because of its potential significance to the case, an inquisitorial agent traveled to Villacorta's home in Hinojosa del Campo to collect those instructions and forwarded them to inquisitors in Cuenca. The document was inserted into Ramírez's trial dossier as folio 89. One side contains the instructions; the other is a brief section, written in rhyming verse, of a longer dramatic work. Two characters appear in the extant lines; the first designated "yo" in the margin (but "Belindoro" in the text) is the vassal of a king designated "sol" in the margin. They converse for roughly half of the lines before Belindoro departs and "sol" begins a soliloquy:[4]

> of the prince, your son, we do not know,
> and this, lord, is the injury we suffer.
> sol: How is that, Belindoro?
> Declare what afflicts me.
> yo: Lord, we do not find your son.
> sol: What? Is it possible? O sad Moor!
> Then, there is no trace of whither he's gone?
> yo: Lord, we have not found him
> I'm afraid I must say.
> sol: Did he have occasion?
> yo: I don't know.
> sol: Did he go by land or sea?
> yo: No one knows, lord.
> sol: This increases my pain all the more.
> Away! Go call to me
> the stable hand, I say,
> or that captive Christian
> immediately, before this hand
> punishes you all.

yo: I will call him right away.
sol: Do not delay.
yo: I go immediately.
sol: What is this? Allah, where am I?
Contentment has finished with me.
There is no secure fortress
if enemies are outside.
What good is it for corsairs
to have fortune on the sea?
For as soon as it fails them
they descend with everything to the depths.
What are these contrasts of the world
that assault every contentment?
Of what worth to Xerxes are
his proud squadrons?
Or his bloody banners,
since it came out the other way?
As for the Macedonian corsair,
Of what value were his victories?
Or that histories of him recount
That he defeated the fierce King Darius?[5]

What can be gathered from this meager offering? A prince, the son
of the king designated "sol," has been lost, which deeply distresses and
unsettles his father. The king dispatches a vassal or retainer, Belindoro,
to summon his groom, a Christian captive. Geographically, the events
occur at a location where a departure of the prince by either land or sea
was possible. The imagery is martial—injury, pain, bloody banners, cap-
tives, and fortresses. Strikingly, the king, who drives the drama in these
lines, is a Muslim. He establishes this identity by calling upon Allah,
keeping a Christian slave, and describing himself as a "sad Moor." The
name of his vassal, Belindoro, evokes the names of various characters
in sixteenth-century chivalric romances—Artemidoro, Belianís, even
Florambel, not to mention Florisdoro, the title character of Ramírez's
chivalric romance, perhaps the missing prince at the drama's center.

The story itself, with its reflections on contentment and the caprice of fortune, surely drew upon Ramírez's own experience, but the narrative may also mirror a loss suffered by the previous Duke Juan de la Cerda (r. 1544–75), whose second son, Gastón (ca. 1547–ca. 1562[?]), was captured by the forces of Ottoman admiral Piali Pasha at the Battle of Djerba (1560). Legend had it that Gastón was taken prisoner and transported to Constantinople, where he died a few years later. The story was well known in Deza, where Román's mother speculated on the fate of the youth in the early 1560s with her neighbors.[6]

The marginal notes in the scrap of paper, "yo" and "sol," may refer to actors who were assigned the parts in a theatrical version of the scene. While "sol" might be a shortened version of the king's own name— perhaps Solomon—"yo" is clearly not an abbreviated form of Belindoro and must instead be read as the first person pronoun.[7] If this is the case, then the document would probably represent an effort to dramatize Florisdoro's story for the stage. Perhaps it was an early version "composed" as a *comedia*, which Román subsequently revised into a "book of chivalry." Sixteenth-century Dezanos did perform such works locally, and the town's Moriscos (and maybe its Old Christians as well) showed repeated interest in *comedias* and *farsas*. Lope Guerrero referred to *farsas* being performed in Deza in the late 1560s, and these were not merely traveling troops that stopped briefly in town.[8] Local Morisco youths rehearsed, made costumes, and performed publicly.[9] Did Román Ramírez compose those plays too?

Folio 89 also has bearing on the question of Román's literacy. Reading and writing were distinct skills and taught separately in early modern Europe. Certainly, a fair percentage of Deza's Moriscos could do one or both thanks to the efforts of local clerics and Old Christians. Many of Román's contemporaries learned to read from the priest Gonzalo de Santa Clara (d. bef. 1570), among them Moriscos Francisco de Arcos (b. ca. 1540), Mateo Romero el viejo (ca. 1530–aft. 1572), Juan de Contreras (ca. 1530–72), Lope Guerrero el viejo (1539–1611), Juan de San Juan (1547–ca. 1592), and Luis de Cebea el menor (1547–1611).[10] No doubt there were other pupils, and Román might have been among them.

He claimed that his mother's medical knowledge had no connections to the world of books and literacy, but his father was a great reader with a penchant for chivalric romances.[11] He often read aloud and may well have acquired many of the volumes found in his son's library. Given this home environment, the literacy of so many of his contemporaries, and his own future literary interests, of all the Moriscos in Deza, Román el menor seems an unlikely candidate for illiteracy. Yet, the playwright Ruiz de Alarcón cast him in that light and his literary pretensions have been dismissed as "suspect in the extreme" because an "illiterate farmer" could not have afforded the various books that Román claimed to possess.[12] But this Morisco was far more complex than his critics have allowed, and his relationship to the written word can best be understood by considering his local context and religious convictions.

Those who question Román Ramírez's ability to read and write do so, principally, on the basis of his own testimony. In 1599, when asked by the Holy Office if he knew how to "write and read and if he has or has had any books," he claimed, "He knows how to read a very little bit and does not know how to write, except only to sign his name." He was not, of course, claiming complete illiteracy. Rather, he explained that he had "known how to read for thirty years, and nobody taught him but rather he was reading on his own bit by bit, a youth having given him the basics from the primer." He went on to name many of the books that he owned and was then asked whether he read from those books clearly and quickly and with ease. To this he responded, "For himself, he reads well but when reading for others he does not read very quickly. Most of what he read was for the purpose of embellishing it and memorizing it in order to recite it afterwards by memory."[13]

Provided with a copy of Juan Huarte de San Juan's *Examen de ingenios para las sciencias* (1575), "he read a little from one chapter of it" but "seemed to read neither quickly nor clearly."[14] The inquisitor then pronounced, "He did not seem to know how to read so clearly or quickly and with the ease that was required and necessary in order to memorize so much and with such precision" as to be able to recite continuously the "chapters, lines, and details" that he claimed to have memorized or "read from memory."[15] In other words, the inquisitors did not deny he could read but asserted the unlikelihood of his having read and memorized so many works. Their question derived principally from a concern about whether his recitations were performed naturally or by virtue of some other power.

Despite Ramírez's claim and the inquisitorial pronouncement, evidence suggests that from at least the 1560s he could read well and may have known how to write. Licentiate Bonifacio testified that Román knew how to read as a youth, since the Morisco had indicated that, "when he was a boy," he had read and memorized some "divine stories." Román himself mentioned that "when he was a boy" he memorized books that he either "read" or "heard read."[16] Referring in 1571 to events that occurred in 1567 or 1568, Ana de Almoravi confessed (under torture) that she had witnessed Román reading to other young men from a "book about things of the Moors," and that he led a group of Moriscos to the duke's garden, where "he instructed them." She saw him "reading to them from a book" about "Moorish things."[17] Further evidence of literacy later in life comes from the testimony of Bartolomé el mozo, who traveled to Deza in 1593. Having arrived late, he dined and slept at the Morisco's home. There, "Román read from some books in his house and he said he was studying from them and he was very well read and knew a great deal."[18]

Román also claimed he did not know how to write, except to sign his name, but this too may have been false. Certainly, many examples of his signature exist from 1570 through to the end of his life. And although no indisputable evidence exists that he could write anything else, Ana de Almoravi described him copying Islamic prayers onto scraps of paper in the mid-1560s.[19] Circumstantial evidence links him to various documents with some degree of likelihood. The earliest of these is undated but belongs to the 1560s when Ramírez was first working as an *hortelano* at the duke's garden.[20] The handwriting is entirely different from that of Gonzalo Martínez, who made regular reports to the duke, and of Martín de la Milla, the rival *hortelano*. Although it found its way into the ducal archive, it lacks an author or addressee. The document, written from the monastery of San Francisco in Medinaceli, indicates that the desired trees (*álamos* or poplars) for the duke's property could not be found there, but it offers suggestions as to where in the garden to place them once located and even includes a small sketch. While it cannot be assigned to Ramírez with certainty, the subject was part of his bailiwick, and the suggestion that poplars be transported in from Aragon likewise hints at the Morisco.

A second document, which dates to 1581, appears in connection with the visit to Deza of the inquisitor Arganda, who summoned Román and Ángela de Miranda to account for their apparent failure to complete the three annual confessions required of them by the Edict of 1570–71. The couple presented Arganda with two confessional receipts that indicated their compliance. The elderly local priest Juanes de Altopica wrote the first one, while the priest Juanes Valles signed the other. The latter receipt attested to confessions made during the entire period between 1571 and "today" (with the exception of a confession to Altopica made in Easter 1572). However, the signatory did not write the receipt.[21]

Arganda immediately saw the receipt as problematic and charged Román with having presented a forgery. Although the Morisco explained his way out of the situation, the handwriting is strikingly similar to that of the *álamo* missive. They also very much resemble two other documents: the incense instructions and the *comedia* lines on the recto and verso sides of folio 89. Since the incense instructions given to Villacorta in June 1594 were written on scrap paper, the play excerpt must antedate them.[22] Although Ramírez might have employed an amanuensis for writing a fair copy of *Florisdoro*, both sides of folio 89 give every indication of having been dashed off in a hurry.[23] Certainly, Villacorta mentioned no amanuensis being present during his consultation with Ramírez in the duke's house.[24] Minor differences are detectable between these writing samples, but over the course of three decades such variances are not remarkable.

Another possible example of the Morisco's writing dates to 1581 and is connected to the same brief inquisitorial examination as the confessional receipt, but the writing style differs substantially from the others. This last is the letter of apology written to Dr. Arganda subsequent to his departure. Román (predictably) lost his temper at some point in the proceedings and, having regained his composure, dispatched a written apology a few days later to Arganda, who had already left town.[25] The hand in this sample is much clearer and more precise than the others, which are little better than scrawls. This letter, however, was more formally written, reflecting the importance of its message and recipient. Either Ramírez wrote it using the clearest, most careful script he could manage, or he paid someone to pen it for him.

None of this proves that Román was a better reader or writer than he claimed to be when he stood before the Holy Office in 1599. But squaring that claim to minimal literacy with the above evidence *and* his ownership of a substantial library—in 1593 Bartolomé el mozo noted the "great quantity of books" in his house[26]—*and* his remarkable familiarity with those books, *and* the idea that he was "composing" his own volume is no simple feat. In fact, his testimony about his ability to read and write, and the poor performance he gave of reading aloud, seem at odds with the rest of the evidence. But why would Román have misled the Holy Office on this matter? A clue may lie in the chronology he provided for having acquired his "very little bit" of literacy. "Thirty years ago," he claimed (i.e., ca. 1569), a lad taught him the basics from a primer and he taught himself the rest of what little he knew.[27] If true, he could not have done any reading (let alone writing) before that date. However, Ana de Almoravi claimed he was both reading and writing earlier in the decade—not chivalric tales but Islamic materials.

Although baptized as an infant and later confirmed by the church, Román Ramírez lived large portions of his life as a secret Muslim. While sometimes he may have felt ambivalence and even been drawn toward Christianity, his heart always inclined toward the Law of Mohammed. This he acknowledged to the Holy Office in 1571 and again in 1599. Numerous witnesses in the Morisco community knew and interacted with him as a Muslim. When it was in his interest, he could speak intelligently and with authority about Islam.

He may, as he claimed in 1599, have initially been exposed to it in ca. 1553 by way of Gerónimo de Villaverde, the migrant farmhand whose moves away from Deza left the youth with no way to fix the date of Ramadan. However, decades earlier, in 1571, Román's confession for the Edict of Grace did not mention Villaverde. Instead he claimed to have been drawn (for the first time, the inquisitor must have assumed) toward Islam in May or June 1566 while in Fuentes de Ebro (Zaragoza), having traveled there with Mateo Romero el menor (b. ca. 1552) and Gerónimo de Obezar (b. ca. 1548). Both men were associated with the Almanzorre-Almoravi circle and had traveled to Aragon to work for Juan de Fuentes, a local Morisco landowner.[28] While there, "on the eve of Trinity Sunday," Román was encouraged by his fellows to shun the "bad" Christian fast and instead keep Ramadan. Mateo Romero and Juan de Fuentes taught him how to perform ritual ablutions in the Muslim fashion and offered to teach him prayers as well but, he claimed, they never got around to the latter.

Near the beginning of Lent 1567, having completed the harvest in Fuentes and traveled to Madrid before returning to Deza, Ramírez claimed to have been approached in the town plaza by Romero, who told him that Ramadan had come. The same thing happened the following year, but this time Ana de Almoravi urged him to make his wife to fast as well.[29] Meanwhile, Román was called upon in his capacity as port guard to travel with an Augustinian, one Father Marcelo, to Torre Loizaga (Biscay) and Serón de Nágima (Soria). Román testified that, as they traveled, the priest "told him all sorts of things from the holy Scriptures" and ultimately convinced him that Christianity was true. "God has miraculously breathed upon me," he purportedly told his wife, "The trip with the friar has illuminated the way for me."[30]

Decades later, during his 1599 trial, Román coordinated the time spent harvesting in "Osera [del Ebro] and Fuentes [del Ebro]" with the period immediately following his duel with Licentiate Páez. While he was "forced to stay away" from Deza, "other Moriscos converted him [*le tornaron*]." He began to fast and continued to do so "until he enjoyed the [Edict of] Grace, as he declared in the confession that he made for the said Grace."[31] Both the 1571 and 1599 accounts agree that Román's turn (or return) to Islam occurred no earlier than mid-1566 and that it happened in Aragon. They also agree that the proselytizers were the Moriscos with whom he interacted in Aragon and that he continued to fast for a time after returning to Deza. Yet the reliability of the 1571 (and, for that matter, the 1599) confession is questionable. Not only does the inquisitorial context naturally foster doubts, but the confession itself gives every indication of being a studied performance. This does not necessarily mean the content was fictitious but does suggest that Ramírez was crafting a story and not offering an unrehearsed confession. Moreover, in her 1570–71 trial, Ana de Almoravi provided key information about Román's Islamic formation and activities in 1565 and shortly thereafter that casts doubt on the narrative he spun.

Ana de Almoravi left Aragon in ca. 1558 along with her husband and son, Mateo Romero el menor. By their industry the "poor" family grew "rich" in Deza.[32] In September 1570 Almoravi was arrested by the Holy Office and made a partial confession that named Román Ramírez as a secret Muslim. On January 31, 1571, she underwent torture, which led to additional confessions and denunciations. Among those denounced were Román, his father-in-law, and several of his friends. A week later, on the morning of February 5, she reaffirmed her previous denunciations and supplied information about the visit of Pedro el Cañamenero in winter 1564–65 to teach a group of local men, including Román Ramírez el mayor, about Islam and especially the *letra de moros*.[33] One night around St. John's Day (June 24), she claimed that she found a group sitting at Cañamenero's feet and listening to him read from one of his two "very good and very excellent books," among them Román the younger. Seeing Almoravi, the reader covered the book and Román, concocting a reasonable fiction, told her that Cañamenero was reading "verses about the Marquis of Mantua."[34]

To judge from Almoravi's description of events, Cañamenero's presence in town sparked an Islamic revival. Observance of Ramadan spread, and several houses became established sites for prayers. As Cañamenero's departure drew near, Velasco de Medrano and Francisco de Miranda convinced him to leave one of his books behind so that the two men "might copy [*trasladasen*] it" for Medrano.[35] Probably it was this same volume, or the copy made from it, to which Almoravi referred under torture when she noted that, while pretending to rehearse *farsas*, Francisco de Miranda "instructs all the youths in [his studio]" and "the son of Román Ramírez, who is called Román, has a book and he also instructs them." Together they taught the "prayers of the Moors, *alhandu* and *colhua*, and the azala," that is, the form of the daily prayers. Román "read from a book and then wrote for them on tiny scraps of paper the surahs of *alhandu* and *colhua*." She added one final piece of information: "Román took them all to the duke's garden, where he is the gardener, and there he instructed them."[36]

The context of these confessions and denunciations demands caution, but many of the details—the reference to verses from the Marquis of Mantua, the rehearsal of *farsas*, and Ramírez's connection to the garden—ring true. Certainly, if Ana de Almoraví's testimony was not a complete fabrication, then the 1571 and 1599 descriptions of Ramírez being reintroduced to Islam while sojourning in Aragon become highly suspect, as does the claim that he only learned to read in 1569 and never to write, except to sign his name. Days before Ana denounced him in Cuenca, he made his own confession in Deza for the 1571 Edict of Grace and in April of that year he was reconciled to the church. Sometime later, the Holy Office in Cuenca belatedly noted Ramírez's failure to address several issues, including Almoraví's accusations, in his confession, but Arganda and Madriz let it drop. They dismissed the accusations for lack of corroborating testimony.[37]

Even in 1599, revealing his literacy to inquisitors remained dangerous since he did not know how much they knew about his activities. Certainly, he had to assume they had reviewed his 1571 confession, but did they know about his interactions with Cañamenero or his activities as an Islamic instructor? If they had that information in front of them, he would need to defend against it, but to explicitly deny the charge without a preceding accusation would merely draw attention to it. If, however, he suggested in both word and deed that he had never been more than a poor reader and was altogether incapable of writing, then he could implicitly contravene any report of literacy before 1569 and reemphasize that his trip to Aragon, years after the arrival Pedro el Cañamenero and his Islamic books, had been the pivotal moment.

Critically, however, in 1571 and all the more in 1599, Román's own well-being was not his only goal. His concern extended to the crypto-Islamic community of Deza and perhaps of the entire border region as well. In his 1571 confession, he denounced several Moriscos, but primarily Aragonese outsiders, like Juan de Fuentes, Ana de Almoraví, and Mateo

Romero. All the Dezanos he denounced belonged to the Almanzorre-Almoravi circle. So, he felt comfortable sacrificing these Moriscos. But he never mentioned Cañamenero's work or his own and Miranda's efforts to instruct Deza's lads in Islam.[38] Similarly, in 1599 he manipulated the course of his own trial to focus attention on outsiders (like Villaverde), the dead (like his grandfather), and the more spectacular elements of his own story, while diverting attention away from ongoing crypto-Islamic activity in town, including his own pedagogical efforts.

Moreover, despite his 1599 claim that when he took the Edict of Grace he had "truly intended to convert to the Catholic faith," Islamic activities were not only a reality in Deza but Román Ramírez played a key role in them. For the more than two decades after the Edict, he claimed, he "performed not a single Moorish ceremony," even though "his heart always inclined toward being a Moor and he vacillated within himself over which was the better Law, that of the Moors or the Christians and in which he would be saved."[39] Determining whether he actually experienced this doubt and uncertainty is, of course, impossible. But as far as his outward observance of Christianity can be judged, at least during the 1570s and 1580s, Ramírez convincingly played the loyal son of the church.

He had always had his children baptized, of course, and the town's sacramental register indicates the confirmation of Lope, Francisco, and Miguel in 1570. In accordance with the terms of the 1571 Edict of Grace, everyone who was reconciled had to confess annually at Easter, Pentecost, and Christmas. When Inquisitor Arganda queried Román about his confessions between 1571 and 1581, the Morisco provided confessional receipts signed by local priests. Arganda challenged their authenticity, noting that Román's itinerary, which included fifteen months in the jail in Molina and frequent travel on behalf of Gerónimo de Salamanca, did not fit the confessional observance described in the receipts. The Morisco responded that, "while he was imprisoned," they had "occasionally" permitted him to travel to Deza, which allowed him to confess. The exception, he noted, was one Pentecost when he failed to comply and one Christmas spent in Madrid. He had confessed both infractions to priests in Deza and performed "penance because he was late in confessing."[40] So, if he was sloppy about fulfilling his penitential obligations, at least he knew how to rectify the situation.

In 1595 Licentiate Bonifacio—no friend of Ramírez—rated his religiosity above average. He had seen him "go to Mass and the sermon very regularly and attend the divine offices with greater frequency" than other Moriscos. Although Bonifacio could not assess Román's heart, he acknowledged that he worked through the beads of the rosary and did all of the external things that "the rest of the Christians" did when they prayed.[41] He rarely communed but this was beyond his control. Beginning in 1584, the bishop had prohibited all of Deza's Moriscos from receiving the Eucharist, except when they were marrying or *in extremis*. If Ramírez performed well before Old Christians, however, clearly more was going on beneath the surface and, as Ana de Almoravi had indicated in 1571, a great deal of it was connected to the duke's garden and house.

It was there, he claimed at his final trial, that he had come to know "Muçali" (presumably, Musa Ali), an unbaptized Turkish slave belonging to one Captain Pedro de Cabrera (d. bef. 1608).[42] The two arrived in Deza in 1590 or 1591 and the slave began "coming frequently to [Román's] garden," where they "struck up a great friendship."[43] Ramírez claimed that one day in June or July 1591 he asked Muçali, "In whom does the Great Turk believe?" The answer: "Allah, which is to say, God." He enquired further, "Does the Great Turk fast? And if so, how?" Muçali responded, "He fasts for Ramadan, and does not eat during the day until it is nighttime." The slave, who had observed Román eating a few days earlier, chided him because, coincidentally, it was the month of Ramadan. The Morisco pleaded ignorance and was told, "Well, look, I tell you on behalf of Allah to fast henceforth because if you don't fast you'll go to hell."[44]

Román professed himself willing but said he did not know how to determine when it was Ramadan. Muçali explained that since the lunar month had begun around St. John's Day that year, the following year the moon would appear "ten or fifteen days earlier and the next year another so-many days earlier," and so on. The following year Muçali advised him when the fast was to begin and "they fasted the whole thing together" and performed the ritual ablutions and daily prayers, dressing in clean clothes and resting at midday. They said *Allahu akbar* "many times, raising and lowering their heads and bowing themselves down to the ground and extending their palms out high when they rose up." They recited surahs together, two of which Ramírez repeated for the inquisitor.[45] When Muçali gained his freedom in ca. 1595, he tried to convince his friend to return with him to Constantinople in order "to be a Moor," and the latter was "very determined to do it" but ultimately failed to follow through.[46]

All of this about Muçali may have been a fig leaf that allowed Román to avoid talking about Deza's crypto-Islamic scene between the Edict of Grace and the early 1590s. Then again, perhaps Román's religious convictions really did waver after taking the Edict. In 1581, when Dr. Arganda visited Deza, local Old Christians denounced several Moriscos but said nothing against Ramírez or about any ongoing activities at the garden.[47] Bonifacio's testimony indicates that, so far as he could tell, Román behaved piously, and although there is a great deal of evidence of his Islamic activities, none of it pertains to the period between the Edict and Muçali's arrival. Like other members of the Cañamenero circle, perhaps Román felt justified conforming to Christianity during this period even if "his heart always inclined toward being a Moor."

If so, the mid-1590s brought an end to accommodation and religious ambivalence, presumably as a consequence of Muçali's influence. Subsequently, Ramírez entered a phase of renewed Islamic zeal. This was accompanied by an effort to realign internal belief and external action as well as a more aggressive stance toward the Spanish Church and monarchy. In mid-1593, for example, while in Tajahuerce, witnesses remembered Ramírez wondering whether "the Turk would make an expedition against the king."[48] The Holy Office interpreted this as evidence of antagonism toward the monarch and support for the greatest Islamic threat in the Mediterranean: the Ottoman Empire.[49]

Additional, and more substantial, evidence of Islamic activities also date to the period after Ramírez's encounters with Muçali. He not only had the fadas performed for his infant daughter María (and presumably for his son Juan the following year) but he also revived the Islamic activities in the garden.[50] Lope Guerrero reported that in early 1596, he, Román, and several other Moriscos gathered there, intending "to game and enjoy themselves," but "Román Ramírez stood up and told everyone there certain things about the Law of Mohammed, in the form of a lecture or sermon, telling them, essentially, that Mohammed had come to reveal the truth and had opened the door to salvation and other things of this sort."[51] Guerrero's description suggests that this was the first time such a thing had happened; they had gone to "enjoy themselves," but Ramírez had turned it into a religious meeting.

If Guerrero was describing the first gathering of this garden *junta*, it was not the last. Old Christians Martín de Estaragón and Catalina López offered reports in 1607 and 1608 respectively to local inquisitorial authorities in Deza about having witnessed similar meetings at the end of the previous century. Both claimed, on separate occasions, to have entered the garden and discovered a group of perhaps ten men. Román alone was on his feet, addressing the others and presumably "teaching them some things about Mohammed," or, as Estaragón put it, "some Islamic silliness."[52] Apart from these moments of intrusion by Old Christians, the site of the duke's garden and house, strategically located outside of the town walls, was a place where the region's crypto-Muslims could forego the "crypto." Nor was this merely a local matter. As Deza's inquisitorial scribe put it, "New Christians gathered [there] and performed their wickedness day and night, it being well situated for such a thing." And, moreover, it was "a place where Aragonese Moriscos gathered and hid."[53]

If Román's encounter with Muçali in 1590 or 1591 sparked a renewal of his religious convictions, then what was he doing between those encounters and early 1596, when he appears to have begun convening the garden *juntas*?[54] He was certainly dealing with tragedy: the deaths of his father (1592) and wife (1594), and the murder of his son (between October 1595 and January 1596). He became co-magistrate, remarried, participated in the Tajahuerce affair, performed in Soria, and was confined in Deza. He may also have proselytized among his own family. His sons Miguel and Francisco, as well as his brother Juan Ramírez (1544–aft. 1609) and brother-in-law Francisco de Miranda, were associated with the garden *juntas* from early on. They also became proselytizers in their own right. Lope Guerrero, who had gone to the garden to game that first time, rather than to hear about Islam, purportedly became "a very firm Moor" thanks to the efforts of Francisco Ramírez.[55] Miguel Ramírez instructed young relatives and presided over the meetings after his father's arrest.[56] And Román's new wife, Ana, who may have been an Old Christian, participated in a fadas ceremony without complaint.

Perhaps the traumatic events of the 1590s, which seemed to culminate in his arrest and then liberation, led Ramírez to view the experiences as God's judgment upon his lukewarm Islamic convictions and to take a firmer and more public stance than he had theretofore. Many of the town's crypto-Muslims interpreted events providentially, seeing tragedy and suffering as evidence of God's displeasure. Aunt Teresa purportedly prophesied impending divine judgment upon those Moriscos who did not follow the Law of Mohammed. And in 1608 María la Jarquina explained the inquisitorial "scourge and punishment" they were suffering as divine punishment for their being "bad Moors."[57] This suggests some uneasiness with *taqiyya* as an appropriate principle for long-term ordering of Morisco religious life. The garden *juntas* provided a physical environment within which Moriscos could reconcile Islamic convictions with the limitations placed upon their ability to conform externally.

Trying to find a way for Dezanos to live—body and soul—as Muslims, even if only within the confines of the garden, was dangerous and Ramírez did not publicize those activities, least of all to the Holy Office. As an Islamic instructor and organizer of the garden *juntas*, he not only knew about the town's but also the entire region's crypto-Islamic activities. During his 1599 trial, diverting attention from his own literacy helped to keep that information secret.[58] When he told the inquisitor that he could read "well" to himself, but not "very quickly" before others, he reinforced the claim that what he knew of Islam came from scattered conversations with a few Aragonese Moriscos and a long-gone Turkish slave. Certainly, this implied, it had no significant literary or pedagogical component.

In fact, during his trial, Román worked hard to suggest he had only a tenuous grasp of Islam. On July 7, for example, he recited the first of two surahs, which seems to be nonsense, then explained that Muçali had told him that by praying it he gained "as many pardons as if he were to go to the house of Mecca, where Mohammed was buried."[59] But Mohammed's tomb is in Medina, not Mecca. The second surah he gave was a garbled version of *Surat al-Fatiha* ("The Opening"), which Muslims recite multiple times each day. When asked about its meaning, he again foregrounded naiveté by offering an absurd explanation:

> Not even in Turkey was there a man who knew what it meant, except that it was the first surah of the Quran. And when Allah was asked what its words meant by some of his servants, he responded to them that he could not tell them but that he who recited [the words] would gain as many pardons as there were stars in the heavens and that he who knew this surah knew everything in the whole world that he needed to know.[60]

In case all of this was too subtle, he then confessed to knowing the phrase *yemauleo yemauleo*, which he would recite seven times. In Arabic, *ya mulay* means simply "O my Lord," but Román suggested an improbably long translation: "Allah spoke and responded to the prayers of his servants, 'You are true and my servant. I am the honorable one and the noble one, and on my honor and nobility I will give you paradise.'"[61]

All of this helps explain Román's claim to minimal literacy on May 19 and his failure to read well before the inquisitor. Faced with a direct question, a simple denial that he could read would not do, for evidence of his bookishness was obvious. But he did not want them to think of him as a man of the written word, much evidence to the contrary, so he hedged his answers, read slowly, and made mistakes. This tactic, however, convinced the inquisitor that he could not have read all the books that he claimed to have, let alone with the care necessary to memorize their contents.[62] This, in turn, suggested that his memory was not natural, as he claimed, but must have had another source. Ultimately the Holy Office followed the logic of that sequence to arrive at the conclusion with which they had begun the trial: demonic aid.

Ramírez's most vibrant period of Islamic activity in decades, then, was the nearly three-and-a-half-year interlude between his release from close confinement in Deza in January 1596 and his final arrest and transportation to Cuenca in May 1599. This window was, in part, a consequence of bureaucratic inefficiency. Getting the denunciations made against him in Soria in October 1595 to Cuenca proved complicated. The commissioner Vinuesa had forwarded them in an incomplete state to Valladolid but without making a copy to keep in Soria or to send to Cuenca.[63] Nevertheless, by early February 1596, and despite Román already enjoying the freedom of the town in Deza, Cuenca's chief prosecutor, Juan de Ochoa, had enough information to pique his interest and requested that Dr. Pedro Cifuentes de Loarte, the tribunal's resident inquisitor, take up the case.[64]

Instead, it languished for a year and a half, then it proceeded fitfully. Yet Ochoa was not the only one interested in it. On July 1, 1597, while pursuing other business in Berlanga de Duero (Soria), Cuenca's senior inquisitor Francisco de Arganda summoned Juan de Ortigosa, the cura of nearby Madruédano, the priest who had twice failed to exorcise Ana Sanz.[65] Arganda, who had visited Deza in 1581, was strongly anti-Morisco and had been on the receiving end of Román's temper, so perhaps he was both personally and professionally interested in the case.

Ortigosa's version of events emphasized Román's demonic ties, and on July 12 Arganda commissioned one Juan de Arnedo, a canon from Berlanga, to travel to Tajahuerce in order to take depositions from the witnesses of the events of 1593–94.[66] This he did, but not for two months. From September 20–22, Arnedo conducted fifteen formal interviews, some quite lengthy, before forwarding the manuscript record to Cuenca. Unable to locate the hidalgo soldier Juan Arias de Villacorta, however, Arnedo then traveled to Soria, where he found his man and took his deposition on October 14. Only then did Arnedo lay hands on what became folio 89, the scrap of paper that contained both the recipe and *comedia* lines. All of this he sent on to Cuenca.[67]

And then, again, nothing. On April 22, 1598, Ochoa wrote to Arganda, now back at Cuenca, and noted the delay, reminding him that more than two years had passed since the request for action. That morning the inquisitor examined the file and ordered it sent out for evaluation (*calificación*), which seems never to have occurred. Almost eight months passed before the *fiscal* again pressed for action. On January 1, 1599, he submitted another letter—this one addressed to both Arganda and

Loarte—and on January 11 they jointly ordered a second *calificación* to evaluate the case's merits.[68] By March 16, Dr. Martín Yáñez, a canon in Cuenca, and Fray Diego de Rojas, a Trinitarian friar, concluded that the deposition suggested an "express pact with the devil." Román Ramírez's arrest was ordered that same day.[69] A week later, the Holy Office sent the warden of the secret jails to sequester his goods and, on April 28, that order was passed onto inquisitorial familiar Juan de Barnuevo Miranda, chief magistrate and alcaide of Arcos de Jalón (twenty-six miles southwest of Deza). He was also charged with arresting the Morisco and transporting him to Cuenca, where he arrived on May 7.

Juan de Ochoa's frustration with this lethargic process is evident. While it is tempting to adduce the intervention of Román's allies, the reality is that the tribunal was understaffed and overworked. Moreover, whatever its merits, the case was irregular, the events having occurred outside of Cuenca's jurisdiction, and based primarily on hearsay. Whether Juan de Barnuevo Miranda was eager to see the trial proceed is unclear. The Barnuevos were important hidalgos with branches throughout Soria, and it was probably this same man who became Deza's castellan and chief magistrate between 1602 and 1611. While he was certainly related in some way to Pedro de Barnuevo, when the new man became alcaide he often cooperated with local Moriscos.

If this Barnuevo bore a grudge against the Morisco on account of the latter's behavior toward his kinsman, then perhaps harsh treatment in transit explains Ramírez's poor condition when he arrived in Cuenca. His biographers have assumed that he was sickly over the course of his life—Caro Baroja described him as "asthmatic," "consumptive," and "a man not given to ardent desire."[70] It is true that in 1589, while an alderman, Román noted that his health was poor.[71] And he told inquisitors that after rediscovering Islam under Muçali in the 1590s he had not always "been able" to fast the entire month of Ramadan "because he was sick."[72] So his health may indeed have been in decline. Yet, his years of fighting, fleeing, and travel suggest a normally robust constitution. And the births of María and Juan indicate that he remained sexually active in the mid-1590s. He continued traveling, performing for audiences, concocting cures, doing council work, and overseeing the garden *juntas* as well.[73]

Whatever his previous condition, he was now poorly. On May 11, at his first audience before the inquisitor, he began with a request for "company" since he was so ill (*malo*).[74] In late June 1599, he complained of his chilly cell and expressed concern about weight loss. He was suffering from tightness of the chest and now had trouble breathing.[75] Inquisitor Loarte rejected a bribe of "forty or fifty" ducats to bring his trial to a speedy conclusion.[76] The following month, on July 7, at the end of an audience in which he had provided nothing of substance to the inquisitors, Ramírez was admonished, the record was read back to him, and he signed his name to it. But rather than return to his cell, he interjected a request to be shown the accusations made against him, so that he could see and acknowledge his guilt. Loarte explained that the only way to expedite the trial was for him to make a full confession. In what proved to be a pivotal moment, the Morisco then asked that, whatever penance he was subsequently given, he be allowed to carry it out in Deza, where "he could find someone to feed and look after him." He feared that, in Cuenca, he would have no caretaker and would die "walking the streets." If Loarte responded, his words are not recorded, but Román followed up this request with the revelation that "his whole life he had been a Moor."[77]

Over the previous two months, Islamic activities had played no role in the trial. Instead, Loarte had explored Ramírez's involvement in the Tajahuerce affair, which had led him to pursue matters specifically related to the presumed demonic pact. The focus was on whether his healing or memory was in any way unnatural, which led to a tortuous discussion of the events in Tajahuerce. Ramírez denied even knowing how to determine whether someone was possessed, let alone how to cure them. All he could offer was a medical description of Ana Sanz's initial malady: excessive melancholic humors had spread to her heart on account of being forced to marry a man she detested. His incense drove the melancholy out of her body and thus restored her.

The matter of Ana's twisted neck also interested Loarte, and Ramírez found it more difficult to explain. He claimed that "in his entire life he had never seen another infirmity like it." It "seemed bad" to him, and others regarded it as a spiritual infirmity. For those reasons, he explained, he told

Ana's family to take her to shrines and have the gospels read to her. That is, during his second visit (although not the first), he suspected that her malady had a spiritual, rather than merely physical, source but again he emphasized his craft's inability to either detect or treat such things. He had difficulty, therefore, accounting for how he had restored her head to its normal position. When pressed by Loarte, he finally avowed, "What do I know, lord? Just as she returned to herself [*volvió en si*] with the incense, her head returned [*volvió*] and took its place."[78] The repetition of the verb suggests Román saw a similarity between the two healings but could not explain the mechanism by which the second had occurred.

Loarte had more success tripping Ramírez up on the topic of his memory, for he found it difficult to explain how he had acquired vast store of literary knowledge (let alone why he possessed a sizeable library), since he could not read well. In an attempt to resolve this contradiction, the Morisco made two claims. First, he asserted that his memory was a "natural thing, not artificial" and not the result of any draughts or medicines.[79] Second, he claimed that his ability to memorize had declined, that "in Spain there was now no man of less memory" than him. While his recall had previously been astonishing, allowing him to recite entire books virtually word for word, after discovering his son's body in ca. 1596, he was "altered" and "lost his memory and has not read from his head except to the duke of Medinaceli a few times."[80]

These two claims allowed Ramírez to explain how he could have memorized so many books, primarily by hearing his father read them aloud decades previously, without being able to read well or quickly. But it also allowed him to explain why he now found memorization to require more interaction with a text than it previously had. Thus, two days after telling Loarte that he had lost his memory, when the inquisitor ordered Ramírez to "recite some of the chapters" that he knew, he revealed he did not possess perfect recall. Instead, seemingly grudgingly, he revealed the "secret" of his reading by memory, something that he had never told "a living soul," nor thought that he ever would: he never actually recited books verbatim but merely knew their outlines and details well enough to provide close renditions of them.[81] Although his abilities now were in decline, this was all he had ever done. Once, he suggested, this had been easy, but now he could only accomplish these feats of memorization by constantly reviewing texts, which is precisely what witnesses described him doing.[82]

If Román thought this explanation would bring his trial to a speedy conclusion, he was mistaken. Instead, following the revelation of this "secret" on May 21, a series of audiences occurred through June and early July dominated by detailed descriptions of the process by which he cured various diseases.[83] Finally on the morning of July 7, after listening to one last cure, Loarte moved the case along. He requested Román's genealogy and asked a series of formulaic questions, which inquisitors asked of all prisoners who appeared before them. That it took seven audiences and almost two months to get around to gathering this information is unusual; typically, the accused provided it immediately after being sworn in. For the first time, Román mentioned his Morisco ancestry and having taken the Edict of Grace.[84] And then, finally, at the end of the audience, he unexpectedly revealed his lifelong inclination toward Islam.

Like his confession for the Edict of Grace, this confession was a performance. Both declarations are nearly the same length and contained similar performative elements of vacillation, conversion, and reconversion. Especially if the follow-up audience on July 9, 1599, is considered, the narrative structure of the later confession ends, like its 1571 counterpart, in a dramatic conversion. Ramírez declared he knew the Holy Office had no evidence of his having Islamized, but he chose to put himself in God's hands and confess everything. This he did with "anguish, tears, sighs, and lamentations."[85] Such dramatic flair does not make either confession false. What it does suggest is that he carefully constructed the narratives and spun them with purpose.

As with his earlier revelation about the secret of his recitation, disclosing his Islamic inclinations failed to improve Román's situation, and Loarte remained unmoved by his conversion performance on July 9. The accused was returned to his cell and not summoned again. On or around August 2, Ramírez finally requested an audience himself. For the first time, both Loarte and Arganda attended. Making reference once again to his health, Román renewed his request to pay a surety in exchange for his release from confinement. Having scoured his memory, he also now denounced two of Deza's Old Christians for blasphemy. The inquisitors responded with an admonishment and returned him to his cell.[86]

Summoned two days later for another audience, Román attempted one last startling revelation. Indicating at the outset that he had nothing new to confess, he received a final formal admonition from the inquisitors. When warned that the *fiscal* was ready to present his accusations, Román responded dramatically that "even if they cut off his head, he didn't have anything else to say."[87] Juan de Ochoa then delivered fifty-five accusations to which the accused responded in turn. The first four of these, which pertained to Islamic activity, Román answered briefly with reference to his previous confessions. But the fifth accusation prompted a longer and peculiar response. He was accused of having entered into an "express pact" with a demon by the "favor, help, and council" of which he "bewitched and cursed [*hechizó y maleficó*] a woman," resulting in her demonic possession along with "a loss of judgment and memory."[88]

Ramírez may have been waiting for this moment, for he offered a monologue on his relationship with a demonic familiar named Liarde that he had inherited from his grandfather.[89] This demon, he explained, first appeared to him after the death of Juan de Luna, who Román understood had "had a pact" with Liarde. But where the demon had been submissive and humble to the grandfather, the grandson found it difficult to manage. Liarde ignored his summonses, spoke condescendingly to him, often refused to help, and asserted it "never spoke the truth." The most he got out of the interactions were occasional medical consultations about the curative power of various herbs.[90]

As with his confession of Islamizing, a follow-up audience requested by Román provided an opportunity to complete the narrative arc of his dealings with Liarde. Three days later, the notary described the Morisco dismounting the stool upon which he sat and kneeling. He told Arganda and Loarte that since his last confession he had been beset by "thoughts and imaginations," and unable to find relief. He begged the inquisitors that, "if he was in danger," to "attend to his soul that he might finish well in his old age." Urged on by them to further confession, he expanded upon his relationship with Liarde. The demon had never helped him read or recite. That, he now admitted, had been a result of the camphor juice he imbibed as a boy and which had almost killed him.[91] With this story, he attempted to shore up the now shaky claim that his memory was neither demonic nor unnatural.

Moreover, Ramírez asserted that when he had been arrested and confined in Medinaceli in 1592, subsequent to his fight with Barnuevo, he had summoned Liarde one last time. When the demon finally appeared (after "three or four" attempts at contact), the Morisco complained that he had not been warned about the arrest. "Must I advise you?" responded the demon. "Why would I let you know they were going to string you up and hang you? I don't have to do anything good for you." "To the devils with you!" replied Ramírez. He no longer wanted to see or hear from the spirit and even hoped his grandfather was suffering in hell for having bestowed such an "evil thing" upon him. He never interacted with Liarde again and claimed to have confessed the whole affair to the guardian of the Franciscan house in Medinaceli, who absolved him thanks to a bull of crusade. He even granted permission for that priest to break the seal of confession if the Holy Office cared to interview him.[92] Like his reconversion from Islam the previous month, Ramírez presumably hoped this would clear the way for his reconciliation.

His hopes, again, were frustrated. Four days later, the inquisitors summoned him and asked whether he had entered into any sort of pact or agreement with the demon. This he denied, and Arganda and Loarte resumed reading out the remaining fifty chapters of the accusation. Seeming dejected now, Ramírez rarely responded with more than a few words, although a reference to Licentiate Bonifacio provoked sharp rejoinders and denials. Yet the critical moment came when the recipe on folio 89 was produced as evidence that Ramírez had used incense to expel demons from Ana Sanz. His response is telling, for instead of responding to the accusation, he responded by asserting that he had not written the recipe but merely dictated it; Villacorta was the author.[93] The inquisitors took this defensiveness as a denial of responsibility for what was written. In fact, confronted with a document in his own hand, Ramírez responded by claiming he could not write, which was hardly the point of the accusation. They had merely wondered whether the recipe used incense to expel demons; he had jumped to his relationship with the written word.

At his final audience before the inquisitors, on August 14, Ramírez reasserted one last time his desire to live and die as a Christian. Death was not far off for him, and he did not sign the record either for that audience or the preceding one, which suggests a further decline in health. One month later, on September 13, the warden of the secret jails notified the inquisitors that a physician had visited the prisoner and pronounced him in danger of death. Ramírez requested a confessor, who came and went.[94] On October 6, subsequent to another medical examination, Arganda approved a transfer to the Hospital of St. James with strict instructions to keep the patient from speaking with "anyone from the outside, nor with Moriscos from Arcos or Deza, nor with anyone who had been reconciled."[95]

His health continued to decline despite the move, and on November 6 he requested another confessor. Inquisitor Arganda summoned Gabriel Núñez, the Jesuit rector in Cuenca and a *calificador* for the Holy Office.[96] The contents of his confession are unknown, of course, but neither of the confessors would have granted absolution. One month later, on December 8, 1599, Ramírez died. His body was buried in unconsecrated ground at the hospital, even as his trial lumbered on. On January 31, 1600, a notice of his death was dispatched to his wife and children, who were ordered to appear at Cuenca to defend his "memory and reputation." Word reached them on February 10, but they never showed. In their absence, a *defensor* was appointed. On February 23, Loarte and an epis-copal representative, in consultation with a group of senior churchmen that included Gabriel Núñez, read the sentence. The Suprema confirmed it three days later. Román Ramírez was condemned as a relapsed Moor-ish heretic and, "adding offense to offense and guilt to guilt," for having entered into "an express accord and pact with the devil."[97]

These two crimes—crypto-Islam and diabolism—proved a potent combination. Bartolomé de Ortega, Ana Sanz's father-in-law, had hinted at the connection and its implication when he claimed in 1597 to have overheard Ramírez ask the demons whether the Ottoman sultan would raise an armada to go against the king of Spain. According to Ortega, the demon had simply responded, "Yes."[98] But in the Morisco's inquis-itorial sentence, the conversation took on new and sinister elements:

The Accused wanted the Great Turk to go to war against the Christians, so, like a great enemy of our holy Catholic faith, he asked the devil *to cause* men and a great Armada to attack the King our lord. In order to satisfy this desire, the devil responded that the Great Turk was arming his men to invade Spain [emphasis added].[99]

Here Islam and diabolism became coordinated forces, made all the more frightening by the threat of a sorcerer who could gather information and cause harm at a distance.

In view of his offenses, the Holy Office ordered Ramírez's bones and effigy relaxed to the secular arm and any "monument or coat of arms . . . taken down and blotted out" in order to erase his memory from "the face of the earth."[100] Yet the principal effort to appropriate the memory of Román Ramírez occurred not in Cuenca but rather in Toledo, the site of his auto de fé. Instead of being conducted under the authority of the conquense tribunal, on February 12, Loarte ordered Román's bones exhumed, placed in a wooden box, and prepared for transportation.[101] This turn of events was orchestrated sometime before January 31, when Arganda wrote to Loarte indicating that the newly installed inquisitor general, Cardinal Fernando Niño de Guevara, was in desperate need of Román's body and a guilty verdict as quickly as possible.[102] The hasty conclusion of the trial and posthumous condemnation occurred specifically so that Ramírez could feature as the main event in an *auto general*, more than one hundred miles away from the place where he was tried and died, and the better part of two hundred miles from his hometown.

That auto occurred on March 5, 1600, in Toledo's Zocodover Plaza. Niño de Guevara presided and the audience included, among other luminaries, young King Philip III, his new wife Margaret of Austria, and royal favorite the Duke of Lerma. Arganda told Loarte that the bit about the demon would "go over well." He was right. One local consequence of this effort to use political theater to frame royal policy toward Moriscos is indicated by the royal couples' subsequent visit to Deza in early 1602.[103] The town was an official border crossing between Castile and Aragon, but very much off the beaten path for monarchs. More broadly, of course, Román's posthumous performance in Toledo informed the king's experience vis-à-vis the Moriscos and contributed to his decision to expel them.

In 1599 and 1600, however, both the royal visit and the expulsion were unimagined and largely unimaginable events in Deza. Whether the townsfolk realized it or not, the legacy of Román Ramírez's inquisitorial trial was a non-event, for, whatever his faults, he had successfully diverted inquisitorial attention away from the town's crypto-Muslim community and avoided a larger inquiry. Although he could have denounced friends, neighbors, and kin (and might have if he had lived longer), he instead repeatedly focused on the Moriscos of Aragon, the deceased, the Turkish Muçali, his Old Christian enemies, and the more spectacular elements of his own story. His trial offered the Holy Office no new targets. Viewed from this perspective, he was the hero of his story. But like every good Spanish chivalric tale, this one has a sequel, and it saw that legacy turn tragic.

9

Small-Town Dreams

Miguel García Serrano's Story

For late-sixteenth-century Dezanos, chief magistrates were controversial figures. Since the 1530s, at least, the dukes of Medinaceli had temporarily named men to that office, typically outsiders and usually for the purpose of performing specific judicial enquiries.[1] But when, in late 1570, Deza's new castellan Francisco López de Rebolledo was also permanently appointed alcalde mayor, it sparked a sort of rebellion among the citizenry. And the same thing happened again two decades later.[2] On both occasions, townsfolk, especially the members of the town council, complained directly to the duke, hoping he would intervene for the sake of the town's "common good and utility" as well as its "general calm." In the 1590s, during the second of these local rebellions, two Dezanos wrote to the duke on behalf of the "rest of the citizens" to inform him of chief magistrate Pedro de Barnuevo's "notorious" behavior. He had "forgotten that he is—as are we all—the vassal of your Excellency." Barnuevo (r. 1584–95), they explained, was "so bad, committing so many and such notorious affronts, that, compelled by the extreme necessity" in which they found themselves, the citizenry had finally turned to the duke.[3]

Beyond disliking him generally, many Dezanos expressed deep concerns about Barnuevo's exercise and abuse of judicial authority. Jurisdictional conflicts cropped up between the town magistrates (who were meant to have precedence in all cases of first instance) and the chief magistrate (who claimed authority to adjudicate all disputes without reference or regard to the rulings of town magistrates). Although technically he wielded magisterial power only over Deza's outlying hamlets—the so-called Four Places of the Recompense—and not over the town itself, the citizenry felt that such nuances mattered little to Barnuevo. What was more, appointing Deza's castellan and the keeper of its arsenal to the office of chief magistrate combined judicial authority and executive muscle in troubling ways. The townsfolk "humbly" suggested to the duke that this union of offices contravened Castilian law for "very just reasons," since "these two things are understood to be incompatible."[4]

The few remaining details about the town's quarrel with Barnuevo survive in an anonymous and undated *memorial* sent to the duke that detailed the ways in which the alcalde mayor, who should have been a "steady, kind, and just judge," was instead flippant and vengeful in his bearing and "poorly disposed to administer justice." In particular, the authors claimed, he spent a great deal of time mistreating "with word and deed" some of the "principal and most honorable men of the town." If they failed to doff their caps quickly enough, he knocked them from their heads and pinned them to the ground. He even placed some under arrest. And when "very great citizens" whom he disliked were proposed for the town council, he crossed off their names out of "enmity and hatred" and forwarded others to the duke for approval.[5]

The *memorial* accused Barnuevo of attacking all sources of local authority likely to challenge him. He affronted the members of the town council in their official capacity when they did not submit to his will, speaking "many and very bad words" to them. He claimed that, if not for him, they would hold no offices at all. When, probably in 1593, he arrested one Miguel García Serrano, then serving as chief bailiff, he first took the man's staff of office and broke it with his own hands, saying that since it was "he who had given the staff, he could take it away and break it."[6] He even scandalized the town by publicly asserting that, but for the clergy, everyone would live in peace.[7] The man was so offensive that he successfully made himself the common enemy not only of the town council but also of large section of the citizenry, both Old and New Christians.

Old Christian Miguel García Serrano (1563–1631), whose arrest by Barnuevo served as hard evidence of the chief magistrate's caprice and tyranny, played a pivotal role in the history of late sixteenth- and early seventeenth-century Deza. Literate and ambitious, he was a man of some means and influence, but his place was not among the town's hidalgo elite or its wealthiest citizens. His paternal grandfather was buried in the church when he died in 1540, but not in the costlier choir, let alone in a private chapel.[8] As his own death approached, Miguel laid out plans for a variety of anniversary and funerary Masses, novenas, and bulls of crusade for himself and his recently deceased wife. The specificity and complexity of his dispositions distinguished him from his poorer neighbors' more perfunctory ones, but his was still the will of a commoner. He was laid to rest in a confraternal chapel and made no grand charitable displays among his bequests.[9]

His father, Juan (ca. 1530–bef. 1604), was a literate farmer who kept an inn (*casa de mesón*).[10] Both his father and his mother, María Hernández (ca. 1534–1611), were natives of Deza.[11] Miguel himself married María de Santa Clara (d. 1631) and fathered at least two children. In the first years of the seventeenth century he sent his daughter María to the house of Ana López, who taught "girls to *labrar*," an uncertain verb that probably refers to needlework and perhaps more specifically to a feminine art form such as embroidery, which was increasingly popular among middle- and upper-class girls.[12] His son was a "student," probably at a university given that his robes cost 200 *reales* in ca. 1607.[13]

Miguel remained connected to the business of his family's inn, but he was increasingly pulled in new directions.[14] After having had his name put forward several times, the duke finally appointed him council bailiff in 1593 and, in that capacity, he came into conflict with Barnuevo.[15] Perhaps García Serrano's willingness to stand up to a bully made him seem a likely candidate to inaugurate a new office: *procurador síndico* (or *del común*) of Deza's commune and republic. This office, distinct from the solicitor general (procurador general) who sat on the town council, was dreamed up in 1597 and formally established by a broad cross section of the town's citizenry—Old Christians and Moriscos, laymen and clergy—in March of the following year.[16]

The procurador síndico was an advocate charged with protecting Deza's citizens from outsiders working against their interests. The office's foundational document specifically referenced judges of the port, customs, and commission, as well as the duke's "magistrates major and minor [*alcaldes mayores y minores*]" as potential adversaries.[17] The officeholder was furthermore responsible for coordinating the town's lawsuits against any and all of the above and even against the duke of Medinaceli himself.[18] García Serrano continued asserting his claim to the office until at least 1607. During that decade, as the town experienced growing stresses and new challenges to its communal identity, he attempted a revolution in local politics and, although his office had been created to protect Deza, he ended up splitting it in two.

The catastrophe was, to be sure, a continuation of processes begun decades earlier. At the beginning of the sixteenth century, Duke Juan de la Cerda (r. 1501–44) had altered the structure of local politics, revoking the hidalgos' control over half of the seats on the town council.[19] But over the course of the century, and especially in the 1560s, the local gentry reasserted itself, primarily by securing statements of hidalgo status via suits litigated in the Royal Appellate Court in Valladolid. It tried both civil and criminal cases, assessed claims of nobility, and asserted an exclusive right to hear cases involving town councils or seigniorial lords.[20] The court proved an indispensable institution for many litigants, since its officials were difficult to bribe and willing to find against the powerful. Some vassals even devised ways to use the court to restrict the exercise of seigniorial power.[21]

As more families secured hidalgo status in Deza—twelve by 1591 and twenty-one by 1606—their members began to reassert themselves in local politics. In 1590 they petitioned for a restoration of the privilege of *mitad de los oficios* and, despite opposition by the town council, Duke Juan Luis (r. 1575–94) granted their request.[22] Thus, beginning in 1592 a hidalgo was appointed annually to one of the co-magistracies, while the other alternated between a Morisco and an Old Christian officeholder. The gentry also gained one of the four deputy seats and, beginning that same year, a hidalgo was appointed to serve as alderman alongside two commoners, a Morisco and an Old Christian.

At the very end of the century, however, a new duke of Medinaceli tinkered with this system again. Although the same number of names for potential office holders were being sent to him as had been sent to his father, in 1597 Duke Juan (r. 1594–1607) returned only two aldermen, a hidalgo and a Morisco. In 1598, after the "principal naming" again returned only two officers, a hidalgo and an Old Christian, the town council petitioned for redress and, subsequently, a third alderman (Morisco Lope de Hortubia) was selected. When the duke named only two aldermen in 1599, the town's new procurador síndico faced his first high profile test. In protest, García Serrano presented the council with a formal judicial notification (*requirimiento*) and requested that an alderman from the Morisco neighborhood be named as well, "just as was done in earlier times."[23] Hidalgo alderman Diego de Ocáriz agreed to submit the request and chief magistrate Velasco de Barnuevo countersigned the document, but the duke refused to budge.

García Serrano and many other Dezanos saw this refusal as part of a frustrating broader trajectory of ducal initiatives and responses. Deza was a town on the rise, growing in wealth, population, and prestige. Civic leaders imagined it at the center of regional commerce and activity, but whenever Deza pursued that agenda or involved itself in regional affairs, the duke intervened. In 1594, for example, at the start of his reign, Duke Juan reiterated a 1571 injunction against municipal efforts to control the grain conveyed north from Cihuela.[24] In 1596 he challenged the propriety of an innovative financial arrangement (approved by his father) that provided a financial cushion for the town in times of dearth or need, perhaps because it reduced Deza's dependence on him.[25] The duke owned most of the revenue-producing rentable lands in and around town, and when the council attempted to establish independent sources of income he intervened to stop them.[26] In the wake of the Barnuevo debacle and the new duke's own heavy handedness, many wondered whether the best interests of their feudal lord were, in fact, aligned with those of Deza's *republica*.

Such tensions between vassals and lords were not unusual in early modern Spain. Some seigniorial towns (*señoríos*) considered themselves fortunate to have the protection of a noble patron, who could shield them from overambitious tax collectors or the frequent billeting of soldiers, or who might bless them by establishing fairs, endowing churches or a university, or attracting craftsmen and industry. "Ordinary people" often preferred having a powerful lord, particularly one who resided in town, to rein in the excesses of a *mayordomo* or other over-mighty subjects.[27] This same pattern played out in Deza, after a fashion, when the council attempted to appropriate common lands in order to rent them out for municipal revenue. Poorer farmers found themselves without winter pastures for their herds and flocks, and a ducal representative stepped in to defend their cause.[28] Nevertheless, the inhabitants of some señoríos, especially hidalgos and prosperous citizens, chafed at the restrictions that came with vassalage. And, all things considered, the majority of towns preferred to assert *realengo* status, direct royal control.

Elsewhere in Soria, when the cash-strapped monarchs of the sixteenth century sold off royal towns, reducing them from realengos to señoríos, some municipalities took it upon themselves to incur debt in order to purchase a return to royal jurisdiction.[29] Similar notions must have been percolating among Dezanos at the end of the 1590s. And such civic mindedness—"good pretensions," they called it—proved attractive not only to Old Christians but also to Moriscos, perhaps especially those who could claim some wealth, social status, and political influence.[30] Initially, at least, many Morisco officeholders convinced themselves that allying with the town (and by extension with the king) to the detriment of their seignior was in their best interest. Such sentiments led them to sign onto a series of appellate court lawsuits organized by Miguel García Serrano and filed against the duke, probably in late 1597.

Although at the end of January 1598, the newly installed town council, with the encouragement of chief magistrate Velasco de Barnuevo, voted to distance itself from any involvement in the affair, the case went forward.[31] Unfortunately, no legal record of the suits exists, presumably because they were eventually resolved out of court. Broadly speaking, it is clear that the litigation focused on disagreements about jurisdictional conflicts, but precisely what the town hoped to gain in the long run is nowhere explicitly stated. Still extant, however, is the negotiated "agreement and concord" that resolved the conflict between the duke and the town "in a peaceful way" in October 1600.[32]

The move to begin negotiations with the duke was itself indicative of an emerging split within the town. Some, like Morisco Lope Guerrero el menor (b. 1571), concluded that the lawsuits against the duke were inherently risky and imprudent. Reflecting upon the affair in 1603, at the end of a term as solicitor general, he argued that it was foolish to waste the town's limited financial resources on "suits that were neither just nor certain of success."[33] The collective voice of the town's Moriscos echoed Guerrero: the suits were "unjust and by pursuing them we did ourselves and the republic [of Deza] great harm."[34] Thus, sometime around the beginning of 1600 the inhabitants of the Morisco Upper Neighborhood revoked the powers of attorney they had previously granted and withdrew from the suits.[35] Consequently, all sides were driven to the negotiating table. Four local men, authorized to represent the town's clergy, *hidalguía*, Old Christians, and Moriscos met to settle with the duke.[36]

Whatever the specific goals of the lawsuits had been at their inception, the town did gain some concessions in the negotiations. On the issues of the relationship between Deza's co-magistrates and other legal authorities appointed by its seignior, Duke Juan confirmed the full jurisdiction of the ordinary magistrates in "civil, criminal, and executive [*ejecutivas*] cases" in the court of first instance. He also conceded that deputies were not ducal appointees, but rather chosen by the council, and that neither he nor his representatives could appoint new magistrates or remove old ones from office before the end of an incumbent's term.[37]

But both sides had to give something, and the duke gained on two significant points. First, he demanded the abolition of the recently established office of procurador síndico. Second, he secured acknowledgment of the chief magistrate's preeminence over the members of the council, his right to participate in council and commune meetings, and his inviolability before local magistrates. In fact, the duke stopped using the title chief magistrate in the wake of the concord, instead granting his castellans the accompanying title of "governor of the four places of the valley."[38] This change reflects the *gobernador*'s diminished claim to the municipal authority implied in the title of alcalde mayor. His purview was now more clearly limited to the town's environs and hamlets than the urban center itself. Some locals saw this as a victory and convinced themselves that, as a result of the negotiations, Deza's former freedoms had been restored.[39] Not everyone agreed.

In particular, Miguel García Serrano and his supporters had expected more. Disgusted that the negotiators had gained so little and given so much, in late spring 1601 García Serrano borrowed the town's copy of the concord from Deza's notary and, together with Old Christian magistrate Francisco Manrique, took it to Ágreda, where they presented it for review to a lawyer, Licentiate Alonso Pérez. Pérez, however, was unwell and unable (or, perhaps, unwilling) to examine the document. He refused to take possession of it while he recovered because he lacked "space." Presumably, then, it remained in the hands of García Serrano, who continued to claim the title procurador síndico despite the office's abolition.

The following year, when the council requested the concord from Gonzalo Martínez el mayor, the town's aged notary, he could not produce it and was arrested for breach of the public trust. Subsequently, Martínez's son appeared before Morisco magistrate Lope de Arcos on his father's behalf and, on October 6, 1602, Arcos summoned García Serrano and two other Old Christians (Juan Desteras and Francisco Manrique)[40] to account for their actions.[41] He demanded the return of the document, but García Serrano refused and threatened legal action if the magistrate issued an arrest warrant, which Arcos did in any case.[42]

Whether the Moriscos's withdrawal from the lawsuits was the wisest course of action, their decision had forced the town to negotiate at a disadvantage. Miguel García Serrano and his cohorts were furious. The procurador síndico remained at large despite the warrant, and the attempt to arrest him only stoked the fires. To some observers, it seemed the duke and his Moriscos had formed a pact that worked to the disadvantage of the town, especially its Old Christians. How else to explain how he favored the Moriscos? He rented key properties to them, like the Liñán pottery works and his own house and garden. (Both were reputed sites of Islamic and anti-Christian activities.)[43] Condemned diabolist and crypto-Muslim Román Ramírez had been the duke's man, and Ramírez's son served on as the duke's alguacil mayor after his father's death.[44] The Moriscos themselves had purportedly promised "never to oppose [the duke] in anything he requested," even if it was to the detriment of the broader community. To put it bluntly, they were "contrary to this town and its Old Christians."[45]

Some Old Christians were explicit in their condemnation of the duke's activities, formally broadcasting before the Royal Appellate Court his preference for Moriscos over Old Christians. Moriscos, they claimed, never held offices on their own merit but only "on account of friendship or some other reason and because the duke of Medinaceli and his judges, favoring the Moriscos, procured" offices for them.[46] Old Christians grew increasingly concerned about the social and economic power wielded, with ducal support, by some Moriscos. They feared that their own rightful place in town was being co-opted. This combination of fears and frustrations proved incendiary. What had formerly been a relatively strong consensus among the population devolved into a factionalism that pitted an Old Christian bloc against the Moriscos. It also nourished the belief that the will of Deza's feudal lord might prove incompatible with the best interests of the town itself, if not with the king and church as well.

By late 1602, the town was in uproar and the factionalism found geographical purchase in the physical divide between the Morisco Upper Neighborhood and the Old Christian Lower Neighborhood. Few stood above the fray. "They have longed to kill us and to do us great harm," explained the residents of the Morisco quarter. "And they put themselves to it, many of [the Old Christians] gathering together with swords and daggers and other weapons, like firearms [*escopetas*] and spears, and other arms, yelling, 'Die! Die, you Moorish dogs!'" Echoing the crusaders' battle cry, the aggressors claimed "it was God's will."[47] Ominously, the sacristan Mateo Navarro put his ecclesiastical credentials to work for the Old Christian cause. In early 1603 Moriscos Francisco de Arcos, Luis de Mendoza, and Miguel Ramírez complained that, when laymen were contentious, "they weren't surprised," but a priest should have pursued "peace" between the parties instead of "stirring them up."[48] Religion and politics had now become deeply intertwined in the dispute.

In January, Duke Juan attempted to rein in a situation that was quickly spiraling out of control. He decreed that all disputes between neighborhoods be brought before his residency judge, Dr. Muñoz de Herrera, who arrived in town on February 13, 1603.[49] Muñoz de Herrera believed that the heart of the problem was the determination of García Serrano and a few other Old Christians to challenge the concord of 1600. Consequently, he reiterated the order for the procurador síndico and his associate Francisco Manrique to produce the missing concord and had them arrested until they complied.[50] Although García Serrano was certainly free by the end of the year, they seem never to have handed over the document. Instead, in April 1606 Deza's solicitor general requested a fresh copy made from the one in the duke's archive.[51] The residency judge's departure in March was followed in April by an episcopal visitation. In an act that further undermined the town's fragile unity, the bishop's representative now ordered that Moriscos's names be read aloud at Mass so they could audibly indicate attendance. Like many of the disciplinary measures imposed upon the Moriscos, this only further alienated them from their Old Christian neighbors.[52]

Moriscos responded to these challenges in two ways: violence and litigation. Sometime before November 1604, explained the Old Christian members of the town council,

On the occasion of a minor dispute [*leve riña*] provoked by a New Christian against an Old Christian, many [Moriscos] assembled and gathered and sought, with great fuss, to distribute weapons, saying, 'Let them die! Now is the time! The hour has arrived!' And they resisted *la justicia* [i.e., either justice generally or the magistrate specifically] and released some of their number who had been arrested, and on other occasions they have done similar things, thus demonstrating that they are the public enemies of this town.[53]

Since the mid-1580s, Old Christian Juan de Peñafiel el mayor (b. ca. 1540) had been charged with going into the Upper Neighborhood on Sundays and holidays to enforce attendance at Mass, for which reason, he claimed, they "disliked him very much." Now, "seven or eight" of them came out against him in the plaza of the *Corrillo*. They "threatened him and said that he and the vicar were from the devil," and if it had not been for a couple of Old Christian passersby, they would have "carried him up a road and mistreated him."[54]

These violent reactions to violence are significant, but the immediate response to the 1602 assault on the Upper Neighborhood was actually more measured. On December 28, the Moriscos gathered en masse, not to fight but rather to take out a loan by granting power of attorney to a group of men for the establishment of a redeemable annuity.[55] Subsequently, they received an investment of 400 ducats from one Diego de Montoya of Medinaceli, which they earmarked for future legal fees.[56] The action was necessary, for Old Christians had already begun to organize a lawsuit against their Morisco neighbors in an effort to bar them from holding "offices of justice or governance."[57]

All that was lacking was a test case and, late in 1603, Miguel García Serrano supplied one. In November, he dispatched Fernando de Ballasteros to the Royal Appellate Court in Valladolid in the name of the Lower Neighborhood with a petition that claimed Moriscos were sitting on Deza's town council contrary to royal law. In particular, the petition suggested that those who had been *penitenciado* (i.e., reconciled for a less serious offense) by the Holy Office, their descendants, and Moriscos of otherwise questionable religiosity were being appointed. In early December the court responded, without further elaboration, that the laws of the realm should be obeyed.[58]

On December 26, by local tradition the day on which the subsequent year's officers would be nominated, García Serrano appeared before the Old Christian magistrates Pedro de Argüello and Francisco Polo.[59] In a moment of staged political theater, he presented the court's opinion and demanded that Moriscos be excluded from the council of 1604.[60] The traditional meeting of the commune was canceled and the Old Christian council members of 1603 remained in office.[61] Moriscos Lope de Arcos, the most recent Morisco magistrate (1602), and Lope Guerrero el menor, the solicitor general of 1603, also maintained a claim to those titles until ducal confirmation of Luis de Cebea and Gonzalo el Burgueño, who were meant to have been selected for the council of 1604, finally arrived, about ten months later, in November of that year.[62]

In the interim, a political and administrative crisis developed. Both sides launched suits and countersuits before the Royal Appellate Court.[63] Using language that often resonated with propaganda written to support the expulsion, these Old Christians dismissed the Moriscos of the Upper Neighborhood as unsuitable for office.[64] They were, claimed the litigants, only a small minority in the town and had never held offices by custom or tradition. They were refused the Eucharist, had little interaction with Old Christians, and most had been condemned or *penitenciado* by the Holy Office. "All or most of them," the Old Christian suit asserted, worked in "mechanical offices and held vile and lowly jobs, which they performed personally."[65] A related document spoke of how Morisco magistrates worked at cobblery and shoed horses while dispensing justice, thereby reducing Deza to a laughingstock for visitors and neighboring towns.[66]

The Moriscos's rebuttal hinged on the fact that they did not hold office by ducal favor but rather by immemorial right and tradition. For although Deza had two neighborhoods, this was merely a function of geography—the two "were the one council." At no time had they ever acted independently from one another. Thus, in alternating years, citizens from the Upper Neighborhood had been elected tithe collector and parish churchwarden, and held offices in all of the town's confraternities. The neighborhoods had always functioned as equals in such matters, and rightly so, since the Upper also boasted "very honorable and wealthy people," while the Lower had its share of "outsiders, the poor, and people who cannot hold or exercise such offices." The rebuttal also painted a picture of solid Catholic religiosity in the Upper Neighborhood, even asserting of the men elected to office that "both they and their parents were very Old Christians [*tan cristianos viejos*]," and that nothing hindered them from sitting on the council.[67]

García Serrano did not sit idle as the suits worked their way through the court. In January 1604 he moved to shore up the case by calling upon a series of senior Old Christian citizens to testify about the quality and reputation of the town's Moriscos before Pedro de Argüello and Francisco Polo, who continued to sit as co-magistrates. The witnesses offered the familiar list of defects, emphasizing the town's proximity to Aragon, the Moriscos's vile offices, and their problematic relationship to the church. Román Ramírez, who was mentioned by each of the witnesses, became the prime example of the dangers posed by the town's New Christians.

"A few years before he was arrested," one of them explained, "he had been the town's magistrate and also an alderman, solicitor general, and deputy." And the year he was arrested and his bones burned, his name had been put forward for the magistracy again.[68] García Serrano probably intended these testimonies to accompany the countersuit filed in the Royal Appellate Court case, but, hedging his bets, also sent a copy to the tribunal of the Holy Office in Cuenca.

Months passed and local conflicts continued to fester. Finally, the Old Christians, impatient for results and presumably following García Serrano's lead, opened up a second front to the attack. In early March, as lawyers were beginning to present powers of attorney, petitions, and counter-petitions at court, Juan Manrique de Peña denounced a group of Moriscos whom he heard complaining about sacristan Mateo Navarro's role in stirring up anti-Morisco sentiments.[69] María Rasa denounced brothers-in-law Gabriel de Saleros and Gabriel Lancero, along with several of their female relatives, for working on a feast day.[70] Librada González denounced Ana la Buena for cooking meat during Lent.[71] In May, Miguel García Serrano's own mother and daughter denounced eleven-year old Ana Guerrera for reciting Arabic prayers. Ana López and her husband Alonso de Santos confirmed and expanded upon those charges.[72] All of these witnesses gave formal testimony before Deza's inquisitorial commissioner, Licentiate Miguel Benito. There may have been other denunciations as well.

In the absence of a clear ruling from the court, life went on, but the disputed election of 1604 produced administrative confusion. In June, for instance, Old Christian co-magistrates Argüello and Polo and alderman Francisco de Ocáriz named Pascual Martínez the collector of tithes (*tercero de los fructos decimales*) for the year. But castellan Juan de Barnuevo Miranda, the vicar Licentiate Benito, Morisco alderman Juan de Deza, and Morisco solicitor general Lope Guerrero settled the office on Morisco Lope de Arcos, who was meant to have been magistrate. In August, the duke stepped in and gave the office to the Morisco.[73] Despite losing the round, Argüello and Polo continued to operate as magistrates, pronouncing later that month on an inheritance dispute over the estate of priest Juan Ruiz.[74]

As 1604 drew to a close and time came to elect new council members, the situation heated up again. The duke and Barnuevo Miranda intended to put Moriscos Luis de Cebea el mayor in the magistracy and name Gonzalo el Burgueño solicitor general. In mid-November Argüello, Polo, and the other Old Christians on the council protested, asserting that the offices ought to be held by "people of quality" and those who were not "opposed to the good pretensions of the town." The proposed appointments, they claimed, were void in any case, since "in ancient towns like this one, the outgoing officials of the republic, who are finishing their term, name successors to those offices and the [duke] must choose from among those names for the following year."[75] Undaunted, the alcaide dismissed their petition, pointing out that the inhabitants of the Lower Neighborhood had often endorsed officeholders from the Upper. Indeed, the Moriscos meant to sit on the council of 1604 had themselves initially been proposed with the support of Old Christians back in 1603.[76]

The 1605 Lenten season was both violent and tragic in Deza. Citizens on both sides of the conflict were arming themselves in order to do harm to their neighbors, and on February 23 Juan Mancebo provoked an internal feud amongst the Moriscos by publicly beating Luis de Cebea el menor in the main plaza.[77] Coincidentally, a trio of clerical deaths occurred as well. The rabble-rousing sacristan Mateo Navarro died in February, presumably of natural causes, and was followed in March by Judeoconverso priest Juan de Ozuel, who had been part of religious life in Deza for more than thirty years. Finally, and more problematically for the Moriscos, in that same month the parish's vicar and inquisitorial commissioner Licentiate Miguel Benito died.

One of Benito's final official acts as commissioner had been to receive a denunciation made by Diego Zamorano. Zamorano, a reconciled Morisco born in Arcos de Jalón in ca. 1535, seems to have experienced a true conversion after a run-in with the Holy Office. He abandoned Islam, drank wine, and presented himself before inquisitorial personnel several times to denounce crypto-Muslims. On February 9, 1605, less than two weeks before his own death, Zamorano had denounced a group of Moriscos from Deza that included his daughter and her husband.[78] But rather than submitting the denunciation to his superiors at the tribunal in Cuenca, Benito buried the document among his papers. It was not the first time he had done this.

In March 1605, as Benito's health was failing and after "many months" of deliberation, the Royal Appellate Court delivered an unequivocal ruling:

We command that the said council and citizens of the Lower Neighborhood . . . no longer exclude the citizens of the Upper Neighborhood from elections for offices of the administration of justice and town governance on account of their being New Christians, but rather that they admit them to the use and exercise [of the offices] just like the rest of the citizenry.[79]

The Lower Neighborhood's lawyer appealed, of course, emphasizing the shortcomings of the Upper's inhabitants and especially their problematic religious status and interactions with Aragonese Moriscos. They had smuggled horses and transported "money from [Aragon] as well as weapons, lead, and other ammunition and prohibited merchandise." They communicated with, provided aid for, and hid Aragonese provocateurs, "all to the great harm and prejudice of the royal crown."[80] Yet, despite the implied danger, the court reaffirmed its original ruling. Moriscos had just as much right as any other citizen to hold municipal office.

Then, as if on cue, within weeks of the Appellate Court's ruling and with the tide of the conflict having turned, decisively it seemed, in the Moriscos's favor, Licentiate Benito's death introduced a new and catastrophic element. While working through the priest's papers, his executor, local notary Pedro de Cisneros (d. 1629), discovered a series of formal denunciations that ought to have been but never were forwarded to Cuenca. Cisneros, a familiar in his own right, had acted as inquisitorial scribe in Deza since his appointment in 1593. He now found at least eight denunciations, written in his own hand and notarized by him, dating as far back as October 1599.[81] Cisneros knew, of course, that other denunciations had been made over the years as well. Benito had properly forwarded some of these to Cuenca in a timely fashion.[82] But others, like one made by Librada González in April 1604 against Morisca Ana la Buena, had been either lost or destroyed by the commissioner and needed redoing.[83]

Benito left no explanation of his motives for withholding the denunciations. The rumor was that he had been taking bribes.[84] But the broader trajectory of his activities suggests Benito was working to de-escalate tensions within the town and doing so in ways that set him at cross-purposes with certain agendas popular in the tribunal at Cuenca. Remarkably, his sympathies often leaned in the direction of the Moriscos. In June 1604, he put himself at odds with the Old Christian faction when he worked with Juan de Barnuevo Miranda to settle the office of tithe collector on Lope de Arcos.[85] That November, he and Lope de Arcos formally witnessed the alcaide's dismissal of a petition that opposed naming Moriscos to the council of 1605.[86] More than once, Benito absolved confessants of sins or dismissed out of hand activities that ought to have been remanded to his inquisitorial superiors. No wonder that, all things considered, María la Carnicera preferred confessing to him than to the confessor regularly assigned to Moriscos.[87]

The Licentiate's death, however, eliminated a key check to effective inquisitorial oversight, and now denunciations flowed freely to Cuenca. Over the next months, Old Christian neighbors denounced Moriscos Lope Guerrero el menor, Leonor de Hortubia, María de Ropiñón, Lope de Obezar, Francisco de Mendoza, María la Carnicera, Miguel Ramírez, Catalina la Valenciana, Hernando Martínez de la Castellana, Francisco de Miranda el menor, Antón Guerrero, Francisco Ramírez, Francisco de Medrano, Lope Guerrero el viejo, Juan Guerrero, and Gabriel de Medina.[88] Few of the denunciations were sufficient to merit formal inquisitions, but they drew Cuenca's attention toward Deza once again and, this time, held it.

Despite the ongoing denunciations and the escalating feud between the Cebea and Romo families within the Morisco community, by mid-1605, with the appellate court trial definitively concluded, the outright violence between neighborhoods actually declined. Perhaps the silencing of sacristan Mateo Navarro also served the peace. By all indications, the Islamic activities of crypto-Muslim Moriscos continued apace and, at times, even took on a slightly more public character, at least among the Moriscos themselves. The fadas ceremony was performed on recently baptized infants before family and friends. And engagement parties attended by Old and New Christians alike were followed by Muslim marriage ceremonies performed in upper rooms before select audiences. Deza's Morisco muleteers continued to expand their network of associates across the peninsula and, in the wake of their father's death, Miguel and Francisco Ramírez took over leadership of the gatherings in the duke's garden and house.

Even so, Miguel García Serrano was not one to let old grudges lie fallow, and when the duke returned the names for the council of 1607, he lodged yet another complaint before that year's hidalgo magistrate, Antonio de Ucedo Salazar. Still styling himself procurador síndico, García Serrano noted that Moriscos Lope de Arcos, Juan de Heredia, and Luis de Hortubia el Jarquino had been named to offices but asserted that this was "against the law and decrees of the realms and against the royal sentence" pronounced in 1605.[89]

It is not clear why García Serrano believed the appointments contradicted the court's ruling, but he may have been troubled by the fact that, since the conclusion of the trial, the duke had selected a preponderance of Moriscos to sit alongside hidalgo officeholders, squeezing out Old Christians who were not part of the gentry. In any case, his complaint was dismissed yet again and the Moriscos stayed in power. Clearly, as long as Juan de la Cerda lived, his Moriscos would reap the benefits of having abandoned their united front with Deza's Old Christians and the prioritization of town interests in order to cast their lot in with the duke. To everyone's surprise and to the dismay of some, a little over nine months later the duke was dead and the first of several waves of *moriscos dezanos* had been transported to the secret jails of Cuenca's inquisitorial tribunal.

Miguel García Serrano's efforts to assert Deza's "good pretensions" divided the citizenry decisively along a New Christian-Old Christian axis. This left the town, and especially its Moriscos, vulnerable in the years that followed to the ministrations of the Holy Office. It eventually also fomented an atmosphere of fear and suspicion that resulted in the depopulation—via arrest or flight—of much of the New Neighborhood. Yet, the decisive blow fell only in 1611, when the royal Edict of Expulsion was enforced in Deza. Without the protection of Duke Juan or the support of local Old Christians, the Moriscos lacked the mechanisms that might have defended them against external threats. In fact, Morisco Deza was doomed.

10

As Much Moors Now as Ever

Ana Guerrera's Story

Toward the end of 1606, in what was by all accounts the highlight of the season, Ana Guerrera (b. 1595) and Diego de Fadrique (b. ca. 1582) celebrated their betrothal. The bride's parents, Juan Guerrero and Francisca de Hortubia, invited almost everyone. Graciously, the bride's father even extended an invitation to María la Burgueña and her husband Juan Mancebo despite the fact that Mancebo and his brothers Francisco and Román el Romo were waging an ongoing and bloody feud with los Cebea, the maternal branch of the groom's family tree. La Burgueña, knowing that many "who were contrary to her husband" would attend, sent her regrets.[1]

But most other Moriscos accepted, and they were not alone: "There were also many Old Christians, and among them some clerics." Music and dancing were on offer. The hosts laid out food both upstairs and down, and "everyone" partook together.[2] Old Christian Juan Miguel (b. 1563), the head of the local branch of the Santa Hermandad, offered this description of the evening:

> Juan Guerrero and his wife spoke with him, requesting his presence that night in their house along with others of the town's *señores* and *gente honrada* at a gathering for the betrothal of their daughter with Diego de Fadrique. . . . [Juan Miguel accepted and] was at Juan Guerrero's house that night for the gathering with many other Old Christians as well as New. He saw them perform and establish the marriage

accords before the notary Francisco García, and he recalls that among other attendees at the betrothal was Luis de Cebea el viejo [the groom's grandfather], who stood up and addressed all who were present at the gathering, according to custom. Luis de Cebea [el menor] was there as well, and [Juan Miguel] saw him and others walking around serving and passing out food and drink. There were also many present from the Cebea clan, the Guerreros and Fadriques—both men and women—all of them content in the way that one often sees at such gatherings among kin.[3]

More than just a celebration of family and friends, this was an effort at rapprochement and reconciliation. No evidence suggests that Miguel García Serrano was invited, let alone present, but hidalgo Pedro de Argüello, who had strongly supported the effort to exclude Moriscos from holding office, attended. Although less effusive in his praise of the good fellowship and food than other Old Christian attendees, he confirmed the presence of many of "the principal people" of Deza. Argüello did his duty as a guest and stayed until the marriage accords had been confirmed and the food consumed. Then he left and dined at his own board. After dinner, strolling onto the plaza, he could still see dancing—in Guerrero's doorway and on the street outside of his house—in full swing.[4]

As the party wound down, Ana Guerrera later reported, "all of the Old Christians and many of the New Christians" took their leave. After their departures, Ana having danced her fill and rested for a time, a smaller group assembled in the upper room, where most of the food had been laid out earlier in the evening. In addition to the couple and their parents, about two dozen Moriscos crowded in and stood while Lope Guerrero el viejo and María la Jarquina presided over a wedding ceremony—in the "style of the Moors"—that joined Ana and Diego as husband and wife. Afterward, the assembly called out blessings on them before departing.[5] Although everyone assumed that a parish ceremony would take place in July, when Ana turned twelve and reached the minimum canonical age for marriage, it never happened.[6] Instead, she came of age as a prisoner in Cuenca, living proof to the Holy Office that crypto-Islam in Deza was not only alive but thriving and that, despite decades of disciplinary work, had become a generational phenomenon already being appropriated by the town's youth.

Ana was a precocious child, intelligent, thoughtful, and devout. Although she had Old Christian great-grandparents on both sides, her own parents, Juan Guerrero (b. ca. 1555) and Francisca de Hortubia (b. ca. 1567), had been married in a Moorish ceremony when her mother was about sixteen.[7] Her father's five brothers and her mother's three sisters, not to mention many of their spouses and in-laws, were committed Muslims, creating a community of belief within which the young girl was reared. On the night after her baptism, she was given the name "Marien" in a fadas ceremony performed by María la Jarquina, and several generations of relatives gathered afterward to celebrate her induction into Deza's Muslim community.[8]

According to her father, Ana was introduced to the Ramadan fast by her grandmother, mother, and aunts when she was only two years old.[9] By the time she was eight, her parents had "made sure" that "she knew the elements of the Law of Mohammed and that she lived in it." Her mother and grandmother taught her "Arabic prayers of the Law of Mohammed and all the rest of it." When other Moriscos visited their home, the girl was trotted out to recite "the prayers that she had learned and whatever she knew about the Law of Mohammed." She bragged to Antón Guerrero, "I know more prayers than you do, uncle," and her parents delighted to see the girl had been well instructed.[10] By age ten, she was fasting the full month of Ramadan and attending the fadas of Morisco infants, perhaps in preparation for the day when she would perform the ceremonies.[11]

Relationships with older women played a formative role in Ana's religious life. Her mother and her grandmother, Cecilia la Montera (1547[?]–1608), were driving forces, but Ana maintained important relationships with many older women, among them her maternal aunts, Catalina (b. ca. 1563), Ana (b. ca. 1577), and Cándida (b. ca. 1580) de Hortubia, as well as María la Jarquina and María de Ropiñón (1577–ca. 1606), her cousin's wife. Ana's next-door neighbor Catalina Zamorano (b. ca. 1585), who had purportedly learned *cosas de Mahoma* from her own aunt Francisca Ropiñón, invited Ana to stay in her house whenever Catalina's muleteer husband was abroad. They shared a bed and discussed Islam.[12] Frequently seeing people perform azala and discussing *cosas de Mahoma*—when she visited neighbors to play with their children or overheard her grandmother and la Jarquina debating the timing of upcoming fasts—also helped normalize Islamic religiosity for Ana.[13] In her experience, practicing Islam was a part of daily life, if a guarded one, for even as a girl she knew not talk about such things and believed that her mother "would kill her" if she discovered Ana had discussed them with outsiders.[14]

She had some sense, then, of the dangers associated with Morisco crypto-Islam. She was also aware, even if only passively, of differences between male and female religiosity within her community. Subsequent to her Moorish marriage with Diego, Ana's parents hired a pair of Moriscos from Aragonese Ariza to perform repairs on their grain storage bins. The workmen Gabriel and Francisco de la Huerta were the son and grandson of Catalina Pérez, who had exerted such a proselytizing influence on the town in the 1550s and 1560s. While they were on the job, the elder Huerta asked Ana if "she knew the prayers of the Law of Mohammed," and she responded by telling them all she knew, much to the pleasure of her mother and grandmother who observed the exchange. Huerta, apparently impressed, agreed that she knew "what was appropriate for the salvation of the soul" and offered to teach her "more things" if she "wanted to come to Ariza." The girl purportedly responded that she "already knew enough and didn't want to learn more lest they take her to the Inquisition."[15]

Sometime later Huerta renewed his offer to the girl and her mother while they were strolling in the plaza, and Ana again demurred. Francisca de Hortubia subsequently mentioned the exchange to Diego de Fadrique, who responded that "if she didn't want to go, he would, so that he might learn what [Huerta] said he was going to teach her concerning the sect of Mohammed." Ana asked him why he wanted to go, and he responded that his aunt had told him "he was an ignorant ass."[16] No evidence suggests Diego spent time in Ariza, but his enthusiasm and her resistance hints at a gendered sense of what risks were considered appropriate among Deza's crypto-Muslims. Ana's family had no problem making sure she was well instructed, and she clearly enjoyed soaking up that knowledge and impressing others with it. But traveling to Aragon to sit at the feet of an instructor was the sort of thing men did.

From Ana's description of the encounters with Huerta, it is unclear whether her family would have supported an Aragonese sojourn for the girl, but they certainly did not isolate her physically or educationally in the home or even within their Morisco community. Instead, they seem to have wanted their daughter to exhibit a certain degree of breadth and polish. She had, for example, undergone Christian as well as Muslim catechization. When asked to do so, she could perform the sign of the cross and the accompanying prayer (*santiguado*) and recite the Pater noster, Ave Maria, Salve Regina, the Creed, Ten Commandments, and at least some of the articles of the faith—all "well said" in the vernacular.[17] And while episcopal demands regarding catechization may explain this element of her education, her parents went further. For about "two years," perhaps beginning as early as age six and in the midst of the conflict between the Upper and Lower Neighborhoods, Ana was sent to the home of Old Christian Ana López, who taught needlework to girls and probably embroidery in particular.[18] Among López's other pupils was María, the daughter of Miguel García Serrano.

Although Ana's parents probably hoped López's instruction would provide their daughter with appropriate feminine adornment, the decision proved disastrous. In spring 1604, still only eight years old, the girl found herself navigating a situation the consequences of which she could not have fully understood. One day during Lent, as they sat before the fire, López's husband Alonso Santos (a basket weaver but also involved in the buying and selling of goods) recited "a prayer that begins 'In the highest heaven where is the Trinity, there is our comfort, etc.'" Ana responded that "she knew another one, which was very good, that they recited every night in her house." She offered to recite it, if they wanted. They did, and "the girl spoke a prayer that was neither in Latin nor in Romance but that seemed [to Alonso] to be in the Arabic tongue and in the whole of it she made no mention of God, Saint Mary, or any saints, male or female."[19]

Several days later, López and Santos asked the girl to repeat the prayer, but she always said it so quickly that they could not catch hold of any particular words. Santos, recently returned from a trip to Anguita (Guadalajara), had a supply of "chokers and many other things," which he promised to give her if she recited "all the prayers her mother said to her at night." Ana offered the usual prayers of the church but also one "that she knew in another language."[20] On at least one occasion, María García (b. 1590), Miguel García Serrano's daughter, was present as well. When prompted to recite her prayer, Ana claimed to have forgotten it. But María García, López, and Santos pressed her over and over until she finally relented. Another day, María asked Ana to say it again so that "when I go to confession I can say it" to the priest. Ana refused and María badgered her: "Well, if you go to confess and the vicar asks you for it, I guess you won't say it." "Certainly not!" responded Ana, "I'll tell him I don't know it."[21] After María left, reported Ana López, the Morisca was "very repentant" about ever having said the prayer in front of María García. She would rather have been "thrown on the coals" than have said it; her mother would kill her if she found out.[22]

Her parents did find out and they acted quickly to control the damage. Surprisingly they seem never to have confronted Ana, let alone killed her. Instead, she was immediately withdrawn from López's instruction, and her aunt Cándida de Hortubia informed the girl that "since she already halfway knew how to sew, she would finish teaching her." Ana was kept in the dark about the real reason, but she immediately suspected her precipitous separation from López happened because "Santos and his wife had denounced her."[23] Whether they had before Ana's removal or only did so afterward is, in fact, unclear. The denunciations occurred in early and mid-May 1604, but the events described purportedly occurred in mid-March. Juan Guerrero told his cellmate that Santos and López only denounced Ana (on May 15 and 16) when her mother refused to pay them a *cuarto* (~1/8 *real*) that they believed the girl to have stolen from them.[24] In other words, he thought they were looking for a bribe, albeit a very modest one.

A week before Santos and López denounced Ana before Licentiate Benito, María García and her grandmother (the latter offering only hearsay evidence) did the same. Somehow word of the denunciation got to the girl's parents and, although the situation was extremely delicate, they judged it more dangerous to do nothing than to take action. They first spoke with a Morisca named María de Deza,[25] who "had been a servant [*criada*] of [Licentiate] Miguel Benito."[26] María accompanied the couple when they met with Licentiate Benito and explained that they "knew what Santos had told him and that he had provided information about it and that if he passed it along" the girl would be sent to the Holy Office. Surprisingly, the commissioner informed his visitors that "he didn't need to make a case out of it" and that "Santos and his wife were despicable folk and had perverse hearts."[27] Benito set these most recent denunciations on top of a stack of similar documents in his study, and there they stayed.

While Ana's mother refrained from killing her, the girl may have been disciplined in other ways. The betrothal to muleteer Diego de Fadrique, in particular, was not something Ana desired. While she offered little specific commentary about her husband or his treatment of her, she did claim the "marriage was not according to her desire but rather against her will" and indicated that it happened "because it pleased her parents." For them, it represented an important union with los Cebea, who were among "the best" families in the Upper Neighborhood.[28] However reluctant she might have been, no one offered any hint that Ana was surly or resistant at the betrothal party or the Moorish wedding ceremony. Rather, she was described as dancing and enjoying herself. And by all accounts Diego doted on the girl. Although they dwelt apart, for the next seven months he frequently visited during the day and ate meals in her parents' house, where he chatted to and spent time with his young bride.[29]

Presumably, the plan was for the couple to establish their own home and begin a married life together sometimes after Ana's twelfth birthday (July 25) and their parish wedding. Instead, in the wake of Licentiate Benito's death and the discovery of the hidden denunciations, the Holy Office shrewdly focused its initial energies on Ana. Her youth meant that torture was not permissible and that she would automatically be assigned a guardian [*curador*], but she was also unlikely to be mentally or physically prepared to endure inquisitorial procedure and life in the secret jails without revealing what she knew. Moreover, of the individuals denounced in the reports received at Cuenca after Benito's death, the case against Ana—which boasted three eyewitnesses and a fourth who offered hearsay evidence—was the strongest of the lot.

Ana's twelfth birthday marked the age at which she was old enough to be tried by the Holy Office. And so, eleven days before her birthday, to the shock of her neighbors, she was arrested. On the night of Saturday, July 14, Juan de Barnuevo Miranda, the man who had transported Román Ramírez to Cuenca eight years earlier and now Deza's alcaide, came to her home and ordered her to accompany him. Barnuevo allowed her to speak neither with her sickly mother (who was abed in the next room), nor with Diego de Fadrique (who had "come to see her"), but he did assure her "she would return afterward." He took her to his home and secured her in a room, where she remained until the next morning. By that time Gil Martínez, the warden of Cuenca's inquisitorial jails, had arrived to escort Ana. As he loaded the mules for their trip, Barnuevo's wife approached the young Morisca and gave her a hat and shawl for the road. She told her an Old Christian taverner named María la Gila had come the previous night with a word of comfort from her mother, which was now passed on to Ana: she need not worry for she "would be returned to her home on Sunday night."[30] The women's optimism proved false.

Whatever her mother had believed, Ana's father was immediately convinced his daughter would be transported to Cuenca. The situation was serious and, overnight, a group of Moriscos had gathered to formulate a plan. Luis de Liñán, who controlled the income associated with the Gorgoz properties, donated 20 ducats for Ana's maintenance and magistrate Lope de Arcos contributed 50 reales.[31] Even Juan Agustín, the Morisco whom everyone considered an assimilator, gave "a certain amount of money" to buy barley for her board.[32] Probably on Sunday, friends and relatives gathered at the home of Juan Guerrero and Francisca de Hortubia. Catalina Zamorano's husband Gabriel de Medina came "to console" with his neighbors about Ana's arrest, which he considered "a great disgrace." Juan's brother Lope el viejo suggested that they should get some money and abandon Deza for Rome.[33] (Ostensibly, the rationale seems to have been to seek a dispensation, but Moriscos sometimes used "Rome" as code for traveling to Constantinople or to the Barbary Coast by way of Marseilles.)[34] The dominant opinion, however, was that "there was nothing else to do but give an account of [the affair] to the Duke of Medinaceli" in the hope of gaining another Edict of Grace. Otherwise, "not a person would remain in Deza." Whether they fled town or were arrested, "they would all go, one after another."[35]

That first impromptu meeting gave way to more concrete plans and action. Almost everyone except the members of the Romo-Mancebo faction were involved: Luis and Gerónimo de Liñán, co-magistrate Lope de Arcos, Luis de Cebea el viejo and el menor, Francisco de Miranda, Francisco and Miguel Ramírez, as well as their uncle Juan (Román's brother), the brothers Lope and Luis de Hortubia, Lope de Cieli, Luis de Hortubia el Jarquino (the son of la Jarquina), and the Guerrero brothers (Juan, Lope, Antón, and Miguel), among others. They gathered to "discuss what they had to do about it," and Juan Guerrero demanded the support of everyone. This matter involved the entire community and he refused to act alone. The others agreed and told him "they would put their estates and persons toward a remedy."[36]

The general fear, repeated several times, was that the Upper Neighborhood would share the fate of the Morisco quarter in Ágreda and of Aguilar del Río Alhama. In the former, between 1577 and 1583, forty Moriscos were reconciled and in 1588 another seventy-five took an Edict of Grace—all on account of "a muchacho."[37] In Aguilar, the pueblo was virtually depopulated in the mid-1580s, with dozens of its inhabitants relaxed to the secular arm.[38] These horror stories were all the more vivid since Deza's Moriscos had relatives in both places. Lope de Arcos had been born in Ágreda and Lope de Deza had married in Aguilar, his wife's hometown.

Everyone assumed Ana would behave "like a little girl and tell the truth about everything" and, so, they agreed to give over part of their fortunes "to the duke" in order to avoid the fate of the other towns.[39] But having gained his neighbors' support, Juan Guerrero now acted upon his honor and averred, "He didn't want to receive anything from them." The responsibility was his and he "wanted to use up his estate" first. The decision was made to send an envoy to the duke in Madrid to see what could be done. Juan provided fifty *reales* and a horse mule for the trip. His brother Miguel Guerrero and Miguel Ramírez (son of Román) were chosen as envoys.

The goal of the trip was to inform the duke that the girl "had been arrested by the Holy Office," so he "might favor them and try to head off what they feared."[40] Unfortunately, Miguel Ramírez, whose father and grandfather had both been central to previous negotiations with the town's seigniors—especially for protection against the Inquisition— refused to go. In his account of these events, Miguel explained that he was asked to speak to the duke on behalf of Ana's parents, who were experiencing great "sentiment and sorrow" at the loss of their daughter. But Miguel "excused himself, saying that it was coming up on August and he had a lot of other work to do thereabouts." They refused to let the matter rest and, a few days later, a group of "four or six" men finally succeeded in "persuading" him to go.[41] The two Miguels departed the following afternoon.

Juan Guerrero's road took him elsewhere. He was eager for word of his daughter's fate and even more to get word to her. Immediately after her arrest, he sold a mule for fifty ducats, but rather than heading to Rome, he and Lope Guerrero el menor approached Gil Martínez, the man who was holding the girl prisoner.[42] Juan gave him half the money from the sale and asked to be allowed to see Ana so he could give her a blessing. In his confession before the Inquisition, Guerrero admitted his true intention had been to "advise her to keep quiet," but Martínez refused his consent in any case.[43] "I know that you have enemies," he explained, "and I don't want them to turn on me." Presumably pocketing the ducats, the warden promised to take special care of the girl. He would lodge her in his house "with his own daughters and granddaughter." He even asked Guerrero to tell him "what she usually ate so that I can give it to her." He responded, somewhat ill-advisedly, that, "She did not eat pork" but was not otherwise picky.[44]

Yet he refused to give up on the idea of speaking with Ana or, at least, laying eyes on her. In August, despite his wife's lingering illness, he left for Cuenca with her encouragement, bearing gifts for the warden—a tooled leather *cordobán* bought in Brea for thirty *reales*, a load of apples and peaches, and an *arroba* of linen cloth. He made it only as far as Arcos before he thought better of the errand and returned home, to his wife's disappointment.[45] In October he steeled himself for another go, but without the gifts. Accompanied by a friend from Arcos and another from Ariza, he made it all the way to Cuenca, where he rendezvoused with Morisco Íñigo de Moraga, another friend, with whom he lodged.[46] Moraga's wife counseled Guerrero, urging him to "turn back because in this Holy Office everything was a secret and he wouldn't learn anything." But her husband opined that if he had brought the "gifts" he had intended to bring to Cuenca, the warden would have accepted them.[47]

After two or three days, his friends prevailed upon Guerrero to return home; he could accomplish nothing. But Íñigo de Moraga promised to do all he could for the Dezano and, true to his word, soon visited the warden's house, which was located next to or within the inquisitorial compound. Ostensibly, he went to enquire whether the warden's wife cared to purchase linen cloth. He brought three *arrobas* with him and presented her with half an *arroba* (about 15 lbs.) of the cloth for which he refused payment, explaining, "He would be reimbursed by Annie's father in Deza." Although Martínez was reluctant to accept the goods, removing them from his wife's hands proved even less desirable and he finally consented to the gift. In return, he led Moraga out onto a small plaza in front of the door from where they could see Ana inside the house. "You can tell Juan Guerrero," said the warden, "I kept my word to him."[48] The news reached Guerrero a few days later. If he had failed to get a message to her, at least he knew she was being well treated. In fact, speaking with Ana and urging her to guard her tongue would have done little good, for trusting the community's security to a twelve-year-old girl was, at best, a risky proposition. More important were the negotiations to bring her case to a speedy and agreeable conclusion.

The Miguels—Ramírez and Guerrero—probably arrived in Madrid in early August 1607 and gained an audience with Duke Juan de la Cerda. Ramírez took the lead and requested "a letter for the Holy Office" that could be used to abbreviate Ana's trial and avoid the outcome they feared was inevitable if she revealed all she knew. As Trevor Dadson has shown in his studies of Villarrubia de los Ojos, a committed noble patron could defend effectively against expulsion efforts and the Dezanos needed every advantage they could get.[49] The duke questioned the envoy about the girl's age and her family, but ultimately, according to Ramírez, refused to get involved. "The duke responded" to his overtures, saying, "it was a great burden to him that the business of the Holy Office had touched upon that Neighborhood in Deza." Unfortunately, "the princes swore always to give favor and aid to the Holy Office" and to provide their support rather than seeking to undermine inquisitorial procedure. He lamented that he was, therefore, unable to provide "any letter." If it were "any other court," he would have been pleased to help.[50] Juan Guerrero supplied an additional detail: the duke had not even delivered the dismissal personally but had sent his secretary to "tell them to depart, which they did," arriving home ten or eleven days after they had left.[51]

Ramírez's account suggests this was the end of the matter, and apparently he took no part in further negotiations, despite his family legacy. Others, however, continued to pursue the matter and, finally, a breakthrough occurred more than two months after their first effort. On October 25, 1607, the nobleman's young second wife, Antonia de Toledo y Dávila (ca. 1591–1625), gave birth to an infant boy who was the duke's heir apparent. The Moriscos saw an opportunity to press their suit. Juan Guerrero gave his brother Miguel and Luis de Hortubia (b. 1569) ten ducats and a mule and, on behalf of the town, they carried a "gift" to Madrid to honor the birth. When they presented it, they also "gave [the duke] a letter and petition" that explained their willingness to mortgage their estates if he would pursue their cause. Apparently won over, the duke agreed to "take it upon himself to resolve the matter."[52]

Yet, the petition that gained his favor barely got out of Deza at all. Late in the day, on November 4, 1607, as Juan Guerrero and Luis de Hortubia discussed the latter's mission to Madrid, an unnamed son of Old Christian Hernando de Molina (b. 1542) came running to the home of Catalina de Hortubia, Juan's sister-in-law. The boy, who had been dispatched by his father, explained "he had seen three people from Cuenca enter the house of familiar Pedro de Cisneros and shut the door" behind them. Catalina rushed to find Juan and, when she did, he was just handing the petition to the messengers.[53] Everyone correctly surmised that the men from Cuenca were inquisitorial agents who had come to make more arrests.

Hortubia and Miguel Guerrero quickly slipped out of town. As for Juan and Francisca, even if they had not expected matters to come to a head so abruptly, they had been planning for this eventuality ever since their daughter's arrest. Anticipating the confiscation of their goods, in September and October 1607 they had buried some of their possessions in the houses of Juan de Hortubia (nicknamed el Soldado) and Lope de Arcos. Foreseeing the possibility of needing to flee, they had transported other goods to a contact in Arcos de Jalón and deposited as much as 1,000 *reales* with associates in Cuenca and Ariza.[54] Now the moment for decision had arrived and the couple gathered with a few friends and relatives to discuss the situation late into the night. Since Juan's wife remained ill, the notion of his fleeing to "Rome" on his own for "a dispensation" was broached. He rejected the plan out of hand, saying, "He did not want to run but rather to stay with his wife and die where she died."[55]

His mother-in-law Cecilia la Montera also dismissed the idea of immediate flight, suggesting that it would likely draw attention. She advised them instead to get a few hours' sleep and then eat a large breakfast. Juan, Francisca, and Antón Guerrero were then to head out of town, ostensibly to gather firewood in the hinterland but, in fact, to go into hiding. Once the situation in town was clear, la Montera would advise them how to proceed. The matriarch having spoken, Francisca considered the matter settled. She rose to her feet, opened the door, and found herself looking into the faces of inquisitorial agents, who arrested her and her husband on the spot. The *familiares* also had warrants for Lope el viejo, Lope el menor, Antón Guerrero, and Cecilia la Montera—all of them conveniently closeted together in the house—as well as Catalina Zamorano and Gabriel de Medina, Francisca's sisters Catalina, Ana, and Cándida de Hortubia, and Ana de Mendoza (b. ca. 1570).[56] Each of them was confined in the home of a trustworthy Old Christian in Deza before being transported to Cuenca, where they arrived on November 12.

Following the arrests, Román's son Francisco Ramírez (b. bef. 1570) and Luis de Cieli went door-to-door collecting funds for the Edict of Grace, which the duke had finally agreed to pursue on behalf of Deza's Moriscos.[57] Tragically, however, by the end of the month Juan de la Cerda was unexpectedly dead.

Deza's seignior had married twice. The first union left a daughter but no son. Then in 1606, only a few months after becoming a widower, he married again, this time to doña Antonia. This strategically important marriage linked him to her father, don Gómez Dávila y de Toledo (1553–1616), the Marquis of Velada, tutor to both the *infante* Carlos and the future King Philip III, and a powerful figure at court from the early 1590s until his death.[58] The marriage was meant to solidify an alliance between the de la Cerdas and Velada, a master courtier and politician, who was even then busy outmaneuvering the royal favorite Francisco Gómez de Sandoval y Rojas, Duke of Lerma.[59] Great things were being planned, but Duke Juan's unexpected death introduced a degree of uncertainty about the future, not least of all for Deza's Moriscos. They could have no hope that the new duke, a mere infant, would pursue their cause. Although their search for a remedy was not quite dead, lacking seigniorial protection, many now felt it prudent to focus on preparing for the very real likelihood of renewed inquisitorial activities.

The Upper Neighborhood went on high alert and several young men—Francisco de Cebea "the Friar" (b. 1584), Luis de Cebea el menor (b. ca. 1584), Alexo de Liñán (b. ca. 1590), and one of Lope de Deza's sons—began "walking at night through the whole town, keeping watch to see if anyone from the Holy Office arrived." The Dezanos had anticipated the arrests of Juan Guerrero and Francisca de Hortubia, but the fate of the other nine came as a surprise and suggested that Ana Guerrera had been very forthcoming in her confessions and denunciations. Would the newly arrested Moriscos do the same? The Friar (and presumably the other men as well) went about armed with "a sword and a firelock pistol." If questioned about his nocturnal ramblings and weaponry, he intended to plead the feud with the Romo-Mancebo clan, claim that "he could not walk around during the day" on account of them, and dared not do so unarmed. In fact, if the Inquisition did return, he intended to put up a fight.[60]

No one, however, stays on guard indefinitely. Cebea's eventual capture, in the early hours of the morning on March 15, 1608, happened when, having kept watch for "many previous nights," he took one off and was discovered asleep and unarmed.[61] In addition to Francisco, twenty-two or twenty-three other Moriscos were arrested in Deza.[62] Another one, Miguel de Deza (b. ca. 1578), a relative of Íñigo de Moraga, had recently

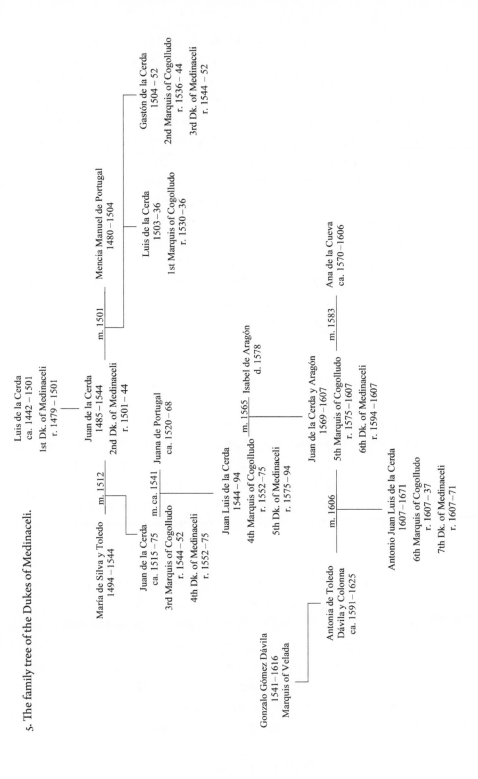

5. The family tree of the Dukes of Medinaceli.

Luis de la Cerda
ca. 1442–1501
1st Dk. of Medinaceli
r. 1479–1501

Juan de la Cerda
1485–1544
2nd Dk. of Medinaceli
r. 1501–44

m. 1501

Mencia Manuel de Portugal
1480–1504

Luis de la Cerda
1503–36
1st Marquis of Cogolludo
r. 1530–36

Gastón de la Cerda
1504–52
2nd Marquis of Cogolludo
r. 1536–44
3rd Dk. of Medinaceli
r. 1544–52

María de Silva y Toledo
1494–1544

m. 1512

Juan de la Cerda
ca. 1515–75
3rd Marquis of Cogolludo
r. 1544–52
4th Dk. of Medinaceli
r. 1552–75

m. ca. 1541

Juana de Portugal
ca. 1520–68

Juan Luis de la Cerda
1544–94
4th Marquis of Cogolludo
r. 1552–75
5th Dk. of Medinaceli
r. 1575–94

m. 1565

Isabel de Aragón
d. 1578

Juan de la Cerda y Aragón
1569–1607
5th Marquis of Cogolludo
r. 1575–1607
6th Dk. of Medinaceli
r. 1594–1607

m. 1583

Ana de la Cueva
ca. 1570–1606

Gonzalo Gómez Dávila
1541–1616
Marquis of Velada

Antonia de Toledo
Dávila y Coloma
ca. 1591–1625

m. 1606

Antonio Juan Luis de la Cerda
1607–1671
6th Marquis of Cogolludo
r. 1607–37
7th Dk. of Medinaceli
r. 1607–71

been placed in custody as well. He had been paid eighteen *reales* a few days earlier to travel to Cuenca and liaise with Moraga about the status of the Dezano prisoners.[63] Unluckily, on March 12 he ran abreast of inquisitorial secretary Alonso de Póveda in El Recuenco (Guadalajara), who placed him under arrest just to be safe.[64] To this list must be added Luis de Cebea el más mozo, Juan de Cebea, and Juan Mancebo, who spent the next two years in Deza's municipal jail, ostensibly on account of their ongoing feud, but in fact at the request of Secretary Póveda, who as yet lacked sufficient evidence to justify their transportation to Cuenca.[65]

The total number of arrests had now reached forty and many feared that these were merely prelude to an even larger culling. In the days following the events of March 15, Old Christian García Cubero found himself talking with Moriscos Diego de Fadrique el mayor (b. 1551) and Juan Mancebo, who would be arrested in a matter of days.[66] Fadrique commented, "If God doesn't do something about it, whether because of arrests or flight, there won't be any of us left in the village over the age of ten."[67] Indeed, some Moriscos had already begun to flee, among them Miguel Guerrero and his wife. Gabriel Lancero (b. ca. 1569) left soon after the arrest of Ana Guerrera's family. Morisco blacksmiths Francisco de Arcos and Juan de Amador Fernández el menor took work in Carabantes and Mazaterón, respectively.[68] Román Ramírez's brother Juan (b. 1544) and his son Francisco (b. ca. 1579) disappeared in the spring or early summer of 1608.[69] Others were selling "what little possessions they had" to make good their escape or avoid having them confiscated upon arrest.[70]

Yet, some in Deza, working under the leadership of Lope de Arcos, continued to pursue an Edict of Grace from the Royal Council in Madrid. On April 8, 1608, local *familiares* Juan de Barnuevo Miranda and Pedro de Cisneros wrote to Cuenca to inform the tribunal that Lope and others were still seeking that remedy. "They are resolved to do it and have great hopes of negotiating [the Edict]," they noted, despite "some difficulty on account of it having been such a short period since the other one was granted to them." Barnuevo and Cisneros worried that to concede a new Edict would be to give the Moriscos license "always to be wicked," for they would merely return to their ways and hold out hope for a third one.[71] A few days later, their fears apparently confirmed, the familiares penned a follow-up. The Moriscos had "dispatched Lope de Cieli [alias el Bueno] and Francisco de Mendoza to Madrid two or three days previously with, they tell us, great hopes of negotiating on account of the help they are sure to receive from the Duchess of Medinaceli and the Marquis of Velada, her father."[72]

Duke Juan Luis's sudden death in November 1607 had left his young wife and her father in mourning—the latter for more political reasons, the former for domestic ones.[73] Velada had lost an important associate in the household of the king; doña Antonia had lost a husband and the father of her infant son. That child, Antonio Juan de la Cerda y Toledo, held title as duke of Medinaceli until his death in 1671, but in 1607 he was ruled by his mother and maternal grandfather. The duchess was hardly a nonentity, even during these years, but at the time of her husband's death she was just seventeen. Her father assumed the lead position and carefully managed his grandson's education and estates until his own death a decade later.

In January 1608, Velada's rival, the Duke of Lerma, had emerged as a proponent of Morisco expulsion. Although discussions within the Council of State remained heated and opinions divided, Lerma's move precipitated a policy reversal within the group, which subsequently also endorsed expulsion.[74] In the moment, Velada resisted the decision.[75] Deza's Moriscos, presumably, knew nothing of these debates but simply trusted that Velada was willing to negotiate with them in good faith and on the basis of the promise received from the previous duke. Even in 1610, some were still clinging to the notion that they had gained the Edict three years previously but had, as yet, been unable to take possession of it (*no lo han podido sacar*).[76]

Others could find no more room for hope. Juan Corazón, who was arrested in late June 1608, informed his cellmate Luis de Cebea el viejo that their efforts were fruitless. He explained that they "sent [Francisco de] Mendoza and another Morisco named Lope el Bueno to negotiate with the Marquis of Velada in order to procure the Grace and solution for Deza's Moriscos." But the two envoys returned with the disappointing news that Velada had dismissed them "with the blessing of God," claiming that "everything that could be done there had already been done." And although he promised to continue doing "what he could," they had nothing concrete to show for their efforts.[77] A plan to negotiate directly with the Holy Office in Cuenca failed even more dramatically. Envoy Lope de Cieli walked into the lion's den with a petition from one Lope de Hortubia.[78] When he presented it to the inquisitors during their morning audience, he was first asked to wait in the hall outside the audience chamber and then summarily arrested.[79]

Despite these many setbacks, efforts to find a solution continued. In October 1608, *bachiller* Bartolomé Montero, Benito's successor as inquisitorial commissioner, sounded the alarm once again.[80] He warned Cuenca that Deza's Moriscos were "proceed[ing] with great care, soliciting the Grace, for a Morisco named Diego de Fadrique hasn't stopped coming and going from Madrid; we can't understand why." Francisco de Miranda el menor (b. ca. 1571), a painter like his father and grandfather, remained on site in Madrid and Lope de Arcos directed affairs back home. Montero went on to explain that he had heard a rumor indicating "they've already gotten the Grace for those who are here [in Deza] and they are seeking it for those who are in your lordship's jails."[81]

In spite of Morisco hopes, the rumor was false or at least overly optimistic. The Marquis of Velada's primary motivation had always been political and he had no sympathy for the Moriscos' cause. In fact, they could hardly have chosen a less enthusiastic patron.[82] Despite his rivalry with Lerma, Velada became one of the "strongest defenders" of the expulsion and proved "inflexible" in his application of policy. In April 1609, when Philip III issued the decree, he did so with the unanimous support of the royal Council of State, including the Marquis. All that remained was to negotiate the process of implementation.[83] Velada firmly believed no exceptions should be made, even for seemingly assimilated Moriscos; and he refused appeals made by the Count of Oropesa, the Duke of Arcos, and representatives of the Aragonese Cortes. A "work so holy and so beneficial for these realms" had to be seen through to the bitter end, he argued.[84] As far as Deza's Moriscos went, the Holy Office was in agreement in no small part thanks to Ana Guerrera.

Her arrival in Cuenca on the night of July 18, 1607, was followed by a first audience the next afternoon. Unable to deny that she knew an Arabic prayer, she recited it and claimed to have learned it some four years previously from an otherwise unknown "old Morisca woman who lived in her neighborhood" named Aunt María de Gabriel, who had since died.[85] Despite a series of warnings and admonitions, Ana made no additional denunciations until early October, when she was presented with the formal Accusation. Although names and other information that would have revealed the identity of those who had denounced her had been removed, she began to grasp the danger in which she found herself. She admitted knowing two more Arabic prayers, which she claimed to have learned from her cousin's now-deceased wife. She returned to Aunt María de Gabriel and even briefly implicated her grandmother, Cecilia la Montera.[86] But a day and a half later, the floodgates opened.

She began by naming her mother, father, and aunts as crypto-Muslims and a few days further on, she widened the circle, naming all the Moriscos in Deza who did not eat pork or drink wine.[87] She told, in particular, of a feast given by Lope de Arcos on the occasion of his being named tithe collector in 1604 over the objections of the Old Christian faction. Although wine and pork were on the table, "none of the [Moriscos] she named ate or drank any," including her husband and uncles. She could not speak for all of the attendees who refused, but as for her immediate family, she was certain that they had abstained "for the sake of keeping the Law of Mohammed." Dozens of names across the generations followed, and they were just the ones she could remember. While Ana acknowledged that some Morisco men drank wine regularly and muleteers did so while on the road on account of the cold, most of the town's New Christians were as much Moors now as they had ever been.[88]

Ana had held out for two and a half months; her father lasted barely two days. After a first audience on November 13, he began to confess in earnest his own sins and those of others on the morning of the fifteenth. In an astonishing series of denunciations that included virtually every Morisco he had ever known, in Deza or outside of it, Juan Guerrero participated in audience after inquisitorial audience until, finally, running out of things to say in August of the following year. In this he was encouraged and egged on by one Gabriel de León, an informant who shared Guerrero's cell until March 1608.[89]

The information provided by daughter, father, and informant—along with the confessions and denunciations offered by many of the other detainees—provided the bedrock for at least forty-six cases against Dezanos, many of which dragged on for years. The Holy Office attempted to make other arrests as well, but at bare minimum thirty Dezanos, including one Old Christian collaborator, fled town in anticipation. For those who lingered, prospects were grim, especially after word of the royal Edict of Expulsion spread. In July 1610, some of the remnant continued to hope against all reasonable hope that "the Duke of Medinaceli would defend them," even as they feared they would be made to "depart like all the rest."[90] The Edict was published in Deza in early August 1610 with the expectation that it would be enforced sixty days later. In late September, *bachiller* Montero wrote to Cuenca explaining that the Moriscos were in a dither. Some refused to believe the order was meant to apply to them since they were "old" Moriscos, not Granadinos.[91] They appealed to the Count of Salazar, who was managing the expulsion, and went through the process of gaining a legal ruling, but it merely confirmed that "they are Moors."[92]

Many of them now gave up on Spain altogether, saying they did not "want to waste anything more on the defense of this but rather depart according to the order of His Majesty." They were selling their goods and buying donkeys.[93] Others were still trying to prove themselves "good Christians." Montero thought it a vain hope on the whole. But among the town's Moriscos were María Navarra, the widowed sister of Bernardino Almanzorre, and her son Gerónimo de Molina. They had moved out of the Upper Neighborhood to live among Old Christians and Gerónimo had taken on the care of several pigs. He was set upon one day by a group of Morisco hooligans, ages twelve to fourteen, who threw rocks and berated him as a scoundrel for "giving up the good law for a bad one."[94] Gerónimo denounced them to commissioner Montero. He and his mother were not the only Moriscos to try to gain a place among the Old Christians, but they were among the few who succeeded. In the flyleaf to the sacramental register, a cleric wrote, "On the eighth day of July 1611, the Moriscos of this town of Deza departed. They were four hundred people on foot." María Navarra died in town sixteen years later.

11

Cleverer than His Father

Miguel Ramírez's Story

In mid-December 1607, as Ana Guerrera and a dozen other Moriscos from Deza were learning about life in Cuenca's secret jails, the infant duke Antonio Juan de la Cerda took formal possession of the town.[1] Barely a month old, he stayed home for the occasion but was legally represented by Licentiate Antonio Sáenz de Verano. The official record repeatedly emphasized that the entire ceremony occurred "quietly and peacefully without any contradictions."[2] As far as appearances go, there is no reason to dispute the claim, but for a town brimming with social, economic, political, and religious tensions, Deza's actual state was neither peaceful nor quiet. These qualities, which reflected the effectiveness of seigniorial authority and the submission of vassals, were key to the central message that the duke's party wanted to convey as it asserted control over local affairs. Yet the ceremony failed to resolve ongoing tensions and restore harmony, for although Dezanos submitted to the will of their lord and accepted the peace he offered, the plans of the crown, episcopacy, and Holy Office were busily working at cross purposes.

The whole town assembled for the ceremony, but especially its office-holders, decked out in official regalia. Upon arrival, Licentiate Verano claimed the keys to the town archive and fortress, which he ceremonially entered, locked, and occupied. He stripped all officeholders of titles, staves of office, and insignias, then took possession of the keys to the magisterial courtroom. He unlocked it, sat on the bench beneath the duke's arms, and held court in his name and with his full authority.

Local executive, judicial, and municipal power were now concentrated in the infant grandee by proxy. At this point in the proceedings during previous possession ceremonies, litigants had sometimes approached the bench seeking justice; not this time.

That silence is noteworthy. Ten months earlier, in February 1607, Miguel García Serrano (still doggedly styling himself procurador síndico) had appeared before Antonio de Ucedo Salazar, the hidalgo co-magistrate, and petitioned for redress of grievances. He pointed out that Duke Juan had named three Moriscos for the council of 1607: Lope de Arcos, Juan de Heredia, and Luis de Hortubia el Jarquino. Those appointments, he claimed, contravened "the laws and edicts of these realms," as well as the executive order (*ejecutiva*) his faction had gained from the Royal Appellate Court several years earlier.[3] The magistrate formally received the grievance and transmitted it to the duke—notarized and witnessed— but the Moriscos stayed in office. Now, with an opportunity to press their case before the seigniorial stand-in, the Old Christian faction was silent. Similarly, the Moriscos left unmentioned the matter of the Edict of Grace that the old duke had recently promised to secure on their behalf.

The previous day, Juan de Barnuevo Miranda had been the town's castellan; Ucedo Salazar and Lope de Arcos had been co-magistrates. Now, divested of their offices, they were mere citizens and whatever pressure various factions might have been willing to bring to bear while the duke was at a distance, a dustup at this crucial moment would have been disastrous. Ceremonies like this were rife with uncertainty, and townsfolk on all sides apparently saw prudence in presenting a united front for the moment; they could renew their disputes after the Licentiate's departure.

Verano had other plans. His first official act on the second day of the possession ceremony was to pass outside of the town walls and visit the infamous garden once controlled by Román Ramírez and which, after his death, had come into the possession of his son Miguel. Verano ambled through the property, evaluated it, then declared that he "likewise also took possession of it in the name of the duke, my lord." This too occurred "quietly and peacefully," with Barnuevo Miranda and Lope de Arcos (the most politically influential Old Christian and Morisco in town) serving as witnesses.[4] This act, without precedent in previous possession ceremonies, suggests that Verano understood at least some of Deza's idiosyncrasies.[5] By asserting ducal control, he took the contentious property out of play in local factional disputes.

Later that day, Verano returned the keys, staves, insignias, and titles. Now restored as castellan, Barnuevo Miranda pledged fealty to the new duke in a ceremony of homage and, in trust, received the fortress and its arsenal. Magistrates, councilmen, officeholders, and scribes were reinstalled. The Moriscos would keep their offices, but apparently not the duke's garden. Although Verano ceremonially restored everything else of which he had taken possession to the men who had previously controlled them, no grant was made for the contentious property.[6] It remained, for the time being at least, under the duke's immediate and direct control.

Licentiate Verano provided no indication of future plans for the garden. By December 1607 the Marquis of Velada knew a Morisco expulsion was possible, perhaps even likely, so he may have been angling to remove Miguel Ramírez in anticipation. But the expulsion was as yet uncertain, so perhaps this was merely a necessary assertion of authority and matters would return to the status quo ante after the situation had cooled down. Or perhaps Velada had decided, once and for all, to bring his son-in-law's overenthusiastic support for the Moriscos to an end.[7] Whatever the plan was, it soon had to be adjusted, for within two months of Verano's departure inquisitorial authorities in Cuenca ordered the arrest of another sixteen of Deza's Moriscos. The circle of denunciations was expanding, threatening to swallow the entire Morisco community, and among those caught up was Miguel Ramírez.

Born sometime around 1569, Miguel was Román's fourth child and the family's third boy. Although no entry appears for him in the parish's sacramental register, in 1608 he was able to name both his godparents and the cleric who baptized him.[8] According to his own testimony, he was born and raised in Deza and lived in his father's house until Román's second marriage in ca. 1595. Miguel then moved into the home of his eldest brother, also Román (b. 1563), where he lived for "about ten years," until his own marriage to María Almotazán (b. ca. 1579) in June 1602.[9] The couple established a home and had two daughters, Ángela in November 1603 and, in January 1606, Isabel, who died eight months later.

When he was in his late thirties, Miguel Ramírez identified himself as a farmer, but this was not the full extent of his activities. From the mid-1590s, following the accession of Juan Luis de la Cerda, he served as the duke's alguacil mayor. This office, distinct from the alguacil who sat annually on the town council, was appointed directly by the seignior to help oversee Deza's hamlets, the so-called Four Places of the Recompense." Miguel held the office for the better part of a decade, at least until his marriage in 1602 and perhaps for a few years after.[10]

In addition to farming and serving as alguacil mayor, Miguel and his brothers Román and Francisco were involved in the goings-on at the duke's house and garden. This certainly entailed agricultural labor—Francisco was seen digging and Román III was described as an *hortelano*—but Miguel's connection to the garden appears to have been focused on Islamic activities.[11] The admittedly limited evidence, then, suggests a division of labor among the brothers in the garden. This does not, however, mean that Miguel was physically weak or infirm. Although in 1611 he claimed a bad heart and a swollen hand, he did so not only in the wake of heavy torture (which he resolutely withstood), after four years in the secret jails, and also while attempting to avoid galley service. And while his examining physicians' evaluation of him may reflect a lack of charity about the patient's ailments, they dismissed his claims to be in poor health and specifically noted his "natural robustness."[12]

Following his father's death, in a process that remains murky, Miguel inherited the duke's house and garden. In November 1607, eight years after Román's death, local familiar Pedro de Cisneros confirmed, in a letter to Cuenca, that the Duke of Medinaceli had given the property to Miguel Ramírez.[13] Cisneros further suggested that this transfer had occurred only very recently—*pocos dias a esta parte*[14]—although others described the brothers (and the juntas) continuing in the garden since Román's death.[15] Cisneros' point, then, was probably that, following the Moriscos' successful negotiations with the duke in early November, he had confirmed their ongoing access to and control over the property.[16]

Presumably, the duke expected the Ramírez brothers to continue paying rent on the property. Specifically where that money came from is unknown, but Miguel was not without financial means. The Holy Office had confiscated Román's estate, thereby eliminating any heritable wealth, although some quantity of goods or coin may have been hidden away. In any case, Miguel owned his own house, a threshing floor, and a field of wheat. He also claimed to have deposited 400 ducats with a "certain woman" in La Alameda, one of Deza's hamlets, in anticipation of his arrest in 1608. Altogether, he informed the Holy Office, his estate was worth around 1,400 ducats.[17] Yet, some claimed that he had access to a great deal more, for he purportedly owned a book containing the location of all hidden treasure in eastern Castile and Aragon.

The discovery of hidden treasure in early modern Spain was often connected to medicine, prophecy, diabolism, divination, and magic generally, especially where Moriscos were involved.[18] Note, for example, the story of Diego de Hurtado, Baron of Bárboles and heir presumptive of the Count of Fuentes. Hurtado, who was executed in 1592 for his ties to Philip II's nemesis, Alonso Pérez, had previously been denounced as a necromancer to the Holy Office for partnering with an Aragonese Morisco to locate a secret hoard using a magical book and the aid of demons.[19] The search came to naught, but the status of Hurtado and Pérez as anti-monarchic figures informs the milieu within which the enemies of Deza's Moriscos likewise branded them enemies of the king. Indeed, many of the elements present in the Hurtado story were recapitulated in late sixteenth- and early seventeenth-century Deza, especially in the Ramírez family's trials.

In an unusual series of inquisitorial denunciations, for example, four witnesses presented hearsay evidence in late 1607 about an unnamed Morisco from Deza whom the town's vicar, Mateo de Luna, decided could only have been Miguel Ramírez.[20] The Morisco purportedly knew the location of a treasure hidden in a cave near Cogolludo that included a golden cup in three pieces out of which three kings had drunk, as well as a hoard of gold and silver that would require fifty mules to haul away. A second cache, in Aragon, was valued at 150,000 ducats.[21] In early modern Spain, obsessed as its inhabitants were with finding hidden treasure,

Moriscos were the acknowledged experts both at finding and at hiding wealth, as witnessed by Cervantes's Morisco Ricote in *Don Quixote,* who returned to Spain from exile in order to recover his secret store of riches.[22] As for the group of men who followed the clues given out by the "Morisco from Deza," after "many days of digging" they determined that they had been hoodwinked.[23]

Assuming, as contemporaries did, that the man referenced in these testimonies was Miguel Ramírez, the episode suggests he had inherited something of his father's showmanship, artfulness, and ability to spin a convincing tale. Inquisitorial familiar Pedro de Cisneros painted this unflattering picture of the son: "He can be suspected of anything, no matter how bad it is, and he continues to follow in the very footsteps of his father." As he considered the denunciations made against Miguel and his "way of proceeding generally," Cisneros concluded, "I understand that he must be even worse [than his father] because he is so much cleverer than he was."[24] This was high, if backhanded, praise.

Miguel Ramírez was highly intelligent and capable. He never served on the town council—his father's legacy made that impossible—but as the duke's alguacil mayor and a member of the commune he was very much involved in local affairs. At least once he acted as legal counsel in a case before local magistrates: Juan Mancebo retained his services after assaulting Luis de Cebea el menor in Deza's main plaza. Ramírez claimed that he had cunningly revealed evidence that Cebea's hostility against Mancebo preceded the attack, thereby calling Cebea's protestations of innocence into question.[25] He knew how to read and write well, skills that he claimed to have learned "while he was a muchacho in the town of Deza" from "some school teachers there and from some clerics."[26] Beyond the presumably fictitious book of treasures, Miguel admitted owning a copy of Bernardo Pérez de Chinchón's *Antialcorano.*[27] He probably had several Islamic books, perhaps even a copy of the Quran.[28]

Perhaps as a result of reading Chinchón, Miguel Ramírez spoke about Christian doctrine using precise language and could clearly distinguish between Islam and Christianity. When, toward the end of his first inquisitorial audience, Dr. Claudio de la Cueva admonished him for not owning up to his heterodoxy, the Morisco responded with a striking statement of faith that must have caught the inquisitor off guard.[29] At first glance it appears to reflect in a clear and orthodox fashion the Spanish Catholic understanding of Christianity. It asserts the perpetual virginity of Mary, the humanity and divinity of Christ, Christ's physical presence in the bread and wine, and so on. It even appears to denounce the "false and wicked Law and sect of the Moors," calling it drivel and a mess. But, read carefully, the grammar of Miguel's statement introduces ambiguities that make authorial intent very difficult to pin down. In fact, rather than referring to his own beliefs and asserting their concordance with Catholic doctrine, the statement can be read merely as a series of claims describing church doctrine without indicating whether Miguel believed them.

Even his seemingly direct condemnation of Islam, which denounced "those [*aquellas*] falsities of that [*aquella*] sect," can be read alternatively as a statement against ecclesial condemnation of Islam. That is, it might be a dismissal of the "Law and sect of the Moors" as "drivel" or, alternatively, the "drivel" here could be the condemnation of Islam by "the holy Councils and doctors of the Church and theologians." His grammar can bear either reading. The Holy Office, too, appears to have been unsure what to make of it, marking that section in the margin and underlining a key phrase ("no human understanding, if it looks with clear eyes, will decry and abandon them as evil . . ."), since the referent for "them" might indicate Islamic beliefs, and the negative construction could indicate that a careful and unbiased consideration of Islam would lead one to acknowledge it as true.

The inquisitorial prosecutor was unimpressed by the profession of faith and regarded it as further evidence of the old Ramírez deceitfulness, which had been manifest most clearly in Miguel's father. It is, the prosecutor concluded, "sure and evident that everything to which the accused referred in the said audience was, imitating his ancestors and his nation, done with particular study and purpose and with particular premeditated affectation, and arranged beforehand for the purpose of deceit."[30] It was, in short, a remarkable application of amphibological speech, grammatical imprecision, and double entendres.

Whatever else the statement of faith reveals about Miguel Ramírez, it indicates a nimble and precise intellect that could grasp subtle theological distinctions. His delivery—whether (as is likely) the speech was memorized beforehand for recitation or concocted on the fly—is further evidence of a sharp mind. It also hints at formidable self-possession, given his circumstances. His confidence and precision suggest a familiarity with speaking as an authority before an audience. Other Moriscos acknowledged that he (and his brother Francisco) presided at Islamic weddings and, although Miguel denied it, Old Christians in Deza denounced him as an Islamic instructor.[31] This latter work he purportedly conducted among adult Moriscos who gathered at the duke's house and garden, but he was also denounced for corrupting the town's Morisco youths, to whom he "gave the Quran to read, telling them it is the Law of Mohammed and a holy thing."[32]

The Holy Office concluded he had made a "regular and great study of the Quran of Mohammed, reading and handling both it and . . . the *Antialcorano* many times." The latter volume, he used to search for "new inventions and false sophistries in order to try to obscure the truth and preserve and confirm" other Moriscos in their "blindness."[33] Miguel and Francisco Ramírez, the Inquisition claimed, were nothing less than "chaplains of Mohammed," Deza's own alfaquíes.[34] If this was true, no one gave any hint that the brothers' training had taken place anywhere other than locally. While their father could have sent them to Aragon to study with a relative or one of his other contacts, the more likely scenario is that they were garden-grown, the fruit of their father's efforts to reinvigorate the local Islamic community.

By March 15, 1608, however, Miguel was in inquisitorial custody, and whatever he had been doing in Deza became less important than what was going to happen to him in the months that followed.[35] Along with twenty others, he was rounded up and prepared for transport to Cuenca. The number of detainees made supervision difficult, and a group of men, which included Miguel, the brothers Francisco and Román el Romo, Francisco de Cebea, his friend Luis de Hortubia el Jarquino, and Juan de Hortubia el Soldado found opportunities to communicate. Despite the blood feud between the Romos and Cebeas, these six entered into a pact along the way, agreeing, as Juan Guerrero explained, "to keep quiet and not confess the truth in this Holy Office," since "three witnesses were necessary to condemn them."[36] They referred to the pact as *lo dicho dicho*, perhaps short for *lo dicho, dicho está*—what is said can't be unsaid—mum's the word.

Word of the pact passed among the prisoners and later between prison cells. Many among the most recent arrivals indicated their determination to "stay tough" (*tener tieso*) and not "let up" (*aflojarse*). On June 1, Francisco el Romo in cell "N" told everyone, "lo dicho dicho and that no one should let up . . . and that no one is letting up but rather lo dicho dicho and everyone should stay tough."[37] The women were in on it too. Those in cell "D" encouraged the men in "C": "Be sure to deny that we are denying. Stay tough."[38] But their neighbors did not respond, and the initial conviction of some eventually began to waver. In October, when the men in "C" were urged to "stay tough" because everyone was denying everything, Antón Guerrero, who had by then been incarcerated for almost a year, responded that there was nothing for it but to go in and tell the truth. The depopulation of the Morisco quarter, he lamented, was a fait accompli; no one was left in the Upper Neighborhood "except the children."[39]

When Gabriel de Medina, also in "C," learned that his sister-in-law had been moved to share a cell with his wife, Catalina Zamorano, he despaired, for he assumed Catalina must have already denounced him. She would tell her sister and then the Holy Office would have two witnesses against him; he would be condemned. "Well, how would you counsel me?" he asked his cellmate, Gabriel de León, who urged Medina to "confess the truth. This was the solution." The Morisco requested an audience in which he denounced both himself and his wife.[40]

As it turned out, León was not the sympathetic counselor that he pretended to be. When Juan Guerrero was processed at the secret jails on the night of November 12, 1607, the warden placed him in cell "P" with León, who had been languishing there for about sixteen months. He immediately sized up the new arrival and convinced him that he too was a Morisco.[41] In fact, he was an erstwhile friar who may or may not have been irregularly ordained in France and may or may not have married a woman in Alcazar de Consuegra. Three days later, León requested an audience with the inquisitor in which he explained the ruse and offered to act as an informant.[42]

In fact, he aided the Holy Office in two distinct ways. First, provided with writing materials and a desk, Gabriel de León recorded the actions and conversations of his cellmates. Astonishingly, he had at least fifty-six audiences with inquisitors over the course of thirteen months in order to make reports. As more Dezanos arrived in Cuenca, several of them—including Juan and Antón Guerrero, Gabriel de Medina, Lope de Deza, Juan de Hortubia el Soldado, and Francisco de Cebea—spent time sharing a cell with him. As the prisoners found ways to communicate between cells using windows, written notes, whispered conversations, and even the building's pipes, he reported on the activities of those outside of his immediate circle.

A second service performed by Gabriel de León was using "various methods and means" to encourage Moriscos to confess their sins and denounce others, especially by emphasizing the dire consequences of being caught in a lie. This, for example, had been the case when he offered counsel to Gabriel de Medina. Covering up the guilt of others, he warned, was dangerous, for if anyone else confessed something León's cellmates had denied or left unmentioned, they would be discovered and their deception made manifest.[43]

Thanks in part to the ministrations of León, Juan Guerrero lasted only a matter of days before he was ready to confess. But what about his family? His wife, brothers, and mother-in-law—not to mention his daughter, Ana—were in custody. If he confessed and they did not, their fate would be sealed. His solution was for everyone to come clean simultaneously. To that end, he asked Gabriel de León to speak to Gil Martínez, the warden of the secret jails, on his behalf and convince him to pass the message along to his family. Guerrero provided León with special "signs" for Martínez to use, so the recipients would know the message was bona fide. Tell them, he urged, to "confess in order to get out of here." He wanted to spare them León's fate of a years-long trial before sentencing.[44] Later, in early fall 1608, the informant was moved from cell "P" to "C," where he worked on Juan's brother Antón and convinced him to confess to keeping Islamic fasts. Their cellmate, Juan de

Hortubia el Soldado, responded by pulling Guerrero's beard and berating him for cowardice.[45]

Huddling in a corner, the humiliated Morisco predicted that Hortubia would eventually do the same. "Soldado, you tell me that I lack courage for having confessed the fasts," but eventually, warned Guerrero, "you'll end up saying what I have said." He reminded Hortubia that his own wife had been arrested and her instruction in Islam had come by way of el Soldado's own mother, Cecilia de Cieli, the "best female teacher in town."[46] But Guerrero was wrong; although Hortubia's own trial docket has gone missing, surviving excerpts indicate he received a sentence—galley service and the confiscation of a fourth of his estate—typical of those who refused to confess their guilt despite torture. Of the original members of the pact, Hortubia and Miguel Ramírez were the only ones who "stayed tough."

The inquisitors must surely have been disappointed. Ramírez's enemies back home would have been too, had they known. Both groups relished the thought of bringing the Morisco to his knees and learning what a full confession would reveal. He had been the subject of an intense series of denunciations by Old Christians immediately following the arrests of Ana's family and close associates in early November 1607, as if to emphasize that he should have been included among the first wave of detainees. Pedro de Cisneros wrote twice to Cuenca to emphasize Miguel's role in local Islamic activities and his connections to Román Ramírez, their mutual associates, and the garden. He even asserted his suspicion that Deza's "Moors" were practicing diabolical witchcraft, for "certain things had occurred in [Cisneros's] house" over the past few years that could be accounted for in no other way.[47]

Nevertheless, over the course of nearly three years, inquisitorial efforts failed to produce any significant confessions. Even after two and a quarter hours of aggressive torture on February 12, 1611—seven turns on the *silla de tormento*, the use of various clamps (*garrotes*) on the rack, and three jars of water poured down his throat (*toca*)—Miguel Ramírez avowed he had already confessed the truth.[48] Five days later, the Holy Office declared him to be gravely suspect of heresy but unanimously endorsed his reconciliation. Like Hortubia, Ramírez's penance included four years rowing in the galleys and the confiscation of (merely) a quarter of his estate.

On February 24, in Cuenca's parish church of San Pedro, Miguel appeared wearing a penitential habit and carrying a lighted taper. The single diagonal band (*media aspa*) on his sanbenito indicated that his abjuration was *de vehementi*, but it distinguished him from those found guilty of formal heresy, who wore a *hábito de dos apsas*.[49] He renounced Islam, attended Mass, and signed the abjuration, although his signature was no longer as confident or smooth as it had once been.[50] Ramírez was subsequently released from the secret jails and transferred to Cuenca's royal jails. There he reunited with a number of reconciled Dezanos, many of whom were awaiting transfer to the galleys. It was likely to be a death sentence.

After years in inquisitorial custody, most Dezanos' cases had been brought to a speedy conclusion in late 1610 and early 1611. The Suprema demanded haste in view of the Morisco expulsions underway in Castile. After Miguel's transfer to the royal jails, the group there numbered about twenty-seven women and fifteen men, among them two non-Dezanos.[51] As the group sorted out who had lived and who had died, compared sentences, and scrabbled to earn their daily bread, they also began laying plans for the future.

Audaciously, in late 1610 or early 1611, Francisco and Román el Romo, two of the detainees, wrote from the royal jails to King Philip III on behalf of the men who had been condemned to the galleys.[52] They petitioned for the commutation of their sentences, claiming they were "ill, broken, crippled in arms and hands" on account of being "so long in prison." The brothers requested a medical examination to verify the groups' incapacity to serve as oarsmen.[53] Someone must have shepherded the appeal through governmental bureaucracy in Madrid, for by January 22 it had found its way to the Suprema.[54] As the Moriscos waited for that plan to bear fruit, they worked to survive and formulated other schemes.

Despite being destitute, they had established lines of communication with friends and relatives back home and were using various contacts to improve their situation and work toward freedom. This otherwise obscure period is partially illuminated by the serendipitous preservation of a cache of letters, dated between March 4 and 14, sent by the prisoners from the royal jails to relatives and friends in Deza. Some thirty-six letters were written—the illiterate often dictated theirs to Francisco el Romo—and surreptitiously handed over to one Fabian de Robles, a sympathetic Morisco from Cuenca, for delivery to Deza, a service he had provided on several previous occasions.

This time at least, however, Roble deputized his son to do the job and, although the boy was young enough to be reckoned a muchacho, his father apparently trusted him to complete a two hundred and fifty-mile solo round-trip. Unfortunately, the boy's mother disagreed and, when she discovered his absence, tracked him to the city's edge. There, in a state of some distress, she happened upon Domingo de Alba, a conquense priest, who reported seeing the boy some miles north of town crossing the Jucar at the Chantre Bridge.

The woman prevailed upon the priest to go in pursuit, and that night he caught up with him at an inn in Collados. When questioned, the boy claimed to be carrying documents dispatched by the *receptor* of the Holy Office, but Alba was suspicious, especially after he leafed through the letters and recognized several names from a recent auto de fé. He decided the prudent course of action was to hand over the cache to inquisitors back in Cuenca. This he did immediately upon his return, thereby ensuring that the letters were never delivered but instead preserved in the inquisitorial archive.[55]

The main purposes of the letters were threefold: to share the writers' latest news and solicit the same from recipients; to request immediate aid in the form of food and clothing for the detainees and care for their children back home; and to urge recipients to pursue a scheme for the prisoners' release and the commutation of their sentences. Whether because previous messages had gone astray or on account of the precarious nature of Morisco life in Deza on the eve of the expulsion, responses to many previous letters home had never arrived in Cuenca. Various writers took this lack of communication personally and now complained of abandonment. While quick to rejoice about the transfer of inquisitorial prisoners to the royal jails, most writers emphasized their own hunger, poverty, and desire to see loved ones.

The plaintive cries for sustenance and information indicate the hardness of their situation and suggest emotional and physical distress. Yet the letters also hint at the sources of support that kept them going. Juan de Cebea, for example, noted that he and his brother Luis were in such dire straits "that we are eating what we get from begging and relying on what my aunt María [la Jarquina] earns spinning at her wheel."[56] La Jarquina, despite being "sick and very weak and needy," not only supplied the brothers from her earnings but also included "two pieces of silk fabric and twelve little needles" with her letter, presents for her granddaughters back in Deza.[57] María de Medina spoke obscurely of mercy showed to them by *la señora alcaidesa*, perhaps the wife of Juan de Barnuevo Miranda back in Deza.[58] Luis de Cebea emphasized the debt they owed to Fabián de Robles' wife, who provided the whole company with food "on many days."[59] Dezano Old Christian Juan Miguel also seems to have played some role as a go-between, and Juan de Hortubia el Soldado felt confident that he could call upon the help of Deza's former alcaide Francisco Fernández Abarca and his wife.[60]

Amidst the struggle to survive, however, the letters also provide evidence of further Morisco schemes to have their sentences commuted. Juan de Hortubia wrote to his uncles Lope and Luis that Alonso de Póveda, an inquisitorial notary, "has reported and informed me that if we have someone in Madrid who acts on behalf of my business (and that of the others), it will be easy to commute the galleys to another penance."[61] Luis de Hortubia el Jarquino likewise reported that their "lawyer [*letrado*] and Secretary Póveda [were] encouraging [them] strongly," saying that if someone were to "solicit" their deliverance (*rescate*) before the Suprema in Madrid, a "remedy" could be gained "with great ease."[62] Others urged relatives to go to Queen Margaret and request their "liberty as alms," which could be had for just fifty ducats.[63] Some hoped that, if approached directly, the king himself would be moved to mercy on account of the Lenten season.[64] Difficult as it is to believe such plans could succeed, the Moriscos placed great hope in the willingness of their loved ones to act. Luis de Cebea even called upon his wife to sacrifice both herself and their daughters' liberty for his own, urging them, if necessary, "to sell yourself and my daughters," since, "God giving me health and liberty, I will get you out of hock and sale."[65]

No specific evidence exists to show that those in Deza ever had the opportunity or will to approach the king, queen, or Suprema, but the sequence of events that occurred soon thereafter suggests something had shifted. On April 11, 1611, the tribunal in Cuenca acknowledged receipt of a brief letter from the Suprema. That letter was accompanied by the petition sent some months earlier by Francisco and Román el Romo, which claimed the Moriscos' poor health made them useless as oarsmen. The Suprema now asked Cuenca for its opinion on the matter.[66] Two days later, physician Dr. Diego de Fernández and surgeon Diego de Morales were summoned to the audience chamber to examine a dozen Morisco men, among them Francisco and Román el Romo, Juan Mancebo, Juan de Cebea, Miguel Ramírez, Juan de Hortubia el Soldado, and Luis de Hortubia el Jarquino. Despite noting a wide array of complaints, illnesses, and injuries, the examiners declared that "none of [the Moriscos] demonstrated any impediment" that would prohibit them from "serving His Majesty in the galleys at the oars."[67]

A few days later, Inquisitor Diego de Quiroga replied to Madrid. He claimed the Moriscos were in fine health, noted the sworn testimony of Fernández and Morales, and reminded the Suprema that "these are a crafty people who have always managed, with lies and fabrications, to hide their sins." And now, he explained, citing the evidence of the confiscated cache of letters and the Moriscos' false claim to ill health, they were "doing it again."[68] The Suprema responded by signaling agreement. The Moriscos remained confined to the royal jails, awaiting transportation to El Puerto de Santa María in Andalusia, where they would be set to rowing as King Philip's newest oarsmen.

All seemed well from Cuenca's perspective until, finally, in early fall 1611, one Pedro Rodríguez Catalán transported the Moriscos to the port of embarkation. Most were received without a fuss, even those who had undergone physical examinations. But four of them—Román el Romo, Juan Mancebo, Miguel Ramírez, and Íñigo de Moraga[69]—were deemed physically unfit for the oars and remanded to Rodríguez's custody. He had no choice but to return them to Cuenca, where the inquisitors received the news with consternation. On October 15, they wrote to Madrid complaining that, based on the "report given by [Rodríguez] as well as the extraordinary formalities that these Moriscos have undertaken in order to free themselves from the galleys before they departed from here," there was every reason to believe the four men had "undertaken negotiations to avoid being received into the galleys."[70]

Indeed, there was. Back in March, for example, Juan de Hortubia el Soldado had written to his uncle and nephew asking them to pursue his liberty, whatever the expense. If, however, "it's our luck that there's no solution, do me the courtesy of making sure to send me letters of favor from doña Paula [del Águila] and Francisco Fernández [Abarca]." The latter was an hidalgo of Deza (who briefly served as interim alcaide following the removal of Pedro de Barrionuevo) and the former was his wife. Hortubia explained that he wanted to give the letters to "Bartolomé del Águila, so that he might show me favor at the port in every way he can."[71] The reference is to one Dr. Bartolomé del Águila, the alcaide and governor of El Puerto de Santa María from 1600 to 1617 and, presumably, a relation of doña Paula.[72] El Puerto was among the many possessions of the dukes of Medinaceli, and Juan Luis de la Cerda himself had appointed Águila.

Although Hortubia's letter to the Fadriques was intercepted, and that attempt to ingratiate himself to the governor was stillborn, his efforts demonstrate that the Dezanos in the royal jails were pursuing such courses of action. Romo, Mancebo, Ramírez, and Moraga somehow outmaneuvered the Holy Office and avoided the fate of their fellows. Incensed that the men had been returned to Cuenca, Licentiate Quiroga and newly appointed inquisitor, Dr. Juan de la Torre, wrote to Madrid emphasizing the offenses committed by the quartet, especially Miguel Ramírez, whom they considered "just as fine a Moor as his father" had been.[73]

The inquisitors in Cuenca surely expected Madrid's support in the face of this new twist, or at least its sympathy. Instead, on October 29, wearied by the trials of Deza's Moriscos and their burden on the treasury, the Suprema ordered Cuenca to set the four remaining prisoners at liberty and send them on their way.[74] Reluctantly, the tribunal complied and on November 3, 1611, released them without guard from the royal jails.[75] Of the men who were pressed into service at El Puerto de Santa María, only one is known to have survived. In March 1616, four and a half years into a three-year stint in the galleys, Juan Corazón (b. 1579) was finally mustered out. Thereafter incarcerated in the public jails of the city of Cartagena, he "suffered great need" before being released to comply with the royal order of expulsion.[76] This is nearly the last scrap of hard evidence about the fate of Deza's Moriscos.

Romo, Mancebo, Ramírez, and Moraga were expected to comply with the decree as well. But if they visited Deza before doing so, they found a town transformed. On July 8, 1611, Deza's remaining Moriscos had been forcibly deported. This was well after the expulsion had been implemented in most other areas, even in Castile, and may suggest that the Dezanos still had friends in high places or that their negotiations were more successful than the extant evidence suggests. As Antiguos, the town's Moriscos were among the select group permitted to sell their property before leaving, thereby avoiding sequestration.[77] They were, however, still expected to hand over one half of their jewels, money, and gold upon leaving Spain.[78]

Nothing suggests their neighbors enacted the vivid scene described in *Don Quixote*, where Old Christians felt solidarity with the expelled and lamented the loss of, at least, one particularly beloved Morisca, whom they "wanted to hide."[79] Other than the death in April 1627 of María Navarra, sister of Bernardino Almanzorre and mother of Morisco swineherd Gerónimo de Molina, no known Moriscos appear in the sacramental register after the expulsion.[80] In contrast to some other locales, notably the Campo de Calatrava, nothing indicates that any exiles returned home or attempted to do so.[81] They left a gaping hole in the life of Deza. The Upper Neighborhood was abandoned and remained largely uninhabited. Some industries, like the Morisco-run pottery works, went dormant for decades.[82] The town suffered economic and demographic decline, which was not fully overcome until the nineteenth century.

Little can be said concretely about the subsequent history of Deza's Moriscos. Bernard Vincent notes that documentation for the pertinent phase of the royal expulsion is "scarce." They might initially have been moved northward toward the checkpoint at Burgos, then over the Pyrenees into southern France.[83] Although the French king closed the crossing at Saint Jean de Luz to Moriscos in June 1610, he reopened it in

September.[84] Even with the detour through Burgos, that route was shorter than the alternative, which would have taken them south to embark at Cartagena in Murcia.[85] If they traveled by way of France, it is possible they remained there, for a small population of Moriscos settled in Languedoc, Provence, Aquitaine, and Bordeaux. These, however, were no freer to practice Islam than they had been in Spain. Instead, they were expected to embrace the "Catholic, Apostolic, and Roman faith." Some eventually settled into Roman obedience; others converted to Protestantism.[86]

A more likely sequence of events takes the Dezanos to North Africa, either by way of the French ports of Agde or Marseille or directly from Cartagena. This was the preferred destination for those who wanted to live as Muslims.[87] Some, like Juan Guerrero, were ready to go and dreamed of Algiers as a place where they could live *en nuestras anchuras*.[88] Others looked toward the Ottoman Empire as a safe haven. In May 1610, with the expulsion of the town's Moriscos just a matter of time, potter Francisco de Medrano announced, "If they took me to the land of the Moors and the Turk told me he would feed me and my children if I denied [*renegue*] God, I say that I'd deny God and Our Lady, for I'm poor and I don't have anything with which to sustain myself and I'll do it for the Turk who sustains me."[89] About two decades later, the Morisco known only as the *Refugiado de Túnez*, claimed to have prayed "night and day" for deliverance for himself and his co-religionists from the "Christian heretics" who had inflicted upon them so much "tribulation and danger." The Refugiado preferred being "in the lands of Islam even if it be naked."[90]

He was, at least, right that life in exile was hardly idyllic, but the realities of that life varied according to numerous factors, especially the point of disembarkation. Local tribes set upon some of the earliest exiles, Valencianos offloaded in Oran.[91] Those who survived the massacre settled in and around Algiers and Tremecén, and spread out along the coastlands, as did subsequent arrivals—principally from Extremadura, Aragon, and La Mancha.[92] The Andalusian émigrés who settled in Tetouan (even before the royal expulsion was enacted) continued to welcome Moriscos but, elsewhere in Morocco, the reception was generally inhospitable. Locals noted the Moriscos' foreign dress and language and expressed "little confidence" that they were true Muslims.[93]

Similarly, the three thousand Moriscos of Hornachos who, in the lead-up to the expulsion, disembarked southwest along the Atlantic coast at Salé received a cool welcome despite their firm commitment to Islam. Culturally and linguistically distinct from the city's inhabitants, the *hornacheros* were rejected and, consequently, established themselves on the other side of the Bou Regreg River, where they refortified a ruined settlement at the site of modern Rabat, the Kasbah of Salé. Subsequently, it swelled as a haven for some fifteen thousand Moriscos from Andalusia and Extremadura as the expulsion accelerated.[94] The community there remained ambivalent toward Spain; sometimes they were violently antagonistic (and became infamous for their piratical activities), but at other times they grew wistful and longed to return. By the early 1630s, several of the *ulama* denounced them for aiding Christians and supporting Spain.[95]

Perhaps the Dezanos' most likely destination was the Ottoman province of Tunisia, which drew in even those who had originally disembarked elsewhere in North Africa.[96] Unlike the more gradual process of arrival that occurred in Morocco and Algiers, perhaps as many as eighty thousand non-Arabic-speaking Moriscos of primarily Castilian and Aragonese origin descended upon and were processed through Tunis beginning in 1610. Those traveling thence from other North African locales were the particular prey of thieves and rarely arrived unscathed. And if they did arrive, their situation seemed little improved. In 1612, one Morisco described the state of affairs in stark, even frightening, terms: "Unfortunate are those who went to Tunis," since it was "a place where the poor could hardly find fresh water." Yet, somehow, it worked. Three decades later, that same commentator noted that what had once been a "purgatory for strangers in search of good land" had become "the best place" for Moriscos to settle.[97]

Assimilation was predictably difficult, but the new arrivals integrated rapidly. They established themselves in separate neighborhoods in Tunis and "ennobled" the kingdom by populating some twenty inland towns and villages.[98] They maintained a linguistic connection to Spain for some time and, in the 1620s and 1630s, constructed what Gerard Wiegers has called a "Maghrebi Morisco" identity that drew upon both Christian and Islamic elements. By the 1650s, however, both in Tunisia and Morocco, the younger generation was fully Arabized and "integrated into North African societies."[99] So, if Miguel Ramírez's daughter Ángela (b. 1603) arrived in Tunisia in 1611, she may well have remained caught between cultures—"cast out of Spain" for being a Moor, "taken for a Christian" in Tunisia—but culturally, at least, her children would have been virtually indistinguishable from those around them.[100]

"They were 400 people on foot," wrote a priest in the flyleaf of Deza's sacramental register, referring to the departure of the town's Moriscos.[101] In exile, they might well have been joined (or preceded) by those who had already fled—either in anticipation of an inquisitorial arrest or of the expulsion itself. There were also the stragglers who spent time in the custody of the Holy Office but were eventually reconciled before being passed onto the royal jails. Others, like Ana Guerrera, remained in penitential confinement for several years only to be released in order to comply with the royal expulsion. The reconciled Moriscos who were condemned to the galleys but, like Juan Corazón, survived the ordeal may have finally reunited with friends and family to embrace French Protestantism or North African Islam.[102] Or perhaps not. As for Miguel Ramírez and his companions, like the rest of the town's Moriscos, they disappear from the sources after their release from the royal jails in November 1611.[103] To the extent that Morisco Deza lived on in Spain, it did so by way of the memory and reputation of Román Ramírez, who became a cultural icon and the subject of legend.

Conclusion

During large portions of his life, Román Ramírez rubbed shoulders with those who cast long shadows: King Philip II, Gerónimo de Salamanca, several dukes of Medinaceli, and, in conjunction with his work as a healer and performer, various nobles, courtiers, *poderosos*, government officials, and inquisitors. Except for the last, perhaps, he liked their company and desired a place among them. Yet, surely, the most evocative point of contact between this singular figure and the wider world was his posthumous participation in the auto de fé celebrated in Toledo on March 5, 1600. Inquisitor General Cardinal Fernando Niño de Guevara needed the Morisco because he had no heretics to burn—either in person or in effigy.[1] The presence of the royal couple, the Duke of Lerma, and other high profile figures demanded a good show, an appropriately sober demonstration to accompany King Philip's oath to defend the faith and his unconditional promise of support for the Holy Office.[2] Coincidentally in Madrid as this crisis unfolded, Francisco de Arganda, the bogeyman of Deza's Moriscos, offered a solution.[3] He brought Ramírez to the Suprema's attention and then repeatedly urged Cifuentes de Loarte, his senior colleague in Cuenca, to conclude the trial with all haste, box up the remains, and have them sent onto Toledo.

As it happened, the auto took place at a critical moment in the Spanish debate about purity of blood (*limpieza de sangre*) and the future of relations between Old Christians and Jewish and Muslim Conversos. Beginning in the mid-1400s a wide range of peninsular institutions and organizations—religious orders, universities, towns and cities, governmental agencies, and so forth—promulgated a series of statutes that restricted the opportunities available to Moriscos and Judeoconversos and prioritized *limpieza de sangre* over other considerations. The Holy Office, in particular, became heavily involved in policing blood purity. In spring 1599, however, just as Ramírez was being transported to Cuenca, Dominican theologian Agustín Salucio published a major critique of the limpieza statutes, his *Discurso . . . acerca de la justicia y buen gobierno de España en los Estatutos de limpieza de sangre.*[4]

The moment seemed right for change. Encouraged by Philip II, Inquisitor General Portocarrero had convened a study group in 1596 to consider how the statutes might be attenuated.[5] Although the king's death in 1598 derailed that project, Salucio could still anticipate strong support for his reforms among senior ecclesiastical officeholders, the royal favorite Lerma, and the members of the Cortes of Castile. Even the Inquisition itself was divided on the issue.[6] Portocarrera's successor, Niño de Guevara, also favored reform and wrote to Philip III in support of Salucio in August 1599.[7] The following year he responded to queries from the Council of State with a *memorial* in which he rejected outright the idea of expulsion for Moriscos and proposed instead a plan of evangelization that would help them internalize Christianity over time.[8] If this truly was his agenda, then the cardinal's inclusion of Ramírez in the auto of March 1600 was a serious and strategic miscalculation. Lerma and others must have been similarly dismayed. The recitation of the Morisco's crimes— above all the way his condemnation tied diabolism, crypto-Islam, and anti-monarchical sentiments together in a fashion that his trial had never established—fell like a bombshell and undermined efforts to move the new king toward integrating his subjects and rolling back purity statutes.

The royal couple had been married less than a year when they attended the auto. The young queen had only recently arrived in Spain and was, perhaps, still unaccustomed to Spanish ways. Yet Queen Margaret had grown up in Austria amidst a looming Ottoman threat; she was predisposed to assume the worst of Moriscos.[9] Ramírez merely confirmed her expectations. After his condemnation, she became more rigid and insistent. Writing in 1613 but reflecting upon the queen's state of mind around the time of the auto, one expulsion apologist explained:

When her most serene highness the Queen saw how much his Majesty favoured the persecution of the Sect of Muhammad (because she had been brought up in constant fear of Turkish invasion of the lands of her father, the Archduke Charles, and of her brother, Don Ferdinand), she earnestly beseeched him to expel them from Spain.

In particular, he claimed, she feared raising children in a land where Moors roamed free and corsairs plied coastal waters.[10]

In the short term, Margaret urged an invasion of Algeria to ease the threat, and even Lerma supported the venture to please the queen. The campaign was a disaster, in part because Aragonese Moriscos conspired with the Ottoman sultan and the kings of Algeria and Morocco. At least that was the rumor. In 1601 the "miracle bell" of Velilla (Zaragoza), which sounded only (and without being acted upon physically) in conjunction with significant events, was heard to ring out, and commentators subsequently and repeatedly connected it to the failure of the Algerian expedition and Morisco treachery.[11] Elsewhere, the years 1602 to 1603 saw numerous "celestial portents" that interpreters read as "indications of God's anger at the sacrilege and blasphemy of the Moriscos."[12] When Philip and Margaret visited Deza in 1602 all of this must have been on their minds. Were they aware that Lope de Arcos, the leader of the Morisco community after the death of Alexo Gorgoz, was town magistrate during their visit? Thanks in part to the queen's continued efforts, by 1609 Philip was ready "to reveal his heart's secret" to the Council of State: the decision to expel the Moriscos.[13]

The opportunity for change had come and gone. Only in June 1611, a few weeks before the Dezanos were expelled, did the Council of State finally address the issue of blood purity by setting a two hundred-year limit to the enforcement of limpieza statutes for Moriscos.[14] The Cortes was even slower to return to the topic, and when they did in 1618 one member noted that while many wanted to see change, "few dared to engage" such a "dangerous and even hateful" topic.[15] In 1621, when Licentiate Bernardino Bonifacio Barnuevo, son and grandson of Román's nemeses and now a canon in Seville, published his account of King Philip's funerary monument in Madrid, he emphasized the monarch's role as triumphant *Maureorum expulsor omnium virtutum exemplar*—expeller of the Moors, exemplar of all virtues.[16]

By way of contrast, the Inquisition expressly ordered all memory of Román Ramírez expunged from "the face of the earth," apart from his sentence and the penitential habit hanging in Deza's parish church.[17] But rather the reverse happened. Instead, the Morisco became a byword in Spanish culture. The tribunal at Cuenca had fixed him to the medieval exegetical tradition, based on 1 John 2:18, of the non-eschatological antichrist—"a human with devilish connections"—a figure often conflated with or connected to Mohammed and to Islam more generally.[18] In Román's case that connection resonated for many who attended his condemnation or heard about it afterward.

Clear early evidence of this appears in Jesuit Martín Delrio's *Disquisitionum magicarum*, originally printed from 1599–1600 in three octavo volumes. But soon after the first edition appeared, the author learned of Ramírez and incorporated a version of his story into a revised edition.[19] Delrio (1551–1608) wrote in Latin rather than Spanish—the language of the trial—but he drew this new material from a manuscript copy of the Morisco's sentencing, which he had received from a now unknown informant. The many repeated details and turns of phrases, as well as Delrio's own comments, testify to the source.[20] Inquisitorial trial documents were not typically available to those unaffiliated with the Holy Office, and it is all the more remarkable that the information traveled from Spain to the Jesuit college in Leuven, where Delrio was working at the time. Nevertheless, all subsequent editions of *Disquisitionum* featured a version of Ramírez's exploits in a section that addressed the question: "What power does magic or an evil spirit have over a soul which is conjoined to a body and animates it?"[21]

The question thus framed may seem abstruse, but it raised a major, even fundamental, issue: whether and how magic and demons interacted with the physical world and, in particular, human beings. Rather than positing a supernatural explanation, Delrio suggested that both magic and demons operated within the preternatural realm, that aspect of creation which "does not go beyond the boundaries of the natural order but is said simply to go beyond reasonable explanation." Nevertheless, "most people" were unaware of this distinction and so "they usually call it 'supernatural' too."[22] Appropriately, Delrio positioned Ramírez here in the murky territory between the natural and supernatural, where "most people" could not clearly discern what was going on.

Delrio emphasized that the Morisco "united in his person several aspects of magic." He was a relapsed heretic, who having been absolved once of Islamizing returned to it later in life. But to that was added "crime to crime and sin to sin": a pact with an evil spirit, whom he "worshipped" and to whom he "dedicated his soul" in exchange for "knowledge of and expertise in the cure of many secret, hidden illnesses, by means of herbs, fumigations, and superstitious incantations." With the "help of the evil spirit," he also "persuaded people that he had a wide and detailed knowledge of both sacred and profane literature, and that he had a good memory." He conducted public recitations and swindled his audience out of money, thereby accumulating "not a little power." A draught given to him by a relative, who likewise "enjoyed the familiarity of an evil spirit," enhanced Ramírez's memory, and Delrio further implicated him in the use of illicit magic to travel great distances quickly, restore the lost (both objects and people), obtain otherwise unknowable information, and command demons to possess and torment people whom he then exorcised at his convenience for financial gain.[23]

Delrio's account of Ramírez's deeds was superficial and lacked many of the details offered by witnesses or the accused in his inquisitorial trial, but that superficiality allowed the story to be reshaped more easily. That is precisely what the playwright Juan Ruiz de Alarcón (1580–1639) did in a second work that cemented the Morisco's notoriety. The date of composition for Alarcón's *Quien mal anda en mal acaba* is debated. Antonio Castro Leal contended that it was written in the first few years of the seventeenth century, immediately following Ramírez's death.[24] But Luis Fernández-Guerra has dated it to ca. 1617, suggesting the play was inspired by the November 1616 auto de fé in Toledo at which Cardinal Bernardo Sandoval y Rojas, the inquisitor general and uncle to the Duke of Lerma, astonished Madrid by pardoning one and all. The court, Fernández-Guerra hypothesizes, buzzed with "stories and anecdotes of the auto of 1600," Ramírez's auto, which had been attended by the cardinal's illustrious nephew.[25]

Whatever the role of the rumor mill, Alarcón probably learned some details about the Morisco directly from Delrio, since the two men briefly overlapped at the University of Salamanca. Delrio began lecturing for the law faculty in summer 1604 (having published his revised version of *Disquisitionum* the previous March) and Alarcón completed studies for a licentiate degree in the same subject in 1605.[26] This may provide some support for Castro Leal's early dating of the play, particularly since Fernández-Guerra offers no specific evidence for his claim that court gossip inspired Alarcón to write the play after November 1616. Even if the later date is correct, the playwright would still have known Delrio's account.

Quien mal anda en mal acaba is a comedy in which "magic takes the form of an express demonic pact entered into by the illiterate *morisco* Román Ramírez out of lust for the beautiful doña Aldonza [de Meneses]," a noblewoman of Deza.[27] An impoverished and shabby version of the Dezano falls for Aldonza and casts himself into the devil's power. In exchange for his soul, the Morisco is made to appear a physician and attempts to eliminate a rival for Aldonza's affection and so gain his *enamorada*.[28] All is set right in the end and Román gets his just desserts, while the lady and her true love are reunited. Alarcón fabricated the entire plot, which bears little resemblance to historical events or even to the accusations made against Ramírez.

The early modern period never saw a published version of the play. Instead, it was compiled in the nineteenth century from various surviving manuscript copies.[29] In fact, outside of the many printings of Delrio, no literary or historical work mentioned Ramírez's name until the late nineteenth century. Yet it is difficult not to find echoes of his story in surprising places. For example, the seventeenth-century plays *Vida y muerte del falso profeta Mahoma* and *El profeta falso Mahoma*, the latter by Francisco de Rojas Zorrilla and first performed in 1635, both reflect elements of Ramírez's story. Unusually for Spain, they depict Mohammed on stage as a central character and, more particularly, as one who knew enough about Christianity to know it was true, and Islam false, but nevertheless vacillated between them.[30] Ultimately, he chose the latter for power and selfish ambition, which drove him to sell his soul to the devil. He was attended in the Rojas play by the demon Luzbel, which granted him magical powers to triumph over his adversaries, and he sought the overthrow of a Christian ruler (the Emperor Heraclius) but was brought low in the end.[31] This Mohammed was, as the Christian character Teodoro comments in *Vida y muerte*, a "false prophet, precursor of the Antichrist" (lines 2730–31). Here we find Mohammed depicted as the non-eschatological antichrist as shaped by the legend of Román Ramírez.

Similarly, the strong resonance between Ramírez and the work of Miguel de Cervantes has struck virtually every student of the Morisco, leading some to suggest that knowledge of what happened at the auto of 1600 fired Cervantes's imagination. This may well be the case. After all, the book's narrator (Cervantes?) claimed to have stumbled upon the full manuscript copy of Quixote's adventures—purportedly composed by the Moorish enchanter and storyteller Cide Hamete Benengeli—in Toledo's Alcaná market, near where Ramírez made his final performance. But gossip may not be the only point of contact, for the information contained in the Morisco's sentence of condemnation cannot account for the surprising number of possible allusions and nods made to him in *Don Quixote*, even if we also bring in Delrio's comments and Alarcón's play (presuming the earlier date of composition). Either we are tilting at windmills or some other interaction must have occurred.

A few striking parallels exist between the two men's lives: both Cervantes and Ramírez worked as tax collectors, frequently found themselves behind bars, and attempted jailbreaks. But nothing suggests they crossed paths during any of these escapades. Cervantes returned from five years of captivity in Algiers at the close of 1580, just as Ramírez wrapped up his most public period. For the years that followed he was, until his transportation to Cuenca, at home far more often than he was away. Cervantes was jailed in 1592 in Castro del Río (Córdoba) and again from 1597 to 1601 in Seville. After his release, he lived in Madrid for a time before resurfacing in Valladolid a few years later. One biographer hypothesized that he worked there "drafting petitions and drawing up statements of claims" for litigants at the Royal Appellate Court.[32] The notion is interesting, for those same years saw Dezanos frequently in Valladolid, the venue for the crucial suits between the town and the duke as well as between the Upper and Lower Neighborhoods. Remarkably, in 1604 Cervantes submitted the first part of *Don Quixote* for approval to Gil Ramírez de Arellano, the very judge who had refused to share Román with his rival a decade earlier in Soria and who, a few years later, had adjudicated the case involving Deza's Moriscos and Ramírez's presumptive father-in-law.[33] But these connections are tenuous. No, the most likely point of contact, if one is to be found at all, is earlier—1567–68 when both Ramírez and Cervantes were in Madrid, at the beginning of their careers as artists and trying to make a place for themselves at court.[34]

Speculating in this way in the absence of any positive historical evidence is rarely profitable, but that has not kept scholars from noting *Don Quixote*'s apparent evocation of the Morisco of Deza, nor should it. Seeking hidden Morisco treasure rarely ends well, but sometimes we find loot. Julio Caro Baroja, Leonard Harvey, Luis Bernabé Pons, Hilaire Kallendorf, and others, noting an apparent indebtedness, have all wondered whether the Ramírez affair was on Cervantes's mind as he drafted the first part of the book in the years immediately following the Morisco's death.[35] Caro Baroja could not help but imagine that Ramírez would have gotten along well with the Knight of the Sorrowful Countenance—*hubiera hecho buenas migas*—far better than the cura or barber. Both Ramírez and Quixote, he explained, were *perdidos por los libros de caballería*.[36] The Morisco too owned and composed chivalric tales, was an amuser and protégé of a duke, and rode upon a magic flying horse. They had similar libraries, dry brains, and hot tempers. Even Cervantes's framing mechanism, by which he made his novel into a translation of a work composed by Benengeli—an enchanter at once Moorish and diabolical[37]—"appears in a new perspective in light of the extraordinary similarities" between Quixote and Ramírez.[38] Was it a coincidence that Ruiz de Alarcón called his Moorish enchanter's fictional ladylove Aldonza, the actual name of the woman whom don Quixote dubbed Dulcinea?

Consider the scene in part one of *Don Quixote*, where the knight errant and his squire come upon a group of manacled convicts being transported to the galleys. The passage echoes with elements of Ramírez's own story—Zocodover Plaza appears and a jailbreak occurs; one convict is a performer, another is a sorcerer and herbalist, yet another is a "great talker" (165–67). The most dangerous of the lot—although his specific crimes remain obscure—is a man of contested identity: Ginés de Pasamonte, alias Ginesillo de Parapilla (although he denies the latter name). He "alone had committed more crimes than all the rest combined," and thereby combines in himself all the others and "respond[s] for all of them" (168, 171). The reader learns that Pasamonte, who has been condemned to ten years in the galleys (i.e., condemned to "civil death" [168]), "wrote his own history himself, as fine as you please," and that he "pawned it for two hundred *reales*." Ramírez tells inquisitors he received three hundred for his unfinished *Florisdoro de Grecia*. *The Life of Ginés de Pasamonte* is no more complete—"How can it be if my life isn't finished yet?" Pasamonte is a "liar," he is "clever" and "unfortunate," for "misfortunes always pursue the talented" (168–69).

When Pasamonte reappears in part two, he comes in the guise of Master Pedro, a puppeteer (and, hence, as a version of Cide Hamete Benengeli himself, the storyteller who pulls the strings throughout the book).[39] "He's a famous puppet master who's been traveling the Aragonese side of La Mancha for some time," the innkeeper informs don Quixote, adding, "He also has with him a monkey with the rarest talent ever seen among monkeys or imagined among men, because if he's asked something, he pays attention to what he's asked, then jumps onto his master's shoulders and goes up to his ear and tells him the answer to the question" (624). The monkey, like Ramírez's Liarde, is fickle about answering; he knows something about the past and the present but can only conjecture about the future.[40] This information keys the innkeeper, who is "amazed that [Pedro] has not been denounced to the Holy Office," into the fact that the puppeteer "must have made some agreement with the devil to grant this talent to the monkey . . . and when he is rich the devil will take his soul" (626). It turns out, however, that just as Ramírez's ability to memorize and recite had a natural explanation, albeit one dependent upon deception, so too the monkey: "Before [Pedro] would enter any village where he was taking his puppet theater and monkey, he would learn in a nearby village, or from anyone he could, what specific things had happened in the village and to whom," then he would "commit them to memory" (637). Ginés-Pedro is no simple calque of Ramírez, but he does reek of him.

In the late seventeenth or early in the eighteenth century a woodcut (perhaps by Diego Obregón [fl. 1658–99] but more likely not) was fashioned to depict the famous scene in which the cura, aided by the barber, conducts an inquisition upon don Quixote's library. They pardon a few of the books, but most are given over to his housekeeper to be burned in a domestic auto de fé. The chapter is brilliant and hilarious. But why does the parish cura in this woodcut bear an uncanny resemblance to Fernando Niño de Guevara, who presided over Ramírez's auto?[41] Did the artist, in thinking about that scene, recall another man who had been *perdido por los libros de caballería* and connect the two as have many others? Did their stories somehow become interwoven in the decades after they became famous? At a yet more folksy level, did Román Ramírez become immortalized, as Grace Magnier Heney proposes, in the famous Spanish tongue twister about Ramón Ramírez, who cut off the tail of San Roque's dog?[42] More than four centuries after his death, our Morisco (like don Quixote) still leads those who seek to uncover his secrets into tortuous byways that end with too many question marks and not enough periods.

The point here is not to suggest that further study of Román Ramírez in particular or the Moriscos of Deza more generally will illuminate the hidden meaning of *Don Quixote* or reveal the secret depths of Philip III's heart. Rather, all of this is to make a point broadly about the value that might be had in the study of local history and the light it can shine on some of the larger scholarly debates about early modern Spain. As Deza's story suggests, studying the local context within which the experiences and expulsions of Spain's Moriscos unfolded pays dividends. After all, although the expulsion successfully did away with the town's Moriscos, elsewhere—in Villarrubia, for example—a rather different context produced substantially different results. Instead of viewing successful expulsions as direct consequences of royal decrees and dismissing failed expulsions as somehow anomalous, the entire process should instead take account the people involved, the distinctive elements of the places in which they lived, and the consequences of those outcomes both locally and more broadly.

For Deza, of course, the patronage offered by Dukes Juan and Juan Luis was critical. And the latter's sudden death, precipitating the accession of an infant son ruled by his grandfather, spelled disaster for the Moriscos. But great nobles were not the only ones pulling the strings. What happened in Deza makes no sense without Bernardino Almanzorre, Ana de Almoravi, and Pedro el Cañamenero extending the influence of Aragonese Islam into Castile; the visits of inquisitors Reynoso, de la Madriz, and Arganda between 1569–81; or the untimely revelation of the denunciations hidden by Licentiate Miguel Benito. Would the town's Old Christians have put up a fight to resist the expulsion of their Moriscos had Miguel García Serrano not already and so thoroughly poisoned the well?

The story of Deza's Moriscos—like their counterparts elsewhere—is not one of monolithic uniformity. Some, like María Navarra, Gerónimo de Molina, and Diego Zamorano embraced Christianity and found themselves wounding and wounded by family members and former friends. But even among those who continued to regard Islam as the better Law for the salvation of their souls, various strategies emerged with predictable consequences in the decades after the Edict of Grace, just as different circles of Islamic instruction had coalesced in earlier years. Some internalized their convictions, making them matters of the heart, but found that doing so led them in the direction of acculturation; others lived out their religion in times and places that enabled them to avoid the watchful gaze of neighbors, but they always longed for more: a broad land where they could be Muslims *en sus anchuras*. Among women, a domestic Islam thrived and spread from generation to generation and house to house, but that inclination to sociability carried risks and endangered the entire community; Ana Guerrera knew too much when she was too young.

Even within the community of crypto-Islamic Moriscos major divisions existed—between the Cebeas and Romos, or between the seigniorial and town factions. But moments of crisis and of celebration could also draw the community together. It took the arrests of 1607 to cool the feud between the Cebeas and Romos but it happened. Nor should we forget that the town did not always divide along expected lines. Recall the Old Christian boy dispatched by his father in November 1607 to warn Juan Guerrero that inquisitorial agents had come to town. Old Christians and Moriscos worked for and with, bought from, and sold to one another; they collaborated in the town council and unified against over-mighty chief magistrates; they attended church and theater together; they sent their children to the same schools and joined the same confraternities. Some became friends. Old Christians—clerics, hidalgos, and commoners—celebrated Morisco betrothals; a few Moriscos married Old Christians. The actions of several Old Christians in town suggest that not everyone felt comfortable about inquisitorial inquiries or the expulsion, even if very few did much to impede them.

In many cases, archival sources exist that would allow scholars to sketch nuanced depictions of Moriscos that improve upon hackneyed portrayals of passivity, monolithic unity, and irreconcilable incompatibility with Old Christian neighbors. Admittedly, approaching Morisco history as local history risks myopia by focusing on the particular at the expense of the general. One all too easily loses sight of the broader historical context when overwhelmed by provincial details. Keeping those elements in balance here has proved challenging. Nevertheless, the utterly unique story of the people who lived in one small town during the Morisco century suggests that a local approach to the Morisco problem offers definite advantages over abstract depictions and top-down analyses, especially for our understanding of social interactions. It shows not only the tensions between Moriscos and Old Christians but also their collaboration. It demonstrates not only a sense of what Moriscos were like in a specific context but also the differences and divisions that existed among them, not least of all between generations, genders, and socioeconomic groups. It reveals how external institutions and individuals interacted with townsfolk, and that the impact of those encounters went in both directions. And it exposes the fact that thinking of something like the Expulsion as a phenomenon brought to bear upon a community by outsiders without understanding the context within which it was to occur takes far too much for granted.

Notes

1. Modern historiography (not to mention the contemporary defenders of the Expulsion or their heirs) bears witness of this. See, for example, Janer, *Condición social*; Danvila y Collado, *La expulsión*; Boronat y Barrachina, *Los moriscos españoles*; and even the more sympathetic portrayal offered by Lea, *The Moriscos of Spain*.

2. "Moriscos of La Mancha," 1068.

3. García Avilés, *Los moriscos del Valle de Ricote*, 27–44.

4. *Pedro de Valencia*, 29–30.

5. On the use of the phrase, see Perceval, *Todos son uno*.

6. Chejne, *Islam and the West*, 174, n. 2. The author provides a useful survey of the older historiographical debates about Moriscos.

7. *Tolerance and Coexistence*, 8.

8. See, for example, Núñez de Muley, *Memorandum*, 1–54 and Barrios Aguilera and García-Arenal, *¿La historia inventada?*, 83–136.

9. *Imperial Spain*, 301.

10. *Imperial Spain*, 302.

11. *Inquisición y moriscos*, 18. See also her "Moriscos de la región de Cuenca," 152. More recently, she has revised her position on this issue. See her "Religious Dissent," 893–94.

12. *Spain under the Habsburgs*, 2:48.

13. *Medicina, ciencia, y minorías marginadas*, 27.

14. Domínguez Ortiz and Vincent, *Historia de los moriscos*; Tapia Sánchez, *La comunidad morisca*; and Benítez Sánchez-Blanco, *Moriscos y cristianos*.

15. Dadson, *Tolerance and Coexistence*, 3. There are, as Dadson notes, a growing number of (especially hispanophone) historians working to place Morisco communities within local contexts (*Los moriscos de Villarrubia*, 17–18). To his

list, I would add García Pedraza, *Actitudes* (on Granada) and Cavanaugh, "The Morisco Problem" (on Valladolid).

16. *Tolerance and Coexistence*, 1.

17. "Testing the Limits," 214.

18. Dadson, *Tolerance and Coexistence*, 35.

19. To this point Dadson comments, "It would be as wrong to claim that all Moriscos in Spain were assimilated by the early seventeenth century as it would be to claim that none was, to deny that numerous groups were assimilated or well on the way to being so. The process is complex and varied, with few obvious patterns to help us. One group of Moriscos in rural Castile or Exremadura might be assimilated while those a few kilometres away were not" (*Tolerance and Coexistence*, 241).

20. Christian, *Local Religion*, 4.

21. Caro Baroja, *Vidas Mágicas*, 309–28; Harvey, "Oral Composition," 270–86; and García-Ballester, *Medicina, ciencia y minorías marginadas*.

22. Barrow, *The Zincali*, 187, proposed that the incantation's title referred to a root used by gypsies and named after Satan, the "good baron" (or *buen barón*). However, the story may also echo the *Isra*, a journey taken by Mohammed from Mecca to Jerusalem on the back of a heavenly steed in a single night. And several commentators have suggested a possible connection to Clavileño, the supposedly magic flying horse in *Don Quixote* (pt. 2, chs. 40–41), 713–27.

23. ADC, leg. 343, exp. 4876, fols. 12v-13r and 232v-33r.

24. ARCV RE, caja 1193, exp. 47.

25. ADM, leg. 43, doc. 100.

26. ADC, leg. 343, exp. 4876, fol. 228r.

27. ADC, leg. 343, exp. 4876, fol. 13v. Román referred to this suit at fol. 197v and linked it explicitly to the animosity of an anti-ducal faction in Deza. Unfortunately, no evidence of the case mentioned by Bonifacio has come to light in the ducal archives.

28. AHMD, caja 26/4, fol. 6r-v. For Bonifacio's role in local politics, see RAH CS, doc. 58.630 M-144, fols. 95–108.

29. Harvey, "Oral Composition," 280.

30. Ramírez identified Bonifacio as an enemy at ADC, leg. 343, exp. 4876, fols. 232v-33r, when asked about the *bon y varón* incantation.

31. See O'Banion, "'They will know our hearts,'" 193–217.

32. ADC, leg. 343, exp. 4876, fol. 212v.

1. TOWNS, CONTOURS, AND KINGDOMS

1. Alcalde, "Los caminos reales," 265–84 and "Caminería histórica," 55–75.

2. Alcalde, *Deza*, 1:158–62.

3. Alcalde, *Deza*, 1:174–75.

4. Alcalde, *Deza*, 1:185–93.

5. Alcalde, *Deza*, 1:197.

6. The details of the story, told by Fernán Pérez de Guzmán, are difficult to credit given Deza's large population of resident *mudéjares* only a few decades later. See *Crónica de los reyes de Castilla*, 2:467 and Alcalde, *Deza*, 1:199–202.

7. Alcalde, *Deza*, 1:208–9.

8. García-Arenal, "Los Moriscos de la región de Cuenca," 193. Similar trends occurred elsewhere, notably Villarrubia de los Ojos (Dadson, *Los moriscos de Villarrubia*, 176–90).

9. AHMD, leg. 238 (Padrones de Repartimiento, 1586–1611).

10. Alcalde, *Deza*, 1:210–11.

11. See, for example, the 1533 inquisitorial case against local apothecary Francisco Núñez, who tried to help his *judeoconverso* father, Diego, avoid an entanglement with the Holy Office. ADC, leg. 148, exp. 1787 (inquisitorial trial of Francisco Núñez, confession of the accused, January 18, 1533). At least two Jewish Conversos, *bachilleres* Juan Ruiz (d. 1589) and Juan de Ozuel (d. 1605), became priests later in the century (ADC, libro 320, fol. 21r).

12. Cantera Montenegro, "La comunidad Morisca de Ágreda," 11–42.

13. Cantera Montenegro, "Las comunidades mudéjares de Osma y Sigüenza," 142–45. This makes Deza's Morisco population roughly equal in size and proportion to that of Villarrubia de los Ojos in the Campo de Calatrava (Dadson, *Los moriscos de Villarrubia*, 59). Proportionally both mirrored the Morisco population of Daimiel although the total number of Moriscos there was greater, around 500 in 1538 (Dedieu, *L'administration*, 87).

14. In 1530 Francisco de Rebolledo claimed to have "turned Christian" in about 1500, two years before Deza's other *mudéjares*. But the statement was made as part of an attack against a rival and Francisco was known as a vicious slanderer. Nevertheless, in favor of his claim, he was also regarded as a drunkard, which suggests that he had moved further away from Islam than most other New Moorish Converts. See ADC, leg. 116, exp. 1590 (inquisitorial trial of Juan López, testimony of Francisco de Rebolledo, September 7, 1530, and testimony of Rodrigo Hernández Abarca, November 22, 1558).

15. Detractors like Damián Fonseca (*Justa expulsión*, 174) and Pedro Aznar Cardona (*Expulsión justificada*, fol. 63r) compared Morisco growth to the multiplication of rabbits and the spread of "bad weeds." They argued that, indifferent to the Christian attachment to the celibate life, religious vocation, or virginity, virtually all Moriscos married young—eleven for girls and twelve for boys—and engaged in polygamy. This growth would, it was feared, overwhelm Old Christians by out-producing them. More recent studies have moderated or contradicted this claim to fecundity. Among them, see Bernard Vincent, "50,000 Moriscos almerienses," 507 and "El Albaicín de Granada,"

133–34 and 136; Tapia Sánchez, *La comunidad Morisca de Ávila*, 400; and Aranda Doncel, *Los moriscos en tierras de Córdoba*, 93.

16. Cardaillac, *Moriscos y cristianos*, 21–31; Harvey, *Muslims in Spain*, 112–13; García-Arenal, *Inquisición y moriscos*, 10; and Tueller, *Good and Faithful Christians*, 206.

17. *Los moriscos de Villarrubia*, 163–68.

18. See Herzog, *Defining Nations*, 17–42.

19. On this issue, see especially the discussions by Bergmann, "The Exclusion of the Feminine," 128; Lehfeldt, *Religious Women*, 200; and Perry, *Gender and Disorder*, 68–69.

20. See, for example, O'Banion, *The Sacrament of Penance*, 124–33; Lehfeldt, *Religious Women*, 2; Poska, *Women and Authority*; and Casey, *Family and Community*, 157.

21. Widows in early modern Spain, especially elite widows, stood in a relatively privileged position that afforded them substantial personal freedom, control over their property, finances, children, and even the ability to litigate on their own behalf. See Coolidge, *Guardianship*, 6–9 and 17–40; and Vassberg, "The Status of Widows," 180–95.

22. ADM, leg. 60, doc. 40, fol. 1r.

23. ADC leg. 375, exp. 5308 (inquisitorial trial of María la Burgueña, testimony of Gerónimo Molino, September 15, 1610) and leg. 372, exp. 5274 (inquisitorial trial of Ana la Buena, testimony of Librada Gonzáles, December 21, 1608).

24. ADC, leg. 367, exp. 5180 (inquisitorial trial of Lope Guerrero el viejo, testimony of Juan Guerrero, February 28, 1608).

25. See Perry, *Handless Maiden*, 27–37.

26. See, for example, AHMD, leg. 16a, doc. 7 (letter dated August 8, 1602).

27. ARCV SH, caja 746, doc. 11; caja 847, doc. 4; caja 705, doc. 10; caja 710, doc. 1; caja 463, doc. 4; caja 318, doc. 8; caja 746, doc. 11; caja 683, doc. 14; caja 1676, doc. 1; caja 777, doc. 23; caja 647, doc. 12; caja 46, doc. 5; caja 630, doc. 19; caja 446, doc. 11; caja 46, doc. 5; ARCV RE, caja 1584, doc. 31; caja 1632, doc. 72; caja 1641, doc. 80; caja 1776, doc. 46.

28. Alcalde, *Deza*, 1:224–26.

29. AHDOS APD, leg. 160, doc. 17; ARCV RE, caja 373, doc. 21; and ARCV PC, caja 203, doc. 5.

30. See ARCV SH, caja, 46, doc. 5 and ARCV RE, caja 1151, doc. 26.

31. ARCV RE, caja 1131, doc. 47.

32. ADC, libro 317, fol. 462v.

33. ADC, libro 317, fol. 462r.

34. ADM AH, leg. 188, doc. 27, fol. 1v.

35. ADC, leg. 375, exp. 5324 (inquisitorial trial of Ana de Hortubia, testimony of Juan Guerrero, December 4, 1607).

36. MacKay, *"Lazy, Improvident People,"* 19.

37. Sánchez León, "Town and country in Castile," 286–87. For a local example, see the efforts of the council to establish a standardized measurement for wheat in town despite the opposition of Deza's millers (AHPS AMD, leg. 26.556, doc. 15).

38. ADM, leg. 60, doc. 29 and Alcalde, *Deza*, 1:242–43.

39. ADC, libro 317, fols. 111r and 122v-23r (*This Happened*, 89–90 and 103–5).

40. Juan de Cieli identified himself as a bricklayer and carpenter: ADC, leg. 247, exp. 3315 and leg. 783, exp. 2932. Francisco de Miranda and several of his relatives were painters: ADC, leg. 763, exp. 1077 (inquisitorial trial of Francisco de Miranda el menor, portada, 1571).

41. ADC, leg. 376, exp. 5333 (inquisitorial trial of Leonor de Hortubia, first audience of the accused, January 28, 1571); leg. 362, exp. 5142 (inquisitorial trial of Miguel Ramírez, testimony of Juan Manrique de Peña, March 7, 1604); leg. 767, exp. 1392 (inquisitorial trial of Miguel Ruiz, testimony of Juan de Frias, [1613]); leg. 785, exp. 3338 (inquisitorial trial of Diego de Ozuel, testimony of Catalina Velasco, April 13, 1624); and leg. 249, exp. 3350 (inquisitorial trial of Diego de Hortubia, testimony of Pedro Rubio, January 10, 1570).

42. ADC, leg. 767, exp. 1392 (inquisitorial trial of Miguel Ruiz, testimony of Juan de Frias, [1613]); and leg. 361, exp. 5131 (inquisitorial trial of Ana Guerrera, testimony of Alonso de Santos, May 16, 1605).

43. ADC, leg. 88, exp. 1283; leg. 789, exp. 2456; leg. 719, exp. 934; leg. 376, exp. 5332; leg. 355, exp. 5042; leg. 785, exp. 3338; leg. 99, exp. 144; leg. 758, exp. 595; leg. 212, exp. 2449; leg. 247, exp. 3327; leg. 783, exp. 2931; leg. 763, exp. 1094; and libro 317, fol. 450r.

44. The taverns of Deza paid 25,0000 mrs. in annual rents and the mesones paid 12,000 (ADM, leg. 44, doc. 19, fol. 1r). In the 1590s both Old Christians and Moriscos (including a woman: Catalina de Almazul) operated *mesones* (AHPS AMD, leg. 26.556, docs. 20 and 23).

45. ARCV RE, caja 2285, doc. 18, fol. 1r-v.

46. ADC, leg. 365, exp. 5166 (inquisitorial trial of Ana Mendoza, response to the accusations [cap. 4], February 26, 1610).

47. ADC, libro 317, fol. 468r. The rent for the *carniceria* was 10,000 mrs. per annum. ADM, leg. 44, doc. 19, fol. 1r and leg. 44, doc. 26, fol. 1r.

48. Clouse, *Medicine, Government, and Public Health*, 148–49.

49. Physicians: ADC, leg. 177, exp. 1598 (inquisitorial trial of María de la Castilla, testimony of Isabel Núñez) and leg. 209, exp. 2414 (inquisitorial trial of María de Hortubia, testimony of Antonio Páez, July 6, 1558); AHMD, caja 238, doc. 15 (Padrón de repartimiento del salario del médico, 1609); and AHN, leg. 1924, exp. 19, fol. 62v. Surgeons: AHN, Inq., leg. 1924, exp. 19, fol. 56v and ARCV RE, caja 1151, doc. 26, fol. 2v. Apothecaries: ADC, leg. 148, exp. 1787 (inquisitorial trial of Francisco Nuñez, January 18, 1533) and ARCV RE, caja 2285, doc. 18, fol. 2r.

Like physicians, apothecaries received remuneration from the town. See AHMD, caja 16a, doc. 6 (February 21, 1595); leg. 15b, doc. 2 (June 1, 1568); and leg. 1, doc. 41 (October 25, 1636).

50. See Blécourt and Usborne, "Situating 'alternative medicine,'" 283–85 and Jütte, "Introduction," 1–10 for helpful comments about the relationship between orthodox and alternative medicine in early modern Europe.

51. See García-Ballester, *Los Moriscos y la medicina*; "Academicism versus empiricism," 246–70; and "Inquisition and Minority Medical Practitioners," 156–91.

52. See also Dadson, "Literacy and Education," 1011–37; Kagan, *Students and Society*, 23; Eisenberg, *Romances of Chivalry*, 105–6; and Bennassar, *Valladolid en el Siglo de Oro*, 468–69.

53. García Díaz, "Escritura y clases populares," 73.

54. ADC, leg. 249, exp. 3363 (inquisitorial trial of Francisco de Arcos, first audience, September 26, 1570). See also, ADC, leg. 250, exp. 3383, fol. 26v (inquisitorial trial of Luis de Cebea el menor, first audience, July 12, 1571).

55. ADC, leg. 248, exp. 3342, fol. 17v (inquisitorial trial of Juan de San Juan, first audience, September 28, 1570).

56. See also Dadson, *Tolerance and Coexistence*, 57–60.

57. ADC, leg. 289, exp. 4049 (inquisitorial trial of Antón Calvo, first audience, June 26, 1581); leg. 372, exp. 5254 (inquisitorial trial of Ana la Buena, testimony of Librada González, December 21, 1608) and leg. 362, exp. 5142 (inquisitorial trial of Miguel Ramírez, testimony of Librada González, January 29, 1609). In 1695 the holder of this post was also the church organist, but this does not seem to have been the case earlier in the century (AHMD, caja 78c, doc. 20).

58. ADC, leg. 249, exp. 3363, fol. 13r (inquisitorial trial of Francisco de Arcos, first audience, September 26, 1570).

59. ADC, leg. 362, exp. 4876, fol. 89v.

60. Alcalde, *Deza*, 1:247–49; ARCV RE, caja 1641, doc. 80, fol. 2v (1570); AHMD, caja 196a, doc. 3 (1611); AHMD, caja 110b, doc. 1 (1581); ARCV RE, caja 1901, doc. 45, fol. 1v (1597); AHMD, caja 71n, doc. 1 (1603); and ADM, leg. 68, doc. 10 (1549).

61. On early modern *escribanos*, see Bejarano Rubio, "Los escribanos públicos," 9–26 and Ybáñez Worboys, "Las escribanías públicas del número," 389–405. In Deza, the same individual often exercised all of these offices, although in larger urban centers they would normally have been divided. Those licensed as royal notaries could perform their office not only within the local confines of Deza but anywhere within the realm.

62. ADC, libro 317, fol. 476r (1569); leg. 719, exp. 938, fol. 1r (1609); ARCV RE, caja 1193, doc. 47 (portada, November 8, 1570); ARCV RE, caja 1999, doc. 90, fol. 5r (November 10, 1603); and ADC, leg. 370, exp. 5241 (inquisitorial trial of Juan de Cebea, testimony of Catalina Sánchez, September 23, 1610).

63. ADM, leg. 111, doc. 39, fol. 1r; ADM AH, leg. 125, doc. 1, fol. 9r; and ADC, leg. 719, doc. 938, fol. 3r.

64. See AHMD, caja 76, doc. 1; ADM, leg. 111, doc. 25, fol. 8r; and ADC, leg. 370, exp. 5241.

65. ADC, leg. 820, exp. 7992, fol. 8v (January 12, 1604).

66. AHDOS APD, LS (1535–1579), fol. 32r and ADC, libro 318, fol. 112r.

67. The local physician Antonio Páez rented the Val de los Homos vineyard from the duke in 1546. ADM, leg. 60, doc. 40, fol. 1v.

68. See the example of the tailors Juan Contreras (Morisco) and Juan Valles (Old Christian) who became friends early in the century. ADC, leg. 99, exp. 1440 (inquisitorial trial of Juan Contreras, testimony of Catalina Valles, February 5, 1524).

69. The same general contours to Morisco-Old Christian relations has been noted by others in different geographical contexts, including Dadson (*Tolerance and Coexistence*, 11) and Mira Caballos ("Unos se quedaron," 470–71).

70. On Morisco muleteers see Tapia Sánchez, "Las redes comerciales," 231–43; "Arrieros, mercaderos, mesoneros," 146–54.

71. See Alcalde, *Deza*, 1:334n88. Juan Febrel, *ollero*, reestablished the pottery works in ca. 1632.

72. See Domínguez Ortiz, *La clase social de los conversos* and Gutiérrez Nieto, "Inquisición y culturas marginadas," 837–1015.

73. ADC, libro 317, fol. 476r (*This Happened*, 47–48).

74. ADC, leg. 116, exp. 1590 (inquisitorial trial of Juan López, testimony of Bernardino Burgueño, November 22, 1558) and leg. 208, exp. 2408 (inquisitorial trial of María de Medina, confession of the accused, December 16, 1557).

75. By the early modern period the town was hardly impregnable, but a medieval wall surrounded the Lower Neighborhood and the entire town could be closed off by securing its six gates. In 1599, during an outbreak of plague, the town council followed this course of action. See AHMD, caja 282, doc. 7b-c (Cuentas del consejo, 1599).

76. Alcalde, *Deza*, 1:247–49.

77. There is no clear indication of the extent to which women, especially female heads of households (like widows or spinsters) were able to participate in the commune. ARCV RE, caja 1999, doc. 90, fol. 6r.

78. See ADC, leg. 820, exp. 7992, fol. 1r and ADM AH, leg. 125, doc. 1 (letter of Antonio de Ucedo Salazar, February 11, 1607).

79. See Alcalde, *Deza*, 1:247–49.

80. Compare Deza's practice with that of the Campo de Calatrava, where Moriscos were also incorporated into local political office (Dadson, *Los moriscos de Villarrubia*, 124–30).

81. ARCV RE, caja 1151, doc. 26, fol. 12v.

82. The earliest explicit reference to a local Morisco (one Jorge Montero) serving as an alcalde ordinario is from 1530 (ADC, leg. 109, exp. 1540 [inquisitorial trial of María Lerma, testimony of Jorge Montero, September 23, 1530]). Juan de Rentellas, who seems to have served as magistrate in 1523 or 1524, was a Morisco but from Almazán. It is unclear whether his neighbors in Deza regarded him as a Morisco before his arrest, since he was charged with having put off his penitential *sanbenito* garb (ADC, leg. 91, exp. 1327 [inquisitorial trial of Gerónimo de Ocáriz, testimony of María de Córdova, October 7, 1525]).

83. No evidence suggests that the Morisco claim to offices in Deza was derived from a privilege granted to a pre-existing Mudéjar *aljama* (self-governing community of Moors). Compare with Dadson, *Tolerance and Coexistence*, 13.

84. On the *mitad de oficios* see Díaz de la Guardia y López, "La mitad de oficios," 43–95.

85. ARCV RE, caja 1999, doc. 90, fol. 6r. For an example of the arrangements arrived at for the office of regidor, see ADM, leg. 111, doc. 25, fol. 8r.

86. AHPS AMD, leg. 26.558, doc. 2, fols. 9v-10r.

87. Purportedly, in just "a few years," the town had been forced to pay out 2,000 ducats to cover the expenses incurred by these inquiries (AHPS AMD, leg. 26.558, doc. 2, fol. 7r-v).

88. Minguela y Arnedo (*Historia*, 1:378–79) provides a transcription of Pope Eugenius III's 1146 bull to the bishops of Sigüenza, Osma, and Tarazona regarding the boundaries of their respective dioceses.

89. On the archpresbytery of Ariza, see Minguela y Arnedo, *Historia*, 3:619–25 and González, *Censo de población*, 342.

90. ARCV RE, caja 1189, doc. 30, fol. 8r and caja 2206, doc. 30, fol. 2r; and AHMD, caja 16b, doc. 2.

91. ADM, leg. 3, doc. 129a (June 13, 1739). The crucifix was processed (for drought) at least as early as 1566 (ADC, libro 317, fol. 360v [*This Happened*, 24–25]).

92. See Martínez Frías, "Una iglesia columnaria," 195–206 and Alcalde, *Deza*, 2:52–63.

93. The first mention of a resident cura is of Francisco de Soria "cura de Deça" who confessed the Morisca Catalina de Hortubia in her house when she was sick on the feast day of St James in 1607. Elsewhere, Soria is designated "teniente de cura" but usually just "presbitero." ADC, leg. 366, exp. 5172 (inquisitorial trial of Catalina de Hortubia, first audience, November 19, 1607).

94. For example, María de Haro, who lived as a beata for perhaps four decades (AHDOS APD, LS [1535–1579], fols. 6r and 152v); Juana de Guzman, whose home was located on the *calle pública* (ARCV RE, caja 966, doc. 30, fol. 3v); and María Ruiz, sister of local priest Juan Ruiz (ARCV RE, caja 2206, doc. 30, fol. 5r).

95. Weber, "Locating Holiness," 61–66.

96. Alcalde, *Deza*, 2:64–72.

97. AHDOS APD, leg. 160, doc. 28.

98. Alcalde, *Deza*, 1:253.

99. ARCV RE, caja 1151, doc. 26, fol. 3r.

100. AHDOS APD, leg. 160, doc. 51 (Libro de la hermandad y cabildo del s.s. Pedro, 1550–1617).

101. ADC, leg. 363, exp. 5150, fol. 1r (inquisitorial trial of Lope de Obezar, 1606) and AHMD, caja 282, doc. 6.

102. ADC, libro 318, fol. 111r and AHDOS APD, leg. 160, doc. 28 (Libro de la Cofradía de Santa Ana, 1594–1661). A single Morisco, Luis de Cebea el mayor (ca. 1524–1609), was initially among the confraters and held office in 1592, 1593, and 1595 before he was excluded.

103. ADC, leg. 363, exp. 5150, fol. 1r (inquisitorial trial of Lope de Obezar, 1606) and AHDOS APD, LS (1580–1605), fol. 113r.

104. Flynn, *Sacred Charity*, 23 and 133.

2. DEZA DIVIDED

1. ADC, leg. 343, exp. 4876, fol. 212v.

2. Note that the pattern of inquisitorial activity against Moriscos in Deza mirrors that of the Cuencan tribunal more broadly. See Carrasco, "Morisques anciens," 198.

3. Additionally, between 1529 and 1537, twelve cases against Judeoconversos were initiated along with an investigation into a series of charges made against Juanes de Altopica, Deza's vicar and the inquisitorial *juez de comisión*. Scattered evidence also points to additional denunciations against New Christians (both Morisco and Judeoconverso) and orders for arrest. If any of these escalated to formal trials, record of them has been lost.

4. *Tolerance and Coexistence*, 63.

5. ADC, leg. 89, exp. 1302 (inquisitorial trial of Ruy Diaz de Mendoza, accusation of *bachiller* Martín Sánchez de Santander, September 22, 1525).

6. ADC, leg. 247, exp. 3316, fol. 8v (inquisitorial trial of María de Almanzorre, testimony of Bernardino Almanzorre, May 24, 1570).

7. Dadson describes the alfaquí of Villarrubia's Moriscos making a similar departure after the conversions of 1502 (*Coexistence and Tolerance*, 15).

8. ADC, leg. 367, exp. 5180 (inquisitorial trial of Juan Guerrero, testimony of Gabriel de León, November 20, 1607).

9. In fact, it is often unclear whether seemingly Islamic activities stemmed from Islamic belief or whether, by the sixteenth century, Mudéjar religion had become "not a belief system but a way of differentiating themselves from their Old Christian neighbors" (Dadson, *Coexistence and Tolerance*, 15).

10. ADC, leg. 209, exp. 2414 (inquisitorial trial of María de Hortubia, testimony of Mari Gil, February 8, 1557).

11. ADC, leg. 209, exp. 2414 (inquisitorial trial of María de Hortubia, request for tachas y abonos, June 13, 1558).

12. On relationship between confessors and their female confessants see Bilinkoff, *Related Lives* and O'Banion, *Sacrament of Penance*, esp. 124–41.

13. ADC, leg. 209, exp. 2414 (inquisitorial trial of María de Hortubia, testimonies for abonos of the accused [Martín Fernández Deza, Juanes Valles, Pedro de la Huerta, Antonio de Melgosa, Rodrigo Fernández Abarca, and Francisco Navarro], July 4–7, 1558).

14. ADC, leg. 209, exp. 2414 (inquisitorial trial of María de Hortubia, testimony for tachas of Mari Gil [Ana de Torres y de Rebolledo], July 6, 1558).

15. ADC, leg. 249, exp. 3369 (inquisitorial trial of Luis de Cebea el viejo, First Audience [April 23, 1608] and response to the Accusation [cap. 3; March 7, 1609]).

16. ADC, leg. 249, exp. 3369 (inquisitorial trial of Luis de Cebea el viejo, confession for the Edict of Grace, January 30, 1571) and AHDOS APD, leg. 160, doc. 28 (July 26, 1592 and July 26, 1594).

17. Santa Ana was a particularly exclusive confraternity. Cebea and his son, also Luis (1547–1611), appear to have been the only Morisco confraters ever admitted. ADC, leg. 209, exp. 2414 (inquisitorial trial of María de Hortubia, confessions of the accused, June 13 and July 5, 1559) and AHDOS APD, leg. 160, doc. 28 (Libro de la Cofradía de Santa Ana de la Parroquia de Deza [1594–1661]).

18. ADC, leg. 209, exp. 2414 (inquisitorial trial of María de Hortubia, confessions of the accused, June 13 and 15, 1559).

19. ADC, leg. 209, exp. 2414 (inquisitorial trial of María de Hortubia, confession of the accused, June 15, 1559). Hortubia noted that the Virgin (rather than the Holy Spirit, as in Navarro's account) "illumined her and she came to an understanding and believed that Our Lady gave birth as a virgin and remained one after the birth."

20. ADC, leg. 209, exp. 2414 (inquisitorial trial of María de Hortubia, testimonies of Alonso Burgueño, María de Gamorra, and Juana de Heredia, July 11, 1559).

21. ADC, leg. 209, exp. 2414 (inquisitorial trial of María de Hortubia, letter of María de Hortubia to the inquisitors of Cuenca, received January 18, 1561).

22. ADC, leg. 367, exp. 5180 (inquisitorial trial of Juan Guerrero, confession of the accused, December 1, 1607).

23. A fifth Morisco tried in 1558, Lope de Deza (alias del Sol; ca. 1499–aft. 1570), had been living in "Molina" (Molina de Aragón?) but had many ties to Deza and may have been raised there. After being reconciled, Lope lived in Deza, where he was denounced a second time and arrested in late 1569. Unfortunately, his second trial has been lost and his fate is unknown. For his first trial, see ADC, leg. 212, exp. 2432.

24. See ADC, leg. 212, exp. 2441 (inquisitorial trials of Luis de Liñán el viejo, 1558 and 1570–71); leg. 208, exp. 2408 (inquisitorial trials of María de Molina, 1557

and 1571–72); and leg. 212, exp. 2449 (inquisitorial trial of Juan de Contreras, 1557–58 and 1570–72). The tribunal at Cuenca sentenced Luis de Liñán (ca. 1521–92) to be relaxed but the Suprema overturned the decision and (despite one dissenting vote on the council) allowed him access to the Edict of Grace granted to Deza's Moriscos in 1570–71 (ADC, leg. 212, exp. 2441 [inquisitorial trial of Luis de Liñán el viejo, sentence of the Suprema, October 6, 1571]).

25. In fact, when Juan de Contreras and Luis de Liñán learned that an inquisitor was in the region in 1570, fearing that they were about to be arrested and charged as relapsed heretics, the duo fled for the Morisco towns of western Aragon, making a circuit that took them through Torrellas and Almonacid de la Sierra before going to ground at the pottery works of Morisco Leonis Fernández in Villafeliche (ADC, leg. 247, exp. 3315, fol. 17r-v).

26. ADC, leg. 116, exp. 1590 (inquisitorial trial of Juan López, Juanes de Altopica's letter to the tribunal of Cuenca, November 6, 1533).

27. See Carrasco Urgoiti, El problema Morisco.

28. AHMD, caja 15C, doc. 1 (Ordenanzas de la villa de Deza, 1534).

29. For example, both Mateo Romero el mayor of Terrer (Zaragoza) and Juan de Contreras of Ariza (Zaragoza) were sent to study with Santa Clara around 1540, returned home, and then moved to Deza decades later. See ADC, leg. 254, exp. 3443, fol. 15v and leg. 212, exp. 2449, fol. 74r.

30. Anes, "The Agrarian 'Depression,'" 61.

31. ADC, libro 317, fol. 462r (This Happened, 27).

32. ADC, leg. 249, exp. 3552, fol. 48v.

33. ADC, leg. 212, exp. 2441 (inquisitorial trial of Luis de Liñán el viejo, first audience of the accused, April 23, 1558).

34. ADC, leg. 249, exp. 3367, fols. 2r and 27r-v.

35. ADC, leg. 250, exp. 3383, fols. 27v-30r.

36. ADC, leg. 249, exp. 3352, fols. 18v-21v.

37. ADC, leg. 249, exp. 3352, fol. 10v.

38. See ADC, leg. 343, exp. 4876, fols. 192r-95r (This Happened, 55–63). Some elements of the story may be true but other evidence suggests that Ramírez knew about Ramadan, guadoc, and azala before his purported interactions with Romero and Almoravi.

39. ADC, leg. 249, exp. 3352, fols. 28r and 48v.

40. ADC, leg. 249, exp. 3552, fols. 29–31v, 39v-40r, and 42v.

41. AHPZ, ms. 27/5, fol. 209v. Was this Mendoza, perhaps, a grandson of Deza's old alfaquí Ruy Diaz de Mendoza?

42. The surname Calemón (or Çalemón) was a common one among the Moriscos of Torrellas. See Ansón Calvo, Torrellas, 33.

43. Bernardino's birth date is slightly uncertain. In 1570, he gave his age as 20 "more or less," but he was probably born in late March 1546, since a son of

Francisco Almanzorre and "Ana" Navarra was baptized on April 5 of that year. As occasionally happened in the entries for the sacramental register, the priest recording the baptism failed to enter the child's name (AHDOS APD, LS [1535–1579], fol. 39v), but this seems to be the couple's only son otherwise unaccounted for. Bernardino was confirmed in Deza on May 16, 1556 (fol. 81r).

44. ADC, leg. 247, exp. 3316, fols. 5v, 8v, 15v-16r and ADC, leg. 250, exp. 3370 (inquisitorial trial of Lope Guerrero el viejo, testimony of Bernardino Almanzorre, June 22, 1570). Unfortunately, Bernardino's 1570 trial has been lost, which leaves some gaps in his biography. Nevertheless, because he denounced many other Moriscos and was, in turn, frequently denounced by them, a coherent, if incomplete, record of his activities can be constructed.

45. ADC, leg. 247, exp. 3317 (inquisitorial trial of Luis de Mendoza, confession of the accused, July 15, 1570). Although the biography of this Alexos Maestro is unknown, the surname was common among the Moriscos of Torrellas. See Ansón Calvo, "La vida cotidiana," 255 and Torrellas, 33 and 128.

46. ADC, 247, exp. 3316, fol. fol. 7r-v and leg. 250, exp. 3370 (inquisitorial trial of Lope Guerrero el viejo, testimony of Bernardino Almanzorre, June 21, 1570).

47. ADC, leg. 247, exp. 3316, fol. 5v.

48. The Antialcoran was a refutation of Islam collected in twenty-six sermons. Polemical works of this sort were valuable to Islamizing Moriscos because they described at least something of what Muslims were supposed to believe.

49. It was not the pamphlet written by Miquel Llot de Ribera and published by Sansón Arbús of Perpignan entitled Verdadera relacion de la vitoria y libertad que alcançaron quatrocientos Christianos captivos de Hazan Baxa, since the events described in that work occurred later, in 1590. The Apologeticus of the Mozarabic abbot Sansón de Córdoba (d. 890) is highly unlikely. One possibility is that "Sansón" here refers to the biblical figure, whom the Quran does not mention but about whom some medieval Muslims nevertheless wrote briefly. See Rippon, "The Muslim Samson," 240–46.

50. For a description, see Bouzineb, "Los consejos al hijo de Ādam," 198.

51. See Mami's scholarly edition of the Sueño in "Otra leyenda Morisca," 387–403. Bernardino briefly referred to it in ADC, leg. 247, exp. 3311 (inquisitorial trial of María de Saleros, testimony of Bernardino Almanzorre [under torture], June 20, 1570).

52. Guillén Robles published a Castilian version of the Recontamiento (based on the 166-folio manuscript cataloged as BNE Mss/5292) in Leyendas de José. See Roberto Tottoli's notes on this text in "Recontamiento de Yuçuf," 200–201.

53. Descriptions of these books are recorded in ADC, leg. 250, exp. 3370 (inquisitorial trial of Lope Guerrero el viejo, testimony of Bernardino Almanzorre, June 21, 1570) and ADC, leg. 250, exp. 3383, fols. 69v-70r.

54. See Wilnet Gil, "Regimiento de las lunas," 156–59.

55. ADC, leg. 247, exp. 3311 (inquisitorial trial of María de Saleros, testimony of Bernardino Almanzorre [under torture; June 20, 1570] and confession of the accused [August 21, 1570]).

56. ADC, leg. 247, exp. 3311 (inquisitorial trial of María de Saleros, testimony of the accused, August 21, 1570). An interest in poetry potentially connects Bernardino to the parish school run by Gonzalo de Santa Clara, who used *coplas* to teach reading; however, this practice was not unusual in early modern Spain.

57. Bernardino dated this interaction to either Easter or the feast of St. John (June 24) 1569, but Lope Guerrero indicated that it happened when he was eighteen years old (i.e., ca. 1565). It might reasonably have occurred any time after Bernardino's return to Deza from Aragon in 1566 and summer 1569 (ADC, leg. 250, exp. 3370 [inquisitorial trial of Lope Guerrero el viejo, testimony of Bernardino Almanzorre, June 22, 1570]).

58. ADC, leg. 250, exp. 3370 (inquisitorial trial of Lope Guerrero el viejo, testimony of the accused, December 15, 1610). Lope's 1610 version of the encounter fits reasonably well with Bernardino's account, given in 1570 (ADC, leg. 250, exp. 3370 [inquisitorial trial of Lope Guerrero el viejo, testimony of Bernardino Almanzorre, June 22, 1570]).

59. ADC, leg. 250, exp. 3370 (inquisitorial trial of Lope Guerrero el viejo, testimony of the accused, December 15, 1610).

60. The hiding of the papers (at least some of them in a compartment under the stairs in his mother's house) was connected with the rumor of the visitation and, subsequently, the presence in Deza of inquisitors during autumn 1569 and winter 1570–71.

61. ADC, leg. 250, exp. 3383, fol. 69v and leg. 247, exp. 3311 (inquisitorial trial of María de Saleros, testimony of Bernardino Almanzorre, June 21, 1570). This was a manuscript book written partly in Arabic and partly in Latin script on quarter-sheet pages of an indeterminate length. The BCLM copy (ms. Toledo 505) contains 57 folios. El Romo briefly alluded to the book in his own trial, but the inquisitors do not seem to have pursued it (ADC, leg. 212, exp. 2449, fol. 56v).

62. ADC, leg. 249, exp. 3363, fol. 14r-v.

63. ADC, leg. 247, exp. 3317 (inquisitorial trial of Luis de Mendoza, confession of the accused, July 15, 1570).

64. ADC, leg. 248, exp. 3329 (inquisitorial trial of Alonso Aliger, confession of the accused [under threat of torture], January 12, 1571).

65. ADC, leg. 254, exp. 3443, fols. 38r-41r. Romero's denunciation here specifically locates his initial Islamic interactions with Bernardino Almanzorre to Ágreda in the spring of 1565 (fol. 38r), during which time Bernardino is known to have been living in Torrellas. Moreover, strong evidence suggests that Romero and his wife Ana de Almoravi, who came to Deza from Aragonese Terrer in 1558, were crypto-Muslims before their arrival.

66. See, for example, the interactions between Almanzorre, Obezar, Arcos, Luis and Diego Martínez, Mancebo, and San Juan when the two different groups they comprised encountered one another while trying to catch sight of the new moon that marked the end of Ramadan in 1569 Ramadan (ADC, leg. 249, exp. 3363, fols. 4r-6r).

67. His sister María Navarra (1551–1627) had some inkling of what the older members of her family were up to as well. After her brother's arrest, she sought the advice of his father-in-law, Íñigo de Saleros, about what to do with one of the Aljamiado books (ADC, leg. 250, exp. 3383, fol. 70v).

68. ADC, leg. 247, exp. 3316, fol. 12v. The claim is difficult to credit given María's religious heritage (as granddaughter of the old alfaquí) and the fact that she must have been involved in sending her son to Aragon. Yet she had lived for a few years (perhaps following the death of her father) with Old Christians in Medinaceli, so a lingering Christian devotion is not impossible (ADC, leg. 247, exp. 3316, fol. 20r).

69. ADC, leg. 247, exp. 3316, fol. 8v.

70. See ADC, leg. 247, exp. 3374 (inquisitorial trial of Mari Gómez, testimony of the accused [July 14, 1570], response to the accusation [July 24, 1570] and response to the publication of additional witnesses [August 26, 1570]). Initially upon their arrest by the Holy Office, Mari Gómez (Bernardino's mother-in-law) and the rest of her immediate family agreed to blame everything on María and Ana de Almanzorre in order to divert attention from Bernardino. Subsequently, however, Mari, Íñigo de Saleros, and their children independently confessed to the conspiracy and admitted that Bernardino had introduced them to and instructed them in Islam.

71. Bernardino described these efforts in ADC, leg. 247, exp. 3311 (inquisitorial trial of María de Saleros, testimony of Bernardino Almanzorre [under torture], June 21, 1570).

72. ADC, leg. 250, exp. 3374 (inquisitorial trial of Mari Gómez, response to the publication of additional witnesses, August 26, 1570).

73. The inquisitorial trials of Íñigo and Francisco de Saleros have not survived. Two younger siblings—Íñigo (b. 1556) and Ana (b. 1560)—went unconverted or, more likely, were considered too young to be trusted with knowledge of *cosas de moros*. Yet even the very youngest son, Gabriel (b. 1562), knew enough to be excited when Bernardino told him Ramadan was over, which suggests the family's children were not kept entirely in the dark (ADC, leg. 249, exp. 3363, fol. 5v).

74. ADC, leg. 367, exp. 5180 (inquisitorial trial of Juan Guerrero, testimony of Gabriel de León, November 20, 1607).

75. ADC, leg. 212, exp. 2449, fol. 47r-v.

76. ADC, leg. 209, exp. 2441 (inquisitorial trial of Luis de Liñán el viejo, testimony of Francisco el Romo, August 3, 1570).

77. ADC, leg. 250, exp. 3383, fol. 40v.

78. Francisco's dates are unknown, but in 1569 he was described as "the eldest" among a group that included a man born in 1504 (ADC, libro 317, fol. 473r [*This Happened*, 45]).

79. This was probably the Francisco de Gonzalo who married, Ana Fernández, another sister of the wives of Pedro and Juan de Deza Cañamenero, but also might have been the husband of Luisa la Viscaina mentioned below.

80. Román was uncle to the wives of Juan and Pedro.

81. Juan was a first cousin of the wives of Juan and Pedro and, in a conversation with Lope de Obezar, mentioned having learned from Pedro (ADC, leg. 247, exp. 3314, fol. 50r).

82. ADC, leg. 249, exp. 3352, fol. 52r.

83. ADC, leg. 249, exp. 3352, fol. 49r.

84. ADC, leg. 249, exp. 3352, fol. 47r. Among the instructed, Ana named Íñigo de Hortubia el Soldado (1540–93), Hernán Mancebo (b. ca. 1535), Luis de Cebea el menor (1547–1611), and "Fadriquillo," perhaps Juan de San Juan (alias de Fadrique; 1547–ca. 1592) or his brother Diego de Fadrique (b. 1554).

85. ADC, leg. 249, exp. 3352, fol. 52r. The watchers included Mateo Almotazán (b. ca. 1540), Jorge Montero (b. ca. 1546), Juan de Hortubia, Velasco de Medrano, Román Ramírez el menor, and Francisco de Miranda.

86. These included the homes of potter Francisco de Baptista, Alexo Gorgoz, and "certain others" (ADC, leg. 249, exp. 3352, fols. 50v–51r). Among the "certain others" mentioned to Ana de Almoravi (by Velasco de Medrano) may have been the homes of Gonzalo el Burgueño and María la Carnicera (which Gerónimo de Molina mentioned as a place for prayer), Gabriel Aliger (which boasted a "painted room" for prayers), and Luis Corazón and María la Marquesa (who had a "very good and very well hidden" room used for the purpose). See ADC, leg. 247, exp. 3320, fols. 31v and 43v; and leg. 248, exp. 3342 (inquisitorial trial of Juan de San Juan, testimony of Luis de Cebea el menor, November 14, 1570).

87. ADC, leg. 247, exp. 3314, fol. 50r. Alonso Ropiñón also recalled receiving instruction about fasting and prayers from "Pedro el Cañamenero, native of Villafeliche" in ca. 1568 while on the road toward Almazán (ADC, leg. 249, exp. 3364 [inquisitorial trial of Alonso Ropiñón, response to publication of witnesses (cap. 3), November 7, 1570]).

88. ADC, leg. 212, exp. 2449, fol. 49v. Román el Romo offered an alternative account of Lope del Sol's statement: "Don't lose heart that they treat you like Moors. What can you do? The Moors, like the Christians, also think that they are being saved in their Law and, in the end, the greater part of the world is of

Moors" (ADC, leg. 212, exp. 2441 [inquisitorial trial of Luis de Liñán el viejo, testimony of Francisco el Romo, July 31, 1570]).

89. ADC, leg. 212, exp. 2449, fols. 49v-50v and leg. 212, exp. 2441 (inquisitorial trial of Luis de Liñán, testimony of Francisco el Romo, July 31, 1570).

90. ADC, leg. 212, exp. 2449, fol. 57r. A similar examination ordeal appears to have been conducted by Pedro el Cañamenero upon Francisco de Miranda el viejo in 1565 (ADC, leg. 249, exp. 3352, fol. 52r).

91. ADC, leg. 212, exp. 2449, fols. 57r-v and 95r.

92. Contreras described the volume as a book that "dealt with matters related to punishments [cosas de castigos] and the rule of the azalas, although it did not contain azoras" and elsewhere he said it was "a book that Juan de Deza gave to him that was in letra moriega and it dealt with what the nations [gentes] would see on the Day of Judgment" (ADC, leg. 212, exp. 2449, fols. 95r and 100v). Perhaps this book was some version of the Alkitāb de preiques. See Roza Candás, "Alkitāb de preiques i exemplo i dotrinas," 196–98 and Fernández Fernández, "Libro de Castigos."

93. Juan de Deza of Villafeliche, nicknamed Rioja, took Dezano Juan Guerrero (b. ca. 1555) on as an apprentice sandal maker and instructed him in cosas de moros in ca. 1581. He claimed to have been a grandson of Deza's former alfaquí and was probably the son of one of the Cañamenero-Dezas of Villafeliche active in Deza in the 1560s. Juan Guerrero, who claimed to be illiterate, proved a poor student for memorizing Arabic prayers but Rioja successfully taught him a number of specific points of theology that challenged Christian doctrine. See ADC, leg. 367, exp. 5180 (inquisitorial trial of Juan Guerrero, confession of the accused [November 15, 1607] and testimony of Gabriel de León [November 20, 1607]).

94. ADC, leg. 247, exp. 3317 (inquisitorial trial of Luis de Mendoza, confession of the accused, July 15, 1570) and ADC, leg. 250, exp. 3383 (inquisitorial trial of Lope de Cieli el menor, confession of the accused under torture, February 10, 1571).

95. ADC, leg. 249, exp. 3352, fols. 28v, 47r-48r, 50r, and 52r.

96. ADC, leg. 343, exp. 4876, fols. 192r-95r (This Happened, 55–60).

97. See, for example, This Happened, 22–23 and 47–48.

98. ADC, libro 317, fols. 473r and 474r (This Happened, 43–44).

99. ADC, leg. 249, exp. 3352, fols. 18v and 22r.

100. ADC, leg. 254, exp. 3443, fol. 36r.

101. ADC, libro 318, fols. 448r-78v (This Happened, 3–51).

102. A precise count is made difficult, since several trials are known to have been lost, and there may yet be others that remain unknown. Cuenca also initiated several more cases, which for lack of corroborating evidence never led to arrests or developed into full-scale trials.

103. ADC, leg. 367, exp. 5180 bis (inquisitorial trial of Juan Guerrero, testimony of Gabriel de León, August 21, 1608).

104. Mateo Romero el menor and el mayor executed a series of daring escapes and remained at large before finally being condemned in absentia in the early 1580s. They may have even returned to Deza, although the evidence is inconclusive. See ADC, libro 318, fols. 102v-3r (*This Happened*, 78–79) for a possible sighting of los Romero in 1581.

105. ADC, leg. 249, exp. 3369 (inquisitorial trial of Luis de Cebea el viejo, testimony of María Navarra, April 5, 1570).

3. GETTING ON WITH THEIR LIVES

1. Fernández Nieva, "Don Diego Gómez de la Madrid," 81 (letter from de la Madriz to Cuenca, January 17, 1571). In secondary literature, the inquisitor's surname is variously spelled "Madrid" or "Madriz." The archival sources used in this book uniformly identify him as "Madriz," so that spelling is retained here.

2. Romero Medina makes the point with reference to Dutch Protestants ("Don Juan de la Cerda," 357).

3. Fernández Nieva, "Don Diego Gómez de la Madrid," 82 (declaration of Miguel Benito to de la Madriz, January 17, 1571).

4. Fernández Nieva, "Don Diego Gómez de la Madrid," 87 (letter from Duke Juan de la Cerda to de la Madriz, January 16, 1571).

5. See, for example, Román Ramírez el menor's fascinating declaration (ADC, leg. 343, exp. 4876, fols. 192r-95r [*This Happened*, 56–60]).

6. Fernández Nieva, "Dr. Diego de la Madrid," 106 (letter of Francisco de Baptista, Gerónimo Gorgoz, Juan de Deza, Francisco Mancebo, and Alexo Gorgoz to Dr. Diego Gómez de la Madrid, April 7, 1571).

7. Younger Moriscos balked at this provision, since they would be required to make three confessions (rather than the usual one) for the rest of their lives. They feared this would cause Old Christian neighbors to stigmatize them (Fernández Nieva, "Dr. Diego de la Madrid," 98–99).

8. ADC, leg. 247, exp. 3322 (inquisitorial trial of Gerónimo Gorgoz, confession for the Edict of Grace, December 1, 1570).

9. ADC, leg. 249, exp. 3552, fol. 49r.

10. ADC, leg. 249, exp. 3552, fols. 50v-51r.

11. ADC, leg. 249, exp. 3552, fol. 48r.

12. ADC, leg. 247, exp. 3322 (confession of Gerónimo Gorgoz for the Edict of Grace, December 1, 1570).

13. ADC, leg. 249, exp. 3552, fol. 50r.

14. The Inquisitor Madriz assessed Gorgoz a fine of 14 ducats subsequent to his taking the Edict of Grace. This was the largest fine assessed to any of the Moriscos and two more than Gerónimo's brother Alexo. See ADC, leg. 247, exp. 3322 (sentence of Gerónimo Gorgoz for the Edict of Faith, February 8,

1571). Deza's Moriscos appear to have generally been poorer than their cousins in nearby Arcos (Carrasco, "Morisques anciens," 212).

15. AHDOS APD, leg. 160, doc. 17 (will of Gerónimo Gorgoz, April 26, 1579).

16. ADC, leg. 249, exp. 3552, fols. 50r-53r.

17. During his inquisitorial trial, Luis de Liñán identified both himself and his father as *olleros* (ADC, leg. 212, exp. 2441 [inquisitorial trial of Luis de Liñán el mozo, confession of the accused, April 23, 1558]). The Liñán family continued to operate the *ollería* through the sixteenth century. See ADC, leg. 355, exp. 5042 (denunciation of Gerónimo de Liñán by María Gil, September 14, 1602), ADM, leg. 60, doc. 29 (escritura original de una huerta y una olleria, 1546), and doc. 40, fol. 1r (relación de algunas escrituras de renta, 1553).

18. ADC, leg. 813, doc. 6657 (letter from Pedro de Cisneros to the inquisitorial tribunal at Cuenca, March 24, 1608).

19. ADC, libro 318, fol. 100r (*This Happened*, 75).

20. ADC, leg. 375, exp. 5324 (inquisitorial trial of Ana de Hortubia, testimony of Gabriel de León, March 28, 1608); AHMD, caja 26, doc. 4, fol. 91r; and AHDOS APD, leg. 160, doc. 17 (will of Alexo Gorgoz, 1599).

21. ADC, leg. 250, exp. 3370 (inquisitorial trial of Lope Guerrero el viejo, confession of the accused, December 18, 1610) and ADC, leg. 364, exp. 5159 (inquisitorial trial of Antón Guerrero, response of the accused to accusation [cap. 61], June 5, 1610).

22. See AHMD, caja 26, doc. 4, fols. 121v and 135v. On these types of annuities, see D'Emic, *Justice in the Marketplace*, 44.

23. AHDOS APD, LS (1535–1579), fol. 179r and ADC, leg. 748b, doc. 106, fol. 21v.

24. ADC, leg. 375, exp. 5324 (inquisitorial trial of Ana de Hortubia, testimony of Gabriel de León [March 28, 1608] and first audience of the accused [December 10, 1607]).

25. Gorgoz settled 11 *yugadas* of farmland and a lease paying out 25 ducats per decade on Corazón. See ADC, leg. 377, exp. 5342 (inquisitorial trial of Juan Corazón, confession of the accused, December 9, 1608).

26. ADC, leg. 367, exp. 5180 (inquisitorial trial of Juan Guerrero, testimony of the accused, June 18, 1608) and ADC, leg. 364, exp. 5159 (inquisitorial trial of Antón Guerrero el viejo, response of the accused to accusation [cap. 61], June 5, 1610).

27. AHDOS APD, LS (1580–1605), fol. 111v.

28. The brothers' wills, which were the legal instruments that formalized these arrangements, are in the unfoliated Libro de fundaciones y capellanías de la parroquia de la villa de Deza, 1537–1671 in AHDOS APD, leg. 160, doc. 17.

29. See ADC, leg. 375, exp. 5324 (inquisitorial trial of Ana de Hortubia, testimony of Gabriel de León, March 8, 1608). The price of commodities fluctuated substantially during these years, but a *fanega* (55.5 liters) of wheat sold for about

one ducat and prices were rising dramatically in the late sixteenth and early seventeenth centuries, approaching 2 ducats per *fanega* in some years.

30. ADC, leg. 250, exp. 3370 (inquisitorial trial of Lope Guerrero el viejo, confession of the accused, December 18, 1610).

31. See ADC, leg. 367, exp. 5180 (inquisitorial trial of Juan Guerrero, testimony of the accused, June 18, 1608).

32. Alcalde, *Deza*, 1:245.

33. López de Rebolledo belonged to one of Deza's hidalgo families, but he seems also to have formerly served as alcaide in the town of Arcos, which was part of the duke's domain.

34. ADM, leg. 44, doc. 21 (undated [but 1571]). See ADM, leg. 44, doc. 22 (undated [but 1571]), which emphasized the "inconveniences" of having competing jurisdictions at play in "such a small place."

35. See AHPS AMD, doc. 1S.12 (1572) and doc. 1S.14 (1577). Fernández Abarca's immediate successors—Gerónimo de Ocáriz (r. 1581–84), Pedro de Barnuevo (r. 1584–95), and Velasco de Barnuevo (r. 1596–ca. 1602)—also used both titles.

36. AHDOS APD, LS (1535–79), fol. 161v.

37. The only disagreement, apparently, was whether to honor the Maccabees (whom the calendar of Sigüenza, and thus Deza, honored on July 15), or St. Bonaventure (whom the "new Roman" calendar, which was being imposed in the wake of Trent, commemorated on that day). Eventually, everyone agreed they did not need to know who was responsible, for they could honor *both* the Maccabees *and* St. Bonaventure.

38. Unable to finish settling his affairs on account of his final illness, Gorgoz granted Licentiate Miguel Benito power of attorney to lay out his wishes for the disposition of his worldly goods on the basis of what Gorgoz had indicated in previous conversations. See AHDOS APD, leg. 160, doc. 17 (will of Alexo Gorgoz, 1599).

39. See the list of Moriscos whom Arganda summoned: ADC, leg. 750, doc. 104, fol. 1r.

40. AHDOS APD, leg. 160, doc. 17 (will of Alexo Gorgoz, 1599).

41. ADC, leg. 375, exp. 5324 (inquisitorial trial of Ana de Hortubia, testimony of Gabriel de León, June 20, 1608).

42. ADM, leg. 188, doc. 27, fol. 2v.

43. ADC, leg. 748b, doc. 106.

44. ADC, leg. 365, exp. 5165 (inquisitorial trial of Gabriel de Medina, testimony of Gabriel de León, October 13, 1608). According to some reports, Carnicero was sexually involved with the wife, María Ramírez (or de Román).

45. ADC, leg. 367, exp. 5180b (inquisitorial trial of Juan Guerrero, response to the accusations [cap. 75], October 27, 1609). Conceivably, as Ana Guerrera's father, Juan was attempting to honor the charity show to his daughter by

keeping silent about Agustín and Carnicero, but this is unlikely as his other denunciations were remarkably comprehensive.

46. ADC, leg. 813, exp. 6657 (letter from Pedro de Cisneros to the inquisitorial tribunal in Cuenca, March 24, 1608).

47. ADC, leg. 367, exp. 5180 (inquisitorial trial of Juan Guerrero, testimony of the accused, June 18, 1608); ADC, leg. 375, exp. 5324 (inquisitorial trial of Ana de Hortubia, response to accusations [cap. 9], November 27, 1609); ADC, leg. 377, exp. 5342 (inquisitorial trial of Juan Corazón, response to the accusations [cap. 6], March 11, 1610); ADC, leg. 364, exp. 5159 (inquisitorial trial of Antón Guerrero el viejo, response to the accusations [cap. 61], June 5, 1610); and ADC, leg. 250, exp. 3370 (inquisitorial trial of Lope Guerrero el viejo, testimony of the accused, December 18, 1610).

48. ADC, leg. 374, exp. 5324 (inquisitorial trial of Ana de Hortubia, response to the accusations [cap. 9], November 27, 1609).

49. ADC, leg. 374, exp. 5324 (inquisitorial trial of Ana de Hortubia, testimony of the accused, September 11, 1610).

50. See ADC, leg. 377, exp. 5342 (inquisitorial trial of Juan Corazón, response to the accusations [cap. 6], March 11, 1610; and response to the publication of witnesses [test. 2, cap. 2], July 30, 1610).

51. ADC, leg. 367, exp. 5180 (inquisitorial trial of Juan Guerrero, testimony of Gabriel de León, March 28, 1608).

52. In fact, Ana de Hortubia did not denounce anyone until September 1610, more than two years after Juan Guerrero's full confession. ADC, leg. 375, exp. 5324 (inquisitorial trial of Ana de Hortubia, testimony of the accused, September 11 and 13, 1610).

53. ADC, leg. 367, exp. 5180 (inquisitorial trial of Juan Guerrero, testimony of Gabriel de León, June 20, 1608). See also Guerrero's account of this conversation in ADC, leg. 367, exp. 5180 (inquisitorial trial of Juan Guerrero, testimony of the accused, June 18, 1608).

54. ADC, leg. 367, exp. 5180 (inquisitorial trial of Juan Guerrero, testimony of the accused, June 18, 1608).

55. ADC, leg. 364, exp. 5159 (inquisitorial trial of Antón Guerrero el viejo, response to the accusations [cap. 61], June 5, 1610).

56. ADC, leg. 250, exp. 3370 (inquisitorial trial of Lope Guerrero el viejo, response to the accusations [cap. 40], March 10, 1609).

57. ADC, leg. 250, exp. 3370 (inquisitorial trial of Lope Guerrero el viejo, testimony of the accused, December 15, 1610). On December 18 Lope Guerrero provided inquisitors with a description of the Gorgoz estate.

58. Devin J. Stewart ("Dissimulation," 135) defines *taqiyya* as an "Islamic legal dispensation that allows the believer to commit an act that would ordinarily be forbidden or to omit an act that would ordinarily be required in cases of dan-

ger from a hostile or potentially hostile audience." Also see Stewart, "Dissimulation in Sunni Islam," 439–90.

59. See Harvey, "Crypto-Islam," 163–78; Molénat, "Le problème de la permanence," 392–400; and Bernabé-Pons, "*Taqiyya, niyya* y el islam," 491–527.

60. I quote from Rosa-Rodrigues's translation of the *fatwa* in her "Simulation and Dissimulation," 176–78.

61. ADC, leg. 250, exp. 3383, fols. 14r-15v (inquisitorial trial of Luis de Cebea el mayor, testimony of Juan de San Juan [alias Fadrique], September 28, 1570).

62. ADC, leg. 247, exp. 3322 (inquisitorial trial of Gerónimo Gorgoz for the Edict of Grace, testimony of the accused, December 1, 1570).

63. ADC, libro 317, fol. 460r (*This Happened*, 22) and ADC, leg. 250, exp. 3383 (inquisitorial trial of Juan de Cebea el menor, testimony of the accused [under torture], February 16, 1611).

64. See the edition of the *fatwa* included in Hendrickson, "The Islamic Obligation to Emigrate," 344.

65. Jurist Yça Gidelli evidenced similar concerns in his mid-fifteenth century *Breviario sunní*, written to Muslims living under Christian rule, when he judged that "it is abhorrent to wear clothing in Christian styles for prayer." See Gayangos, ed., *Tratados de la legislación musulmana*, 282.

66. Quoted in Harvey, "Political, Social and Cultural History," 219.

67. I have argued that their establishment of the obra pía was (probably) an effort to follow the Mufti's advice on almsgiving in O'Banion, "'They will know our hearts,'" 205–17.

68. See AHDOS APD, Libro de la Obra Pía . . . fundada por Gerónimo Gorgoz, 1647–1827 and, for the early records of the brothers' obra pía, see AHDOS APD, leg. 160, doc. 17.

69. For Paciencia: ADC, leg. 364, exp. 5159 (inquisitorial trial of Antón Guerrero el viejo, testimony of Gabriel de León, October 13, 1608) and ADC, leg. 365, exp. 5165 (inquisitorial trial of Gabriel de Medina, testimony of Gabriel de León, November 7, 1608). For María Navarra and Gerónimo de Molina el menor: ADC, leg, 375, exp. 5308 (inquisitorial trial of María la Burgueña, testimony of Gerónimo de Molina, September 15, 1610).

70. ADC, libro 321, fols. 121v-34v. Compare the situation in Villarrubia, where the Moriscos who remained after the attempted expulsion faced gossip and drunken insults by a few rowdy Old Christians (and a Morisco collaborator) but received the support of others, especially local authorities (Dadson, *Tolerance and Coexistence*, 70–78).

4. SEEKING A FREER LAND

1. Haliczer, *Inquisition and Society*, 260.

2. On Sunday, June 25 an anathema was read from the pulpit along with a supplemental edict on "simple fornication." The supplemental edict was intended to correct the widespread belief that fornication with an unmarried woman, especially a prostitute, was either not a sin or, at worst, a venial sin. This prompted multiple denunciations against Old Christian Juan Navarro (e.g., ADC, libro 318, fols. 116, 118v-20v [bis] [*This Happened*, 95–96, 98–101]).

3. See, for example, Licentiate Antonio Páez's 1569 description of the negotiation ceremony (ADC, libro 317, fol. 459r-v [*This Happened*, 20–22]). They had not stopped occurring, for similar betrothal celebrations were still being performed in town four decades later (ADC, leg. 361, exp. 5131 [inquisitorial trial of Ana Guerrera, testimony of Juan Guerrero, August 9, 1608]).

4. ADC, libro 318, fol. 110v (*This Happened*, 89). More alarming, perhaps, was the reported exhumation in 1578 of a Morisca from Deza's parish cemetery to be reinterred amongst Muslims in Ariza. In this case, however, both the dead woman and her sister (who purportedly transported the body) were Aragonese Moriscos sojourning in Deza (ADC, libro 318, fols. 121r-22v [*This Happened*, 101–3]).

5. ADC, libro 318, fol. 111r (*This Happened*, 90).

6. ADC, libro 317, fol. 473r (*This Happened*, 43–44).

7. The boy's father described him as a lazy scoundrel and an inveterate liar, and he claimed that he did not "know how to determine whether his son was telling the truth about this" (ADC, libro 317, fol. 475v [*This Happened*, 47]). For his part, Lope Guerrero claimed, decades later, that he had not even been in town during that period. See ADC, leg. 250, exp. 3370 (inquisitorial trial of Lope Guerrero el viejo, response to the accusations [cap. 4], March 9, 1609).

8. For the orders to arrest the two Lopes, see ADC, leg. 250, exp. 3370 (inquisitorial trial of Lope Guerrero el viejo, June 27, 1570) and ADC, leg. 375, exp. 5321 (inquisitorial trial of Lope de Deza, August 19, 1570). Both men presented themselves before Inquisitor Madriz on February 4, 1571, in Deza and confessed for the Edict of Grace. Record of those confessions and of their reconciliations is contained in the dossier of their respective inquisitorial trials.

9. ADC, leg. 375, exp. 5321 (inquisitorial trial of Lope de Deza, examinations before Francisco Arganda, July 4–26, 1581).

10. Even Luis de Cebea el menor, who claimed he had never been informed about his responsibility to confess thrice annually (and therefore had not done it), was merely admonished to do better and fined 1,500 mrs. He took the advice to heart and for the next twenty-eight years confessed as required and at other times as well, keeping his receipts in a book, which he left in the possession of the local inquisitorial commissioner. ADC, leg. 250, exp. 3383 (inquisitorial trial of Luis de Cebea el menor, testimony of the accused [July 11, 1581] and responses to the accusation [cap. 3] [October 13, 1609]).

11. Arganda fined most Moriscos between 300 and 3,000 mrs. (roughly 1–11 ducats). A few (presumably because of their poverty) were merely assigned spiritual penances. At the other extreme, Román Ramírez el menor was fined 6,000 mrs., perhaps because he lost his temper during his interview with the inquisitor. ADC, leg. 707, exp. 625 (*This Happened*, 116–17).

12. ADC, libro 318, fols. 122v-23v (*This Happened*, 103–5).

13. In later years, this Lope Guerrero was sometimes known as "el viejo" or Lope el Guerrero to distinguish him from his nephew Lope Guerrero el mozo or el menor (b. 1571), the son of Francisco Guerrero (1543–91). Unless otherwise indicated, references to "Lope Guerrero" are to our Lope, Lope Guerrero el viejo.

14. ADC, leg. 250, exp. 3370 (inquisitorial trial of Lope Guerrero el viejo, first audience of the accused, December 4, 1607).

15. ADC, leg. 364, exp. 5159 (inquisitorial trial of Antón Guerrero el viejo, testimony of the accused, September 3, 1608).

16. ADC, leg. 367, exp. 5180 (inquisitorial trial of Juan Guerrero, testimony of Gabriel de León, December 20, 1607).

17. ADC, leg. 367, exp. 5180 (inquisitorial trial of Juan Guerrero, response to the accusations [cap. 86], August 19, 1608).

18. ADC, leg. 367, exp. 5180 (inquisitorial trial of Juan Guerrero, testimony of Gabriel de León, December 20, 1607).

19. ADC, leg. 378, exp. 5356 (inquisitorial trial of María la Jarquina, testimony of Gabriel de León, May 13, 1608).

20. ADC, leg. 250, exp. 3370 (inquisitorial trial of Lope Guerrero el viejo, confession of the accused, December 15, 1610). Guerrero admitted this having been transferred to the inquisitorial torture chamber but before undergoing any physical torture.

21. Isabel del Valdelagua's husband, Antón de Deza, was the half-brother of Ana de Deza (Lope's wife). ADC, leg. 367, exp. 5180 (inquisitorial trial of Juan Guerrero, response to the accusations [cap. 55], August 13, 1608).

22. ADC, leg. 376, exp. 5334 (inquisitorial trial of María de Cebea, testimony of Gabriel de León, October 10, 1608).

23. ADC, leg. 249, exp. 3369 (inquisitorial trial of Luis de Cebea el viejo, response to the accusation [cabeza], March 27, 1609) and ADC, leg. 367, exp. 5334 (inquisitorial trial of María de Cebea, testimony of Gabriel de León, October 10, 1608). A "Lope Guerrero" served as *procurador del común* between 1602–04, but this was certainly Lope Guerrero el menor (b. ca. 1571), our Lope's nephew.

24. ADC, leg. 250, exp. 3383 (inquisitorial trial of Luis de Cebea el menor, testimony of Francisco de Cebea, May 2, 1608).

25. Because Guerrero offered contradictory statements to the Holy Office and was intentionally deceptive, some details of that journey are obscure but the general sequence of events is clear enough.

26. ADC, leg. 250, exp. 3370 (inquisitorial trial of Lope Guerrero el viejo, testimony of Bernardino Almanzorre, June 22, 1570).

27. This timeline corresponds roughly with what Lope Guerrero confessed to the Holy Office in 1610 when he acknowledged having gone over to the "sect of Mohammed" with "all his heart" about forty years previously. See ADC, leg. 250, exp. 3370 (inquisitorial trial of Lope Guerrero el viejo, confessions of the accused, November 13 and December 15, 1610).

28. ADC, leg. 250, exp. 3370 (inquisitorial trial of Lope Guerrero el viejo, confession of the accused, December 15, 1610).

29. During his seventeenth-century trial, when asked whether the accusation was true, Lope Guerrero claimed it could not have been since he was living in Torrubia de Soria during the time of the Alpujarras Revolt. This defense seems to be an evasion, since other sources indicate that Lope regularly traveled between Torrubia and Deza during his apprenticeship. See ADC, leg. 250, exp. 3370 (inquisitorial trial of Lope Guerrero el viejo, response to the accusations [cap. 4], March 9, 1609).

30. ADC, leg. 365, exp. 5165 (inquisitorial trial of Gabriel de Medina, testimony of Gabriel de León, November 7, 1608).

31. ADC, leg. 364, exp. 5159 (inquisitorial trial of Antón Guerrero el viejo, testimony of Gabriel de León, October 13, 1608).

32. ADC, leg. 250, exp. 3370 (inquisitorial trial of Lope Guerrero el viejo, testimony of the accused, November 13, 1610).

33. ADC, leg. 250, exp. 3370 (inquisitorial trial of Lope Guerrero el viejo, testimony of Diego Zamorano, August 23, 1601). Several decades earlier, an inquisitor in Áreval had noted the danger posed by Morisco tavern keepers and suggested that it prohibit Moriscos from holding the office (Tapia Sánchez, "Arrieros, mercaderes, mesoneros," 152).

34. Apparently the Old Christians (both of whom were Dezanos) and Gabriel de Medina's Morisco father-in-law Diego Zamorano (ca. 1535–1605) joined the party unexpectedly. Zamorano had previously been reconciled by the Holy Office and subsequently collaborated by denouncing Moriscos, including his daughter and son-in-law. See ADC, leg. 250, exp. 3370 (inquisitorial trial of Lope Guerrero el viejo, testimony of Diego Zamorano, August 23, 1601) and leg. 358, exp. 5103 (inquisitorial trial of Catalina Zamorano, testimony of Diego Zamorano, August 18, 1604, and February 9, 1605).

35. ADC, leg. 250, exp. 3370 (inquisitorial trial of Lope Guerrero el viejo, testimony of Juan Guerrero, August 9, 1608).

36. ADC, leg. 367, exp. 5180 (inquisitorial trial of Juan Guerrero, testimony of Gabriel de León, March 13, 1608).

37. ADC, leg. 364, exp. 5159 (inquisitorial trial of Antón Guerrero el viejo, testimony of Gabriel de León, October 9, 1608) and leg. 367, exp. 5180 (inquisitorial trial of Juan Guerrero, testimony of Gabriel de León, October 29, 1608).

38. For example, the *ordinario* (a specialized muleteer who carried mail between two major cities) who traveled to Zaragoza on behalf of students at the University of Salamanca between 1589–1610 was a Morisco from Árevalo. His regular route took him through Deza (Tapia Sánchez, "Arrieros, mercaderes, mesoneros," 154).

39. The entourage also included the son (Antón) and nephew (Pascual) of Antón Guerrero, Luis de Hortubia (known as el Jarquino), Pedro Zamorano (the son of Diego Zamorano), Francisco Ramírez (the nephew of Román Ramírez el menor), and Juan de Hortubia (son of Pedro de Hortubia).

40. Contradictory evidence exists regarding Juan's presence on the trip, but he denied having participated (ADC, leg. 370, exp. 5241 [inquisitorial trial of Juan de Cebea, response to the publication of witnesses (cap. 5), August 11, 1610]). His brothers' trials, which presumably would provide clarity, have been lost. If he did participate, as a youth, he probably would not have been expected to engage in Islamic activities.

41. Additional details about Luis de Arride, his three brothers, and their families in Brea was provided independently in 1608 by an inquisitorial spy in the secret jails of Cuenca, where several of Deza's Moriscos were then confined. See ADC, leg. 364, exp. 5159 (inquisitorial trial of Antón Guerrero, testimony of Gabriel de León, November 8, 1608).

42. Antón Guerrero claimed Francisco fasted under pressure from his brother. ADC, leg. 367, exp. 5180 (inquisitorial trial of Juan Guerrero, testimony of Antón Guerrero el viejo, September 6, 1608). Compare with the testimony of Gabriel de León, who reported that his cellmate Juan Guerrero named the Moriscos who fasted on this trip but did not mention Francisco (ADC, leg. 367, exp. 5180 [inquisitorial trial of Juan Guerrero, testimony of Gabriel de León, November 22, 1607]), and of Gabriel de Medina who indicated that two of the men on the trip told him Francisco did not fast (ADC, leg. 364, exp. 5159 [inquisitorial trial of Antón Guerrero el viejo, testimony of Gabriel de Medina, September 2, 1608]).

43. ADC, leg. 366, exp. 5174 (inquisitorial trial of Luis de Hortubia el Jarquino, testimony of Francisco de Cebea, April 21, 1608).

44. ADC, leg. 367, exp. 5180 (inquisitorial trial of Juan Guerrero, testimony of Antón Guerrero el viejo, December 20, 1608).

45. ADC, leg. 364, exp. 5159 (inquisitorial trial of Antón Guerrero el viejo, testimony of Luis de Cebea el más mozo, May 26, 1610).

46. Antón Guerrero and Antón el menor, Francisco Ramírez, Pedro Zamorano, and Juan de Hortubia continued on and were joined by Juan Guerrero (Antón el viejo's nephew).

47. ADC, leg. 364, exp. 5159 (inquisitorial trial of Antón Guerrero el viejo, testimony of Pedro Zamorano, August 17, 1610) and ADC, leg. 367, exp. 5180 (inquisitorial trial of Juan Guerrero, testimony of Antón Guerrero el viejo, September 6, 1608).

48. ADC, leg. 250, exp. 3383 (inquisitorial trial of Luis de Cebea el menor, testimony of Francisco de Cebea, 30 April 30 and May 2, 1608).

49. Ironically, Francisco had previously carried on an affair with Isabel Martínez (b. 1564), María's aunt (ADC, leg. 378, exp. 5356 [inquisitorial trial of María la Jarquina, testimony of Gabriel de León, June 20, 1608]).

50. Perhaps evidence that locally the fiction was known for what it was, the sacramental register correctly records Francisco and María as the girl's parents (AHDOS APD, LS [1605–1646], fol. 6v).

51. ADC, leg. 364, exp. 5159 (inquisitorial trial of Antón Guerrero el viejo, testimony of María la Carnicera, November 19, 1610).

52. ADC, leg. 364, exp. 5159 (inquisitorial trial of Antón Guerrero el viejo, testimony of Lope Guerrero el viejo, December 15, 1610) and ADC, leg. 250, exp. 3370 (inquisitorial trial of Lope Guerrero el viejo, testimony of Juan Guerrero, August 9, 1608). The church solemnized Juan and María's union on March 15, 1607 (AHDOS APD, LS [1605–1647], fol. 5).

53. ADC, leg. 362, exp. 5142 (letter from Pedro de Cisneros to the Holy Office in Cuenca, November 26, 1607). See also Díaz Migoyo, "Memoria y fama," 50–52.

54. ADC, leg. 364, exp. 5159 (inquisitorial trial of Antón Guerrero el viejo, testimony of Gabriel de León, October 11, 1608).

55. ADC, leg. 250, exp. 3370 (inquisitorial trial of Lope Guerrero el viejo, testimony of the accused, December 15, 1610).

56. Standard inquisitorial procedure included asking a series of set questions during the accused person's first audience, among them a question about literacy. Usually, when the accused indicated the he could read or write, he was asked to explain how he had learned to do so. This follow-up question was either omitted or the answer was not recorded during Lope's trial. See ADC, leg. 250, exp. 3370 (inquisitorial trial of Lope Guerrero el viejo, first audience, December 4, 1607).

57. ADC, leg. 249, exp. 3363 (inquisitorial trial of Francisco de Arcos, first audience, September 26, 1570). Sources do not allow for the calculation of literacy rates for Deza generally or its Moriscos specifically. But based on anecdotal evidence Morisco literacy (among men) was not uncommon. This claim corresponds with what Trevor Dadson and Serafín de Tapia Sánchez have concluded about Morisco literacy in their respective studies of the Moriscos in

(rural) Villarrubia de los Ojos and (urban) Ávila. See Dadson, "Literacy and Education," 1011–37 and *Tolerance and Coexistence*, 37–64; as well as Tapia Sánchez, *La comunidad morisca de Ávila*, 338.

58. In the 1580s Miguel de Deza learned to read and write from a pair of Old Christians and from the cleric Pedro Jiménez (ADC, leg. 370, exp. 5225 [inquisitorial trial of Miguel de Deza], first audience, May 29, 1608). Layman Miguel Sánchez was the *maestro de niños* by 1597 (AHMD, caja 282, doc. 6).

59. ADC, leg. 364, exp. 5159 (inquisitorial trial of Antón Guerrero el viejo, testimony of Gabriel de León, October 10, 1608).

60. ADC, leg. 116, exp. 1590 (inquisitorial trial of Juan López, testimony of Bernardino Burgueño, November 22, 1558).

61. ADC, leg. 116, exp. 1590 (inquisitorial trial of Juan López, testimony of Francisco Navarro, November 14, 1558).

62. Luis's father, Luis el viejo (1524–1609) was serving as co-magistrate in 1605. No sources mention his involvement in the investigation, so he may have recused himself.

63. Juan (b. 1567) was the son of Francisco el Romo (ca. 1533–ca. 1571) and Ana la Corazona (b. ca. 1542). It is unclear why he used the surname Mancebo, since his brothers Francisco (b. 1564) and Román (b. 1570) used el Romo. However, a paternal grand-aunt's husband (Hernán) was surnamed Mancebo.

64. AHDOS APD, leg. 160, doc. 28 (Libro de la Cofradía de Santa Ana de la Parroquia de Deza [1594–1661]).

65. Compare the Cebea's failure with the success of Morisco social climbers in the Campo de Calatrava who held relatively high offices in various confraternities. Elsewhere, however, Old Christian brotherhoods could be, as they were in Deza, more exclusive (Dadson, *Tolerance and Coexistence*, 61–63, 206–8).

66. ADC, leg. 250, exp. 3383 (inquisitorial trial of Luis de Cebea el menor, testimony of Baltasar de Ocáriz, September 24, 1610).

67. ADC, leg. 371, exp. 5246 (inquisitorial trial of Juan Mancebo, testimony of Francisco de Cebea, May 7, 1608).

68. ADC, leg. 250, exp. 3383 (inquisitorial trial of Luis de Cebea el menor, testimony of Juan Miguel, September 24, 1610).

69. Román claimed he was plotting his revenge, but the Holy Office arrested him before he could carry it out. ADC, leg. 369, exp. 5216 (inquisitorial trial of Román el Romo, first audience, June 15, 1608).

70. ADC, leg. 250, exp. 3383 (inquisitorial trial of Luis de Cebea el menor, testimony of Baltasar de Ocáriz, September 24, 1610).

71. ADC, leg. 250, exp. 3370 (inquisitorial trial of Lope Guerrero el viejo, testimony of Juan Guerrero [August 9, 1608] and testimony of Francisco de Cebea [July 9, 1610]).

72. ADC, leg. 250, exp. 3383 (inquisitorial trial of Luis de Cebea el menor, testimony of Pedro de Cisneros, October 2, 1610). Juan Mancebo claimed in his own trial that he had never lived outside of Deza, which suggests (but does not prove) that the authorities failed to enforce the sentence (ADC, leg. 371, exp. 5246 [inquisitorial trial of Juan Mancebo, first audience, October 9, 1609]).

73. ADC, leg. 375, exp. 5321 (inquisitorial trial of Lope de Deza, first audience, May 23, 1608).

74. ADC, leg. 367, exp. 5179 (inquisitorial trail of María la Burgueña [alias Carnicera], testimony of the accused, February 19, 1610) and ADC, leg. 367, exp. 5180 (inquisitorial trial of Juan Guerrero, testimony of Gabriel de León, December 20, 1607). Exchanging bulls of crusade in this fashion was prohibited but doing so was common.

75. ADC, leg. 250, exp. 3383 (inquisitorial trial of Luis de Cebea el menor, testimony of Pedro de Cisneros, October 2, 1610).

76. ADC, leg. 250, exp. 3383 (inquisitorial trial of Luis de Cebea el viejo, testimony of Pedro de Cisneros, October 2, 1610).

77. Luis and Juan were fined and exiled "for a time." The same punishment (but again in unknown quantities) was meted out to their father, mother, brother, and to Juan de Deza (for failing to appear). ADC, leg. 250, exp. 3383 (inquisitorial trial of Luis de Cebea el viejo, testimony of Pedro de Cisneros, October 2, 1610).

78. ADC, leg. 370, exp. 5225 (inquisitorial trial of Miguel de Deza, testimony of Gabriel de León, June 20, 1608) and ADC, leg. 250, exp. 3383 (inquisitorial trial of Luis de Cebea el menor, request for defense, September 18, 1610). Francisco was actually keeping a watch for the arrival of inquisitorial personnel, but the feud was a believable cover story to explain his skulking.

79. ADC, leg. 250, exp. 3383 (inquisitorial trial of Luis de Cebea el viejo, testimony of Pedro de Cisneros, October 2, 1610).

80. ADC, leg. 370, exp. 2541 (inquisitorial trial of Juan de Cebea, statement of Alonso de Póveda, March 22, 1608) and ADM, leg. 111, doc. 39, fol. 5r.

81. ADC, leg. 367, exp. 5180 (inquisitorial trial of Juan Guerrero, testimony of Gabriel de León [August 21, 1608] and response to the accusations [cap. 69] [October 27, 1609]).

82. ADC, leg. 367, exp. 5180 (inquisitorial trial of Juan Guerrero, testimony of Gabriel de León, November 27, 1607).

83. ADC, leg. 366, exp. 5174 (inquisitorial trial of Luis de Hortubia el Jarquino, testimony of Gabriel de León, May 13, 1608). See also ADC, leg. 366, exp. 5174 (inquisitorial trial of Luis de Hortubia el Jarquino, response to the accusation [cap. 30], April 24, 1610). Although Bayonne was hardly the utopia that the Dezanos imagined, Moriscos settled there both before and after the expulsions of 1609–14. See Gil Herrera and Bernabé Pons, "The Moriscos Outside Spain," 230–32 and Muchnik, "Judeoconversos and Moriscos," 437–38.

84. Quoted from Harvey's translation of the Mancebo's *Breve compendio* in *Muslims in Spain*, 184.

85. See Molénat, "Le problème de la permanence," 392–400; Bernabé-Pons, "*Taqiyya, niyya* y el islam de los moriscos," 491–527; and Rosa-Rodriguez, "Simulation and Dissimulation," 143–80.

5. THE GUARDIANS OF MORISCO CULTURE

1. See ADC, leg. 378, exp. 5356 (inquisitorial trial of María la Jarquina, testimony of Francisco el Romo [November 11, 1610] and response of the accused to the second Accusation [November 13, 1610]).

2. See Bramón, "El rito de las fadas," 33–37 and García-Arenal, *Inquisición y moriscos*, 56–59.

3. Dadson, *Tolerance and Coexistence*, 84–85 and Vincent, "Las mujeres moriscas," 592.

4. Perry, *Handless Maiden*, 69–73 and 82.

5. Perry, *Handless Maiden*, 72.

6. ADC, leg. 820, exp. 7992, fol. 8v.

7. Perry, *Handless Maiden*, 67.

8. Poska's *Women and Authority* argues that early modern Spanish women exercised a much greater degree of liberty than the moralists would otherwise lead one to expect.

9. ADC, leg. 358, exp. 5103 (inquisitorial trial of Catalina Zamorano, first audience, December 1, 1607). Catalina's autobiographical *discurso de vida* is unusual for its degree of detail; most Dezanas tried by the Holy Office provided only a few sentences of autobiography when queried by inquisitors. The amount of travel she undertook is also unusual, since most Moriscas merely described themselves as living at home with their mothers until they married and then living with their husbands until their arrest. Despite these idiosyncrasies—indeed, because of them—her *discurso* is helpful for reading other, less detailed, accounts because it suggests both the range of possibilities available and also some of the limits.

10. For a version of the legend, see Guillén Robles, *Leyendas Moriscas*, 1:182–221. For an application of the Carcayona tale to the plight of the Moriscos, see Perry, *Handless Maiden*, 27–37.

11. ADC, leg. 250, exp. 3370 (inquisitorial trial of Lope Guerrero el viejo, first audience of the accused, December 4, 1607).

12. This was young by any standard, but Moriscas, on average, married a year earlier than Old Christian women. This, in part, led Old Christians to fear that Moriscos would grow like "bad weeds" and soon overrun the entire Peninsula. The threat was exaggerated but, as Tapia Sánchez has shown in his study

of Ávila, the town's Morisco community was outpacing the Old Christians. See *La comunidad morisca de Ávila*, 400, and Perry, *Handless Maiden*, 50–51.

13. María la Jarquina never mentioned living anywhere other than Deza, but their son claimed to have been born in Morata (ADC, leg. 366, exp. 5174 [inquisitorial trial of Luis de Hortubia el Jarquino, first audience of the accused, June 6, 1608]).

14. ADC, leg. 366, exp. 5174 (inquisitorial trial of Luis de Hortubia el Jarquino, testimony of Juan Guerrero, August 13, 1608). For her part, María evaded questions about her relationship with Guerrero when it was broached during her inquisitorial trial (ADC, leg. 378, exp. 5356 [inquisitorial trial of María la Jarquina, response to the Accusations (cap. 8), July 28, 1609]).

15. ADC, leg. 378, exp. 5356 (inquisitorial trial of María la Jarquina, first audience of the accused, June 10, 1608).

16. See ADC, leg. 366, exp. 5174 (inquisitorial trial of Luis de Hortubia el Jarquino, testimony of the accused, June 12, 1610).

17. See García-Arenal, *Inquisición y moriscos*, 57–58.

18. ADC, leg. 366, exp. 5174 (inquisitorial trial of Luis de Hortubia el Jarquino, testimony of Catalina Zamorano, January 11, 1610).

19. ADC, leg. 369, exp. 5214 (inquisitorial trial of Isabel de Liñán, confession of the accused, March 1, 1610).

20. ADC, leg. 364, exp. 5159 (inquisitorial trial of Antón Guerrero el viejo, testimony of Catalina Zamorano, January 11, 1610). Purportedly, when Gerónimo de Leonis asked what name the boy should be given, his father responded, "Luis, like me," to the amusement of attendees (ADC, leg. 364, exp. 5159 [inquisitorial trial of Antón Guerrero el viejo, testimony of Luis de Hortubia el Jarquino, April 24, 1610]).

21. ADC, leg. 367, exp. 5180 (inquisitorial trial of Juan Guerrero, response to the Accusation [cap. 8], August 9, 1608). When he arrived home that evening, Guerrero was informed that the fadas had been performed. A party of both men and women gathered the following night "in honor and celebration" of the ceremony.

22. ADC, leg. 378, exp. 5356 (inquisitorial trial of María la Jarquina, testimony of Francisco el Romo, November 11, 1610).

23. ADC, leg. 376, exp. 5332 (inquisitorial trial of Lope de Cieli, testimony of Gabriel de León, December 20, 1607). Luis de Hortubia el Jarquino claimed that, like Gerónimo de Leonis, Francisco el Romo knew how to fix the date of Ramadan. But subsequently he retracted the denunciation and claimed that he had meant Fabián de Deza, who was already dead, rather than el Romo, who was currently being tried by the Holy Office. The retraction seems dubious given the circumstances. See ADC, leg. 366, exp. 5174 (inquisitorial trial of Luis de Hortubia el Jarquino, confession of the accused, May 6, 1610).

24. La Jarquina performed the fadas for Miguel Ramírez's daughter "Marien" in ca. 1606 (ADC, leg. 378, exp. 5356 [inquisitorial trial of María la Jarquina, confession of the accused, February 11, 1611]).

25. García-Arenal claims that only a single example (occurring in 1569) of such marriages exists in the records of the Conquense tribunal (*Inquisición y moriscos*, 59–60). In fact, there are several, among them the 1605 marriage of Francisco de Cebea and María Martínez by Luis de Arride Lumán of Brea (Zaragoza) (ADC, leg. 250, exp. 3383 [inquisitorial trial of Luis de Cebea el menor, testimony of Francisco de Cebea, April 30 and May 2, 1608]).

26. ADC, leg. 367, exp. 5180 (inquisitorial trial of Juan Guerrero, testimony of Gabriel de León, May 13, 1608).

27. ADC, leg. 364, exp. 5159 (inquisitorial trial of Antón Guerrero el viejo, testimony of Gabriel de León, October 11, 1608).

28. When Francisco de Cebea was arrested by the Holy Office, he had in his possession a necklace of very similar description, which he valued at twenty ducats. Because he was not immediately searched, he successfully hid it under his clothes and later handed it off to his father-in-law, Hernando Martínez. See ADC, leg. 370, exp. 5241 (inquisitorial trial of Juan de Cebea, testimony of Miguel Ramírez, October 3, 1609).

29. ADC, leg. 361, exp. 5131 (inquisitorial trial of Ana Guerrero, response to the Accusation [cap. 6], July 12, 1610). No positive evidence indicates that Deza's Moriscas underwent a ritual bathing and clothing in the presence of their female relatives on their wedding day or that their bodies were adorned with henna as occurred among the Moriscas of Valencia. See Alcaina Fernández, "La inquisición en el marquesado de los Vélez," 30.

30. ADC, leg. 375, exp. 5322 (inquisitorial trial of María la Carnicera, testimony of Gabriel de León, May 13, 1608). Juan Guerrero confirmed this in ADC, leg. 367, exp. 5180 (inquisitorial trial of Juan Guerrero, response to the Accusation [cap. 102], August 20, 1608).

31. García-Arenal, *Inquisición y moriscos*, 62.

32. ADC, leg. 378, exp. 5356 (inquisitorial trial of María la Jarquina, testimony of Lope Guerrero el menor, November 26, 1610). Bernardino was a Morisco from Ariza (Zaragoza) but married to Ana de Baptista, a Dezana (ADC, leg. 252, exp. 3414 [inquisitorial trial of María de Medina, testimony of Juan Guerrero, August 13, 1608]).

33. ADC, leg. 367, exp. 5334 (inquisitorial trial of María de Cebea, response to the publication of witnesses [test. 2; cap. 6], July 20, 1610) and ADC, leg. 375, exp. 5322 (inquisitorial trial of María la Carnicera, ratification of the confession of the accused, November 19, 1610). On Morisco preparations for burial, see Longás, *La vida religiosa de los moriscos*, 285–87 and García-Arenal, *Inquisición y moriscos*, 62–63. See also Dadson, *Tolerance and Coexistence*, 212, where

enshrouding played a similarly significant role in demarcating Morisco practice from Old Christian. He also offers a rich description of what a Morisco shrouding entailed in Villarrubia (*Los moriscos de Villarrubia*, 1135–77).

34. Juan Guerrero claimed that la Jarquina had performed the fadas for Ana, but Francisco de Cebea believed that it was María la Carnicera. La Jarquina herself was evasive in her description of the event, claiming that she had "seen" the ceremony. She noted the presence of Cecilia la Montera but made no mention of la Carnicera. ADC, leg. 378, exp. 5356 (inquisitorial trial of María la Jarquina, testimonies of Gabriel de León [May 13, 1608] and Juan Guerrero [August 9, 1608]; and confession of the accused [under threat of torture] [February 11, 1611]).

35. ADC, 378, exp. 5356 (inquisitorial trial of María la Jarquina, testimony of Ana Guerrera, August 9, 1610).

36. ADC, 378, exp. 5356 (inquisitorial trial of María la Jarquina, confession of the accused [under threat of torture], February 11, 1611).

37. ADC, leg. 378, exp. 5356 (inquisitorial trial of María la Jarquina, testimony of Gabriel de León, June 20, 1608).

38. García-Arenal, *Inquisición y moriscos*, 110; Lobo Cabrera, *Los libertos*, 120–21; and Goodman, *Power and Penury*, 36–37.

39. ADC, leg. 378, exp. 5356 (inquisitorial trial of María la Jarquina, testimony of Gabriel de León, October 14, 1608).

40. López Terrada, "Medical Pluralism," 7–8. On the relationship between orthodox and "alternative" medicine, see Blécourt and Usborne, "Situating 'alternative medicine,'" 283–85 and Jütte, "Introduction," 1–10.

41. ADC, leg. 716, exp. 861 (Pedro de Barnuevo's denunciation of María de Luna, October 16, 1599).

42. ADC, leg. 367, exp. 5180 (inquisitorial trial of Juan Guerrero, testimony of Gabriel de León, December 19, 1607).

43. ADC, leg. 362, exp. 5142 (inquisitorial trial of Miguel Ramírez, letter of Pedro de Cisneros, November 12, 1607).

44. See ADC, leg. 375, exp. 5322 (inquisitorial trial of María la Carnicera, testimony of Juan Guerrero, August 8, 1608) and ADC, leg. 378, exp. 5356 (inquisitorial trial of María la Jarquina, testimony of Gabriel de León, May 13, 1608).

45. ADC, leg. 375, exp. 5322 (inquisitorial trial of María la Carnicera, response to the Accusation, June 12, 1609).

46. ADC, libro 317, fols. 467r-68r (*This Happened*, 34–35).

47. The exception to this rule, apparently, was that only men butchered animals "according to the ceremony of the said Law." Gabriel de Medina confessed that when their husbands were ill, Deza's Moriscas sometimes summoned him to slaughter animals, especially fowl. ADC, leg. 367, exp. 5179 (inquisito-

rial trial of María la Burgueña, testimony of Gabriel de Medina, October 10, 1608). See likewise, ADC, leg. 246, exp. 3306, fol. 52v.

48. See, for instance, ADC, libro 318, fols. 111r-v and 122v-23r (*This Happened*, 89–90 and 103–5).

49. ADC, leg. 368, exp. 5196 (inquisitorial trial of María la Carnicera, testimony of Juan Guerrero, December 4, 1607).

50. ADC, leg. 367, exp. 5180 (inquisitorial trial of Juan Guerrero, response to the Accusation [cap. 5], August 9, 1608). See also ADC, leg. 367, exp. 5180 (inquisitorial trial of Juan Guerrero, testimony of Gabriel de León, November 23, 1607).

51. ADC, leg. 367, exp. 5180 (inquisitorial trial of Juan Guerrero, confession of the accused, January 10, 1608).

52. ADC, leg. 378, exp. 5356 (inquisitorial trial of María la Jarquina, confession of the accused, February 11, 1611).

53. ADC, leg. 378, exp. 5356 (inquisitorial trial of María la Jarquina, testimony of Diego Zamorano [August 18, 1604], testimony of Juan Guerrero [December 15, 1607], and confession of the accused [under threat of torture] [February 11, 1611]).

54. Little is known of María la Flamenca, who died ca. 1603 and was never tried by the Holy Office. Of her children whose births can be dated, the eldest was born in 1568, which would suggest a birth date of ca. 1550 for the mother, making her a rough contemporary of María la Jarquina. La Flamenca's daughter, Ana la Buena (b. ca. 1578), married in Deza and continued to run a Moorish household, keeping to the dietary practices she learned from her mother. See ADC, leg. 372, exp. 5254 (denunciation of Ana la Buena by Librada González, December 21, 1608).

55. She called the midday prayer (*salat az-zuhr*) the "azala de adogar," the afternoon prayer (*salat al-asr*) "al azar," and the evening (*salat al-magrib*) "al magre." Less faithfully, the night prayer (*salat al-isa*) became "Argueytre." The inaccuracy of pronunciation may, of course, also be blamed on the inquisitorial scribe who recorded her statement. ADC, leg. 378, exp. 5356 (inquisitorial trial of María la Jarquina, confession of the accused, November 11, 1610).

56. ADC, leg. 378, exp. 5356 (inquisitorial trial of María la Jarquina, confessions of the accused, July 28, 1609, and November 11, 1610).

57. This interest was not unique to María la Jarquina. While in inquisitorial custody, Gabriel de Medina and Antón Guerrero indicated to their cellmate that Deza's Moriscas were always eager to learn Islamic prayers and intimated that it would "go very well with them" if they passed along any new ones. ADC, leg. 364, exp. 5159 (inquisitorial trial of Antón Guerrero el viejo, testimony of Gabriel de León, October 10, 1608).

58. Jora (*Ashura*) occurred on the tenth day of the month *Muharram* and commemorated the death of Mohammed's grandson Husain. Carnero (*'Arafah*) occurred on the ninth day of the month of *Dhul Hijja*, seventy days after the

end of Ramadan, and was followed by a four-day feast recalling Abraham's willingness to sacrifice his son and God's provision of a ram, hence *carnero*. The six White Days were fasted beginning the second day of the month of *Shawwal*. See García-Arenal, *Inquisición y moriscos*, 48–49 and Vincent, *Historia de los Moriscos*, 91.

59. Juan Guerrero described la Flamenca's daughter María (b. 1568) and Cecilia de Cieli (1546–1607) as frequent hosts of Aragonese Moriscos (ADC, leg. 367, exp. 5180 [inquisitorial trial of Juan Guerrero, response to the Accusation (cap. 73), August 19, 1608]). In the fall of 1608 Lope Guerrero claimed that Cecilia de Cieli had been the best female teacher (*maestra*) in town and the one who "knew the most" about Islam (ADC, leg. 364, 5159 [inquisitorial trial of Antón Guerrero el viejo, testimony of Gabriel de León, October 11, 1608]).

60. ADC, leg. 249, exp. 3552 (inquisitorial trial of Ana de Almoravi, confession of the accused, February 5, 1571).

61. ADC, leg. 378, exp. 5356 (inquisitorial trial of María la Jarquina, testimony of Gabriel de León, May 13, 1608).

62. ADC, leg. 376, exp. 5334 (inquisitorial trial of María de Cebea, testimony of Ana Guerrero, July 10, 1610).

63. ADC, leg. 250, exp. 3383, fols. 26v-33r.

64. ADC, leg. 367, exp. 5180 (inquisitorial trial of Juan Guerrero, testimony of Gabriel de León, December 20, 1607).

65. ADC, leg. 375, exp. 5322 (inquisitorial trial of María la Carnicera, confession of the accused for Edict of Grace [January 16, 1571]; testimonies of Gerónimo de Molina [May 29, 1570, and June 6, 1570] and Ana de Almoravi [January 11, 1571]).

66. ADC, leg. 375, exp. 5322 (inquisitorial trial of María la Carnicera, confession of the accused for Edict of Grace [January 16, 1571]; testimonies of Gerónimo de Molina [May 29, 1570, and June 6, 1570] and Ana de Almoravi [January 11, 1571]).

67. ADC, leg. 367, exp. 5180 (inquisitorial trial of Juan Guerrero, testimony of Gabriel de León, November 28, 1607).

68. Francisco (b. ca. 1548) was the elder brother of Lope de Arcos (b. ca. 1559), who was associated with Román Ramírez's Islamic meetings at the duke's garden and became an important leader of the Morisco community in Deza following the death of Alexo Gorgoz. As a young man, Francisco took the Edict of Grace, having already been denounced and arrested for following the Law of Mohammed. He served three years rowing in the galleys (and probably participated in the Battle of Lepanto) before returning home to establish his own forge and an estate valued at more than 500 ducats in 1594 (ARCV RE, leg. 1901, doc. 45, fol. 11v). In 1609 he and his family were living in Mazaterón (just north of Deza), where Francisco worked as blacksmith, but he continued to maintain his home in Deza (ADM, leg. 188, doc. 27, fol. 6r).

69. ADC, leg. 367, exp. 5180 (inquisitorial trial of Juan Guerrero, testimony of Gabriel de León, August 21, 1608). This does not appear to have been a formal dame school as may have existed in Almagro from 1573 (Dadson, *Coexistence and Tolerance*, 56).

70. The accusation made by an Old Christian all of Deza's Moriscos, both women and men, wore "different clothes and dress, of such a style that they are known to be Moriscos" is a curious one (ARCV RE, caja 1990, doc. 90, fol. 8v). No other indication of unusual dress exists in the entire corpus of primary source documents relating to Deza's Moriscos, and this claim was offered by a hostile Old Christian attempting to emphasize the Moorish behavior of the Moriscos in order to win a lawsuit. If not altogether false, then, it might well be an exaggeration. For Morisco dress, see Martínez Ruiz, *Inventario de bienes* and Vincent, "Las mujeres moriscas," 588–89.

71. Labarta, "La mujer morisca," 225.

72. ADC, leg. 378, exp. 5356 (inquisitorial trial of María la Jarquina, testimony of Gabriel de León, June 20, 1608).

73. ADC, leg. 375, exp. 5322 (inquisitorial trial of María la Carnicera, testimony of Francisco de Cebea, July 9, 1610). In point of fact, la Carnicera lasted more than two years in the secret jails and underwent heavy torture before confessing anything. Only after having withstood six turns of the cord on the chair of torture and having been moved onto the rack did she finally break her silence. Francisco de Cebea, who was more than thirty years her junior, began confessing and denouncing after about a month in the jails.

74. ADC, leg. 375, exp. 5308 (denunciations of María la Burgueña by Gerónimo de Molina and Ana García, September 15, 1610).

75. ADC, leg. 249, exp. 3368 (inquisitorial trial of Ana de Almanzorre, confession of the accused, June 5, 1570).

76. ADC, leg. 343, exp. 4876, fol. 193r (*This Happened*, 59).

77. ADC, leg. 364, exp. 5159 (inquisitorial trial of Antón Guerrero el viejo, testimony of Gabriel de León, December 17, 1608) and leg. 250, exp. 2270 (inquisitorial trial of Catalina Zamorano, testimony of Diego Zamorano, August 23, 1601).

6. FAVOR AND FAME

1. After the death of his first wife, Román the elder married twice more but neither woman's name is known, except that his second wife was *fulana* ("so-and-so") de Arcos.

2. For his hair: ADC, libro 317, fol. 465v.

3. ADC, leg. 343, exp. 4876, fol. 202v.

4. ADC, libro 317, fols. 460r and 465v (*This Happened*, 23 and 32). Another witness, a former servant of Ramírez, accused him of having eaten an egg during

Lent and of failing to say "Jesus" or cross himself when his son sneezed (fol. 467r [*This Happened*, 34]).

5. See Fernández Nieva, "Don Diego Gómez de Lamadrid," 81–87.

6. Fernández Nieva, "Don Diego Gómez de Lamadrid," 106. Román el menor claimed that his father had taken the Edict, but no evidence of this has otherwise come to light (ADC, leg. 343, exp. 4876, fol. 210r). Perhaps some sort of private deal was arranged while he was in Madrid.

7. Not *María* la Ferrara as reported in Palencía, "El curandero," 230 and Caro Baroja, *Vidas mágicas*, 1:314. An Ana de Ferrara (but no one surnamed de Luna) lived in Burbáguena in 1538. By 1581 both families had either emigrated or died out (Halavais, *Like Wheat to the Miller*, 160).

8. ADC, leg. 343, exp. 4876, fol. 12r and 200r; and ADC, leg. 367, exp. 5180 (inquisitorial trial of Juan Guerrero, testimony of Gabriel de León, December 20, 1607).

9. ADC, leg. 367, exp. 5180 (inquisitorial trial of Juan Guerrero, testimony of Gabriel de León December 20, 1607).

10. In addition to Román the younger, the couple's children were Juan (b. 1544), Lope (b. 1547), Gerónimo (b. 1550), Miguel (b. 1551), María (b. 1554), and Francisco (b. 1556).

11. ADC, leg. 343, exp. 4876, fols. 12r and 225v.

12. ADC, leg. 343, exp. 4876, fols. 12v, 225v, and 228r.

13. ADC, leg. 343, exp. 4876, fol. 12r.

14. ADC, leg. 343, exp. 4876, fol. 228r.

15. ADC, leg. 343, exp. 4876, fol. 202v. Here and frequently elsewhere, Ramírez used the word *decorar* to describe his memorization of works for recitation. While *decorar* has a secondary meaning of learning a lesson by memory, it primarily relates to taking something simple and adorning or beautifying it. Embellish, then, is not a strict translation of the word but connotes something of how the storyteller used the books, "adding and removing phrases as he liked" (203v).

16. ADC, leg. 343, exp. 4876, fol. 16r. Or, as he told the inquisitors, he could read for "three months" without a paper or anything else before him (fol. 203r).

17. The encounter probably took place in Torrubia (Guadalajara), about forty-five miles south of Deza, but possibly Torrubia de Soria (Soria), sixteen miles to the north. Ávila made a record of the encounter, he claimed, and recounted it to inquisitorial authorities in October 1595.

18. ADC, leg. 343, exp. 4876, fol. 55v.

19. ADC, leg. 343, exp. 4876, fol. 22v. A similar claim is made at fol. 6v, that Román could recite "the Bible or sacred writing [*escritura*]" and at fols. 7v-8r, that he knew the "sacred writings [*escrituras*]" and that he claimed he could satisfy requests to recite "any part of the sacred writings [*escrituras*], even if it were from the Bible."

20. ADC, leg. 343, exp. 4876, fol. 210v.

21. ADC, leg. 343, exp. 4876, fols. 200r and 225v.

22. ADC, leg. 343, exp. 4876, fol. 201r. González Palencia, "El curandero," 248 and García-Ballester, *Medicina*, 79 interpret this as referring to María's father Juan de Luna. But the addition of the title "doctor," his citizenship in Daroca (rather than Burbáguena), and the fact that María is described as Dr. Juan de Luna's *nieta* strongly suggest that when Román spoke of *su abuelo*, he did not mean his own grandfather but rather María's, which, in any case, makes better sense given the context.

23. ADC, leg. 343, exp. 4876, fol. 201r-v.

24. ADC, leg. 343, exp. 4876, fol. 204r-209v. González Palencia transcribes these in "El curandero," 251–61.

25. ADC, leg. 343, exp. 4876, fol. 211v.

26. In the 1560s, for example, Román the elder was purportedly seen performing ritual ablutions in the local creek and eating dairy during Lent (ADC, libro 317, fols. 460r, 465v, and 467r [*This Happened*, 23, 32, and 34]).

27. ADC, leg. 343, exp. 4876, fol. 226r. Unfortunately, no archival record exists of Juan de Luna's trial.

28. García-Arenal, *Inquisición y moriscos*, 65–66.

29. ADC, leg. 343, exp. 4876, fol. 211v. Román el menor frequently made dramatic references to hellfire, especially to emphasize his sincerity.

30. ADC, leg. 343, exp. 4876, fol. 212r.

31. ADC, leg. 343, exp. 4876, fol. 212v.

32. ADC, leg. 343, exp. 4876, fol. 212v. Note that Villaverde moved to Teruel, not Ramírez, as suggested in Harvey, "Oral Composition," 275 and Caro Baroja, *Vidas mágicas*, 1:314.

33. ADC, leg. 343, exp. 4876, fol. 212v. See González Palencia, "El curandero," 232; Harvey, "Oral Composition," 275; and Caro Baroja, *Vidas mágicas*, 1:314.

34. ADC, leg. 343, exp. 4876, fol. 225v.

35. ADC, leg. 343, exp. 4876, fol. 13r. In 1599, with Ramírez's trial ongoing, the Morisco's nemesis Pedro de Barnuevo (having been removed from his offices) dredged up (or concocted?) a rumor that Ramírez's long-deceased mother had conversed "on Sundays" with a demon, thereby adding another chapter in the family's history of demonic pacts. See ADC, leg. 716, exp. 861 (Pedro de Barnuevo's denunciation of María de Luna, October 16, 1599).

36. ADC, leg. 343, exp. 4876, fol. 225v.

37. Compare with Cardaillac-Hermosilla, *Los nombres del diablo*, 121 and Caro Baroja, *Vidas mágicas*, 1:322.

38. ADC, leg. 343, exp. 4876, fol. 226r.

39. ADC, leg. 343, exp. 4876, fol. 226r.

40. ADC, leg. 343, exp. 4876, fol. 226r-v. Román's assertion at this juncture that "he was not trying to heal (*no trataba de curar*)" anyone but rather was interested in treasure hunting, has been taken to imply a rejection of the family tradition of medicine; his words need not carry that weight.

41. ADC, leg. 343, exp. 4876, fol. 210r. A son named Román was born and baptized in August 1563, a daughter María in February 1565, and Lope sometime in 1566. Román III certainly survived until after 1609. María probably died young, since her father gave a second daughter the same name in 1596. Lope was confirmed in 1570 but "died a young man" sometime before 1599.

42. ADC, leg. 343, exp. 4876, fol. 192r (*This Happened*, 56).

43. ADC, leg. 343, exp. 4876, fol. 226v. Román dated these events to "four or five years" after his first interaction with Liarde (ca. 1562).

44. ADC, leg. 343, exp. 4876, fols. 226v-27r.

45. ADC, leg. 343, exp. 4876, fol. 48v.

46. Deza's Moriscos also had important interactions with Juan Luis's father, Duke Juan de la Cerda, but Román the elder was the point of contact rather than Román the younger and, moreover, evidence suggests that the old duke was not at all sympathetic toward the Morisco healer. Assuming that the "duke" in question was Juan Luis, then the most likely candidate for healing is his daughter Antonia, born in Medinaceli in 1567, although María (b. 1583) is possible as well.

47. The marquisate of Cogolludo, which had been Duke Luis's before his elevation, entailed lordship over the towns of Deza and Enciso.

48. Martín de Milla is otherwise unknown, but the Mellas were Old Christian merchants who asserted their status as hidalgos beginning in the late 1560s and gained it toward the end of the century (ARCV SH, caja 446, doc. 11 and ARCV RE, caja 1584, doc. 31).

49. ADM, leg. 44, doc. 31 (letter from Gonzalo Martínez to Duke Juan de la Cerda, March 28, 1566).

50. ADM, leg. 44, doc. 30 (undated letter from Martín de Milla to Duke Juan de la Cerda).

51. ADC, leg. 249, exp. 3352, fols. 47v-48r and leg. 343, exp. 4876, fol. 59r. In later years, Román paid an annual rent of 200 *reales* for the property but it is not clear what, if anything, he was charged initially. Moreover, it has been assumed—and may well be the case—that Román used the duke's garden to cultivate herbs for his cures, but no specific evidence suggests this. In 1599, he told inquisitors that he spent his days "farming and cultivating (*en cultivar*) a garden that the duke had given him and searching (*en buscar*) for the herbs . . . for his cures" (ADC, leg. 343, exp. 4876, fol. 211r).

52. ADM, leg. 44, doc. 30 (undated letter from Martín de Milla to Duke Juan de la Cerda).

53. ADC, leg. 343, exp. 4876, fol. 211r. These persons of quality included, of course, the knight Carlos López, the duke of Medinaceli's daughter, and the lord of Cabezuelos mentioned above as well as Licentiate Antonio Villegas de Guevara, the *alcalde de sacas* in Gómara (ADC, leg. 343, exp. 4876, fol. 32v), and a knight in Alfaro (fol. 75r).

54. For reasons discussed below, Román probably erred in his dating here. He suggests that la Fuente visited Deza in ca. 1570, but it was more likely 1567.

55. ADC, leg. 343, exp. 4876, fol. 228r.

56. ADC, leg. 343, exp. 4876, fol. 192v (*This Happened*, 57). "Medina" here is presumably Medinaceli. Román habitually abbreviated the names of towns and cities.

57. ADC, leg. 707, exp. 625 (inquisitorial examination of Román Ramírez el menor, July 4, 1581) (*This Happened*, 114).

58. ADC, libro 317, fol. 455r (*This Happened*, 17).

59. ADC, leg. 254, exp. 3429 (inquisitorial investigation into the flight of Mateo Romero el mozo, testimony of Román Ramírez el menor, April 11, 1570).

60. ADC, leg. 343, exp. 4876, fol. 202r.

61. He did not, however, give up on medicine. While in Madrid in ca. 1569 he purchased a copy of Andrés Laguna's expensive 1555 Castilian translation of Dioscorides's *De materia medica*. The book was subsequently "stolen" from him in ca. 1589 (ADC, leg. 343, exp. 4876, fol. 201v).

62. Carlos Morales, "La Hacienda Real," 70.

63. ADC, leg. 707, exp. 625 (inquisitorial investigation of Román Ramírez el menor, July 4, 1581) (*This Happened*, 114).

64. ADC, leg. 343, exp. 4876, fol. 203v.

65. ADC, leg. 343, exp. 4876, fol. 8r.

66. ADC, leg. 343, exp. 4876, fol. 197r.

67. ADC, leg. 343, exp. 4876, fol. 202v.

68. ADC, leg. 343, exp. 4876, fols. 6v, 7v-8r, and 22v. Whether he owned a Bible in the vernacular is unknown. A Castilian copy of the gospels ("un libro de evangelios de Romançe") was in Bernardino Almanzorre's possession in the 1560s but was never linked to Román. See ADC, leg. 250, exp. 3370 (inquisitorial trial of Lope Guerrero el viejo, testimony of Bernardino de Almanzorre, May 2, 1570).

69. ADC, leg. 343, exp. 4876, fol. 202r. *Espejo de consolación*, which contained the lives of Old Testament saints, seems a better fit for Román's library than Dueñas's *confesionario* the *Remedio de pecadores* (Valladolid, 1545), but the reference could be to either work.

70. See Surilla Fernández, *Chariots of Ladies*, 203–50. A critical edition has been produced by Clausell Nácher, "*Carro de las donas* (Valladolid, 1542)." Alternatively, perhaps Román was interested in the *Carro* because it was helpful in navigating interactions with women at court and at the *saraos de damas*.

71. ADC, leg. 343, exp. 4876, fol. 89v.

72. ADC, leg. 249, exp. 3552, fol. 50r. The *Marquis de Mantua* was sometimes also connected to the *Romance de Valdovinos*, another Spanish *chanson* set in the Carolingian era. (See, e.g., *Don Quixote* [pt. 1; ch. V], 41–45.) In 1568, at roughly the same time that Román referred to the Marquis, María la Carnicera (ca. 1551–1611), a Morisca of Deza, was remembered to have sung the portion of *Valdovinos* that goes: "tan clara sale la luna como el sol a mediodia quando sale Valdovino por los caños de Sevilla" (ADC, leg. 375, exp. 5322 [inquisitorial trial of María la Carnicera, testimony of Gerónimo de Molina, May 5, 1570]).

73. See Eisenberg, *Romances of Chivalry*, which remains essential reading for making sense of the proliferation of the genre in early modern Spain. Many of Eisenberg's conclusions about Román Ramírez, however, are incorrect (105n70).

74. ADC, leg. 343, exp. 4876, fol. 203v. Oddly, as Cacho Blecua has noted, Román's claim to having recited the "first chapter of the second book" is problematic for in neither the 1545 nor the 1587 edition does that chapter contain much in the way of battles ("Introducción al estudio de los motivos," 30).

75. González Palencia ("El curandero," 262–63) suggests that "don Duardo" is a reference to a distinct book, the Portuguese romance *Terceira parte da chronica de Palmeirim de Inglaterra na qual se tratam as grandes cavallarias de seu filho o principe dom Duardos segundo* (Lisbon, 1587), the seventh book of the Palmerín de Oliva cycle, but Eisenberg (*Romances*, 106) argues that here Duardo refers to "Duardos, prince of England," whose deeds were included in Francisco Vásquez's *Primaleón*. See also, Harvey, "Oral Composition," 281–82.

76. See ADC, leg. 343, exp. 4876, fol. 202r. I follow Eisenberg (*Romances*, 105–6) for the identification of many of these works.

77. ADC, leg. 343, exp. 4876, fol. 202r. Román also mentioned in this list his copy of Dioscorides's *De materia medica*, but since he presumably did not perform it in the same way as he did the other books it is excluded from the present discussion.

78. Harvey, "Oral Composition," 283.

79. ADC, leg. 343, exp. 4876, fol. 6v.

80. ADC, leg. 343, exp. 4876, fol. 203r.

81. ADC, leg. 343, exp. 4876, fol. 203r. This may reflect the "high somatic component" that Ong connects to oral memory (*Orality and Literacy*, 65–66).

82. ADC, leg. 343, exp. 4876, fol. 202v.

83. ADC, leg. 343, exp. 4876, fol. 203r-v.

84. ADC, leg. 343, exp. 4876, fol. 203v.

85. ADC, leg. 343, exp. 4876, fols. 7v-8r. See also Francisco de Ávila's testimony to similar effect (fol. 16r).

86. ADC, leg. 343, exp. 4876, fol. 11v.

87. ADC, leg. 249, exp. 3352, fol. 28v.

88. ADC, leg. 343, exp. 4876, fol. 12v. A similar claim regarding dishonesty was made four decades later by Morisco Juan Guerrero about Román's son, Román III (ADC, leg. 367, exp. 5180b [inquisitorial trial of Juan Guerrero, October 27, 1609, response to the accusation (cap. 58)]).

89. In this, Román seems to take after his own father whose behavior was described as confrontational and aggressive. See ADC, libro 317, fol. 467v and libro 318, fol. 100r (*This Happened*, 34 and 75).

90. ARCV RE, caja 1193, exp. 47.

91. AHMD, caja 23, docs. 13 and 25; caja 15a, doc. 4; and caja 15, doc. 19.

92. AHMD, caja 26, exp. 31 and RAH SC, doc. M-144, fols. 81–89.

93. ADC, libro 317, fols. 457v-58v (*This Happened*, 20–21). Páez (ca. 1510–77) was born in Atienza and of Jewish descent. His father was tried by the Holy Office and absolved of "incredulity and concealment" in 1524. The son came to Deza in about 1535 and served there as the town's physician until his death.

94. ADC, leg. 343, exp. 4876, fol. 212v.

95. ADC, leg. 707, exp. 625 (letter from Román Ramírez el menor to Dr. Francisco de Arganda, received July 15, 1581) (*This Happened*, 117).

96. ADM, leg. 44, exp. 23, fol. 1r.

97. ADC, leg. 343, exp. 4876, fol. 228r.

98. In typical fashion, Román abbreviates the town's name making it difficult to pinpoint, but this may be Molina de Aragón (Guadalajara), about fifty miles south of Deza, or (less likely) Molinos (Teruel) about one hundred miles southeast of Deza.

99. ADC, leg. 707, exp. 625 (inquisitorial examination of Román Ramírez el menor, July 4, 1581) (*This Happened*, 114).

100. ARCV RE, leg. 1999, exp. 90, fol. 6r.

101. AHPS AMD, leg. 26.558/2, fol. 10v.

102. ADC, leg. 343, exp. 4876, fol. 197v.

103. AHMD, caja 76, doc. 1 (letter of Román Ramírez el menor to Duke Juan Luis de la Cerda, November 16, 1582). In 1592 Román traveled to Soria and Almazán on business related to similar subsequent bonds (AHMD, caja 282, docs. 4 and 5 [July 21 and October 1592]).

104. AHMD, caja 76, doc. 1 (letter of Duke Juan Luis de la Cerda to the town of Deza, December 1, 1582).

105. AHPS AMD, leg. 26.556, doc.15 (letter from Juan Donoso el menor and other millers to the town council of Deza, August 24, 1585).

106. AHPS AMD, leg. 26.556, doc 15 (letter from Juan de Deza to Juan Donoso el menor, August 26, 1585).

107. ADC, leg. 343, exp. 4876, fol. 13r.

108. ADM, leg. 44, doc. 23. In 1594 Barnuevo appears to have arrested a second alguacil mayor (ADM, leg. 111, doc. 25, fol. 10r-v).

109. ADM, leg. 44, doc. 24.

110. ADM, leg. 44, doc. 23.

111. Presumably it was to this arrest that Ramírez referred on September 17, 1597 (and not another detainment in Medinaceli), when he sought to deflect blame about the mismanagement of town finances by claiming that he could not have been involved since he was in jail (AHMD, caja 26, doc. 4, fol. 63r).

112. See AHMD, caja 282, doc. 4 (February and June 1592).

113. AHMD, caja 282, docs. 4 and 5 (June 21, October, and November 1592).

114. Román noted his concerns about paying the rent in 1593 while involved in the Tajahuerce affair (ADC, leg. 343, exp. 4876, fol. 59r), and a 1609 record of ducal income indicates that the annual rent for the *huerta* was 8,976 mrs. (264 *reales*) (ADM, leg. 68, doc. 36, fol. 16r.). An earlier but undated record of ducal rents does not list the *huerta* as a source of income (ADM, leg. 44, doc. 14).

115. ADC, leg. 343, exp. 4876, fols. 15v-16r and 197r.

116. ADC, leg. 343, exp. 4876, fols. 31r and 53v. A *juez* (or *alcalde*) *de las sacas* was a Castilian judge with jurisdiction over cases related to the exportation of prohibited articles, especially precious metals.

7. THE DEMONS OF TAJAHUERCE

1. ADC, leg. 343, exp. 4876, fols. 39r and 48v.

2. ADC, leg. 343, exp. 4876, fol. 64v.

3. ADC, leg. 343, exp. 4876, fol. 198v.

4. ADC, leg. 343, exp. 4876, fol. 51v.

5. ADC, leg. 343, exp. 4876, fols. 17r and 63r.

6. ADC, leg. 343, exp. 4876, fol. 30v.

7. ADC, leg. 343, exp. 4876, fol. 30v.

8. ADC, leg. 343, exp. 4876, fol. 39r.

9. ADC, leg. 343, exp. 4876, fol. 199r.

10. ADC, leg. 343, exp. 4876, fol. 31v.

11. Román's account of events implies that Ortega had heard about him directly from Miguel de Deza in Torrubia but he was probably just telescoping a longer process (ADC, leg. 343, exp. 4876, fol. 198r).

12. ADC, leg. 343, exp. 4876, fol. 15v. Ávila claimed that he had met Román in Torrubia "more than a year and a half" before October 26, 1595 (i.e., early 1594), but early 1593 makes more sense, since that would have given Ávila time to mention the Morisco to Villacorta before Román's services were requested in mid-1593.

13. ADC, leg. 343, exp. 4876, fols. 31r and 56r.

14. ADC, leg. 343, exp. 4876, fol. 198r.

15. Another witness remembered Ángela de Miranda saying that Román was caring for a "knight" in Alfaro rather than his son (ADC, leg. 343, exp. 4876, fol. 75r).

16. ADC, leg. 343, exp. 4876, fols. 31r and 75r. It is possible that the "youth from Ortega" who accompanied Miguel de Deza was Labajo, but Román's account of his interaction with his cousin suggests that they spoke face-to-face (fol. 198r), while Labajo clearly indicates that Román was in Alfaro when he spoke to Ángela de Miranda (fol. 75r).

17. ADC, leg. 343, exp. 4876, fol. 75r. An additional explanation for this delay may be that Román was waiting for permission to enter the territory around Soria. He claimed to have received license to perform cures there from the corregidor before going to Soria, but securing permission would have taken at least a few days, unless Ortega had acquired it preemptively, before sending for the healer (fol. 231r).

18. ADC, leg. 343, exp. 4876, fols. 31r-v and 39v.

19. ADC, leg. 343, exp. 4876, fols. 48v and 52v.

20. ADC, leg. 343, exp. 4876, fol. 53r.

21. ADC, leg. 343, exp. 4876, fol. 32r.

22. ADC, leg. 343, exp. 4876, fols. 53r and 75r. Following one use of the incense, Bartolomé el mozo commented that no one could stay in the befouled room for two weeks (fol. 61v).

23. ADC, leg. 343, exp. 4876, fols. 32r and 40r.

24. ADC, leg. 343, exp. 4876, fols. 32r, 40v, 53v, and 75r.

25. ADC, leg. 343, exp. 4876, fol. 53v.

26. Purportedly, while on his way to Deza, Bartolomé met with a young hidalgo—a curious man who spoke oddly, carried no sword, and claimed (correctly) that Román would be found in the duke's garden. Later, Bartolomé persuaded himself this hidalgo had actually been a demon (ADC, leg. 343, exp. 4876, fols. 54r-55v).

27. ADC, leg. 343, exp. 4876, fol. 196v.

28. ADC, leg. 343, exp. 4876, fols. 32v and 63r.

29. ADC, leg. 343, exp. 4876, fols. 32v-33r.

30. ADC, leg. 343, exp. 4876, fol. 33r.

31. ADC, leg. 343, exp. 4876, fols. 33r-34r and 79r. This episode is a particularly convoluted part of the narrative with witnesses offering somewhat distinct but difficult to reconcile versions of events. Compare fols. 34r, 57r, 67v, and 76v.

32. This point, which the Holy Office extrapolated upon in Ramírez's condemnation to serve as proof that he sought the overthrow of King Philip's Spain by the forces of Islam, was not mentioned by Bartolomé el mozo or Ana Sanz but only by Bartolomé el viejo, who claimed to have heard about it from Ana.

33. ADC, leg. 343, exp. 4876, fols. 34r, 41r, and 68r.

34. ADC, leg. 343, exp. 4876, fol. 57r-v.

35. ADC, leg. 343, exp. 4876, fol. 24r. Quite possibly Román—who claimed to have memorized many sermons (fol. 55v)—was overheard muttering these words to himself.

36. ADC, leg. 343, exp. 4876, fols. 34v-35r. See also fol. 59r, where Bartolomé el mozo suggests that Román had gotten wind of his father's plan to have him arrested and, consequently, demanded immediate payment so that he could depart.

37. ADC, leg. 343, exp. 4876, fols. 41v, 44v, 59r, and 76v.

38. ADC, leg. 343, exp. 4876, fol. 24r.

39. ADC, leg. 343, exp. 4876, fol. 42r.

40. ADC, leg. 343, exp. 4876, fols. 34v, 42r, and 58v.

41. ADC, leg. 343, exp. 4876, fols. 35r and 42v.

42. ADC, leg. 343, exp. 4876, fols. 25r, 42v, and 59v. Further early evidence of Bartolomé el mozo's affliction was that he had forgotten where he was going on his way to Madruédano. He had to ask a stranger to read Ortigosa's name and address on the letter that he carried because he was unable to make sense of them himself (fol. 17r).

43. ADC, leg. 343, exp. 4876, fols. 35r-v, 42v, 44r, and 59v.

44. ADC, leg. 343, exp. 4876, fol. 42v.

45. ADC, leg. 343, exp. 4876, fols. 59v-60r.

46. ADC, leg. 343, exp. 4876, fol. 42v.

47. ADC, leg. 343, exp. 4876, fol. 35v.

48. ADC, leg. 343, exp. 4876, fols. 22v and 30r.

49. ADC, leg. 343, exp. 4876, fol. 17r.

50. *Bachiller* Rueda emphasized the he had personally witnessed the tokens emerging from Bartolomé's mouth (ADC, leg. 343, exp. 4876, fol. 47r).

51. ADC, leg. 343, exp. 4876, fol. 45r-v. *Bachiller* Ortigosa offered one more detail of note about the tokens. Subsequent to the exorcism the objects were given to *bachiller* Rueda, whose return home was marked by the appearance of an unnaturally menacing cloud. Rueda prayed for God's protection and arrived unscathed. As a memorial of the deliverances—both Bartolomé's and his own—he nailed the tokens to the church door in Tajahuerce (fol. 23r).

52. ADC, leg. 343, exp. 4876, fols. 23v and 60r.

53. ADC, leg. 343, exp. 4876, fol. 36r.

54. ADC, leg. 343, exp. 4876, fol. 17v.

55. ADC, leg. 343, exp. 4876, fol. 61v.

56. ADC, leg. 343, exp. 4876, fol. 68r.

57. ADC, leg. 343, exp. 4876, fol. 36r.

58. ADC, leg. 343, exp. 4876, fols. 37v and 43r.

59. ADC, leg. 343, exp. 4876, fols. 24v and 43r.

60. ADC, leg. 343, exp. 4876, fols. 24v and 36r.

61. ADC, leg. 343, exp. 4876, fols. 17v, 46r, and 60v.

62. ADC, leg. 343, exp. 4876, fol. 37v.

63. ADC, leg. 343, exp. 4876, fol. 24v.

64. Both Bartolomé el viejo and el mozo communicated the story of the witches causing Ana pain as well as the claim that Román controlled the demons (ADC, leg. 343, exp. 4876, fols. 37v-38r and 60v).

65. ADC, leg. 343, exp. 4876, fols. 36v and 84r.

66. ADC, leg. 343, exp. 4876, fol. 46v.

67. ADC, leg. 343, exp. 4876, fol. 84v.

68. ADC, leg. 343, exp. 4876, fols. 46v-47r and 85r.

69. ADC, leg. 343, exp. 4876, fol. 89r. The instructions here differ substantially from the version of them recorded in Román's inquisitorial sentence, which describes them as a "magical formula." See *This Happened*, 126–27.

70. ADC, leg. 343, exp. 4876, fol. 197r.

71. ADC, leg. 343, exp. 4876, fol. 85r-v.

72. ADC, leg. 343, exp. 4876, fols. 85v-86r.

73. ADC, leg. 343, exp. 4876, fol. 25r.

74. Whether the alguacil mayor referenced here was the alguacil of the town council (an office held that year by Morisco Juan Ramírez Ropiñón) or the alguacil mayor appointed by the duke to patrol Deza's hamlets is unclear. The former is more likely, but the latter office, which was sometimes given to Román's relatives, could be in view. See ADM, leg. 111, doc. 25, fol. 10r; ADC, leg. 343, exp. 4876, fol. 210r; and leg. 362, exp. 5142 (inquisitorial trial of Miguel Ramírez, first audience of the accused, June 2, 1608).

75. ADM, leg. 111, doc. 25, fol. 10r.

76. ADM, leg. 111, doc. 25, fol. 10v.

77. ADC, leg. 362, exp. 5142 (inquisitorial trial of Miguel Ramírez, first audience, June 2, 1608).

78. ADM, leg. 44, doc. 23. See also ADM, leg. 44, doc. 24 and AHMD, caja 15b, doc. 9.

79. ADC, leg. 343, exp. 4876, fol. 202v.

80. Although removed from his offices and briefly absent from Deza, Pedro de Barnuevo continued to serve in other capacities, including as the town's hidalgo magistrate in 1598. See AHMD, caja 282, doc. 6 and ADC, leg. 796, exp. 4706 (denunciation of Pedro Ropiñón by Pedro de Barnuevo, April 26, 1598).

81. She received all the sacraments, but no posthumous expressions of Christian devotion are mentioned. The absence of reference to having been buried inside the church suggests she was interred in the small cemetery adjacent to the parish (AHDOS APD, LS [1580–1605], fol. 86r).

82. ADC, leg. 343, exp. 4876, fol. 76r. In 1594, one witness called the muchacho "Romanico," a diminutive for Román, but the only Román among our Morisco's near relatives young enough to fit was a grandson born in 1592, which makes him too young to be a traveling companion. Another witness (fol. 56r)

claimed that the boy was called "Francisquillo" and was Román's nephew. A Francisco was born to Juan Ramírez, Román's brother, in ca. 1579.

83. ADC, leg. 343, exp. 4876, fol. 210r.

84. ARCV RE, leg. 1901, exp. 45, fol. 2v.

85. ARCV RE, leg. 1901, exp. 45, fol. 13r.

86. ARCV RE, leg. 1901, exp. 45, fol. 8r-v.

87. What precisely Román meant by calling Ucedo a "captain" is unclear, nor can we know whether his new wife was a Morisco or an Old Christian. To judge from Román's use of the past tense in 1599, his father-in-law predeceased him.

88. ADC, leg. 343, exp. 4876, fol. 197r. Arellano later became involved in adjudicating the case that ensued when Dr. López de Rebolledo died unexpectedly. That death in 1596 or 1597 left his financiers, including the Moriscos from Deza and Juan de Ucedo, in a difficult position. Duke Juan expected them to make good on the debts incurred, but the financiers balked. Ucedo either settled with the duke privately or died before the conclusion of the suit, but in early 1600 the appellate court found in favor of the Morisco financiers and against the duke. In autumn 1595, when Román accepted the invitation to perform in Soria, he could not have anticipated the *receptor's* death, let alone Arellano's involvement in the case. Yet this was a period of increasing litigiousness in Deza, so perhaps the opportunity to cultivate a potentially useful connection was appealing. (ARCV RE, leg. 1901, exp. 45, fols. 17r and 19r-20r).

89. ADC, leg. 343, exp. 4876, fol. 197r.

90. ADC, leg. 343, exp. 4876 fol. 197v.

91. ADC, leg. 343, exp. 4876, fol. 6r-v.

92. ADC, leg. 343, exp. 4876, fols. 6v-7r.

93. ADC, leg. 343, exp. 4876, fol. 14r.

94. ADC, leg. 343, exp. 4876, fol. 11r.

95. Ávila claimed that he had not made the denunciation earlier because "he had been absent" (ADC, leg. 343, exp. 4876, fol. 15v).

96. ADC, leg. 343, exp. 4876, fols. 8r and 12r.

97. ADC, leg. 343, exp. 4876, fol. 15v.

98. ADC, leg. 343, exp. 4876, fol. 231r.

99. ADC, leg. 343, exp. 4876, fol. 233r.

100. ADC, leg. 343, exp. 4876, fol. 21r.

101. ADC, leg. 343, exp. 4876, fols. 15r and 21r. González de Rueda retorted that his "title and commission" afforded authority to gather information related to inquisitorial trials "in all parts and places, wherever they might be, within this district of Valladolid" (fol. 21r).

102. ADC, leg. 343, exp. 4876, fols. 2r and 21r.

103. ADC, leg. 343, exp. 4876, fol. 21r.

104. ADC, leg. 343, exp. 4876, fol. 4r.

105. ADC, leg. 343, exp. 4876, fols. 3r, 19r, and 197v.

106. ADC, leg. 343, exp. 4876, fols. 4r and 197v. In addition to writing to Licentiate Benito, González de Rueda also wrote to the inquisitors at Cuenca on October 19 appraising them of the situation (fol. 2r).

107. ADC, leg. 343, exp. 4876, fol. 5r. Late in 1595 castellan Pedro de Barnuevo was replaced (briefly) by Francisco Gonzalo Fernández Abarca. Early the next year Pedro de Argüello took over the office. Both men were local hidalgos. It is not clear which of them granted Ramírez freedom of the town but having been appointed merely as acting castellans (*tenientes de alcaide*), presumably neither would have granted him such liberty without the duke's approval.

108. ADC, leg. 343, exp. 4876, fol. 202v.

109. ADC, leg. 748b, doc. 106, fols. 16r-24r and ADC, leg. 343, exp. 4876, fol. 210r. The identity of the murdered son is obscure. Most likely the victim was Lope (b. 1566) who, Román noted in 1599, "died a young man." But Lope was left off of a census of the town's Moriscos completed in 1594, suggesting that he died before the murder occurred. The other possible candidate, Juan (b. 1570), went unmentioned not only in the 1594 census but also in the list of children that Román provided during his inquisitorial trial, which suggests that he probably had not survived into adulthood.

110. ADC, leg. 343, exp. 4876, fol. 80v. The solution, in this case, was for the messenger to bring the patient's urine to Román for analysis. The son, who like Ana Sanz was described as suffering from a "demoniac melancholy," received a similar, if not identical, prescription of incense. In this case, however, the treatment was less successful. Curiously, Juan Arias de Villacorta who played an important role in the Tajahuerce affair was a citizen of Hinojosa del Campo. (fols. 80v-81v).

111. AHMD, leg. 282, doc. 6 (June 16, 1597).

112. AHMD, leg. 26, exp. 4, fols. 2v, 28r, and 61r and leg. 282, doc. 6 (October 29, 1596; June 16, 1597; and May 28, 1598).

113. AHPS AMD, leg. 56.228, doc. 10, fols. 74r and 79r. For the lingering memory among Old Christians that the duke had intended to appoint Ramírez, see ADC, leg. 820, exp. 7992, fol. 11r.

8. THE BETTER LAW

1. ADC, leg. 343, exp. 4876, fol. 80v. In spring 1597, Román mentioned that the Tajahuerce affair had cost him "more than 100 ducats," then explained, "They had arrested him and he had given bonds [*dadas fianças*] of a great quantity and as a result he had lost even more than the 100 ducats."

2. ADC, leg. 343, exp. 4876, fol. 204r. The wording here is sometimes taken to suggest that the 300 *reales* were received as an advance on the writing of his book—*treçientos reales por lo que tiene escrito*—as though he had written part

but the rest remained to be completed. Yet he also claimed that had composed (*tiene compuesto*) the book already. Perhaps by this he merely meant that he had the whole story in his head (or in the form of a dramatic work) but had not yet put it down on paper.

3. The sixth book of the Amadís of Gaul cycle, *Florisando* (1510), was dedicated to Duke Juan's great-grandfather, the second duke of Medinaceli, and *Amadís de Grecia* (1530), the ninth book, was dedicated to another great-grandfather, Diego Hurtado de Mendoza, third Duke of the Infantado. Predictably, the library of Duke Juan's own son included copies of the Amadís cycle both in Castilian and in French. See Eisenberg, *Romances*, 111 and Álvarez Márquez, "La biblioteca," 309.

4. González Palencia, "El curandero," 238–39, noted the lines and reproduced them but did not grasp their significance.

5. ADC, leg. 343, exp. 4876, fol. 89v.

6. ADC, libro 317, fol. 460r (*This Happened*, 23).

7. The notion that "sol" could be Solomon was suggested to me by Gonzalo Díaz Migoyo. If "yo" is read as referring to Román himself, then an alternative interpretation of "sol" is to read it as "soldado," the nickname of Román's old friend (and father-in-law to his eldest son) Íñigo de Hortubia (1540–93).

8. ADC, leg. 250, exp. 3370 (inquisitorial trial of Lope Guerrero el viejo, confession of the accused for the Edict of Grace, February 4, 1571).

9. ADC, leg. 249, exp. 3352, fol. 47r and leg. 248, exp. 3342 (inquisitorial trial of Juan de San Juan, testimony of Luis de Cebea, November 14, 1570). Morisco Francisco de Arcos mentioned having played the part of a shepherd in a *comedia pastoral* on Trinity Sunday 1570 and even recited a few of his lines. A *representación de Jacob* was performed on the same feast day (ADC, leg. 249, exp. 3363, fol. 13r).

10. Whatever else these Moriscos were reading, Francisco de Arcos had been exposed to books of chivalry (ADC, leg. 249, exp. 3363 [inquisitorial trial of Francisco de Arcos, First Audience, September 26, 1570]).

11. ADC, leg. 343, exp. 4876, fol. 202v.

12. Eisenberg, *Romances*, 105–6. Harvey suggests that perhaps Ramírez's "quick wits" and "glib tongue" helped him "hide his lack of fluency in reading," to say nothing of his ability to write ("Oral Composition," 281). Others have suggested that he was semi- or barely literate.

13. ADC, leg. 343, exp. 4876, fol. 202r.

14. The choice of *Examen de ingenios* is a fascinating one, particularly since Huarte argued therein that the ability to recall from memory and the ability to create were incompatible. Román, of course, claimed to do both simultaneously.

15. ADC, leg. 343, exp. 4876, fol. 202v.

16. ADC, leg. 343, exp. 4876, fols. 11v–12r.

17. ADC, leg. 249, exp. 3352, fols, 47v-48r.

18. ADC, leg. 343, exp. 4876, fol. 55v. An ambiguous line follows this declaration in which Bartolomé claims that "en un libro pequeño le hizo leer alto, y trataba de cosas de Nuestro Señor, y le parecio a este testigo que heran cosas buenas." The subject of the phrase is unclear but the easiest reading suggests that Román made Bartolomé read aloud to him. However, other evidence suggests that Bartolomé could not read well if at all (e.g., fol. 17r), and he testified of his ignorance of "what was in [Ramírez's] books" (fol. 55v). Perhaps, then, the meaning is that Bartolomé picked out a small book from the library and "made" Román read it. In any case, since Román then went on to describe the range of his Christian knowledge to the visitor, he clearly wanted to communicate to Bartolomé that the small book was part and parcel of the orthodoxy of his knowledge and of his library's contents.

19. ADC, leg. 249, exp. 3352, fols. 47v-48r.

20. ADM, leg. 44, doc. 31 (notice regarding groves and poplars, no date).

21. ADC, leg. 707, exp. 625 (inquisitorial examination of Román Ramírez el menor, receipt signed by Miguel Benito, June 6, 1581) (*This Happened*, 119).

22. In fact, if the marginal notation "sol" did (as I have hypothesized) refer to Ramírez's friend "el Soldado," then the verso side of folio 89 must have been written before his death in 1593.

23. The verso (*comedia*) side of fol. 89 even has, in the same hand as the rest but written yet more sloppily, the direction for delivery of the recipe: "Tajahuerce, from Deza, for Bartolomé de Ortega." Harvey ("Oral Composition," 284) proposes the notion of an amanuensis while trying to make sense of how Román could have "composed" a book without being able to write.

24. When challenged directly about the instructions on August 12, 1599, Román claimed that he had dictated the lines to Villacorta. This claim, discussed below, fits the evidence no better than the claim to illiteracy he made on May 19 (ADC, leg. 343, exp. 4876, fol. 232r-v).

25. ADC, leg. 707, exp. 625 (inquisitorial examination of Román Ramírez el menor, letter from Román Ramírez el menor to Dr. Francisco de Arganda, July 16, 1581[?]) (*This Happened*, 117–18).

26. ADC, leg. 343, exp. 4876, fol. 55v.

27. ADC, leg. 343, exp. 4876, fol. 202r.

28. Both Mateo and Gerónimo de Obezar were, at the time of Román's statement, under arrest by the authority of the Holy Office.

29. ADC, leg. 343, exp. 4876, fols. 192r-93r (*This Happened*, 57–58).

30. ADC, leg. 343, exp. 4876, fol. 193r-v (*This Happened*, 59).

31. ADC, leg. 343, exp. 4876, fol. 212v. This sequence generally squares with Román's 1571 telling, but it offers a somewhat divergent account of the timing of his duel with Páez. The 1571 record dates his time as a migrant laborer in

Fuentes del Ebro to 1566, while the later account suggests that the fight (and flight) occurred around 1568–69, "eleven or twelve years" after Román lost contact with Gerónimo de Villaverde in ca. 1557.

32. ADC, libro 317, fol. 462r (*This Happened*, 27).

33. ADC, leg. 249, exp. 3352, fols. 48v-49r.

34. ADC, leg. 249, exp. 3352, fol. 50r.

35. ADC, leg. 249, exp. 3352, fol. 52r-v.

36. ADC, leg. 249, exp. 3352, fol. 47r-v. Almoravi added that the book from which Román read had come from Villafeliche and that he told her his "uncle" had brought it to him (fol. 48r).

37. ADC, leg. 751, exp. 7 (June 17, 1573).

38. ADC, leg. 343, exp. 4876, fol. 214v. When asked with whom else he had communicated or performed Islamic ceremonies, Román responded, "He does not know about other people except for those whom he has declared."

39. ADC, leg. 343, exp. 4876, fol. 212v.

40. ADC, leg. 707, exp. 625 (inquisitorial examination of Román Ramírez el menor, response to the charge, July 6, 1581) (*This Happened*, 115).

41. ADC, leg. 343, exp. 4876, fol. 11v.

42. Harvey (*Muslims in Spain*, 195) suggests that Muçali was perhaps a fabrication to draw attention away from local crypto-Muslims. While the idea of misdirection is correct, other evidence confirms Muçali's and Cabrera's presence in Deza. Morisco Juan Guerrero notes that he had "heard it said that there was a Moorish slave in Deza who belonged to Captain Cabrera, who later gave the slave his freedom (ADC, leg. 367, exp. 5180b [inquisitorial trial of Juan Guerrero, response to the Accusation (cap. 82), August 19, 1608]). This fits Román's claim that after four years (i.e., in 1595) Muçali returned to his home, Constantinople (ADC, leg. 343, exp. 4876, fol. 241v). Finally, in ca. 1610 the Holy Office attempted to ratify a statement Cabrera made against Morisco Francisco el Romo on October 3, 1608, but the accuser had died in the interval (ADC, leg. 748b, doc. 108b). Unfortunately, Francisco el Romo's trial record is lost, so the content of Cabrera's original testimony is unknown.

43. Intriguingly, Muçali was not the first Turk associated with the garden. Before January 1566 a Turk (presumably baptized) named Francisco de Esperanza was employed as *jardinero* in the duke's garden, where he continued to work until at least Lent 1567, after which he disappears from the record (ADM, leg. 44, doc. 31 [letter from Gonzalo Martínez to Duke Juan de la Cerda, January 23, 1566] and ADC, leg. 247, exp. 3315, fols. 18v-19r). See the author's forthcoming essay, "Román's Garden."

44. ADC, leg. 343, exp. 4876, fol. 213r.

45. ADC, leg. 343, exp. 4876, fols. 213r-14r (*This Happened*, 129).

46. ADC, leg. 343, exp. 4876, fol. 214v. Román's 1599 condemnation asserted that he had stayed in Spain on account of his family, but this rationale does not appear elsewhere in the trial record (ADC, leg. 343, exp. 4876, fol. 257v [*This Happened,* 130]). Morisco converts to Islam were very welcome in Istanbul in the 1590s. Their "raising of the turban to their heads" was greeted with gifts of new clothes or their cash equivalents. See Kristić, "Moriscos in Ottoman Galata," 274.

47. ADC, lib. 318, fol. 94r-124v (*This Happened,* 65–108).

48. ADC, leg. 343, exp. 4876, fol. 34r. This statement was supplied in 1597 by Bartolomé the elder, who claimed to have heard it from Ana Sanz. Petronila Hernández, Ana's mother, also mentioned it, claiming to have heard about it from Ana herself (fol. 41v). Ana only incompletely recalled the exchange and she "did not understand the words well." She admitted that her mother and father-in-law had filled in the details (fols. 67v-68r).

49. ADC, leg. 343, exp. 4876, fol. 255r (*This Happened,* 126).

50. ADC, leg. 378, exp. 5356 (inquisitorial trial of María la Jarquina, testimony of Francisco el Romo [November 11, 1610] and response of the accused to the second Accusation [November 13, 1610]). While fadas ceremonies may have been performed for the children born to Ángela de Miranda, no evidence of them exists.

51. ADC, leg. 250, exp. 3370 (inquisitorial trial of Lope Guerrero el viejo, confession of the accused under threat of torture, December 15, 1610). Speaking fifteen years after the events he described, Lope noted that the garden had been uprooted—he called it an "enclosure that had previously been a garden."

52. ADC, leg. 250, exp. 3370 (inquisitorial trial of Lope Guerrero el viejo, testimony of Catalina la Valencia [alias, López], March 19, 1608, and testimony of Ana Montero October 17, 1607) and leg. 364, exp. 5159 (inquisitorial trial of Antón Guerrero el viejo, testimony of Martín de Estaragón, November 26, 1607).

53. ADC, leg. 362, exp. 5142 (inquisitorial trial of Miguel Ramírez, letter from Pedro de Cisneros to the Cuencan Tribunal, November 26, 1607). The description offered here was of the period after Román's death. Presumably, the garden also drew Aragonese Moriscos while he was alive.

54. The possible exception to this timeline is Lope Guerrero's account of what was potentially the first Islamic *junta* in the garden. He dates it to "about fifteen years" before December 1610, which could mean that it preceded the events in Soria and Román's arrest in late 1595. However, given that all other evidence is clustered in the period subsequent to his January 1596 release from close confinement, it is more likely that the *junta* described by Guerrero took place soon afterward.

55. ADC, leg. 364, exp. 5159 (inquisitorial trial of Antón Guerrero el viejo, testimony of Gabriel de León, October 11, 1608) and leg. 362, exp. 5142 (inquis-

itorial trial of Miguel Ramírez, testimony of Librada González [January 29, 1609] and Accusation [cap. 7] [May 5, 1610]).

56. ADC, leg. 362, exp. 5142 (inquisitorial trial of Miguel Ramírez, January 29, 1609, testimony of Librada González).

57. ADC, leg. 378, exp. 5356 (inquisitorial trial of María la Jarquina, testimony of Gabriel de León, June 20, 1608).

58. Perhaps an excavation of the dilapidated house of the duke will reveal it to have been a site for the production and dissemination of Islamic literature, as was famously the case in Almonacid de la Sierra. See Codera y Zaidín, "Almacén de un librero morisco," 269–76.

59. ADC, leg. 343, exp. 4876, fol. 213v.

60. ADC, leg. 343, exp. 4876, fol. 214r.

61. ADC, leg. 343, exp. 4876, fol. 214r. Possibly, *yemauleo yemauleo,* repeated seven times, was an oblique reference to a portion of the second surah (v. 163), which was to be prayed "seven times" and began with the words "O my God" (Longás, *Vida religiosa de los moriscos,* 59–60). But, if so, by suggesting an unaccountably lengthy translation of the phrase Román indicated to the Holy Office his failure to grasp the subtleties of Islam.

62. ADC, leg. 343, exp. 4876, fol. 202v.

63. ADC, leg. 343, exp. 4876, fol. 15v.

64. ADC, leg. 343, exp. 4876, fol. 1r.

65. ADC, leg. 343, exp. 4876, fols. 22r-25v. Berlanga de Duero was (barely) inside of Cuenca's jurisdiction; Madruédano was outside of it.

66. ADC, leg. 343, exp. 4876, fol. 26r.

67. ADC, leg. 343, exp. 4876, fols. 82r-86v and 88v.

68. ADC, leg. 343, exp. 4876, fols. 90r-91r.

69. ADC, leg. 343, exp. 4876, fol. 92r.

70. Caro Baroja, *Vidas mágicas,* 313. Likewise, Magnier Heney described him as "elderly" and "frail" ("Román Ramírez, Villain or Victim," 450).

71. AHMD, caja 26, doc. 4, fol. 63r.

72. ADC, leg. 343, exp. 4876, fol. 213v.

73. In September 1597 the Council's account books have Ramírez inspecting various fields and lands around Deza, so he was certainly quite mobile at that point (AHMD, leg. 282, doc. 6).

74. ADC, leg. 343, exp. 4876, fol. 196r.

75. ADC, leg. 343, exp. 4876, fol. 208v. He also mentioned his poor health on May 11 and June 14 (ADC, leg. 343, exp. 4876, fols. 196r and 204v).

76. ADC, leg. 343, exp. 4876, fol. 208v. In the event that the fifty ducats was insufficient, Román requested permission to pay a surety and have the "city as his jail."

77. ADC, leg. 343, exp. 4876, fol. 211v.

78. ADC, leg. 343, exp. 4876, fols. 199r-200v.

79. Only later, when attempting to disassociate his ability to memorize from his familiar spirit, did Román introduce the story of the camphor juice, a story that multiple witnesses had already shared with the Holy Office (ADC, leg. 343, exp. 4876, fol. 228r).

80. ADC, leg. 343, exp. 4876, fol. 202v. Here Román notes that he "has neither embellished any more books nor does he have them anymore [*ni ha decorado más libros ni los tiene ya*]." This could mean either that he had disposed of his physical library or, more likely, that he could no longer access those books mentally as he had previously.

81. ADC, leg. 343, exp. 4876, fol. 203r-v.

82. ADC, leg. 343, exp. 4876, fol. 12r. Licentiate Boniface had compared one of Román's recitations to a printed copy of the same story and noted variances. Bartolomé el mozo, while lodging at Román's home, had described the Morisco "reading" and "studying" the books in his home (fol. 55v).

83. ADC, leg. 343, exp. 4876, fols. 204r-9v. These are transcribed in González Palencia, "El curandero," 249–61.

84. Presumably the Holy Office already knew both of these facts, but although some witnesses identified Román as a Morisco, none mentioned Islamic activities or the 1571 reconciliation. No specific evidence indicates that Arganda had connected the healer of Tajahuerce to the Morisco he met two decades earlier, although there are two pieces of circumstantial evidence: 1) Arganda's interest in reviving the case by meeting with Juan de Ortigosa in Berlanga in 1597, and 2) Arganda's absence from Román's first ten audiences may hint that he *did* remember the Morisco and chose to remain aloof from the proceedings for the time being. He began attending audiences on August 2—in the wake of Román's confession of crypto-Islam—and was present for all subsequent audiences.

85. ADC, leg. 343, exp. 4876, fol. 215r.

86. ADC, leg. 343, exp. 4876, fols. 215r-16r.

87. ADC, leg. 343, exp. 4876, fol. 217r.

88. ADC, leg. 343, exp. 4876, fol. 218r.

89. The familiar's name is puzzling. No previous reference to it appears either in popular or literary culture. Perhaps Román drew daringly upon the name of his inquisitor as inspiration: Pedro Cifuentes de *Loarte*.

90. ADC, leg. 343, exp. 4876, fol. 226v. Large sections from this portion of Román's trial (fols. 225v-28r) are transcribed in González Palencia, "El curandero," 268–72. But note that he draws upon information from the August 4 and 7 audiences without signaling a break between them.

91. Here he noted his mother's warning that he would "have a great memory as a result" but, with time, would lose it (ADC, leg. 343, exp. 4876, fol. 228r).

92. ADC, leg. 343, exp. 4876, fol. 228r-v.

93. ADC, leg. 343, exp. 4876, fol. 232r-v. No sample of Villacorta's writing is extant other than his signature (fols. 18r and 86v).

94. The Jesuit Francisco Escudero, who had "experience with what should be done in such a case," was assigned the task. The inquisitors may well have hoped that Escudero would elicit some new information for their ears but, after returning from the jails, he said that he "did not have anything particular of which to advise their lordships" (ADC, leg. 343, exp. 4876, fol. 236r).

95. ADC, leg. 343, exp. 4876, fol. 236v.

96. ADC, leg. 343, exp. 4876, fols. 236v-37r.

97. ADC, leg. 343, exp. 4876, fol. 253v (*This Happened*, 123).

98. ADC, leg. 343, exp. 4876, fol. 34r.

99. ADC, leg. 343, exp. 4876, fol. 255r-v (*This Happened*, 126).

100. ADC, leg. 343, exp. 4876, fols. 251r-v and 259v (*This Happened*, 132).

101. ADC, leg. 343, exp. 4876, fols. 243r and 259v (*This Happened*, 133).

102. Díaz Migoyo, "Memoria y fama," 39–42.

103. AHMD, caja 16a, doc. 7 (letter from the Duke of Medinaceli to Deza's town council, August 8, 1602).

9. SMALL TOWN DREAMS

1. Often, the men designated alcaldes mayores (or sometimes *justicias mayores*) were simultaneously appointed as residency judges (*juezes de residencia*).

2. Alcalde, *Deza*, 1:247 and 275.

3. ADM, leg. 44, doc. 24 (letter of Juan Manrique Peña and Juan Manrique Navarro to the duke of Medinaceli, no date).

4. ADM, leg. 44, doc. 21. See too AHMD, leg. 15b, doc. 9 and ADM, leg. 44, doc. 22, the latter of which was drawn up by the entire concejo and emphasized the "inconveniences" of having competing jurisdictions at play in "such a small place."

5. ADM, leg. 44, doc. 23. The official record of exchanges between the duke and commune regarding election and appointment of officials gives no indication that this last claim was true (AHPS AMD, leg. 26.558, doc. 10).

6. Around the same time, Barnuevo also, apparently, ordered the arrest of alguacil mayor Juan Ramírez (ADM, leg. 111, doc. 25, fol. 10r-v). This was probably Morisco Juan Ramírez Ropiñón who became alguacil in 1594, the year after Miguel García Serrano and was nominated by him for the office (AHPS AMD, leg. 26.558, doc. 10, fol. 63r).

7. ADM, leg. 44, doc. 23.

8. AHDOS APD, LS (1535–1579), fol. 166v.

9. He died on August 17, 1631 (AHDOS APD, LS [1605–1646]). His wife predeceased him by less than a month on July 26.

10. That inn served as the makeshift jail from which Mateo Romero el menor escaped in April 1570. The following August, when Romero was captured in

Aragonese Sabiñán, Juan García Serrano and another Old Christian were tasked with transporting him to Cuenca, but they allowed the Moriscos to escape again. Perhaps these early memories played into Miguel García Serrano's subsequent distrust of Moriscos. See ADC, leg. 249, exp. 3369 (inquisitorial trial of Luis de Cebea el viejo, testimony of María de Almanzorre, April 5, 1570) and leg. 254, exp. 3429 (inquisitorial trial of Mateo Romero el menor, testimony of Juan García Serrano, August 22, 1570).

11. ADC, leg. 361, exp. 5131 (inquisitorial trial of Ana Guerrera, testimony of María Hernández, May 14, 1604). The evidence from the parish register is problematic: AHDOS APD, LS (1605–1646) gives María Hernández as the widow of *Miguel* García Serrano at her death in 1611. The scribe probably erred in writing the name of the son for that of the husband.

12. ADC, leg. 361, exp. 5131 (inquisitorial trial of Ana Guerrera, testimony of María García [May 14, 1604] and first audience of the accused [July 19, 1607]). See Wiesner, *Women and Gender*, 177–79.

13. ADC, leg. 367, exp. 5180 (inquisitorial trial of Juan Guerrero, testimony of Gabriel de León [January 29, 1608] and response to the accusation [cap. 46; August 13, 1608]).

14. He was still involved in the business in 1591 when he and several other local innkeepers petitioned for royal licenses in exchange for paying the *millones* tax (AHPS AMD, leg. 26.556, doc. 20). But he was not named on a similar series of documents dated to 1598–99, which may indicate that he moved away from the hospitality industry (AHPS AMD, leg. 26.556, doc. 23).

15. García Serrano's had been among the names submitted to the duke by the commune for each of the years from 1589–92, but a different man was always selected. As it happened, Duke Juan Luis died during his term and the new seignior did not appoint the council of 1594 until August of that year. Consequently, García Serrano's term was unusually long and his successor's unusually short (AHPS AMD, leg. 26.556, doc. 10, fol. 63r).

16. AHMD, leg. 76, exp. 1, fol. 122r-v. Among those who signed as witnesses to the creation of the office were *bachilleres* Ozuel and Navarro, *maestro* Barba (clergy); Lope de Cieli, Juan Ramírez, Francisco de Miranda, Francisco el Romo, and Diego Fadrique (Moriscos); several Old Christians; and even Francisco Fernández Abarca, a hidalgo. The town council does not appear to have passed a resolution in support of the new office, but solicitor general Lope de Cieli took part in its creation and magistrate Pedro de Argüello and alderman Juan de Peñafiel el mayor likely also favored it.

17. AHMD, leg. 76, exp. 1, fols. 119v-22v.

18. AHPS AMD, leg. 26.558, doc. 11, fol. 57v.

19. ARCV RE, caja 1151, doc. 26, fol. 12v.

20. Kagan, *Lawsuits and Litigants*, 103.

21. Kagan, *Lawsuits and Litigants*, 89, 99–100, 115–16, 138. The litigiousness of Dezanos—both Old Christian and, especially, Moriscos—generally mirrors the patterns Dadson describes in his study of the Campo de Calatrava, but Deza's Moriscos successfully navigated the courts despite their lower level of education and less formal legal training (*Tolerance and Coexistence*, 64–78).

22. AHMD, leg. 16a, doc. 4.

23. AHMD, leg. 15a, doc. 6.

24. AHMD, leg. 111b, doc. 3.

25. AHMD, leg. 26, doc. 4, fol. 61r-v. In 1585, with the permission of Duke Juan Luis, the council had established a grain store (*cámara y pósito*), which provided wheat at fair prices during times of dearth but was also used by the council to raise money (*dineros ascensos*) to pay for lawsuits, visitations, the billeting of soldiers, and other forced expenditures (*gastos forzosos*). The funds derived from "a kind of redeemable annuity—the sale of the right to an annual flow of revenue that the seller could redeem at will. In its most straightforward form the purchase and redemption involved the lump sum payments [of] equal amounts of cash. The salient characteristic of the contract was that the revenue flow in question emanated from a specific property, such as an estate or a farm. It was 'an annual return based on a fruitful good'" (D'Emic, *Justice in the Marketplace*, 44). See also Casey, *Early Modern Spain*, 129.

26. AHMD, leg. 76, doc. 1.

27. Domínguez Ortiz, *The Golden Age of Spain*, 158–61.

28. AHMD, leg. 76, doc. 1 (testimonies of Pedro de Afuera, Miguel Ramírez, and Domingo Calvo, March 8, 1603). Representatives of the town council retorted that, given the financial constraints under which they were forced to operate and the demands of soldiers billeted nearby, their only option was leasing the land (testimonies of Lope Guerrero and Juan de Deza, March 9, 1603).

29. Vassberg, *Land and Society*, 97–99.

30. AHMD, leg. 15a, doc. 7, fol. 1v.

31. AHPS AMD, leg. 26.558, doc. 11, fol. 56r. This council included Pedro de Barnuevo and Francisco Manrique (co-magistrates), Luis de Mella, Pedro Barba, and Morisco Luis de Hortubia (aldermen), Morisco Diego de Medina (solicitor general), Juan de Argüello, Juan Manrique, and Morisco Alexo Gorgoz (deputies).

32. Two contemporary copies of this document exist(ed) but I have been unable to consult either. Attempts to access the copy in the ducal archive (ADM, leg. 3, doc. 104) have not met with success. A second copy, belonging to the town, was noted in the manuscript catalog of Deza's municipal archive completed in 1925 by Eugenio Moreno Ayora and Blas Taracena Aguirre but has since disappeared. Fortunately, an 1829 transcription of the town's copy survives as AHPS AMD, leg. 26.558, doc. 2.

33. AHMD, leg. 76, doc. 1, fol. 18r.

34. ARCV RE, caja 1999, doc. 90, fol. 2r.

35. During the conflicts that ensued, town gossips conveniently forgot that the (Old Christian-dominated) council of 1598 had separated itself from the lawsuits well before the Moriscos withdrew.

36. The representatives were: *bachiller* Juan de Ozuel (d. 1605), hidalgo Francisco Gonzalo Fernández Abarca (ca. 1548–aft. 1611), Juan Desteras (the Old Christian co-magistrate for 1600), and Morisco Lope de Arcos (ca. 1559–aft. 1611). None of them were hardliners. See AHPS AMD, leg. 26.556, doc. 2, fols. 1r and 15v.

37. AHPS AMD, leg. 26.558, doc. 2, fols. 6v-14r.

38. In the official record of correspondence between town and seignior regarding the appointment of officeholders, for example, Juan de Barnuevo Miranda was, from 1601, identified as *alcaide de la fortaleza y gobernador de los quarto lugares de la valle* (AHPS AMD, leg. 26.556, doc. 10, fol. 88v), although his predecessor had been styled *alcaide y alcalde mayor* the previous year (fol. 85v).

39. AHMD, leg. 76, doc. 1, fols. 17r-20r.

40. Desteras, one of the delegates who negotiated the concord, had served as the Old Christian magistrate in 1600 as did Manrique in 1601. For unknown reasons, no Morisco magistrate was appointed in either of those years.

41. Gonzalo Martínez el mayor died a few weeks later, presumably still under arrest (AHDOS APD, LS [1580–1605], December 22, 1602). His death further complicated efforts to recover the concord by muddling the document's chain of transmission (AHMD, leg. 76, doc. 1, fol. 20v).

42. AHMD, leg. 76, doc. 1 (execution of *auto* against Miguel García Serrano and Francisco Manrique by Lope de Arcos, October 17, 1602).

43. From early January 1602, for example, a series of Old Christians denounced Gerónimo de Liñán (who rented the pottery works) for having hung a cross on the horns of a goat and then whipped it about his property. A few months earlier, Old Christian Diego Valero, who lived next to Liñán, moved because he feared his neighbors would murder him (ADC, leg. 355, exp. 5042).

44. ADC, leg. 343, exp. 4876, fol. 210r. This office was distinct from the alguacil (who was sometimes also called an alguacil mayor) who sat on the town council. The alguacil mayor in view here was appointed by the duke and worked as chief constable in the *cuatro lugares de la recompensa*.

45. AHMD, leg. 15a, doc. 7, fol. 1v.

46. ARCV RE, caja 1999, doc. 90, fol. 5v.

47. ARCV RE, caja 1999, doc. 90, fol. 2r.

48. ADC, leg. 362, exp. 5142 (inquisitorial trial of Miguel Ramírez, testimony of Juan Manrique de Peña, March 7, 1604).

49. AHMD, leg. 76, doc. 1, fols. 13r-14v.

50. AHMD, leg. 76, doc. 1 (March 10, 1603).

51. ADC, leg. 820, exp. 7992, fol. 1r and AHPS AMD, leg. 26.558, doc. 2, fol. 15v.

52. ADC, leg. 820, exp. 7992, fols. 1v, 4r-v, 6r-v, 8v, 10r-v.

53. AHMD, leg. 15a, doc. 7, fol. 1v.

54. ADC, leg. 820, exp. 7992, fol. 6r-v.

55. Morisco gatherings of both the entire community and the leadership continued to occur during the crisis years. Old Christians connected these *juntas* to crypto-Islamic activities, but Juan Guerrero was adamant in his inquisitorial trial that they were merely convened to discuss the lawsuits and had nothing to do with *cosas contra la fe* (ADC, leg. 367, exp. 5180b [inquisitorial trial of Juan Guerrero, response to the Accusation (cap. 59), August 3, 1608]).

56. ADC, leg. 250, exp. 3383 (inquisitorial trial of Luis de Cebea el menor, testimony of Pedro de Argüello for the *probanza*, September 27, 1610) and ARCV RE, caja 1999, doc. 90, fol. 1. Sixty-six Morisco heads of household gathered and granted power of attorney on behalf of the rest of the "New [i.e., Upper] Neighborhood" to Lope de Arcos, Juan Martínez de la Castellana, Lope Guerrero (probably el menor), Francisco de Arcos, Juan de Deza, Juan Ramírez Ropiñón, Francisco de Mendoza, Juan de Heredia, and Pedro de Hortubia. Deza's retired alcaide Velasco de Barnuevo (acting now in his capacity as the duke's *mayordomo mayor*) was also named.

57. ADC, leg. 362, exp. 5142 (inquisitorial trial of Miguel Ramírez, testimony of Juan Manrique de Peña, March 7, 1604).

58. ADC, leg. 820, exp. 7992, fols. 1v-2v.

59. In a striking coincidence, this meeting occurred two days after the Great Conjunction of 1603, which came to be viewed as a portent of the Morisco expulsion after Francisco Navarro connected it to the imminent destruction of Islam and rise to glory of Spain in his 1604 *Discvrso sobre la conivncion maxima*. See Magnier, *Pedro de Valencia*, 129–36.

60. ADC, leg. 820, exp. 7992, fol. 1r. The context in which García Serrano made this demand is unclear. García Serrano is simply described as appearing before the co-magistrates but presumably this took place in front of the entire commune.

61. ARCV RE, caja 1999, doc. 90, fol. 3v.

62. ARCV RE, caja 1999, doc. 90, fol. 1r and AHPS AMD, leg. 26.558, doc. 10, fol. 97r.

63. Although the duke never intervened directly in the lawsuits, some evidence (such as the naming of Velasco de Barnuevo on the Morisco power of attorney) hints at which side he favored.

64. On the expulsion treatises, see Talavera Cuesta and Moreno Díaz del Campo, eds., *Juan Ripol y la expulsión*, 25–46 and Magnier, *Pedro de Valencia*, 119–72. On the role of propaganda in the expulsion, see Dadson, *Tolerance and Coexistence*, 101–22.

65. ARCV RE, caja 1999, doc. 90, fol. 5v.

66. ADC, leg. 820, exp. 7992, fol. 7v.

67. ARCV RE, caja 1999, doc. 90, fols. 6r-7r.

68. ADC, leg. 820, exp. 7992, fols. 4v-5r and 11r and AHPS ADM, leg. 26.558, doc. 10, fol. 79r.

69. ADC, leg. 362, exp. 5142 (inquisitorial trial of Miguel Ramírez, testimony of Juan Manrique de Peña, March 7, 1604).

70. ADC, leg. 719, exp. 923 (María Rasa's denunciation of Gabriel de Saleros and other Moriscos, March 13, 1604).

71. ADC, leg. 372, exp. 5254 (Librada González's denunciation of Ana la Buena, December 21, 1608).

72. ADC, leg. 361, exp. 5131 (inquisitorial trial of Ana Guerrera, testimony of Ana López, May 15, 1604).

73. AHMD, leg. 16a, doc. 8.

74. ARCV RE, caja 2206, exp. 30, fol. 3v

75. AHMD, leg. 15a, doc. 7, fol. 1r-v.

76. AHMD, leg. 15a, doc. 7, fol. 3r-v.

77. ADC, leg. 250, exp. 3383 (inquisitorial trial of Luis de Cebea el menor, letter of Pedro de Cisneros, October 2, 1610).

78. ADC, leg. 358, exp. 5103 (inquisitorial trial of Catalina Zamorano, testimony of Diego Zamorano, February 9, 1605).

79. ARCV RE, caja 1999, doc. 90, fol. 7r. The Old Christian council members of 1604 had noted the leisurely pace of the Royal Appellate Court in deciding on their suit; however, this was a period of transition and relocation for the chancillería (AHMD, leg. 15a, doc. 7, fol. 2r). Normally, the court was located in Valladolid, but between 1601–06 Philip III settled his capital in that city and relocated the chancillería first to Medina del Campo, then briefly to Burgos. When the capital was transferred to Madrid in 1606, the appellate court was reestablished in Valladolid.

80. ARCV RE, caja 1999, doc. 90, fols. 7r-v, 8v.

81. ADC, leg. 716, exp. 861 (Pedro de Barnuevo's denunciation of María de Luna, October 26, 1599); leg. 362, exp. 5142 (Juan Manrique de Peña's denunciation of Miguel Ramírez, Luis de Mendoza, and Francisco de Arcos, March 6, 1604); leg. 719, exp. 923 (María Raso's denunciation of Gabriel de Saleros, Gabriel de Lancero, and others, March 13, 1604); leg. 361, exp. 5131 (María Hernández, María García, Ana López, and Alonso de Santos's denunciations of Ana Guerrera, May 14–15, 1604); and leg. 358, exp. 5103 (Diego Zamorano's denunciation of Catalina Zamorano and Gabriel de Medina, February 9, 1605).

82. This was true, for example, of the January 1602 testimonies against Morisco Gerónimo de Liñán (ADC, leg. 355, exp. 5042). Twelve witnesses were involved in the enquiry into Liñán's erratic religious behavior, which turned out to be mere hearsay. Their statements were received in Cuenca on April 15, 1602.

83. ADC, leg. 372, exp. 5254 (Librada González's denunciation of Ana la Buena, December 21, 1608).

84. ADC, leg. 361, exp. 5131 (inquisitorial testimony of Ana Guerrera, testimony of Gabriel de León, November 22, 1607).

85. AHMD, leg. 16a, doc. 8.

86. AHMD, leg. 15a, doc. 7, fol. 3r-v.

87. ADC, leg. 375, exp. 5322 (inquisitorial trial of María la Carnicera, confession of the accused, May 29, 1608).

88. ADC, leg. 363, exp. 5150 (inquisitorial trial of Lope de Obezar, testimonies of Luis de Mella, July 25, 1606); leg. 366, exp. 5168 (inquisitorial trial of Francisco de Mendoza, testimony of Pedro Navarro, June 19, 1607); leg. 375, exp. 5322 (inquisitorial trial of María la Carnicera, testimonies of Catalina Desteras and Juana de Mena, July 15, 1607); leg. 362, exp. 5142 (inquisitorial trial of Miguel Ramírez, testimonies of Mateo de Luna, Ana Montero, and Martín Destaragon, October 3 and November 13 and 26, 1607); leg. 376, exp. 5333 (inquisitorial trial of Leonor de Hortubia, testimonies of Juana Escudero and Catalina López, January 2 and March 19, 1608); leg. 367, exp. 5180 (inquisitorial trial of Juan Guerrero, testimonies of Juan de Hernán Martínez and Juan Rodríguez el sordo, January 18, 1608).

89. ADM AH, leg. 125, doc. R1 5 (petition of Miguel García Serrano, February 11, 1607).

10. AS MUCH MOORS NOW AS EVER

1. ADC, leg. 367, exp. 5179 (inquisitorial trial of María la Burgueña, response to the publication of witnesses [test. 1, cap. 2], July 30, 1610). Ana Guerrera, however, claimed that la Burgueña and her mother (but not Mancebo) did attend (ADC, leg. 375, exp. 5322 [inquisitorial trial of María la Carnicera, testimony of Ana Guerrera, July 12, 1610]).

2. ADC, leg. 375, exp. 5322 (inquisitorial trial of María la Carnicera, testimony of Ana Guerrera, July 12, 1610).

3. ADC, leg. 250, exp. 3383 (inquisitorial trial of Luis de Cebea el menor, testimony of Juan Miguel, September 25, 1610).

4. ADC, leg. 250, exp. 3383 (inquisitorial trial of Luis de Cebea el menor, testimony of Pedro de Argüello, September 24, 1610). Among the other Old Christian attendees were the notary Francisco García, priest Gerónimo Barba, hosier Juan Ramírez, and hidalgo Baltasar Ocáriz.

5. ADC, leg. 369, exp. 5131 (inquisitorial trial of Ana Guerrera, response to the accusations [cap. 6], July 12, 1610).

6. In 1607 Ana claimed that the marriage had been consummated following the Moorish ceremony. Three years later, however, she retracted that statement and claimed she had not understood what "carnal knowledge" meant at the time of her initial confession. She maintained that her husband "did not know if she was a man or a woman, and if they didn't believe her, let them go ask him" (ADC, leg. 369, exp. 5131 [inquisitorial trial of Ana Guerrera, testimony of

the accused (July 19, 1607) and response to the second accusation (cap. 6; July 12, 1610)]).

7. Juan Guerrero's maternal grandmother, María de Sepulveda, was an Old Christian as was Catalina de Tejada, Francisca de Hortubia's maternal grandmother. Tejada was presumably related to Tristán de Tejada, the Argentine conquistador and native Dezano. See Alcalde, *Deza*, 1:265–68.

8. ADC, leg. 378, exp. 5356 (inquisitorial trial of María la Jarquina, testimony of Juan Guerrero, August 9, 1608).

9. ADC, leg. 365, exp. 5166 (inquisitorial trial of Ana de Mendoza, testimony of Juan Guerrero, December 4, 1607).

10. ADC, leg. 366, exp. 5172 (inquisitorial trial of Catalina de Hortubia, testimony of Juan Guerrero, August 9, 1608) and ADC, leg. 369, exp. 5131 (inquisitorial trial of Ana Guerrera, testimony of Antón Guerrero el viejo, September 4, 1608).

11. ADC, leg. 367, exp. 5180 (inquisitorial trial of Juan Guerrero, testimony of Gabriel de León, November 20, 1607) and ADC, leg. 369, exp. 5131 (inquisitorial trial of Ana Guerrera, testimony of Antón Guerrero el viejo, September 6, 1608).

12. ADC, leg. 369, exp. 5131 (inquisitorial trial of Ana Guerrera, testimony of Juan Guerrero [December 4, 1607]; response to the second accusation [cap. 8] [July 12, 1610]; and response to the publication of witnesses [test. 3, cap. 11] [August 9, 1610]).

13. ADC, leg. 369, exp. 5131 (inquisitorial trial of Ana Guerrera, confession of the accused [October 2, 1607] and response to the second accusation [cap. 2] [July 10, 1610]).

14. ADC, leg. 369, exp. 5131 (inquisitorial trial of Ana Guerrera, testimony of Alonso Santos [May 16, 1604] and response to the accusation [caps. 3 and 5] [October 3, 1607]).

15. ADC, leg. 369, exp. 5131 (inquisitorial trial of Ana Guerrera, response to the second accusation [cap. 3], July 10, 1610). Guerrera also claimed that Huerta wrote out and distributed sections of the Quran "so that they would have them with them and so Mohammed would have mercy on their souls when they died." He charged between two and four *reales* for the service.

16. ADC, leg. 369, exp. 5131 (inquisitorial trial of Ana Guerrera, response to the second accusation [cap. 5], July 10, 1610).

17. ADC, leg. 369, exp. 5131 (inquisitorial trial of Ana Guerrera, first audience of the accused, July 19, 1607).

18. ADC, leg. 367, exp. 5180 (inquisitorial trial of Juan Guerrero, testimony of Gabriel de León, November 20, 1607). No details exist about how many pupils attended this dame school or whether López was sanctioned by the consejo as a *maestra de niños*. See also Dadson, *Tolerance and Coexistence*, 56–57.

19. ADC, leg. 369, exp. 5131 (inquisitorial trial of Ana Guerrera, testimony of Alonso Santos, May 16, 1604).

20. ADC, leg. 369, exp. 5131 (inquisitorial trial of Ana Guerrera, confession of the accused [July 19, 1607] and response to the accusation [cap. 2] [October 2, 1607]). There is some disagreement here about the sequence of events. Ana initially claimed she only recited the prayer once, when she was alone with López and Santos. Later, she amended this to say that she recited the prayer exactly twice and that María García had been present. Neither of her accounts seems to be correct in view of the timeline provided by María García, María Hernández (Miguel García Serrano's mother), Ana López, Alonso Santos, and Gabriel de León (Ana's father's cellmate in Cuenca).

21. ADC, leg. 369, exp. 5131 (inquisitorial trial of Ana Guerrera, testimony of María García, May 4, 1607).

22. ADC, leg. 369, exp. 5131 (inquisitorial trial of Ana Guerrera, testimony of Ana López, May 15, 1607).

23. ADC, leg. 369, exp. 5131 (inquisitorial trial of Ana Guerrera, first audience of the accused, July 19, 1607).

24. ADC, leg. 369, exp. 5131 (inquisitorial trial of Ana Guerrera, testimony of Gabriel de León, November 20,1607). According to León's report of Juan Guerrero's account, a gap of some "two years" elapsed between Ana's recitation and the denunciations by López and Santos.

25. Identifying this individual has proved difficult since at least fourteen women bearing that name lived in town at the end of the sixteenth century—five of them could potentially be the one mentioned here.

26. Unfortunately, nothing more is known about the nature of the relationship between Benito and María de Deza but since she "had been" his servant it can be surmised that she no longer was by May 1604.

27. ADC, leg. 369, exp. 5131 (inquisitorial trial of Ana Guerrera, testimony of Gabriel de León, November 20, 1607).

28. ADC, leg. 250, exp. 3383 (inquisitorial trial of Luis de Cebea el menor, testimony of Baltasar de Ocáriz, September 24, 1610). Ana's father believed Luis de Cebea el viejo, the groom's grandfather, was extremely wealthy and that Diego de Fadrique would inherit his estate (ADC, leg. 367, exp. 5180 [inquisitorial trial of Juan Guerrero, testimony of Gabriel de León, May 17, 1608]).

29. ADC, leg. 369, exp. 5131 (inquisitorial trial of Ana Guerrera, response to the second accusation [cap. 6], July 12, 1610).

30. ADC, leg. 369, exp. 5131 (inquisitorial trial of Ana Guerrera, first audience, July 19, 1607).

31. ADC, leg. 367, exp. 5180 (inquisitorial trial of Juan Guerrero, testimony of Gabriel de León, December 21, 1607).

32. ADC, leg. 364, exp. 5159 (inquisitorial trial of Antón Guerrero el viejo, testimony of Gabriel de León, October 13, 1608).

33. ADC, leg. 367, exp. 5180 (inquisitorial trial of Juan Guerrero, testimony of Gabriel de León, November 23, 1607).

34. Wiegers, "Managing Disaster," 143 and 153.

35. ADC, leg. 364, exp. 5159 (inquisitorial trial of Antón Guerrero el viejo, testimony of Gabriel de León, October 8, 1608).

36. ADC, leg. 249, exp. 3369 (inquisitorial trial of Luis de Cebea el viejo, testimony of Gabriel de León, March 29, 1608) and leg. 367, exp. 5180 (inquisitorial trial of Juan Guerrero, response to the accusation [cap. 58], August 13, 1608).

37. ADC, leg. 249, exp. 3369 (inquisitorial trial of Luis de Cebea el viejo, testimony of Gabriel de León, March 29, 1608). See Cantera Montenegro, "La comunidad morisca de Ágreda," 111–42.

38. For the "Morisco conspiracy of Aguilar," see Monter, Frontiers of Heresy, 151–56.

39. In Villarrubia, the Holy Office also targeted potentially weak links within the Morisco community and isolated them from their families in hopes of encouraging confessions and denunciations (Dadson, Tolerance and Coexistence, 84–85).

40. ADC, leg. 367, exp. 5180 (inquisitorial trial of Juan Guerrero, response to the accusation [cap. 58], August 13, 1608).

41. ADC, leg. 362, exp. 5142 (inquisitorial trial of Miguel Ramírez, response to the accusation [cap. 10], May 5, 1610).

42. ADC, leg. 367, exp. 5180 (inquisitorial trial of Juan Guerrero, confession of the accused, August 8, 1608). Fifty ducats seem a high price, but the cost of a pair of mules was roughly twice that of a yoke of oxen between 1550–1650 (Anes y Álvarez, Cultivos, cosechos y pastoreo, 27).

43. Using the pretense of delivering food (some cheese, a muffin, and apples), Ana's mother-in-law also attempted (unsuccessfully) to communicate the importance of keeping quiet as the girl was departing Deza. See ADC, leg. 367, exp. 5180 (inquisitorial trial of Juan Guerrero, testimony of Gabriel de León [November 23, 1607] and response to the accusation [cap. 29] [August 11, 1608]).

44. ADC, leg. 367, exp. 5180 (inquisitorial trial of Juan Guerrero, testimony of Gabriel de León [November 23, 1607] and response to the accusation [cap. 30] [August 11, 1608]).

45. ADC, leg. 367, exp. 5180 (inquisitorial trial of Juan Guerrero, testimony of Gabriel de León [November 23, 1607] and response to the accusation [cap. 31] [August 11, 1608]).

46. Moraga's connection to Deza's Moriscos went back some years. In October of 1603 or 1604 he met up with Luis de Hortubia el Jarquino, Antón Guerrero, and Lope Guerrero el mozo at the fair in Torrija. They laid plans to marry Moraga's son to Hortubia's daughter, declared themselves Moors, and discussed moving to Arcos "so they could all be close to one another." (ADC, leg. 364, exp. 5159 [inquisitorial trial of Antón Guerrero el viejo, testimony of

Gabriel de León, October 13, 1608] and leg. 366, exp. 5174 [inquisitorial trial of Lope de Hortubia, testimony of Antón Guerrero el viejo, October 13, 1608]).

47. ADC, leg. 367, exp. 5180 (inquisitorial trial of Juan Guerrero, response to the accusation [cap. 33], August 11, 1608).

48. ADC, leg. 367, exp. 5180 (inquisitorial trial of Juan Guerrero, testimony of Gabriel de León [November 23, 1607] and response to the accusation [cap. 41] [August 12, 1608]). It is not clear how long Ana remained in Martínez's home, but she had certainly been moved into the secret jails before November 10, 1607, on which date she was transferred from cell "F" to "L" (ADC, leg. 369, exp. 5131 [inquisitorial trial of Ana Guerrera, auto de mudanza de carcel, November 10, 1607]).

49. Dadson, *Tolerance and Coexistence*, 184–86.

50. ADC, leg. 362, exp. 5142 (inquisitorial trial of Miguel Ramírez, response to the accusation [cap. 10], May 5, 1610).

51. ADC, leg. 367, exp. 5180 (inquisitorial trial of Juan Guerrero, response to the accusation [cap. 58], August 13, 1608).

52. ADC, leg. 249, exp. 3369 (inquisitorial trial of Luis de Cebea el viejo, testimony of Gabriel de León, March 29, 1608).

53. ADC, leg. 366, exp. 5172 (inquisitorial trial of Catalina de Hortubia, testimony of Gabriel de León, November 22, 1607) and ADC, leg. 367, exp. 5180 (inquisitorial trial of Juan Guerrero, response to the accusation [cap. 20], August 11, 1608).

54. ADC, leg. 367, exp. 5180 (inquisitorial trial of Juan Guerrero, testimony of Gabriel de León, [November 26, 1607, January 26 and August 21,1608] and response to the accusation [cap. 32] [August 11, 1608]). When questioned by inquisitors, Guerrero denied having hidden any money in Ariza or Cuenca (ADC, leg. 367, exp. 5180 [inquisitorial trial of Juan Guerrero, response to the accusation (caps. 37 and 43), August 11 and 12, 1608]).

55. ADC, leg. 367, exp. 5180 (inquisitorial trial of Juan Guerrero, testimony of Francisca de Hortubia, December 10, 1608). Juan Guerrero also asserted that, although they had made preparations for flight, "neither he nor any of the others had the courage to run away" (response to the accusation [cap. 22], August 11, 1608).

56. ADC, leg. 367, exp. 5180 (inquisitorial trial of Juan Guerrero, response to the accusation [cap. 20], August 11, 1608). Ana de Hortubia's arrest came a few days after the rest. Following their own arrests, her mother Cecilia la Montera and sister Francisca de Hortubia tried to send messages to her. Although they had meant to encourage Ana, who was pregnant, to flee for safety, instead they tipped off inquisitors and prompted her arrest (ADC, leg. 368, exp. 5196 [inquisitorial trial of Cecilia la Montera, testimony of Andrés Martínez, November 11, 1607] and leg. 375, exp. 5324 [inquisitorial trial of Ana de Hortubia, testimony of Juan Martínez de Montoya, November 11, 1607]).

57. Lope de Cieli noted he contributed about 70 *reales* to the cause (ADC, leg. 376, exp. 5332 [inquisitorial trial of Lope de Cieli, confession of the accused, October 23, 1609]).

58. On Gómez Dávila, see Martínez Hernández, "La hacienda del Marqués de Velada," 35–71 and *El Marqués de Velada*.

59. Duke Juan de la Cerda's aunt, Catalina de la Cerda (1551–1603), married Sandoval (at that time merely Marquis of Denia) in 1576. She was the mother of Cristóbal Gómez de Sandoval Rojas, Duke of Uceda, who worked in the 1610s, along with other *poderosos*, to supplant his father as royal favorite.

60. ADC, leg. 370, exp. 5240 (inquisitorial trial of Miguel de Deza, testimony of Gabriel de León, June 20, 1608).

61. ADC, leg. 370, exp. 5240 (inquisitorial trial of Miguel de Deza, testimony of Gabriel de León, June 20, 1608).

62. ADC, leg. 371, exp. 5246 (inquisitorial trial of Juan Mancebo, testimony of García Cubero, December 25, 1608).

63. Miguel Guerrero, who had initially accepted the commission to travel to Cuenca, ultimately determined it was too risky and returned the money, leading the organizers—Lope de Arcos, Luis de Cebea el viejo, Juan Martínez el cojo, Francisco Martínez, Juan de Heredia, Luis de Cebea, Luis and Gerónimo de Liñán, Luis de Hortubia el Jarquino, Agustín Ramírez, Alonso de Cieli, Lope de Hortubia, Luis de Hortubia, Gonzalo el Burgueño, Francisco de Mendoza and his brothers, and "other Moriscos"—to turn to Miguel de Deza. Miguel Guerrero went into hiding and evaded arrest (ADC, leg. 366, exp. 5174 [inquisitorial trial of Luis de Hortubia el Jarquino, testimony of Gabriel de León, May 13, 1608]).

64. ADC, leg. 370, exp. 5240 (inquisitorial trial of Miguel de Deza, letter of Alonso de Póveda to inquisitorial tribunal in Cuenca, March 12, 1608). The order for Miguel's arrest was issued after the fact (along with one for his wife, Ana de Mendoza) on March 15, 1608, the day after Póveda's letter arrived in Cuenca.

65. ADC, leg. 370, exp. 2541 (inquisitorial trial of Juan de Cebea, request of Alonso de Póveda, March 22, 1608).

66. That Mancebo and Fadrique, who were on opposite sides of the feud between the Cebeas and Romo-Mancebos, could engage in civil conversation suggests just how badly the arrests had unsettled the pattern of life in the Upper Neighborhood.

67. ADC, leg. 371, exp. 5246 (inquisitorial trial of Juan Mancebo, testimony of García Cubero, December 25, 1608).

68. ADM, leg. 188, doc. 27, fol. 6r (census of Deza's Moriscos, November 9, 1609) and ADC, leg. 785, exp. 3218 (denunciations of Juan de Amador Fernández by Mateo Miguel and María Esteban, April 26, 1609). Although both men were denounced in various contexts, neither was arrested.

69. ADM, leg. 188, doc. 27, fol. 2v.

70. ADC, leg. 719, exp. 937 (letter of Juan de Barnuevo y Miranda and Pedro de Cisneros to tribunal in Cuenca, April 8, 1608).

71. ADC, leg. 719, exp. 937 (letter of Juan de Barnuevo y Miranda and Pedro de Cisneros to tribunal in Cuenca, April 8, 1608).

72. ADC, leg. 719, exp. 937 (letter of Juan de Barnuevo y Miranda and Pedro de Cisneros to tribunal in Cuenca, April 14, 1608).

73. On the fallout from his death, see Martínez Hernández, "Don Gómez Dávila y Toledo," 585.

74. Dadson discusses the divisions within the Council of State in *Tolerance and Coexistence*, 118–20 and 136–40.

75. Domínguez Ortiz and Vincent, *Historia de los Moriscos*, 170–71. On Velada's rivalry with Lerma, especially regarding the Morisco problem, see Martínez Hernández, "Don Gómez Dávila," 602–24.

76. ADC, leg. 375, exp. 5308 (inquisitorial trial of María la Burgueña, letter from Bartolomé Montero to the Holy Office, September 22–23, 1610).

77. ADC, leg. 249, exp. 3369 (inquisitorial trial of Luis de Cebea el viejo, response to the accusation [cap. 11], March 28, 1609).

78. This reference to Lope de Hortubia is peculiar. While a wealthy Morisco by that name lived in Deza at the time, he is not known to have been central to the negotiation efforts. Perhaps the notary meant to write *Luis* de Hortubia, known as el Jurado for having served as municipal counselor in 1602 and 1607. El Jurado, who was Lope's brother, was much more actively involved. Alternatively, perhaps Lope de *Arcos* was the intended referent.

79. ADC, leg. 376, exp. 5332 (inquisitorial trial of Lope de Cieli, first audience, June 29, 1608). Unfortunately, the petition is not extant and its contents were never described.

80. Montero (ca. 1551–ca. 1616) was appointed Deza's commissioner in 1606 to replace Licentiate Miguel Benito. He had served in town since at least 1569, initially as sacristan. Over time he gained a benefice and an appointment as lieutenant vicar. By the early seventeenth century he was assigned to confess Moriscos, although María la Carnicera expressed frustration with his confessional demeanor, since he had little time for her and rarely paid attention (ADC, leg. 375, exp. 5322 [inquisitorial trial of María la Carnicera, first audience, May 29, 1608]). On clerical comportment in confession, see O'Banion, "'A priest who appears good,'" 333–48.

81. ADC, leg. 363, exp. 5150 (inquisitorial trial of Lope de Obezar, letter from Bartolomé Montero, October 17, 1608). Montero's reference to Diego de Fadrique is ambiguous and could mean either Diego el mayor (b. 1554) or his son Diego el menor (b. ca. 1582), Ana Guerrera's husband. Both men were muleteers.

82. Compare the support given by some nobles to their Moriscos (and not merely for economic reasons) described in Dadson, *Tolerance and Coexistence*, 109–11.

83. Martínez Hernández, "Don Gómez Dávila," 622–24.

84. AGS, Estado (Castilla), leg. 2.641, fol. 122.

85. ADC, leg. 369, exp. 5131 (inquisitorial trial of Ana Guerrera, first audience, July 19, 1607).

86. ADC, leg. 369, exp. 5131 (inquisitorial trial of Ana Guerrera, response to the accusation [cabeza], October 1, 1607).

87. ADC, leg. 369, exp. 5131 (inquisitorial trial of Ana Guerrera, confessions of the accused [October 2 and 6, 1607] and response to the accusation [October 3, 1607]).

88. ADC, leg. 369, exp. 5131 (inquisitorial trial of Ana Guerrera, confession of the accused, October 6, 1607). The Moriscos' failure to fully embrace Islamic prohibitions against wine (unlike pork) mirrors the situation in La Mancha. See García-Arenal, *Inquisición y moriscos*, 69.

89. See O'Banion, "Prisoners' Dilemma," 277–89.

90. ADC, leg. 375, exp. 5314 (letter from Bartolomé Montero to Cuenca tribunal, July 19, 1610).

91. See Dadson, *Tolerance and Coexistence*, 136–37.

92. ADC, leg. 375, exp. 5308 (inquisitorial trial of María la Burgueña, letter of Bartolomé Montero to Cuenca, September 22–24, 1610).

93. ADC, leg. 375, exp. 5308 (inquisitorial trial of María la Burgueña, letter of Bartolomé Montero to Cuenca, September 22–24, 1610).

94. ADC, leg. 375, exp. 5308 (inquisitorial trial of María la Burgueña, testimony of Gerónimo de Molina, September 15, 1610).

11. CLEVERER THAN HIS FATHER

1. On Spanish possession ceremonies (albeit royal ones), see Ruiz, *A King Travels*. Rather than seeing them merely as articulations of ideological aims and social statements, Ruiz emphasizes the complexity of such ceremonies and the elements of uncertainty connected to them such that sometimes "kingly power was the loser or princely authority diminished" (7). Much the same is true of feudal lords.

2. ADM, leg. 111, doc. 39, fols. 1v, 3r (three times), 5v, and 8v.

3. ADM AH, leg. 125, doc. R1(s), fol. 6r.

4. ADM, leg. 111, doc. 39, fol. 5v. Coincidentally, Miguel Ramírez's presence in town during these proceedings is established by the fact that he acted as a formal witness at another point in the ceremony (fol. 4v).

5. See, for example, ADM, leg. 111, doc. 25 for the possession ceremony of 1594.

6. In fact, unlike the other acts of possession, the official record of the ceremony left unmentioned who had occupied the property prior to Verano's assertion of control over it.

7. Yet, both Velada and doña Antonia continued to support the appointment of Moriscos to council offices up to the very eve of expulsion. See AHPS AMD, leg. 26.558, doc. 10, fols. 104r, 106r, 108r, and 110r.

8. ADC, leg. 362, exp. 5142 (inquisitorial trial of Miguel Ramírez, first audience, June 2, 1608). Tempting as it is to imagine that Román chose not to have Miguel baptized, this is unlikely. His failure to comply would surely have been noticed by local clerics and, moreover, the sacramental register is an imperfect document, not only in its current state of deterioration but also on account of the many errors detectable in the records themselves.

9. Several people also accused Miguel of having carried on an illicit relationship with his first cousin María Ramírez (the daughter of Román's brother, Juan, and wife of Diego de Medina) from the late 1590s. See, for example, ADC, leg. 362, exp. 5142 (inquisitorial trial of Miguel Ramírez, testimony of Juan Guerrero, August 13, 1608). But compare with ADC, leg. 365, exp. 5165 (inquisitorial trial of Gabriel de Medina, testimony of Gabriel de León, October 13, 1608), where León claimed that Antón Guerrero el viejo told him that María Ramírez was involved with Agustín Carnicero.

10. In 1608, Miguel explained that he lived with Román III for "ten years more or less, while he was the duke of Medinaceli's alguacil mayor. And at the end of that time he married his wife and established his home." This suggests that, perhaps, he surrendered his office when he married (ADC, leg. 362, exp. 5142 [inquisitorial trial of Miguel Ramírez, first audience, June 2, 1608]). In 1599 his father confirmed that Miguel was then currently *alguacil mayor del duque* (ADC, leg. 343, exp. 4876, fol. 210r).

11. ADC, leg. 364, exp. 5159 (inquisitorial trial of Antón Guerrero el viejo, testimony of Martín Destaragán, November 26, 1607) and leg. 365, exp. 5165 (inquisitorial trial of Gabriel de Medina, confession of the accused, August 30, 1608).

12. ADC, libro 227, fols. 165v-66r (*This Happened*, 150).

13. ADC, leg. 362, exp. 5142 (inquisitorial trial of Miguel Ramírez, letter of Pedro de Cisneros, November 26, 1607). Other Old Christians suggested that "after the death of [their father], Román Ramírez [III] and Miguel Ramírez and Francisco Ramírez, all brothers and the sons of Román," had charge of the property (testimonies of Pedro de Argüellos, Miguel de Yxea, Cristóbal de Ureña, Antonio de Ucedo Salazar, September 29– October 1, 1610).

14. The timing of the transaction described here is unclear. Cisneros's words could be interpreted figuratively to mean "not long ago" or could be read more literally to indicate that the property was gifted a few days before the letter was written.

15. ADC, leg. 362, exp. 5142 (inquisitorial trial of Miguel Ramírez, testimonies of Pedro de Argüellos, Miguel de Yxea, Cristóbal de Ureña, Antonio de Ucedo Salazar, September 29–October 1, 1610).

16. This reading of the chronology described in Cisneros's letters sees the confirmation of the Ramírez brothers' control of the garden coming on the heels of the successful meeting of Miguel Guerrero and Luis de Hortubia with the duke following his son's birth, this despite Miguel Ramírez's unwillingness to participate in those negotiations. See ADC, leg. 249, exp. 3369 (inquisitorial trial of Luis de Cebea el viejo, testimony of Gabriel de León, March 29, 1608).

17. ADC, leg. 362, exp. 5142 (inquisitorial trial of Miguel Ramírez, loose letter from the accused to the Holy Office, no date).

18. See Kallendorf, *Exorcism and Its Texts*, 163–67 and García-Arenal and Rodríguez Mediano, *Orient in Spain*, 95.

19. See Llorente, *History of the Inquisition*, 178 and Menéndez y Pelayo, *Historia de los heterodoxos españoles*, 2:663–65.

20. The inclusion in Miguel's proceso of these testimonies mirrors the way that evidence related to the Tajahuerce affair affected his father's trial a decade earlier. In both trials, the interactions occurred outside of Deza (Sigüenza, in Miguel's case) and the denunciations were made by men who were (seemingly, at least) otherwise unconnected to local affairs. In Miguel's trial, the Holy Office determined that they had no legal weight (designating them *nihil* in the margins and crossing out the numbers assigned to these unreliable witnesses). Nevertheless, the Holy Office drew upon the testimony to accuse Miguel of having inherited the demon Liarde, which helped him locate treasures. See ADC, leg. 362, exp. 5142 (inquisitorial trial of Miguel Ramírez, testimonies of Mateo de Luna, Juan de Chariteo, Pedro de Mendoza, Bartolomé de Mingo, Juan de Martín [October 3 and December 30–31, 1607]; Accusation [cap. 4] [May 5, 1610]).

21. ADC, leg. 362, exp. 5142 (inquisitorial trial of Miguel Ramírez, testimony of Pedro de Mendoza, December 31, 1607). Presumably, all this about treasures was a fiction but the Holy Office took it seriously and ordered Ramírez to disclose "where the said book of treasures is and who has it at present." He denied any knowledge of it. See ADC, leg. 362, exp. 5142 (inquisitorial trial of Miguel Ramírez, Accusation and response to the Accusation [cap. 18], May 5–6, 1610).

22. On treasures and treasure hunting, see Tausiet, *Urban Magic*, 30–57. Ricote appears in *Don Quixote* (pt. 2, ch. 54), 809–16.

23. ADC, leg. 362, exp. 5142 (inquisitorial trial of Miguel Ramírez, testimony of Juan de Martín, December 31, 1607).

24. ADC, leg. 362, exp. 5142 (inquisitorial trail of Miguel Ramírez, letter of Pedro de Cisneros, November 12, 1607).

25. ADC, leg. 362, exp. 5142 (inquisitorial trial of Miguel Ramírez, statement of the accused, January 12, 1611).

26. ADC, leg. 362, exp. 5142 (inquisitorial trial of Miguel Ramírez, first audience, June 2, 1608).

27. ADC, leg. 362, exp. 5142 (inquisitorial trial of Miguel Ramírez, response to the Accusation [cap. 6], May 5, 1610). Ramírez claimed that he bought the *Antialcorano* in Zaragoza in order to *aprovecharse del en su poesía*, which is difficult to credit. A copy of this book was in the possession of Moriscos in Deza as far back as the 1560s (ADC, leg. 247, exp. 3316, fol. 5v).

28. Old Christian Librada González, the wife of the town's schoolmaster, testified to having overheard Morisco youths discussing a book owned by Ramírez that "said so many things about Mohammed," and that he made them kiss (ADC, leg. 362, exp. 5142 [inquisitorial trial of Miguel Ramírez, testimony of Librada González, January 29, 1609]). The Holy Office understood this book to be a Quran, although Miguel denied ever owning one (ADC, leg. 362, exp. 5142 [inquisitorial trial of Miguel Ramírez, response to the Accusation (caps. 6–7), May 5, 1610]).

29. ADC, leg. 362, exp. 5142 (inquisitorial trial of Miguel Ramírez, first audience, June 2, 1608).

30. ADC, leg. 362, exp. 5142 (inquisitorial trial of Miguel Ramírez, Accusation [cap. 22], May 5, 1610).

31. ADC, leg. 362, exp. 5142 (inquisitorial trial of Miguel Ramírez, testimonies of Juan Guerrero [August 18, 1608] and Gabriel de León [October 11, 1608]). Miguel's wife, María Almotazán, was also denounced, for playing the female officiant at Morisco weddings.

32. ADC, leg. 362, exp. 5142 (inquisitorial trial of Miguel Ramírez, testimony of Librada González [January 29, 1609] and Accusation [caps. 5 and 7] [May 5, 1610]).

33. ADC, leg. 362, exp. 5142 (inquisitorial trial of Miguel Ramírez, Accusation [cap. 6], May 5, 1610).

34. ADC, leg. 362, exp. 5142 (inquisitorial trial of Miguel Ramírez, Accusation [caps. 8–9], May 5, 1610).

35. The fates of Francisco and Román III are unclear. The prosecutor in Cuenca requested their arrests sometime in 1608 but apprehended neither. Francisco (but not Román) was numbered among a group of Moriscos who fled (ADC, leg. 719, exp. 931 and 966). Curiously, the census of Moriscos taken in November 1609 indicates that the two men (who had both become widowers) were living in Deza in the house of María de Deza (Francisco's mother-in-law) along with Román III's two sons (ADM, leg. 188, doc. 27, fol. 5r). Either Francisco returned, the census takers erred, or the inquisitors were misled.

36. ADC, leg. 366, exp. 5174 (inquisitorial trial of Luis de Hortubia el Jarquino, testimony of Juan Guerrero, June 18, 1608).

37. ADC, leg. 369, exp. 5216 (inquisitorial trial of Román el Romo, testimony of Gabriel de León, June 20, 1608).

38. ADC, leg. 369, exp. 5159 (inquisitorial trial of Antón Guerrero el viejo, testimony of Gabriel de León, October 11, 1608). Another possible translation of the quotation is: "Be sure to deny. We are denying. Stay tough."

39. ADC, leg. 364, exp. 5159 (inquisitorial trial of Antón Guerrero el viejo, testimony of Gabriel de León, October 11, 1608).

40. ADC, leg. 358, exp. 5103 (inquisitorial trial of Catalina Zamorano, testimony of Gabriel de León, October 11, 1608).

41. Although the charade seems far-fetched, the same period saw at least one other Old Christian successfully pass as a Morisco. See García-Arenal, "Moriscos in Morocco," 302–3.

42. No trial record exists for Gabriel de León in the inquisitorial archives at Cuenca. Yet it is clear from his statements, which were included in the case files of other prisoners, that testimony was gathered against him, he had been processed into the secret jails, and he had participated in multiple audiences before the inquisitors. His case file could have been lost, damaged over time, destroyed accidentally, or removed. On León and the usefulness of his testimony as a source for the Moriscos's activities in the secret jails see O'Banion, "The Prisoners' Dilemma," 277–89.

43. ADC, leg. 364, exp. 5159 (inquisitorial trial of Antón Guerrero el viejo, testimony of Gabriel de León, October 8, 1608).

44. ADC, leg. 250, exp. 3373 (inquisitorial trial of Lope Guerrero el viejo, testimony of Gabriel de León, November 18, 1607). No evidence indicates whether Martínez actually delivered these messages, but it is not impossible. Although capricious in discipline, the warden was sometimes lenient and accommodating.

45. ADC, leg, 364, exp. 5159 (inquisitorial trial of Antón Guerrero el viejo, testimony of Gabriel de León, October 11, 1608).

46. ADC, leg. 364, exp. 5159 (inquisitorial trial of Antón Guerrero el viejo, testimony of Gabriel de León, October 11, 1608).

47. ADC, leg. 362, exp. 5142 (inquisitorial trial of Miguel Ramírez, letters of Pedro de Cisneros, November 12 and 26, 1607).

48. ADC, leg. 362, exp. 5142 (inquisitorial trial of Miguel Ramírez, torture of the accused, February 12, 1611).

49. See Lea, *History of the Inquisition*, 3:163.

50. Ramírez's signature typically corresponds to Soubeyroux Level A—written with ease and decorated with a terminal flourish—but his final signature would be better categorized as Level B. See Soubeyroux, "L'alphabètisation," 231–54.

51. Sources mention the following Moriscos by name, although there must have been others as well. The women: Francisca de Hortubia, Ana de Hortubia, María la Burgueña, María de Cebea, Leonor de Hortubia, María la Jarquina, and María de Medina. The men: Lope Guerrero el viejo, Lope Guerrero el menor [el mozo], Francisco de Cebea, Miguel Ramírez, Román el Romo, Luis de Hortuiba el Jarquino, Francisco el Romo, Juan de Hortubia el Soldado, Juan de Cebea, Luis de Cebea el más mozo, Juan Mancebo, Pedro Zamorano, and Juan Corazón. The non-Dezanos: Rodrigo Fajardo (a *morisco granadino* from Tarancón) and Íñigo de Moraga (from Cuenca and Arcos).

52. These included all males in the group except Lope Guerrero el viejo (reckoned too old for the galleys), Miguel Ramírez and Íñigo de Moraga (not yet released when the letter was written), and Francisco de Cebea (perhaps on account of his feud with the authors' family).

53. ADC, libro 227, fol. 163r (*This Happened*, 147–48).

54. ADC, libro 227, fols. 165r-67r (*This Happened*, 149–51).

55. ADC, leg. 813, exps. 6676 and 6677 (*This Happened*, 135–45).

56. ADC, leg. 813, exp. 6676 (letter of Juan de Cebea to Francisca de Baptista, March 11, 1611) (*This Happened*, 140).

57. ADC, leg. 813, exp. 6676 (letter of María la Jarquina to Francisca Ropiñón, March 11, 1611) (*This Happened*, 137).

58. ADC, leg. 813, exp. 6676 (letter of María de Medina and Ana de Hortubia to Luis de Hortubia and Bartolomé Aliger, March 11, 1611). The wife of Deza's alcaide was regularly afforded this title, but it might also refer to the wife of Gil Martínez, the warden of the secret jails or even the wife of the warden of the royal jails.

59. ADC, leg. 813, exp. 6676 (letter of Luis de Cebea el más mozo to Isabel de Liñán, March 13, 1611).

60. ADC, leg. 813, exp. 6676 (letters of Francisco el Romo to unknown [March 4, 1611]; María de Medina and Ana de Hortubia to Luis de Hortubia and Bartolomé Aliger [March 11, 1611]; Juan Corazón to Ana Guerrera and Diego de Fadrique [March 12, 1611]; and Juan de Hortubia el Soldado to Diego de Fadrique el mayor and Diego de Fadrique el menor [March 12, 1611]). Although nothing came of it, the Holy Office opened a file on Juan Miguel in 1609, apparently for communicating with Ana de Hortubia, who was being held in his home while awaiting transfer to Cuenca (ADC, leg. 719, exp. 939 and leg. 375, exp. 5324 [inquisitorial trial of Ana de Hortubia, confession of the accused, December 11, 1607]).

61. ADC, leg. 813, exp. 6676 (letter of Juan de Hortubia el Soldado to Lope and Luis de Hortubia, March 12, 1611) (*This Happened*, 142). An inquisitorial agent noted the significance of this statement, underlining it upon review.

62. ADC, leg. 813, exp. 6676 (letter of Luis de Hortubia el Jarquino to Diego de Medina, March 1611 [no day]). See also ADC, leg. 813, exp. 6676 (letter of Luis de Cebea el más mozo to María de Hortubia, March 11, 1611).

63. ADC, leg. 813, exp. 6676 (letter of Francisco el Romo to unknown, March 4, 1611).

64. ADC, leg. 813, exp. 6676 (letter of Juan de Cebea to Francisca de Baptista, March 11, 1611).

65. ADC, leg. 813, exp. 6676 (letter of Luis de Cebea el más mozo to María de Hortubia, March 11, 1611).

66. The Suprema's very brief letter to Cuenca that prompted the subsequent medical examinations was accompanied by the petition from the Romo brothers (ADC, libro 227, fol. 161r), but Cuenca's immediate response is lost (see fols. 165r-67r [*This Happened*, 148–50]). Curiously, although the Suprema's letter was dated January 22, 1611, it only arrived in Cuenca on April 11. Even more curiously, although the letter from Francisco and Román to the king is undated, it indicates that all of the Moriscos named in it were, at the time of composition, *presos en la carcel real desta ciudad de Cuenca* and, therefore, not in inquisitorial custody. Presumably, it was sent to Madrid *before* the Suprema composed the letter of January 22, which ordered Cuenca to conduct medical examinations, but Francisco el Romo (one of the purported authors) was not transferred from the secret jails to the royal jails until January 30. Further complicating the chronology and chain of transmission, Miguel Ramírez, whose name had at some point been inserted to replace that of Luis de Hortubia el Jarquino (which was crossed out), was not released until March. The emendation was presumably made subsequent to his transfer, but this suggests that the Suprema's order was either in the possession of someone interacting with the Moriscos in Cuenca between its composition and reception in April or that someone in Madrid made the change while the request was already in process.

67. ADC, libro 227, fol. 167r (*This Happened*, 151).

68. ADC, libro 240, fol. 16r (*This Happened*, 152).

69. Probably in June 1611 Moraga had petitioned the Suprema for a commutation of his galley sentence on the basis of poor health. Cuenca ordered an examination, which noted that a badly wounded arm would likely be fully healed in two months and otherwise confirmed his ability to serve in the galleys (ADC, libro 240, fols. 20r-21v).

70. ADC, libro 240, fol. 26r (*This Happened*, 153).

71. ADC, leg. 813, exp. 6676 (Juan de Hortubia el Soldado to Diego de Fadrique el mayor and Diego de Fadrique el menor, March 12, 1611) (*This Happened*, 141).

72. See Suárez Ávila, "Comentario cordial al artículo," 97–98 and Bermejo Cabrero, *Poder político y administración*, 530. Whether this Bartolomé or doña

Paula were related to the Morisco Bartolomé del Águila who served as castellan of Arcos in 1559 is unknown (Carrasco, "Morisque anciens," 207).

73. ADC, libro 240, fol. 27r (*This Happened*, 154).

74. In May and June 1610 the Suprema had requested a speedy conclusion to all trials (ADC, libro 227, fols. 132r and 135r). Cuenca responded that they were proceeding as quickly as possible given their inadequate staff (ADC, libro 240, fols. 2r and 21v).

75. ADC, libro 227, fols. 227r-28r (*This Happened*, 154–56).

76. ADC, leg. 377, exp. 5342 (inquisitorial trial of Juan Corazón, notice signed by Drs. Ayala and Fadrique Cornet, March 8, 1616).

77. Gil Herrera, "Los bienes raíces," 96 and 116.

78. ADM AH, leg. 188, doc. 28, fols. 30r-31r. See Wiegers, "Managing Disaster," 145.

79. Cervantes, *Don Quixote* (pt. 2, ch. 54), 816. Dadson suggests that similar scenes played out "all over Spain" (*Tolerance and Coexistence*, 112).

80. In the Valle de Ricote and Villarrubia, some Moriscas avoided expulsion by arranging hasty marriages with Old Christians. No evidence of this exists for Deza. See Márquez Villanueva, *Moros, moriscos y turcos*, 234 and Dadson, *Los moriscos de Villarrubia*, 369–72.

81. Dadson, *Tolerance and Coexistence*, 161–82.

82. Alcalde, *Deza*, 1:243.

83. Vincent, "Geography of the Morisco Expulsion," 26.

84. El Alaoui, "Moriscos in France," 256.

85. Lapeyre, *Geografía*, 198–201. Travel to Cartagena was not only longer as the crow flies—perhaps three hundred and fifty miles as opposed about two hundred and seventy-five—but also entailed a less direct route since Castilian Moriscos could not pass through Aragon or Valencia.
To argue the contrary, however, in January 1611 the Count of Salazar notified King Philip that he planned to round up the Moriscos of Benquerencia and Magacela (in Extremadura) and Deza and Arcos de Jalón (in Soria) before finishing off the expulsion process with the Moriscos of Murcia. This final major sweep of Moriscos could have converged at Cartagena (Lapeyre, *Geografía*, 176).

86. Wiegers, "Managing Disaster," 152.

87. García-Arenal, "Moriscos in Morocco," 303.

88. ADC, leg. 367, exp. 5180 (inquisitorial trial of Juan Guerrero, testimony of Gabriel de León, November 27, 1607).

89. ADC, leg. 375, exp. 5314 (inquisitorial trial of Francisco de Medrano, testimony of Francisco Donoso, May 21, 1610).

90. Carr, *Blood and Faith*, 291.

91. Vincent, "Geography of the Morisco Expulsion," 22.

92. Epalza, *Los Moriscos antes y después de la expulsión*, 218–32.

93. García-Arenal, "Moriscos in Morocco," 317.

94. Friedman, "North African Piracy," 13–14 and García-Arenal, "Moriscos in Morocco," 324–28.

95. Bookin-Weiner, "Corsairing in the Economy and Politics of North Africa," 12.

96. Wiegers, "Managing Disaster," 158.

97. The quotation is from Ahmed ibn Qasim al-Hacharî (Ahmed Bejarano) as given in Bernabé Pons, "La nación en lugar seguro," 107–8.

98. Epalza, "Nuevos documentos," 224 and *Los Moriscos antes y después de la expulsión*, 263–64; and Villanueva Zubizarreta, "Moriscos in Tunisia," 369–87.

99. Wiegers, "Expulsion of 1609–1614," 411–12.

100. Villanueva, "Moriscos in Tunisia," 387.

101. AHDOS APD, LS (1605–1646), fol. 1v. A similar note is inserted in the margin of the baptismal section of the register between the baptisms of a Morisca on July 4 and an Old Christian boy on July 10 (fol. 25v). No evidence suggests that Deza's Moriscos were separated from their children or that the latter were handed over to Old Christian neighbors to be raised as Christians.

102. Such a reunion would have been facilitated by the various nodes that developed among the Morisco diaspora. They allowed information to spread and enabled communication between various Morisco communities in exile and at home. See Muchnik, "Judeoconversos and Moriscos," 413–39.

103. Harvey, "Oral Composition," 284–85 speculates (although he acknowledges he does so without evidence) about a relative or even "son of our Román" remaining in Spain under an assumed name—Luis Remírez de Arellano—on the basis of a contemporary reference to a *mancebo grandamente memorioso* who could memorize entire plays in just three hearings and correct their recitation. See Suárez de Figueroa, *Plaza universal*, fol. 237r.

CONCLUSION

1. ADC, leg. 813, exp. 6571, fols. 1r-2r. Ultimately, Niño de Guevara located four unfortunates, including Ramírez, to be relaxed to the secular arm at the auto—three in effigy and one in person (Sierra, *Procesos de la Inquisición*, 486–87).

2. Díaz Migoyo, "Memoria y fama," 42.

3. Moriscos remembered Arganda and his 1581 visitation decades after it occurred and sometimes blamed him for their fate. See ADC, leg. 364, exp. 5159 (inquisitorial trial of Antón Guerrero, testimony of Gabriel de León, [November 7, 1608]; testimony of Gabriel de Medina [June 18, 1610]; and response to the accusation [cap. 52; June 5, 1610]); and leg. 367, exp. 5180b (inquisitorial trial of Juan Guerrero, confession of the accused, [March 30, 1609] and testimony of Francisco de Cebea [April 7, 1609]).

4. BNE, Mss/4501. Salucio did not seek to eliminate the statutes altogether but rather to moderate them, eliminate corruption, and impose statutes of limitations after which ancestry would not be considered.

5. Sicroff, *Los estatutos*, 221.

6. Rawlings, "Agustín Salucio's Rehabilitation," 1655–56.

7. Rawlings, "Agustín Salucio's Rehabilitation," 1658.

8. Boronat y Barrachina, *Los moriscos*, 1:20–22.

9. See Magnier, *Pedro de Valencia*, 5–6, 102–3

10. Marcos de Guadalajara y Javier, *Memorable expvlsion*, fol. 66r-v. I quote from Magnier's translation (*Pedro de Valencia*, 170).

11. Magnier, *Pedro de Valencia*, 170–71.

12. Magnier, *Pedro de Valencia*, 167–69.

13. Guzmán, *Reyna católica*, fol. 192v.

14. Tueller, *Good and Faithful*, 195.

15. Rawlings, "Augstín Salucio's Rehabilitation," 1661.

16. Magnier, *Pedro de Valencia*, 51 and Varnuebo de Soria [*sic*], *Relacion verdadera*, fol. 2r.

17. ADC, leg. 343, exp. 4876, fol. 194v.

18. Magnier, *Pedro de Valencia*, 155–56 and Emmerson, *Antichrist*, 14.

19. Delrio's *Disquisitionum* was frequently reprinted, but the Mainz, 1603 edition is the first to mention Ramírez.

20. See ADC, leg. 343, exp. 4876, fols. 253r-60r (*This Happened*, 121–34) for Ramírez's sentence.

21. *Disquisitionum*, 1:180. I quote from Maxwell-Stuart's translation of Question 24 (*Investigations into Magic*, 104).

22. *Disquisitionum*, 1:41 (*Investigations into Magic*, 57).

23. *Disquisitionum*, 1:105–7 (*Investigations into Magic*, 183–85).

24. Martínez Blasco, *Quien mal anda*, 8 and 71.

25. *Don Juan Ruiz de Alarcón*, 219–20. More recently, Martínez Blasco has followed Fernández-Guerra's dating (*Quien mal anda*, 8).

26. On Delrio's career, see Machielsen, *Martin Delrio*.

27. Whicker, *The Plays of Juan Ruiz de Alarcón*, 108. No "Aldonza" is known to have been living in early modern Deza or to have figured into the life of the historical Román.

28. Note here an echo (or is it the source?) of the interpretation given in *Don Quixote* by the mad Cardenio of the relationship between Queen Madásima and the physician Elisabat in *Amadís of Gaul* (*Don Quixote* [pt. 1, chs. 24–25], 188–89 and 191).

29. The historical Román Ramírez was only rediscovered in the late 1920s when Ángel González Palencia located his proceso in the Archivo Diocesano de Cuenca ("El curandero Morisco," 217–84). González Palencia published long

extracts from the trial record in his article but omitted significant portions of the 260-folio document. Díaz Migoyo traces the threads of literary and historical scholarship flowing out of Delrio, Ruiz de Alarcón, and González Palencia in "Memoria y fama," 39–53.

30. *Vida y muerte del falso profeta Mahoma* was attributed to Rojas y Zorilla as well when it was first published (1642), but recent research ties it to either Antonio Mira de Amescua (1577–1636) or to an unknown Morisco author. See La Granja, "Comedias censuradas," 442–43 and Mami, *El poeta morisco*. Mami argues that *Vida y muerte* was written in response to Zorilla's work, but La Granja alleges evidence dating its premiere to 1609.

31. Julio, "Demonios, brujas y magos," 313–16; Auladell, "Francisco de Rojas Zorilla," 328–29.

32. Watts, *Miguel de Cervantes*, 163. Watts bases the claim on a statement made by Cervantes's sister in 1604 that he *escribía y trataba negocios*, which need not connote Watts's interpretation. Compare with McCrory, *No Ordinary Man*, 186–89.

33. Bouza and Rico, "'Digo que yo he compuesto,'" 13.

34. On this period, see Byron, *Cervantes*, 71–78.

35. Caro Baroja, *Vidas Mágicas*, 349–58; Harvey, "Oral Composition," 270, 285–87 and *Los Moriscos and Don Quixote*, 15; Bernabé Pons, "De los moriscos a Cervantes," 164–65; Alcalá Galán, "El libro como objeto," 25–27; Díaz Migoyo, "Memoria y fama," and Kallendorf, *La rétorica del exorcismo*, 304–6.

36. *Vidas mágicas*, 1:347–48.

37. See Ly, "Literalidad cervantina," 651.

38. Harvey, "Oral Composition," 270. For Cide Hamete Benengeli as enchanter, see *Don Quixote* (pt. 2, ch. 2), 472–73. Several scholars have connected Benengeli to the figure of Miguel de Luna and the Lead Books of Granada (e.g., Case, "Cide Hamete Benengeli," 9–22 and García-Arenal, "Miguel de Luna," 262). I would merely add that at the end of the sixteenth and beginning of the seventeenth centuries, as Spaniards grappled with the Morisco question, both the Lead Books and the Ramírez affair informed the discussion. I find it entirely plausible that Cervantes incorporated and intermixed elements of both in *Don Quixote*.

39. Percas de Ponseti, "Authorial Strings," 51–62.

40. Although never stated explicitly, Liarde appears to suffer from the same limitation. For example, he could tell Ramírez that the Ottoman sultan was raising an armada to attack Spain but did not predict the outcome. Likewise, he could tell Ramírez that a client was wealthy but not how much he would pay. As the innkeeper explains to don Quixote, "future things cannot be known [by the devil] except through conjecture, and only occasionally, for knowing

all times and moments is reserved to God alone, and for Him there is no past or future: everything is present" (626).

41. BNE, Invent/47895. This image can be accessed online via the BNE's Biblioteca Digital Hispánica. See also Ashbee, *Iconography*, 5–6 but note that the BNE image does not appear in the 1674, 1706, 1714, or 1723 editions mentioned by Ashbee nor is it among the illustrations in the 1657 Dordrecht edition upon which the "Obregón" woodcuts were based. The BNE image referenced above is an undated loose leaf but part of a set that includes the 1674 "Obregón" woodcuts. The first edition that I have found to include the image of the bibliographical inquisition is the Madrid, 1735 edition (see *Iconography*, 17–18), which appears to be the source for the BNE image.

42. The tongue twister goes: "El perro de San Roque no tiene rabo porque Ramón Ramírez se lo ha cortado." See Magnier Heney, "Román Ramírez," 449.

Bibliography

ARCHIVES AND MANUSCRIPT MATERIALS

ADC: Archivo Diocesano de Cuenca, Sección Inquisición, Cuenca
  Legajos: 88, 89, 91, 99, 109, 116, 148, 177, 189, 208, 209, 212, 246, 247, 248, 249,
    250, 252, 254, 343, 355, 358, 361, 362, 363, 364, 365, 366, 367, 368, 369, 370,
    371, 372, 374, 375, 376, 377, 378, 707, 716, 719, 748b, 750, 751, 758, 763, 767,
    783, 785, 789, 796, 813, 820
  Libros: 227, 240, 317, 318, 320, 321
ADM: Archivo Ducal de Medinaceli, Toledo
  Legajos: 3, 43, 44, 60, 68, 111, 188
AH: Archivo Histórico
  Legajos: 125, 188
AGS: Archivo General de Simancas, Consejo del Estado, Simancas
  Legajo: 2.641
AHDOS APD: Archivo Histórico Diocesano de Osma-Soria, Archivo Parroquial de
  Deza. El Burgo de Osma.
  Legajo: 160
  Libro de la Obra Pía . . . fundada por Gerónimo Gorgoz, 1647–1827
  LS: Libros Sacramentales
AHMD: Archivo Histórico Municipal de Deza, Deza
  Cajas: 1, 1s, 15a, 15b, 15c, 16a, 23, 26, 26/4, 71n, 76, 78c, 110b, 111b, 196a, 238, 282
AHN: Archivo Histórico Nacional, Sección Inquisición, Madrid.
  Legajo: 1924
AHPS AMD: Archivo Histórico Provicial de Soria, Archivo Municipal de Deza, Soria
  Legajos: 26.556, 26.558, 26.558/2
AHPZ: Archivo Histórico Provincial de Zaragoza, Sección Inquisición, Zaragoza
  Manuscript: 27/5

ARCV: Archivo de la Real Chancillería de Valladolid
PC: Pleitos Civiles
Caja: 203
RE. Registros de Ejecutorías
Cajas: 373, 966, 1131, 1151, 1189, 1193, 1584, 1632, 1641, 1776, 1901, 1999, 2206, 2285
SH: Sala de Hijos de Algo
Cajas: 46, 318, 446, 463, 630, 647, 683, 705, 710, 746, 777, 847, 1676
BCLM: Biblioteca de Castilla–La Mancha, Toledo
Manuscript: Toledo 505
BNE: Biblioteca Nacional de España, Madrid
Inventario: 47895
Manuscripts: 4501, 6016, 5292
RAH SC: Real Academia de la Historia, Colección Salazar y Castro, Madrid
Documento: 58.630 M-144

PUBLISHED WORKS

Alcaina Fernández, Pelayo. "La inquisición en el marquesado de los Vélez. La visita de 1561." *Revista velezana* 7 (1988): 24–32.

Alcalá Galán, Mercedes. "El libro como objeto en el Quijote." In *El ingenioso hidalgo: estudios en homenaje a Anthony Close*, edited by Rodrígo Cacho Casal, 23–41. Alcalá de Henares: Centro de Estudios Cervantinos, 2009.

Alcalde, Vicente Alejandre. "Caminería histórica de la comarca de Calatayud: caminos de Ateca a Soria y Almazán." *Cuarta provincial* 1 (2018): 55–75.

———. *Deza: Entre Castilla y Aragón*. 2 vols. Soria: Excma. Diputación Provincial, 2011.

———. "Los caminos reales de Madrid a Zaragoza entre los siglos XVI y XIX según las guías de la época y su incidencia en la comarca de Calatayud," 265–84. *Actas del IX Encuentro de Estudios Bilbilitanos*. Calatayud: CEB, 2016.

Álvarez Márquez, María Carmen. "La biblioteca de don Antonio Juan Luis de la Cerda, VII Duque de Medinaceli, en su palacio del Puerto de Santa María (1673)." *Historia. Instituciones, Documentos* 15 (1988): 251–390.

Anes, Gonzalo. "The Agrarian 'Depression' in Castile in the Seventeenth Century." In *The Castilian Crisis of the Seventeenth Century*, edited by I. A. A. Thompson and Bartolomé Yun Casalilla, 60–76. Cambridge: Cambridge University Press, 1994.

———. *Cultivos, cosechos y pastoreo en la España moderna*. Madrid: Real Academia de la Historia, 1999.

Ansón Calvo, María del Carmen. "La vida cotidiana entre los moriscos." *Cuadernos de Historia Moderna. Anejos* 8 (2009): 241–68.

———. *Torrellas: Del esplendor Morisco a la decadencia y la tendencia a su recuperación*. Torrellas: Ayuntamiento de Torellas, 2014.

Aranda Doncel, Juan. *Los moriscos en tierras de Córdoba*. Cordoba: Publicaciones del Monte de Piedad y Caja de Ahorros de Córdoba, 1984.

Ashbee, Henry Spencer. *An Iconography of Don Quixote: 1605–1895*. London: University Press, Aberdeen, 1895.

Auladell, Miguel Ángel. "Francisco de Rojas Zorrilla." In *Christian-Muslim Relations: A Bibliographical History. Volume 9. Western and Southern Europe (1600–1700)*, edited by David Thomas and John Chesworth, 326–32. Leiden: Brill, 2009.

Aznar Cardona, Pedro. *Expulsión justificada de los moriscos españoles y suma de las excelencias Christianas de Nuestro Rey Don Felipe el Catholico*. Huesca, 1612.

Barrios Aguilera, Manuel, and Mercedes García-Arenal. *¿La historia inventada?: Los libros plúmbeos y el legado sacramontano*. Granada: Editorial Universidad, 2008.

Barrow, George Henry. *The Zincali: An Account of the Gypsies of Spain*. London: John Murray, 1872.

Bejarano Rubio, Amparo. "Los escribanos públicos en Castilla: el condado de Ledesma en el siglo XVI." *Miscelánea Medieval Murciana* 19–20 (1995–1996): 9–26.

Benítez Sánchez-Blanco, Rafael. *Moriscos y cristianos en el Condado de Casares*. Córdoba: Excma. Diputación Provincial de Córdoba, 1982.

Bennassar, Bartolomé. *Valladolid en el Siglo de Oro. Una ciudad de Castilla y su entorno agrario en el siglo XVI*. Valladolid: Fundación Municipal de Cultura, 1983.

Bergmann, Emilie. "The Exclusion of the Feminine in the Cultural Discourse of the Golden Age: Juan Luis Vives and Fray Luis de León." In *Religion, Body and Gender in Early Modern Spain*, edited by Alain Saint Saëns, 124–36. San Francisco CA: Mellen Research University Press, 1991.

Bermejo Cabrero, José Luis. *Poder político y administración de justicia en la España de los Austrias*. Madrid: Ministerio de Justicia, 2005.

Bernabé-Pons, Luis F. "De los moriscos a Cervantes." *eHumanista/Cervantes* 2 (2013): 156–82.

———. "La nación en lugar seguro: los Moriscos hacia Túnez." *Actas del Coloquio Internacional "Los Moriscos y Túnez," Cartas de La Goleta* 2, edited by Raja Yassine Bahri, 107–18. Tunis: Embajada de España, 2009.

———. "*Taqiyya, niyya* y el islam de los moriscos." *Al-Qantara* 34 (2013): 491–527.

Bernal, Beatriz. *Comiença la hystoria de los innitos y magnanimos cavalleros don Cristalian de España principe de Trapisonda y del infante Luzesciano su hermano*. Valladolid, 1545.

Bilinkoff, Jodi. *Related Lives: Confessors and Their Female Penitents, 1450–1750*. Ithaca NY: Cornell University Press, 2005.

Blécourt, Willem de and Cornelie Usborne. "Situating 'alternative medicine' in the modern period." *Medical History* 43 (1999): 283–85.

Bookin-Weiner, Jerome. "Corsairing in the Economy and Politics of North Africa." In *North Africa: Nation, State, and Religion*, edited by George Joffé, 3–33. London: Routledge, 1993.

Boronat y Barrachina, Pascual. *Los moriscos españoles y su expulsion*, 2 vols. Valencia: Francisco Vives y Mora, 1901.

Bouza, Fernando, and Francisco Rico. "'Digo que yo he compuesto un libro entitulado *El ingenioso hidalgo de la mancha*.'" *Cervantes* 29 (2009): 13–30.

Bouzineb, Hossain. "Los consejos al hijo de Ādam." In *Memoria de los Moriscos: Escritos y relatos de una diáspora cultural*, edited by Alfredo Mateos Paramio, 198. Madrid: Sociedad Estatal de Conmemoraciones Culturales, 2010.

Bramón, Dolors. "El rito de las fadas, pervivencia de la ceremonia pre-islámica de la 'Aqiqa.'" In *Actas del III Simposio Internacional de Estudios Moriscos. Las Prácticas Musulmanas de los Moriscos Andaluces (1492–1609)*, edited by Abdeljelil Temimi, 33–37. Zaghouan: CEROMDI, 1989.

Byron, William. *Cervantes: A Biography*. Garden City NY: Doubleday, 1978.

Cacho Blecua, Juan Manuel. "Introducción al estudio de los motivos en los libros de caballerías: La memoria de Román Ramírez." In *Libros de caballerías (de "Amadís" al "Quijote"): Poética, lectura, representación e identidad*, edited by Eva Belén Carro Carbajal, Laura Puerto Moro, and María Sánchez Pérez, 27–53. Salamanca: Seminario de Estudios Medievales y Renacentistas, 2002.

Cantera Montenegro, Enrique. "La comunidad Morisca de Ágreda (Soria) a fines del siglo XVI." *Espacio, Tiempo y Forma, Serie IV. Historia Moderna* 7 (1994): 11–42.

———. "Las comunidades mudéjares de Osma y Sigüenza a fines de la Edad Media." *Revista de la Facultad de Geografía e Historia* 4 (1989): 137–74.

Cardaillac, Louis. *Moriscos y cristianos. Un enfrentamiento polémico (1492–1640)*. Madrid: Fondo de Cultura Económica, 1977.

Cardillac-Hermosilla, Yvette. *Los nombres del diablo*. Granada: Universidad de Granada, 2005.

Carlos Morales, Carlos Javier de. "La Hacienda Real de Castilla y la revolución de los Genoveses (1560–1575)." *Chronica Nova* 26 (1999): 37–78.

Caro Baroja, Julio. *Vidas mágicas e Inquisición*, 2 vols. Madrid: Ediciones Istmo, 1992.

Carr, Matthew. *Blood and Faith: The Purging of Muslim Spain*. New York: The New Press, 2009.

Carrasco, Raphaël. "Morisques anciens et nouveaux morisques dans le district inquisitorial de Cuenca, première partie." *Mélanges de la Casa de Velásquez* 21 (1985): 193–217.

Carrasco Urgoiti, María Soledad. *El problema morisco en Aragón al comienzo del reinado de Felipe II*. Madrid: Editorial Castalia, 1969.

Case, Thomas E. "Cide Hamete Benengeli y los *Libros plúmbeos*." *Cervantes* 22 (2002): 9–24.

Casey, James. *Family and Community in Early Modern Spain: The Citizens of Granada, 1570–1793*. Cambridge: Cambridge University Press, 2007.

Cavanaugh, Stephanie M. "The Morisco Problem and the Politics of Belonging in Sixteenth-Century Valladolid." PhD diss., University of Toronto, 2016.

Cervantes, Miguel de, *Don Quixote,* translated by Edith Grossman. New York: Harper Collins, 2005.

Chejne, Anwar G. *Islam and the West: The Moriscos.* Albany NY: SUNY Press, 1983.

Christian, William. *Local Religion in Sixteenth-Century Spain.* Princeton NJ: Princeton University Press.

Clausell Nácher, Carmen. "*Carro de las donas* (Valladolid, 1542): Estudio preliminar y edición anotada." PhD diss., Universidad Autónoma de Barcelona, 2004.

Clouse, Michele L. *Medicine, Government, and Public Health in Philip II's Spain.* Ashgate: Aldershot, 2011.

Codera y Zaidín, Francisco. "Almacén de un librero morisco descubierto en Almonacid de la Sierra." *Boletín de la Real Academia de la Historia* 5 (1884): 269–76.

Coolidge, Grace E. *Guardianship, Gender, and the Nobility in Early Modern Spain.* Farnam: Ashgate, 2011.

Crónica de los reyes de Castilla desde don Alfonso el sabio hasta los Católicos don Fernando y doña Isabel. 2 vols. Madrid: Cayetano Rosell, 1898.

Dadson, Trevor. "Literacy and Education in Early Modern Rural Spain: The Case of Villarrubia de los Ojos." *Bulletin of Spanish Studies* 81 (2004): 1011–37.

———. *Los moriscos de Villarrubia de los Ojos (Siglos XV–XVIII): historia de una minoría asimilada, expulsada y reintegrada,* 2nd ed. Madrid: Iberoamericana, 2015.

———. *Tolerance and Coexistence in Early Modern Spain: Old Christians and Moriscos in the Campo de Calatrava.* Woodbridge: Tamesis, 2014.

Danvila y Collado, Manuel. *La expulsión de los moriscos españoles.* Madrid and Seville: Librería de Fernando Fe, 1889.

Dedieu, Jean-Pierre. *L'administration de la foi, L'Inquisition de Tolède (XVIe-XVIIIs siècle).* Madrid, Bibliothèque de la Casa de Velazquez, 1989.

Delrio, Martín. *Disquisitionum magicarum libri sex.* Mainz, 1603.

———. *Investigations into Magic.* Translated by P. G. Maxwell-Stuart. Manchester: Manchester University Press, 2000.

D'Emic, Michael Thomas. *Justice in the Marketplace in Early Modern Spain: Saravia, Villalón and the Religious Origins of Economic Analysis.* Lanham MD: Lexington, 2014.

Díaz de la Guardia y López, Luis. "La mitad de oficios en consejos. Madridejos y otros casos entre el Medievo y la Edad Moderna." *Espacio, Tiempo y Forma, Serie III, Historia Medieval* 20 (2007): 43–95.

Díaz Migoyo, Gonzalo. "Memoria y fama de Román Ramírez." In *Memoria de la palabra. Actas del VI Congreso de la Asociación Internacional Siglo de Oro (Burgos-La Rioja 15–19 de julio de 2002),* 2 vols., edited by M. L. Lobato and F. Domínguez Matito, 1: 39–54. Madrid and Frankfurt: Iberoamericana and Vervuert, 2004.

Dioscorides Anazarbeo, Pedacio. *Acerca de la materia medicinal.* Antwerp, 1555.

Domínguez Ortiz, Antonio. *La clase social de los conversos en Castilla en la Edad Moderna.* Madrid: CSIC, 1955.

————. *The Golden Age of Spain, 1516–1659*, translated by James Casey. New York: Basic Books, 1971.

Domínguez Ortiz, Antonio, and Bernard Vincent. *Historia de los moriscos. Vida y tragedia de una minoría*. Madrid: Alianza Editorial, 1985.

Dueñas, Juan de. *Espejo de consolación de tristes*. Burgos, 1540.

————. *Remedio de pecadores por otro nombre confessionario*. Valladolid, 1545.

Eisenberg, Daniel. *Romances of Chivalry in the Spanish Golden Age*. Newark DE: Juan de la Cuesta, 1982.

Eiximenis, Francesc. *Carro de las donas*. Valladolid, 1542.

El Alaoui, Youssef. "The Moriscos in France after the Expulsion: Notes for the History of a Minority." In *The Expulsion of the Moriscos from Spain: A Mediterranean Diaspora*, edited by García-Arenal and Gerard Wiegers, 239–68. Leiden: Brill, 2014.

Elliott, J. H. *Imperial Spain, 1469–1713*. New York: St. Martin's, 1963.

Emmerson, Richard K. *Antichrist in the Middle Ages: A Study of Medieval Apocalypticism, Art, and Literature*. Seattle: University of Washington, 1981.

Epalza, Míkel de. *Los Moriscos antes y después de la expulsión*. Madrid: Mapfre, 1992.

————. "Nuevos documentos sobre descendientes de moriscos en Túnez en el siglo XVIII." In *Studia Historica et Philologica in Honorem M. Batllorí*, 195–228. Rome: Instituto Español de Cultura, 1984.

Fernández Fernández, María José. "Libro de Castigos (ms. no. 8 de la Junta). Edición, studio lingüístico, glosario y notas." 3 vols. PhD diss., Universidad de Oviedo, 1987.

Fernández-Guerra, Luis. *Don Juan Ruiz de Alarcón y Mendoza*. Madrid: BAE, 1871.

Fernández Nieva, Julio. "Don Diego Gómez de la Madrid, Inquisidor apostólico en Cuenca (1566–1578) y obispo de Badajoz (1578–1601)." *Revista de estudios extremeños* 36 (1980): 68–107.

Flynn, Maureen. *Sacred Charity: Confraternities and Social Welfare in Spain, 1400–1700*. Ithaca NY: Cornell University Press, 1989.

Fonseca, Damián. *Justa expulsión de los moriscos de España*. Rome, 1612.

Friedman, Ellen G. "North African Piracy on the Coasts of Spain in the Seventeenth Century: A New Perspective on the Expulsion of the Moriscos." *The International History Review* 1 (1979): 1–16.

García-Arenal, Mercedes. *Inquisición y moriscos: Los procesos del Tribunal de Cuenca*, 3rd ed. Madrid: Siglo XXI, 1987.

————. "Los Moriscos de la región de Cuenca según los censos establecidos por la Inquisición en 1589 y 1594." *Hispania (Madrid)* 38 (1978): 151–201.

————. "Miguel de Luna y los Moriscos de Toledo: 'No hay en España mejor moro.'" *Chronica Nova* 36 (2010): 253–62.

————. "The Moriscos in Morocco: From Granadan Emigration to the *Hornacheros* of Salé." In *The Expulsion of the Moriscos from Spain: A Mediterranean Dias-*

pora, edited by Mercedes García-Arenal and Gerard Wiegers, 286–328. Leiden: Brill, 2014.

——. "Religious Dissent and Minorities: The Morisco Age." *Journal of Modern History* 81 (2009): 888–920.

García-Arenal, Mercedes, and Fernando Rodríguez Mediano. *The Orient in Spain: Converted Muslims, the Forged Lead Books of Granada, and the Rise of Orientalism.* Leiden: Brill, 2013.

García Avilés, José María. *Los moriscos del Valle de Ricote.* Alicante: Universidad de Alicante, 2007.

García-Ballester, Luis. "Academicism versus empiricism in practical medicine in sixteenth-century Spain with regard to Morisco practitioners." In *The Medical Renaissance of the Sixteenth Century*, edited by Andrew Wear, Roger K. French, and Ian M. Lonie, 246–70. Cambridge: Cambridge University Press, 1985.

——. "The Inquisition and Minority Medical Practitioners in Counter-Reformation Spain: Judaizing and Morisco Practitioners, 1560–1610." In *Medicine and the Reformation*, edited by Ole Peter Grell and Andrew Cunningham, 156–91. London: Routledge, 1993.

——. *Los Moriscos y la medicina: un capítulo de la medicina y la ciencia marginadas en la España del siglo XVI.* Barcelona: Labor, 1984.

——. *Medicina, ciencia, y minorías marginadas: los moriscos.* Granada: Universidad de Granada, 1977.

García Díaz, Isabel. "Escritura y clases populares en Murcia en el tránsito de la Edad Media a la Moderna." In *Cultura escrita y clases subalternas: una mirada española*, edited by Antonio Castillo Gómez, 57–85. Ioartzun: Sendoa, 2001.

García Pedraza, Amalia. *Actitudes ante la muerte en la Granada del siglo XVI: Los moriscos que quisieron salvarse.* Granada: Universidad de Granada, 2002.

Gayangos, Pascual de, ed. *Tratados de la legislación musulmana.* Madrid: RAH, 1853.

Gil Herrera, Jorge. "Los bienes raíces de los moriscos expulsados." *Sharq al-andalus* 19 (2008–2010): 91–119.

Gil Herrera, Jorge, and Luis F. Bernabé Pons. "The Moriscos Outside Spain: Routes and Financing." In *The Expulsion of the Moriscos from Spain: A Mediterranean Diaspora*, edited by Mercedes García-Arenal and Gerard Wiegers, 219–38. Leiden: Brill, 2014.

González, Tomás. *Censo de población de las provincias y partidos de la Corona de Castilla en el siglo XVI.* Madrid: Imprenta Real, 1829.

González Palencia, Ángel. "El curandero morisco del siglo XVI, Román Ramírez." In *Historias y leyendas*, 215–84. Madrid: CSIC, 1942.

Goodman, David C. *Power and Penury: Government Technology and Science in Philip II's Spain.* Cambridge: Cambridge University Press, 1988.

Guadalajara y Javier, Marcos de. *Memorable expvlsion y iustissimo destierro de los Moriscos de España.* Pamplona, 1613.

Guillén Robles, Francisco. *Leyendas moriscas sacadas de varios manuscritos existentes en la Bibliotecas Nacional, Real, y de D.P. de Gayangos*. 3 vols. Seville: Tipografía de la Región, 1896.

Gutiérrez Nieto, Juan Ignacio. "Inquisición y culturas marginadas: conversos, moriscos y gitanos." In *El siglo de Quijote (1580–1680)*, 2 vols., edited by Ramón Menéndez Pidal, 1:837–1015. Madrid: Espasa Calpe, 1996.

Guzmán, Diego de. *Reyna catolica. vida y muerte de D. Margarita de Austria Reyna de Espanna*. Madrid, 1617.

Halavais, Mary. *Like Wheat to the Miller: Convivencia and the Construction of Morisco Identity in Sixteenth-Century Aragon*. Ithaca NY: Cornell University Press, 2001.

Haliczer, Stephen. *Inquisition and Society in the Kingdom of Valencia, 1478–1834*. Berkeley: University of California Press, 1990.

Hamilton, Earl. *American Treasure and the Price Revolution in Spain, 1501–1650*. Boston MA: Harvard University Press, 1934.

Harvey, L. P. "Crypto-Islam in Sixteenth Century Spain." In *Actas del Primer Congreso de Estudios Árabes e Islámicos*, 163–78. Madrid: Comité Permanente del Congreso de Estudios Arabes e Islamicos, 1964.

———. *Los Moriscos and Don Quijote*. London: King's College, 1974.

———. *Muslims in Spain, 1500–1614*. Chicago: University of Chicago Press, 2005.

———. "Oral Composition and the Performance of Novels of Chivalry in Spain." *Forum for Modern Language Studies* 10 (1974): 270–86.

———. "The Political, Social and Cultural History of the Moriscos." In *The Legacy of Muslim Spain*, edited by Salma Khadra Jayyusi, 201–34. Leiden: Brill, 1992.

Hendrickson, Jocelyn N. "The Islamic Obligation to Emigrate: Al-Wansharīsī's *Asnā al-matājir* Reconsidered." PhD diss., Emory University, 2009.

Herzog, Tamar. *Defining Nations: Immigrants and Citizens in Early Modern Spain and Spanish America*. New Haven CT: Yale University Press, 2003.

Huarte de San Juan, Juan. *Examen de ingenios para las sciencias*. Baeza, 1575.

Janer, Florencio. *Condición social de los moriscos de España*. Madrid: RAH, 1857.

Julio, Teresa. "Demonios, brujas y magos en la dramaturgia de Francisco de Rojas Zorrilla." In *Brujería, magia y otros prodigios en la literatura española del Siglo de Oro*, edited by María Luisa Lobato, Javier San José, and Germán Vega, 305–31. Alicante: Biblioteca Virtual Miguel de Cervantes, 2016.

Jütte, Robert. "Introduction." In *Historical Aspects of Unconventional Medicine: Approaches, Concepts, Case Studies*, edited by Robert Jütte, Motzi Eklöf, and Marie C. Nelson, 1–10. Sheffield: EAHM and Health Publications, 2001.

Kagan, Richard. *Lawsuits and Litigants in Castile, 1500–1700*. Chapel Hill: University of North Carolina Press, 1981.

————. *Students and Society in Early Modern Spain*. Baltimore MD: Johns Hopkins University Press, 1974.

Kallendorf, Hilaire. *Exorcism and Its Texts: Subjectivity in Early Modern Literature of England and Spain*. Toronto: University of Toronto Press, 2003.

————. *La rétorica del exorcismo. Ensayos sobre religión y literatura*. Madrid: Vervuert-Iberoamericana, 2016.

Kamen, Henry. "Testing the Limits of Braudel's Mediterranean." In *Early Modern History and the Social Sciences*, edited by John A. Marino, 205–22. Kirksville MO: Truman State University Press, 2002.

Kristić, Tijana. "Moriscos in Ottoman Galata, 1609–1620s." In *The Expulsion of the Moriscos from Spain: A Mediterranean Diaspora*, edited by Mercedes García-Arenal and Gerard Wiegers, 169–85. Leiden: Brill, 2014.

Labarta, Ana. "La mujer morisca: sus actividades." In *La mujer en al-andalus: Reflejos históricos de su actividad y categorías sociales*, edited by María J. Viguera, 219–31. Madrid: Ediciones de la Universidad Autónoma, 1989.

La Granja, Agustín de. "Comedias del Siglo de Oro censuradas por la Inquisición (Con noticia de un texto mal atribuido a Rojas Zorrilla)." In *El Siglo de Oro en escena: Homenaje a Marc Vitse*, edited by Odette Gorsse and Frédéric Serralta, 435–48. Toulouse: Presses Universitaires du Mirail, 2006.

Lapeyre, Henry. *Geografía de la España morisca*. Valencia: Universitat de València, 2009.

Lea, Henry Charles. *A History of the Inquisition of Spain*, 4 vols. New York: Macmillan, 1906.

————. *The Moriscos of Spain: Their Conversion and Expulsion*, 2 vols. Philadelphia: Lea Brothers, 1901.

Lehfeldt, Elizabeth. *Religious Women in Golden Age Spain: The Permeable Cloister*. Aldershot: Ashgate, 2005.

Llorente, Juan Antonio. *The History of the Inquisition in Spain*. Philadelphia: James M. Campbell, 1843.

Llot de Ribera, Miquel. *Verdadera relacion de la vitoria y libertad que alcançaron quatrocientos Christianos captivos de Hazan Baxa*. Perpignan, 1590.

Lobo Cabrera, Manuel. *Los libertos en la sociedad canaria del siglo XVI*. Madrid: CSIC, 1983.

Longás, Pedro. *La vida religiosa de los moriscos*. Madrid: Imprenta Ibérica, 1915.

López Terrada, María Luz. "Medical Pluralism in the Iberian Kingdoms: The Control of Extra-Academic Practitioners in Valencia." *Medical History Supplement* 29 (2009): 9–13.

Ly, Nadine. "Literalidad cervantina: encantadores y encantamientos en el *Quijote*." In *Actas del X Congreso de la Asociación Internacional de Hispanistas: Barcelona, 21–26 de agosto de 1989*, edited by Antonio Vilanova, 641–52. Barelona: Promociones y Publicaciones Universitarias, 1992.

Lynch, John. *Spain under the Habsburgs*, 2nd ed., 2 vols. New York: New York University Press, 1984.

Machielsen, Jan. *Martin Delrio: Scholarship and Demonology in the Counter Reformation*. Oxford: Oxford University Press, 2015.

MacKay, Ruth. *"Lazy, Improvident People": Myth and Reality in the Writing of Spanish History*. Ithaca NY: Cornell University Press, 2006.

Magnier, Grace. *Pedro de Valencia and the Catholic Apologists of the Expulsion of the Moriscos: Visions of Christianity and Kingship*. Leiden: Brill, 2010.

Magnier Heney, Grace. "Román Ramírez, Villain or Victim." *Mèlanges Louis Cardaillac* 1 (1995): 449–55.

Mami, Ridha. *El poeta morisco. De Rojas Zorrilla al autor secreto de una comedia sobre Mahoma*. Madrid: Pigmalión, 2010.

———. "Otra leyenda Morisca." In *Romania Arabica: Festschrift für Reinhold Knotzi zum 70*, edited by Jens Lüdtke, 387–403. Tübingen: Gunter Narr Verlag, 1996.

Márquez Villanueva, Francisco. *Moros, moriscos y turcos de Cervantes. Ensayos críticos*. Barcelona: Bellaterra, 2010.

Martínez Blasco, Ángel. *Quien mal anda en mal acaba*. Kassel: Reichenberger, 1993.

Martínez Frías, J. M. "Una iglesia columnaria en la provincial de Soria: la parroquial de Deza." *Celtiberia* 52 (1976): 195–206.

Martínez Hernández, Santiago. "Don Gómez Dávila y Toledo, II Marqués de Velada, y la corte en los reinados de Felipe II y Felipe III (1553–1616)." PhD diss., Universidad Complutense de Madrid, 2002.

———. *El Marqués de Velada y la Corte en los Reinados de Felipe II y Felipe III: Nobleza Cortesana y Cultura Política en la España del Siglo de Oro*. Salamanca: Junta de Castilla y León, 2004.

———. "La hacienda del Marqués de Velada. Perfiles de una economía cortesana, 1561–1616." *Cuadernos de Historia Moderna* 28 (2003): 35–71.

Martínez Ruiz, Juan. *Inventario de bienes moriscos del reino de Granada (Siglo XVI)*. Madrid: CSIC, 1972.

Maxwell-Stuart, P. G. *Martín del Rio: Investigations into Magic*. Manchester: Manchester University Press, 2009.

McCrory, Donald. *No Ordinary Man: The Life and Times of Miguel de Cervantes*. New York: Dover, 2002.

Menéndez Pelayo, Marcelino. *Historia de los heterodoxos españoles*, 2 vols. Madrid: Librería Católica de San José, 1880.

Mexía, Pedro. *Historia imperial y cesárea*. Seville, 1545.

Minguela y Arnedo, Toribio. *Historia de la diócesis de Sigüenza y de sus obispos*, 3 vols. Madrid: Tip. de la Revista de Archivos, Bibliotecas y Museos, 1910.

Mira Caballos, Esteban. "Unos se quedaron y otros volvieron: moriscos en la Extremadura del siglo XVII." In *XXIX Coloquios Históricos de Extremadura dedica-*

dos al arte románico en Extremadura: Trujillo del 20 al 26 de septiembre de 2010, 459–88. Trujillo: Asociación Cultural Coloquios Históricos de Extremadura, 2011.

Mira de Amescua, Antonio. *Vida y muerte del falso profeta Mahoma*. Valencia, 1642.

Molénat, Jean-Pierre. "Le problème de la permanence des musulmans dans les territoires conquis par les chrétiens, du point de vue de la loi islamique." *Arabica* 48 (2001): 392–400.

Monter, E. William. *Frontiers of Heresy: The Spanish Inquisition from the Basque Lands to Sicily*. Cambridge: Cambridge University Press, 1990.

Muchnik, Natalia. "Judeoconversos and Moriscos in the Diaspora." In *The Expulsion of the Moriscos from Spain: A Mediterranean Diaspora*, edited by Mercedes García-Arenal and Gerard Wiegers, 413–39. Leiden: Brill, 2014.

Navarro, Francisco. *Discvrso sobre la conivncion maxima*. Valencia, 1604.

Núñez de Muley, Francisco. *A Memorandum for the President of the Royal Audiencia and Chancery Court of the City and Kingdom of Granada*, edited and translated by Vincent Barletta. Chicago: University of Chicago Press, 2007.

O'Banion, Patrick J. "'A priest who appears good': Manuals of Confession and the Construction of Clerical Identity in Early Modern Spain." *Dutch Review of Church History* 85 (2005): 333–48.

———. "The Prisoners' Dilemma: Strategies and Ruses in the Inquisitorial Jails of Early Modern Cuenca." In *Playthings in Early Modernity: Party Games, Word Games, Mind Games*, edited by Allison Levy, 277–89. Kalamazoo MI: Medieval Institute Publications, 2017.

———. "Román's Garden: Places, Spaces, and Religious Practice among the Moriscos of Deza." In *Conversos and Moriscos in Late Medieval Spain and Beyond*, edited by Kevin Ingram. Leiden: Brill, forthcoming.

———. *The Sacrament of Penance and Religious Life in Golden Age Spain*. University Park: Pennsylvania State University Press, 2012.

———. "'They will know our hearts': Practicing the Art of Dissimulation on the Islamic Periphery." *Journal of Early Modern History* 20 (2016): 193–217.

———. *This Happened in My Presence: Moriscos, Old Christians, and the Spanish Inquisition in the Town of Deza, 1569–1611*. Toronto: University of Toronto Press, 2017.

Ong, Walter, J. *Orality and Literacy: The Technologizing of the Word*, 2nd ed. London: Routledge, 2002.

Percas de Ponseti, Helena. "Authorial Strings: A Recurrent Metaphor in Don Quijote." *Cervantes* 1 (1981): 51–62.

Perceval, José María. *Todos son uno. Arquetipo, xenophobia y racismo. La imagen del morisco en la Monarquía Española durante los siglos XVI y XVII*. Almería: Instituto de Estudios Almerienses, 1997.

Perry, Mary Elizabeth. *Gender and Disorder in Early Modern Seville*. Princeton NJ: Princeton University Press, 1990.

————. *The Handless Maiden: Moriscos and the Politics of Religion in Early Modern Spain*. Princeton NJ: Princeton University Press. 2005.

Philips, Carla Rahn. "The Moriscos of La Mancha, 1570–1614." *The Journal of Modern History* 50 (1978): 1067–95.

Poska, Allyson. *Women and Authority in Early Modern Spain: The Peasants of Galicia*. Oxford: Oxford University Press, 2005.

Rawlings, Helen. "Agustín Salucio's Rehabilitation of the *converso* and the Revisionist Debate over Racial and Religious Discrimination in Early Seventeenth-Century Spain." *Bulletin of Spanish Studies* 94 (2017): 1650–67.

Rippon, Andrew. "The Muslim Samson: Medieval, Modern and Scholarly Interpretations." *Bulletin of the School of Oriental and African Studies* 71.2 (2008): 239–53.

Rojas Zorilla, Francisco de. *El profeta falso Mahoma*. Madrid, 1640.

Romero Medina, Raúl. "Don Juan de la Cerda (c. 1515–1575), IV duque de Medinaceli. El hombre, el político y el mecenas en la Corte del Rey Prudente." *Tiempos Modernos* 34 (2017): 350–71.

Rosa-Rodrigues, Maria del Mar. "Simulation and Dissimulation: Religious Hybridity in a Morisco Fatwa." *Medieval Encounters* 16 (2010): 143–80.

Roza Candás, Pablo. "Alkitāb de preiques i exemplo i dotrinas." In *Memoria de los Moriscos: Escritos y relatos de una diáspora cultural*, edited by Alfredo Mateos Paramio, 196–98. Madrid: Sociedad Estatal de Conmemoraciones Culturales, 2010.

Ruiz, Teofilo F. *A King Travels: Festive Traditions in Late Medieval and Early Modern Spain*. Princeton NJ: Princeton University Press, 2012.

Sánchez León, Pablo. "Town and country in Castile, 1400–1650." In *Town and Country in Europe, 1300–1800*, edited by S. R. Epstein, 272–91. Cambridge: Cambridge University Press, 2001.

Sicroff, Albert A. *Los estatutos de limpieza de sangre. Controversias entre los siglos XV y XVII*. Madrid: Taurus, 1985.

Sierra, Julio. *Procesos en la Inquisición de Toledo (1575–1610): Manuscrito de Halle*. Madrid: Editorial Trotta, 2005.

Soubeyroux, Jacques. "L'alphabétisation dans l'Espagne moderne: bilan et perspectives de recherche." *Bulletin Hispanique* 100 (1998): 231–54.

Stewart, Devin J. "Dissimulation." In *The Princeton Encyclopedia of Islamic Thought*, edited by Gerhard Böwering, 135. Princeton NJ: Princeton University Press, 2013.

————. "Dissimulation in Sunni Islam and Morisco *Taqiyya*." *Al-Qantara* 34 (2013): 439–90.

Suárez Ávila, Luis. "Comentario cordial al artículo 'Nuevas aportaciones al estudio de Santa María de España.'" *Revista de Historia de El Puerto* 7 (1991): 93–101.

Súarez de Figueroa, Cristóbal. *Plaza universal de todas ciencias y artes*. Madrid, 1615.

Surilla Fernández, Nuria. *Chariots of Ladies: Francesc Eiximenis and the Court Culture of Medieval and Early Modern Iberia*. Ithaca NY: Cornell University Press, 2015.

Talavera Cuesta, Santiago, and Francisco J. Moreno Díaz del Campo, eds. *Juan Ripol y la expulsión de los moriscos de España*. Zaragoza: Instituitición Fernando el Católico, 2008.

Tapia Sánchez, Serafín de. "Arrieros, mercaderes, mesoneros . . . La movilidad de los moriscos de Castilla la Vieja." In *Circulación mudéjares y moriscas: redes de contacto y representaciones*, edited by Alice Kadri, Yolanda Moreno, and Ana Echevarría, 129–66. Madrid: CSIC, 2018.

———. *La comunidad morisca de Ávila*. Salamanca: Gráficas Varona, 1990.

———. "Las redes comerciales de los moriscos de Castilla la Vieja: un vehículo para sus 'complicidades.'" *Studia Histórica. Historia Moderna* 11 (1993): 231–43.

Tausiet, María. *Urban Magic in Early Modern Spain: Abracadabra Omnipotens*, translated by Susannah Howe. Houndmills, Basingstoke UK: Palgrave Macmillan, 2014.

Terceira parte da chronica de Palmeirim de Inglaterra na qual se tratam as grandes cavallarias de seu filho o principe dom Duardos segundo. Lisbon, 1587.

Tottoli, Roberto. "Recontamiento de Yuçuf." In *Memoria de los Moriscos: Escritos y relatos de una diáspora cultural*, edited by Alfredo Mateos Paramio, 200–201. Madrid: Sociedad Estatal de Conmemoraciones Culturales, 2010.

Tueller, James. *Good and Faithful Christians: Moriscos and Catholicism in Early Modern Spain*. New Orleans LA: University Press of the South, 2002.

Varnuebo de Soria, Bernardino Bonifaz. *Relacion verdadera y general de todo lo sucedido en la Corte, desde que murio su Magestad, hasta diez y seys de mayo*. Seville, 1621.

Vassberg, David E. *Land and Society in Golden Age Castile*. Cambridge: Cambridge University Press, 1984.

———. "The Status of Widows in Sixteenth-Century Castile." In *Poor Women and Children in the European Past*, edited by John Henderson and Richard Wall. London: Routledge, 1994.

———. *The Village and the Outside World in Golden Age Castile: Mobility and Migration in Everyday Rural Life*. Cambridge: Cambridge University Press, 1996.

Vázquez, Francisco. *Libro segundo del emperador Palmerin en que se recuentan los grandes & hazañosos fechos de Primaleon & Polendus sus fijos*. Salamanca, 1512.

Villanueva Zubizarreta, Olatz. "The Moriscos in Tunisia." In *The Expulsion of the Moriscos from Spain: A Mediterranean Diaspora*, edited by Mercedes García-Arenal and Gerard Wiegers, 369–87. Leiden: Brill, 2014.

Villegas y Selvago, Alonso de. *Flos sanctorum. Primera parte*. Toledo, 1578.

Vincent, Bernard. "El Albaicín de Granada en el siglo XVI (1527–1587)." In *Andalucia en la edad moderna: economía y sociedad*, 123–62. Granada: Diputación Provincial, 1985.

———. "50,000 Moriscos almerienses." In *Almería entre culturas siglos XIII al XVI*, 489–516. Almería: Instituto de Estudios Almerienses, 1990.

————. "The Geography of the Morisco Expulsion: A Quantitative Study." In *The Expulsion of the Moriscos from Spain: A Mediterranean Diaspora*, edited by Mercedes García-Arenal and Gerard Wiegers, 17–36. Leiden: Brill, 2014.

————. *Historia de los Moriscos: vida y tragedia de una minoría*. Madrid: Alianza Editorial, 1985.

————. "Las mujeres moriscas." In *Historia de las mujeres en Occidente, Vol. 3: Del Renacimiento a la Edad Moderna*, edited by Natalie Zemon Davis and Arlette Farge, 585–96. Madrid: Taurus, 1992.

Watts, Henry Edward. *Miguel de Cervantes: His Life & Works*. London: Adam and Charles Black, 1895.

Weber, Alison. "Locating Holiness in Early Modern Spain: Convents, Caves, and Houses." In *Structures and Subjectivities: Attending to Early Modern Women*, edited by Adele Seeff and Joan E. Hartman, 50–74. Cranbury NJ: Rosemont, 2007.

Whicker, Jules. *The Plays of Juan Ruiz de Alarcón*. Woodbridge: Tamesis, 2003.

Wiegers, Gerard. "The Expulsion of 1609–1614 and the Polemical Writings of the Moriscos Living in the Diaspora." In *The Expulsion of the Moriscos from Spain: A Mediterranean Diaspora*, edited by Mercedes García-Arenal and Gerard Wiegers, 389–412. Leiden: Brill, 2014.

————. "Managing Disaster: Networks of Moriscos during the Process of the Expulsion from the Iberian Peninsula around 1600." *Journal of Medieval Religious Cultures* 36 (2010): 141–68.

Wiesner, Merry E. *Women and Gender in Early Modern Europe*, 2nd ed. Cambridge: Cambridge University Press, 2000.

Wilnet Gil, Monika. "Regimiento de las lunas." In *Memoria de los Moriscos: Escritos y relatos de una diáspora cultural*, edited by Alfredo Mateos Paramio, 156–59. Madrid: Sociedad Estatal de Conmemoraciones Culturales, 2010.

Ybáñez Worboys, Pilar. "Las escribanías públicas del número en Málaga durante la etapa Carolina." *Baetica* 24 (2006): 389–405.

Index

Page numbers in italics indicate illustrations.

ablutions. See *guadoc*

Alcaide, 25–26, 32, 70, 152, 179, 228–29

alcalde mayor. See chief magistrate

alcalde ordinario. See magistrate

alcohol, 30, 41–42, 79, 89, 111, 202, 225, 261n14, 325n88

alfaquí, 14, 40, 49, 50, 53, 54, 66, 90, 101–2, 106

Algiers, 98–99, 244, 253

alguacil mayor, 303n74, 312n6, 315n44

Aljamiado, 50, 52, 54–56, 58, 61, 66, 94, 170, 272n67

Almanzorre, Ana de, *51*, 53, 58, 272n70

Almanzorre, Bernardino, 14, 40, 49–54, *51*, 58, 60–61, 88–89, 94, 257, 269n43, 270n44, 271n65, 272n66, 272n70, 297n68

Almanzorre, María de, 47, *51*, 53, 272n68, 272n70

Almoravi, Ana, 27, 46, *51*, 58, 60–61, 170, 257; accusations made by, 48, 56, 58, 168, 170–71; inquisitorial trial of, 48–49, 66, 170; as Islamic instructor, 58, 114

Almotazán, María de, 229, 328n31

almsgiving, 42, 48, 54, 65–66, 77–78, 98, 240

Altopica, Juanes de, 34, 45, 167, 267n3

animal slaughter, 57, 101, 106, 290n47

annuity, 68–69, 199, 314n25

Arabic language, 22–23, 40, 50, 52, 54, 88–89, 94, 101, 106, 108–9, 112–15, 177, 201, 209, 211, 225, 271n61, 274n93

Aragon, 20, 31, 84, 91; Dezanos in, 22, 31, 40, 46–47, 49, 52, 65, 89, 168–71; Moriscos from, 13–15, 21–23, 27, 45–47, 82, 90–91, 93, 113, 123, 175, 203, 244, 249, 257, 292n59; as place of Islamic study, 40, 88, 123, 210. *See also* Spain

archives, 5, 7–9, 239, 258, 334n29

Arcos, Francisco de, 46, 53, 81–84, 114, 164, 197, 222, 292n68, 306nn9–10, 316n56

Arcos, Lope de, 93, 97, 196, 199, 201, 204–5, 214–15, 219, 222, 224–25, 228, 249, 292n68, 315n36, 316n56, 323n63

Arganda, Francisco de, 72, 81–85, 133, 167, 171–72, 178, 182–86, 247, 281n11, 311n84, 333n3

Argüello, Pedro de, 199–202, 208, 305n107, 313n16

Arias de Villacorta, Juan, 142, 149, 156, 162, 178, 305n110

Arride Lumán, Luis de, 90–92, 283n41, 289n25

Aunt Teresa, 48, 54, 58–59, 61, 79, 115, 176

authority: formal, 25–26, 32–36, 103, 137–38, 151–52, 189–91, 227–30; informal, 24, 54–55, 65, 67, 103, 105–7, 112, 115–16

auto de fé, 16, 186, 238–39, 247–48, 251–53, 256, 333n1

Ávila, Francisco de, 122, 142, 155–58, 300n12

ayuntamiento. See Deza

azala, 12, 40, 48–49, 52, 56, 66, 77, 88–89, 98, 103, 112–13, 170, 173–74, 211–12, 291n55, 291n57

azora, 50, 53, 66, 170–71, 174, 176–77, 310n61. *See also* Quran

baptism, 12, 22, 31, 40, 101, 106

Baptista, Francisca de, 56, 106, 108–9, 113

Baptista, Francisco de, 55, 67, 78, 273n86

Barnuevo, Pedro de, 10–11, 26, 132–35, 134, 137–38, 151–52, 158–59, 189–91, 277n35, 295n35, 300n108, 303n80, 305n107, 312n6

Barnuevo Miranda, Juan de, 179, 201–2, 204, 214, 222, 228–29, 315n38

bathing. See *guadoc*

beatas, 25, 36, 266n94

Beltrán de Ocáriz, Francisco. *See* Ocáriz, Gerónimo de

Benito, Miguel: as inquisitorial commissioner, 201–4, 213; relationship with Alexo Gorgoz, 72

Bishop of Sigüenza, 6, 35, 72–73, 85, 96–97, 173, 198

Bonifacio de Soria, Bernardino, 10–11, 124, 132–33, 134, 137, 152, 155–57, 166, 173–74, 184, 260nn27–28, 260n30

books, 94, 129–31, 146, 165–68, 231, 250–56, 297n61, 297nn68–70; *Antialcoran,* 50, 232, 234, 270n48, 328n27; of chivalry, 28, 94, 120, 129–31, 154, 161–64, 254, 298nn74–75, 306n3, 306n10, 328n28; Islamic, 12, 50, 52–53, 54–56, 58, 113, 168, 170–71, 232, 270nn51–53, 271n61, 274n92

bulls of crusade, 28, 94, 97, 184, 286n74

Burgueña, María la, 109, 115, 207, 318n1, 330n51

Burgueño, Gonzalo el, 48, 199, 202, 273n86, 323n63

burial customs, 82, 105, 108, 249–50, 280n4, 289n33

Cabrera, Pedro de, 30, 308n42

calendar, Church, 37, 71, 92, 95–96, 277n37

Cañamenero-Deza. *See* Deza, Juan de (el Cañamenero); Deza, Pedro de (el Cañamenero)

captivity. *See* slavery

Carcayona, 25, 104

Carnicera, María la, 46, 48, 106, 109–10, 114–15, 204, 273n86, 290n34, 293n73, 298n72, 324n80

castellan. See *alcaide*

Cebea, Francisco de, 75–76, 79, 90–92, 98–99, 115, 220, 234, 236, 286n78, 289n25, 289n28, 293n73, 330nn51–52

Cebea, Juan de, 96–97, 222, 240–41, 286n77, 330n51

Cebea, Luis de (el más mozo), 78, 90–91, 96–97, 222, 240, 286n77, 330n51

Cebea, Luis de (el menor), 86, 95–97, 164, 202, 208, 220, 232, 268n17, 273n84, 280n10

Cebea, Luis de (el viejo), 43–44, 48, 60, 63, *86*, 87, 93–97, 114, 208, 223, 320n28; as confrater, 267n102, 268n17; as council member, 71, 199, 202, 215

Cebea, María de (ca. 1545), *86*, 87, 106, 330n51

Cerda, Don Gastón de la, 164, *221*

Cerda, Juan Antonio de la, 218, *221*, 223, 227, 257

Cerda, Juan de la (ca. 1569–1607), 6, 129, 151, 161, 192–97, 201, 205, 214–20, *221*, 257

Cerda, Juan de la (ca. 1515–75), 63–64, 119, 126, 164, *221*, 296

Cerda, Juan Luis de la, 125–26, 137, 151, *221*, 230, 242, 257

Cervantes, Miguel de, 253–54, 335n32. See also *Don Quixote (Cervantes)*

Chancillería. See Royal Appellate Court

chief magistrate, 26, 29, 32, 70–71, 152, 189–90, 195, 277nn33–35, 305n107

Christianization, 12, 23, 28, 39–40, 248, 257

Cieli, Cecilia de, 237, 292n59

Cieli, Juan de, 46, 60, 263n40

Cieli, Lope de (el Bueno), 215, 223–24, 313n16, 323n57

Cieli, Luis de, 219

Cifuentes de Loarte, Pedro, 178–86, 247, 311n89

Cisneros, Pedro de, 73–74, 110, 203, 218, 222, 230, 232, 237

clothing, 22, 41, 47, 54, 78, 108, 115, 173, 244, 279n65, 289n29, 293n70. See *sanbenito*

commissioner (inquisitorial), 29, 42, 45, 154–59, 178, 201–4, 213, 224, 226, 267n3, 280n10, 304n101, 324n80

commutation of sentence, 60, 238, 240, 331n69

confession (sacramental), 7, 36, 42, 43–44, 64, 72, 83–84, 167, 172–73, 184, 204, 212, 275n7, 280n10

confraternities, 26, 36–37, 67, 69, 71, 191, 200

consejo. See Deza

Constantinople, 99, 164, 174, 214, 308n42, 309n46

Contreras, Juan de, 45, 55, 57–58, 60–61, 164, 269n25, 269n29, 274n92

convertido. See Judeoconversos; Moriscos

Corazón, Juan, 27, 68, 74, 76, 223, 243, 246, 276n25, 330n51

crucifix, 35, 315n43. *See also* sacred images

cuatro lugares de la recompensa. See Four Places of the Recompense

cursing (witchcraft), 110, 146–47, 183. *See also* swearing

Dadson, Trevor, 3–5, 23, 40, 102, 217, 259n15, 260n19, 267n7, 284n57, 314n21

Dávila y de Toledo, Gómez, 220, 221, 223–24, 229, 257, 324n75, 326n7

Day of Judgment, 58–59, 78, 176, 295n29

death, 45, 60, 82, 108–9, 159, 191, 249–50, 277n38. *See also* burial customs

Delrio, Martín, 250–52

Deza: citizenship in, 24, 27, 30, 33, 45; clergy, 21, 31, 32, 35–36, 84, 92, 197, 212–13, 261n11, 266n93; council, 32–35, 67, 70–71, 87, 133–37, 151, 189–90, 192–93, 195, 199–203, 205; as dry port, 21, 27, 29, 69–70, 127–28; economy of, 27–28, 69, 193, 243, 263n44, 263n47; finances, 68, 136–37, 193, 195, 266n88, 300n111, 314n25, 314n28; flight from, 214, 219, 222, 226, 322n55, 323n63; geography of,

Deza (*cont.*)

19–20, 23, 32; *hidalgos*, 21–22, 25–26, 31, 32, 34, 43, 192–93; inquisition interest in, 6, 7, 14, 16, 38, 60–61, 84, 204, 229, 267n3, 274n102; Islamic revival, 49, 56, 58, 61, 116–17; Judeoconversos, 8, 28, 31, 60, 261n11; lawsuit between neighborhoods in, 199, 203, 205, 228, 316nn55–56, 316n63, 317n79; Morisco expulsion from, 5–7, 17, 79, 225, 243–46, 332n85, 333n101; noncitizens, 21, 27; Old Christians, 16, 30, 34; parish church, 35, 67–69, 71–72, 135, 191; Philip III's visit to, 186, 249; physical environment, *xiv*, 19, 26–28, 32, 33, 35–37, 40, 69, 197, 243, 265n75; political structure, 26, 29, 32–35, 70–71, 137–38, 151–52, 189–93, 195, 199–202, 203, 205, 227–38, 266nn82–83; population of, 21–22, 25, 46, 65, 69, 193, 243, 261n11; relationship between Old and New Christians in, 5–6, 14–17, 30, 39–41, 44, 58–59, 70–72, 82, 95, 194–203, 205, 207–8, 229, 258; relationship with dukes of Medinaceli, 16, 25, 34–35, 63–64, 70–71, 96, 136–38, 151–53, 189–90, 192–97, 205, 217–18; social structure of, 24–27, 192; women, 24–26, 37, 265n80

Deza, Inés de. *See* Montera, Cecilia la

Deza, Juan de (el Cañamenero), 55, 57–59, 61, *121*

Deza, Lope de. *See* Sol, Lope del

Deza, Miguel de (blacksmith), 87, 142, 300n11, 301n16

Deza, Miguel de (ca. 1578), 220–21, 285n58, 323nn63–64

Deza, Pedro de (el Cañamenero), 55–57, 60–61, 66, 113, *121*, 170–72, 257

diabolism, 6, 15–17, 109–11, 124–25, 145–49, 154, 177–80, 183–86, 196, 231, 237, 248, 250–55, 295n35, 301n26, 305n110, 327n20. *See also* Liarde; Ramírez, Román (el menor)

dispensation, 87, 92, 214

Disquisitionum magicarum. See Delrio, Martín

divination, 109, 111, 124–25, 249

Don Quixote (Cervantes), 3, 232, 243, 254–56, 260n22, 334n28, 335n38, 336n41. *See also* Cervantes, Miguel de

dry port, 21, 27, 127–29

Duke's house and garden, 69, 93–94, 98, 103, 125–26, 149, 159, 162, 166–67, 171, 173–76, 196, 205, 228–30, 234, 237, 308n43, 309n51, 326nn13–14

edicts of expulsion, 5, 16, 226, 249, 256

education, 28, 45–46, 50, 94, 165, 191, 285n58; catechesis, 102, 211; of girls, 191, 210–11, 293n69, 319n18; Islamic, 48–49, 52–53, 54, 55, 66, 93–94, 98, 111–12, 170–71, 175, 237, 292n59

El Puerto de Santa María, 153, 241–42

Eucharist, 42, 72–73, 85, 96–97, 173, 233

exorcism. *See* possession

factionalism, 15–16, 58, 94–98, 136–38, 194–202, 204–5, 227–30, 257–58, 260n27

fadas, 101–2, 106–7, 174, 209, 288nn20–21, 289n24, 290n34

Fadrique, Diego de (el mozo), *86*, 93, 96, 107, 115–16, 207–8, 210, 213–14, 224, 320n28, 323n66

familiar (inquisitorial), 26, 73, 158, 179, 203, 222, 232

familiar spirit. *See* diabolism; Liarde; Ramírez, Román (el menor) fasting. *See* foodways; Ramadan

fatwa, 77–78

Fernández Abarca, Francisco, 240, 242, 313n16

Fernández Abarca, Francisco Gonzalo, 305n107, 315n36

Fernández Abarca, Gonzalo, 70, 277n35

feuding, 94–96, 132–33, 151, 196–98, 202, 207, 220, 228–29, 232, 234, 257–58, 323n66

Flamenca, María la, 112–14, 291nn53–54, 292n59

Florisdoro de Grecía, 161–64, 167, 255, 305n2

foodways: as breaking of Lenten fast, 201, 293n4; Friday fasts related to, 111; Islamic dietary practices in, 41, 45, 73, 78, 83, 88–89, 111, 216, 225, 290n47, 325n89; for Muslim holy days, 31, 50, 54, 74, 113, 291n58. *See also* animal slaughter; Ramadan

fornication, 25, 48, 87, 281n21, 326n9

Four Places of the Recompense, 29, 70, 161, 190, 230

Fradique, Juan de. *See* San Juan, Juan de

France, 99, 214, 244–45, 286n83

galleys, 14, 17, 60, 96, 230, 237–38, 240–41, 246, 255, 331n69

García Serrano, Miguel, 16, 190–94, 196–201, 205, 211–12, 228, 312n6, 312nn9–10, 313n11, 313nn14–15, 316n60

Gil, Mari, 41–42, 44

Gómez de la Madriz, Diego, 63–65,171, 257, 275n1, 275n14, 280n8

Gómez de Sandoval y Rojas, Francisco, 5, 186, 220, 223, 247, 249, 251–52, 323n59

González de Rueda, Francisco, 154–58, 304n101, 305n107

González Palencia, Ángel, 298n75, 334n29

Gorgoz, Alexo, 14, 63–69, 273n86, 275n14, 276n25, 277n38, 278n58; as councilmember, 67, 71, 314n31; religious identity of, 72–77, 79, 81, 85, 88–89, 98. *See also obra pía*

Gorgoz, Gerónimo, 55, 65–67, 69, 73–76, 78, 81, 275n14; as councilmember, 67, 71. *See also obra pía*

Granada: Kingdom of, 2, 20; Moriscos from, 2, 6, 23, 59, 99, 226, 244–45; Resettlement of Moriscos from, 4, 6, 13, 23. *See also* Second Revolt of the Alpujarras

guadoc, 48, 52, 56, 77–78, 88–89, 91–92, 98, 108, 112, 119, 169, 173

Guerrera, Ana, 16, *86*, 107–8, 207–18; denunciation of, 75, 212, 320n24; family life, 209; inquisitorial custody of, 214, 217, 220, 224–25, 246, 322n48; knowledge of Islam, 114, 209, 257, 320n20; marriage, 93, 96, 107–8, 207–9, 213, 318n1, 318n4, 318n6

Guerrero, Antón, 76, 85, *86*, 89–90, 92, 97, 116, 204, 209, 215, 219, 235–36, 284n46, 321n46

Guerrero, Juan, 75–76, 79, *86*, 89–90, 96–98, 107–8, 112, 115–16, 204, 207–9, 214–19, 225, 234–37, 244, 274n93, 290n34

Guerrero, Lope (el menor), *86*, 194–95, 199, 201, 204, 216, 281n13, 281n23, 321n46, 330n51

Guerrero, Lope (el viejo), 15, 52–53, 59, 71, 76, 83, 85–88, *86*, 89, 92–97, 105, 107–8, 164, 174–76, 204, 214–16, 219, 271n58, 280n7, 281n13, 282n26, 282n29, 309n54, 316n55, 330nn51–52; as officiant, 92–94, 96

Guerrero, Miguel, *86*, 215–16, 217–19, 222, 323n63

Harvey, L. P., 11, 130, 254, 307n23, 308n40
health: mental, 42–44, 125, 141–50; physical, 75–77, 139–43, 179–80, 185, 230
Hernández, Petronila, 141–43, 146, 148, 309n48
Holy Office of the Inquisition. *See* Inquisition
Hortubia, Ana de, 68, 74–76, *86*, 209, 219, 278n52, 322n56, 330n51, 330n60
Hortubia, Cándida de, *86*, 209, 212, 219
Hortubia, Catalina de, *86*, 209, 214, 219, 266n93
Hortubia, Francisca de, *86*, 112, 207, 209–10, 214, 220, 322n56, 330n51
Hortubia, Íñigo de, ix, 273n88, 306n7
Hortubia, Juan de, 219, 234, 236–37, 240–42, 330n51
Hortubia, Luis de (b. 1569), 218, 314n31, 327n16
Hortubia, Luis de (el Jarquino), 99, 105, 205, 215, 228, 234, 240–41, 283n39, 288n23, 321n46, 323n63, 331n66
Hortubia, María de (ca. 1526–92), 41–45, *86*, 268n19
Huerta, Francisco and Gabriel de la, 113, 210, 319n15
humilladero. *See* shrine
hunting. *See* animal slaughter

images, sacred, 43, 90
Inquisition: bureaucracy, 7, 73–74, 152, 157–59, 177–79, 241–43; Cuenca tribunal, 41, 60, 72, 81–82, 97–98, 158–59, 177–79, 203–4, 214, 225, 234–41, 274n102, 331n66, 332n74; Edict of Faith, 82, 85, 280n2; Edict of Grace,

7, 14, 61, 63–65, 71, 83, 103, 214–15, 219, 222–24, 228, 257, 280n8; examination of reconciled Moriscos, 83–84, 238, 241, 280n10; Judeo-converso focus, 31, 247–48, 261n11; jurisdiction, 82, 84, 157–59, 179, 204, 310n65; Morisco focus, 6, 11, 31, 38, 60, 82, 158, 204, 213, 215, 226, 247–48; sources, ix, 7–9; *Suprema*, 7, 17, 64, 238, 240, 242–43, 247, 268n24, 331n66, 332n74; use of torture, 38, 43, 49, 66, 74, 76, 213, 230, 237, 281n20, 293n73; visitations in Deza, 6, 8, 14, 41, 57, 60–61, 65, 72, 81, 133, 257, 271n60. *See also* auto de fé
Isabella I, 20, 129
Islam, 23, 31, 47, 48, 53–54, 57, 59, 93–94, 98, 117, 233, 250; Old Christian fears about, 6, 22, 39, 45, 58–60, 174–75, 185–86, 248–49. See also *alfaquí*; *azala*; foodways; *guadoc*; Moriscos; Ramadan
Istanbul. *See* Constantinople

jails: civil, 97, 135, 151, 172, 222, 243, 253; inquisitorial, 41, 60, 74, 158–59, 179, 213–14, 230, 235–37; royal, 238–42, 330n51, 331n66
Jarquina, María la, 15, 28, 87, 101–2, 104–5, 209–10, 240, 288nn13–14; as officiant, 96, 105, 107–8, 209, 289n24, 290n34; as widow, 105, 113
Judeoconversos, 8, 21–22, 26, 261n11. *See also* Deza; Jews
juez de comisión. *See* commissioner (inquisitorial)

León, Gabriel de, 115–16, 225, 235–36, 283n42, 329n42
Leonis, Gerónimo de, 93, 106, 288n20, 288n23

Lepanto, Battle of, 5, 60–61, 292n68
Lerma, Duke of. *See* Gómez de Sandoval y Rojas, Francisco
Liarde, 124–25, 183–84, 255–56, 311n89, 327n20, 335n40
limpieza de sangre. See purity of blood
Liñán, Gerónimo de, 68, 215, 315n43, 317n82, 323n63
Liñán, Luis de (ca. 1547), 69, 214
Liñán, Luis de (el viejo), 25, 45, 56–57, 60, 268–69n24, 269n25, 276n17
Liñán pottery works, 27, 57, 67–68, 84, 103, 196, 276n17, 315n43
local history, 1–2, 4, 6–7, 11, 17, 165, 256–58, 259n15
lo dicho dicho, 234–35, 237
López de Rebolledo, Francisco, 70, 189, 277n33
Luna, Juan de, 120–25, *121*, 183, 295n22
Luna, María de, 85, 110, 114, 120–23, *121*, 164–65, 295n35
Luna, Miguel de, 3, 335n38

Maghreb. *See* North Africa
magic, 9–11, 28, 80, 109–11, 231, 237, 248, 250–54, 260n22, 303n69. *See also* cursing (witchcraft); divination; witches
magistrate, 34, 67, 70–71, 97, 189–90, 195. *See* chief magistrate
Mancebo, Juan, 95–98, 202, 207, 222, 232, 241–43, 285n63, 286n72, 323n66
Mancebo de Arévalo, 3, 99
Margaret of Austria, 186, 240, 247–49
Marquis of Mantua, 129, 170
Marriage customs, 25, 30, 46, 72, 82, 87, 92, 104, 107–8, 141, 207–9, 261n15, 280n3, 287n12, 289n25
Martínez, Diego, 53, 78, 272n66
Martínez, Gil, 214, 216–17, 236, 322n48, 329n44

Martínez, Gonzalo, 126, 166
Martínez, Luis, 53, 60
Martínez, María, 92, 289n25
Martínez de la Castellana, Hernando, 90, 97, 204, 289n28
medicine, 28, 43, 47, 120, 122, 125–27, 141–44, 149–50, 180–81, 264n61, 305n110
Medina, Gabriel de, 73, 88–89, 103, 204, 214, 219, 235–36, 282n34, 283n42, 290n47, 291n57
Medinaceli, dukes of, 6, 15–16, 24–25, 32, 34–35, 63–64, 125–26, 136, 164, 189, 242, 306n3; Deza's lawsuit against, 136, 192, 194–95, 314n32, 315nn35–36
Medrano, Francisco de, 56, 204, 224
Medrano, Velasco de, 48, 56, 59, 170, 273nn85–86
Mendoza, Francisco de, 204, 223, 316n56, 323n63
Mendoza, Luis de, 53, 58, 60, 197
miracles, 35, 71, 169, 249, 302n51
Miranda, Ángela de, *121*, 123–24, 135, 142, 152, 167, 301nn15–16, 303n81, 309n50
Miranda, Francisco de (el menor), 93, *121*, 149, 175, 204, 215, 238, 263n40, 313n16
Miranda, Francisco de (el viejo), 56, 61, *121*, 123, 170, 263n40, 273n85, 274n90
mitad de los oficios, 34, 192
Mohammed, 175, 176–77, 250, 252–53, 260n22, 319n15
Molina, Gerónimo de (el mayor), 47–48, *51*, 53, 273n86
Molina, Gerónimo de (el menor), *51*, 79, 115, 226, 243, 257, 279n69
Molina, María de, 32, 45, 48, 60
Montera, Cecilia la, 76, *86*, 106–9, 112–14, 116, 209, 219, 225, 290n34, 322n56

Montero, Bartolomé, 224, 226, 324n80
Moraga, Íñigo de, 217, 222, 241–43, 321n46, 330nn51–52, 331n69
Moriscas, 15, 94, 101–6, 114–15, 209–11, 235, 257, 287n12, 290n47, 291n57; as healers, 109–10, 120; as Islamic authorities, 47–48, 110–17, 120, 209–10, 237, 292n59
Moriscos: of Aragon, 6, 13–15, 21–23, 27, 31, 45–49, 82, 113–73, 244, 249, 257, 292n59; assimilation of, 1–3, 5–6, 13, 23, 40, 72, 78–80, 81, 95, 101, 172, 226, 244, 257, 260n19; of Castile, 3–4, 7, 22–23, 244–45; conversion of, 22, 31, 40, 61, 72, 106; crypto-Islam, 6, 12–15, 31, 40, 63, 72–80, 85, 102, 172, 174, 185–86, 202–5, 209–10; dissimulation by, 12, 14, 65, 72–80, 85, 88–89, 99, 173–74, 212, 233, 241, 257; expulsion from Spain, 1–3, 17, 23, 187, 223–25, 229, 238, 243–46, 248–49, 256–58, 316n59; homogeneity of, 2–3, 11, 94, 257–58, 260n19; Inquisition and, 6, 11, 14, 26, 31, 63; letters from prison, 238–40; marriage customs, 30, 72, 87, 92, 107; Old Christian relations with, 5, 15, 22–23, 43, 70–72, 258, 265n69; Old Christian suspicions of, 6, 45, 58–60, 65, 70–72, 81, 109–11, 199–201, 203, 233, 237, 241–42, 312n11; population densities of, 22–23, 46, 261n13; population growth of, 4, 22, 46, 261, 287n33; threats against Old Christians by, 59, 83, 145, 198. *See also* animal slaughter; burial customs; foodways; galleys; Granada; *guadoc*; Islam; Ramadan
Muçali, 30, 173–76, 187, 308nn42–43
mudéjares 23, 31, 261n6, 267n9. *See also* Moriscos

muleteers, 4, 14, 21, 30–31, 47, 69–70, 89–92, 205, 225; caravan to Reus, 90–92, 283nn38–42, 284n46
Muslims. *See* Islam; Moriscos

naming ceremony. See *fadas*
Navarra, María, *51*, 61, 79, 226, 243, 257, 272n67
Navarro, Francisco, 42–44, 268n19, 313n16, 316n59
Navarro, Mateo, 197, 201, 202, 204
networks, 47, 89–90, 93, 98, 171–72, 176, 187, 238–39, 282n33, 283n38, 333n102; Morisco, 16, 116–17, 80, 205
New Christians. *See* Judeoconversos; Moriscos
Niño de Guevara, Fernando, 186, 247–48, 256, 333n1
North Africa, 20, 98–99, 214, 244–46
notary. *See* scribe

Obezar, Gerónimo de, 57, 60, 169, 307n28
Obezar, Lope de, 46, 49, 53, 57, 60, 204, 272n66, 273n81
obra pía, 69, 74–75, 79, 214, 276n25
Ocáriz, Gerónimo de, 151, 277n35
Ochoa, Juan de, 178–79, 183
Orozco, Diego de, 138, 153–57, 159–60
Ortega, Bartolomé de (el mayor), 141–50, 185, 300n11, 301n17
Ortega, Bartolomé de (el mozo), 141–50
Ortigosa, Juan de, 145–50, 178, 302n51, 311n84
Ottoman Empire, 59–61, 98–99, 144, 164, 173–74, 185–86, 244, 248–49, 335n40
Ozuel, Juan de, 71, 202, 261n11, 313n16, 315n36

Paciencia, Alonso de, 79, 88–89, 98
Páez, Antonio, 28, 133, 135, 169, 265n67,
   280n3, 299n93, 307n31
patronage, 6, 43, 125–26, 217, 224, 257
Peñafiel, Juan de, 102, 198, 313n16
penance, 60, 240, 281n11
penitential habit. See sanbenito
Pérez, Catalina, 47–48, 54, 114, 210
Pérez de Chinchón, Bernardo, 50, 232
Philip II, 15, 29, 64, 119, 128, 231, 248,
   301n32
Philip III, 1–2, 5, 185–87, 225, 238, 240,
   247–49; and Dezanos, 185–86,
   238, 240, 247; and expulsion of
   Moriscos,1–2, 5, 187, 225, 249
pious work. See obra pía
Port of Santa María. See El Puerto de
   Santa María
possession: ceremony, 151, 227–29,
   325n1, 326n6; demonic, 142, 145–49,
   154, 180, 184, 251, 302n42, 302n50
pottery, 30–31, 67, 165n71, 243. See also
   Liñán pottery works
Póveda, Alonso de, 222, 240, 323n64
poverty, 27, 73, 239–40, 244, 252
procurador síndico, 191–92, 195–96, 205,
   228, 313n16. See also García Serrano,
   Miguel
Protestantism, 244, 246, 275n2
puerto seco. See dry port
purity of blood, 28, 247–49

Quien mal anda en mal acaba. See Ruiz
   de Alarcón, Juan
Quran, 52, 57, 106, 177, 232, 234, 270n49,
   319n15, 328n28. See also azora

Ramadan, 31, 49; breaking fast of, 78,
   91–92, 272n73; fasting during, 48–
   49, 53, 65–66, 75–76, 84, 89, 91, 98,
   111–13, 169, 173, 209; fixing date

of, 40, 50, 53, 56, 66, 106, 123, 173,
   288n23
Ramírez, Francisco, 94, 121, 172, 205,
   219, 234, 328n35
Ramírez, Miguel, 228–38, 241–43,
   328n50; as alfaquí, 17, 107, 176, 205,
   230, 234, 328n28; as alguacil mayor,
   196, 230, 232, 326n10; family life,
   121, 172, 229–30, 246, 326n10; interactions with Inquisition, 17, 230,
   232–35, 237–38, 326nn20–21; letter to Philip III, 238, 241, 330n52;
   medical examination of, 230, 238,
   241, 331n66; patronage of dukes of
   Medinaceli, 151–53, 161, 196, 205,
   215–16, 217–18, 230–31; release and
   expulsion from Spain, 17, 241–43
Ramírez, Pedro, 129, 153–54, 158, 161
Ramírez, Román (el mayor), 55, 63–64,
   105, 119–20, 121, 123, 293n4, 294n6,
   295n26
Ramírez, Román (el menor): accusation of diabolism and sorcery,
   6, 9–11, 15–16, 109–11, 124, 145,
   148, 154–57, 177–79, 183, 185, 196,
   248; accusation of Islamic activities,12–13, 109, 166, 168–71, 175, 183,
   185, 248, 251; accusations made by,
   48, 58, 171–72; as alfaquí, 16, 93–94,
   170–72, 174–76, 309n54; auto de fé,
   16, 186, 200–201, 247; confession
   for Edict of Grace, 58, 169, 171–72,
   182, 251; confession of Islamic practices, 12–13, 123, 168–72, 179–80, 182,
   308n38, 311n84; demonic familiar,
   10, 15–16, 124–25, 144–45, 148, 183–
   84, 251, 255–56; family life, 47, 101–2,
   107, 119–20, 121, 123–24, 152–53, 159,
   175, 293n1, 294n10, 296n41, 303n82,
   305n109; as guard at dry port, 127–
   28, 169; as healer, 10–11, 15–16, 122,

Ramírez, Román (el menor) (*cont.*)
125, 127, 139, 142–44, 149–50, 154, 159,
179–82, 251, 296n40, 297n53, 297n61,
305n110; health of, 16, 179–80, 182,
185, 310n70, 310n73, 310n75; letter
of apology to Arganda, 133, 167–68;
literacy of, 162, 164–68, 171, 176–
77, 181, 184, 297n61, 306n12, 307n18,
307nn22–24; memory of (faculty),
16–17, 120–22, 127–32, 154, 159, 165–
66, 181–82, 184, 251, 255–56, 294n15,
294n19, 298n81, 306n14, 311nn79–80,
311n91; memory of (posthumous),
187, 196, 200–201, 237, 247, 250–56,
305n113, 335n38, 336n42; patronage
of dukes of Medinaceli, 15, 64, 93,
125–26, 129, 136, 138, 151–53, 161, 196;
as politician, 15, 135–38, 151–52, 160,
175, 179, 200–201, 299n103; possession of duke's garden, 93, 125–26, 138,
159, 173–76, 179, 296n51, 300n114;
receiving Islamic instruction, 56, 12,
122–23, 168–71, 173–74; as storyteller,
13, 15–16, 127–32, 138–39, 153–54, 159,
169–70, 181–82, 251, 294nn15–16,
304n88, 311n82; in Tajahuerce, 142–
45, 154–55; violent behavior of, 10–
11, 15, 116, 132–35, 169, 281n11, 299n89
Ramírez de Arellano, don Gil, 153–54,
158, 161, 254, 304n88
receipts (confessional), 64, 83, 167, 172,
280n10
Reynoso, Alonso Jiménez de, 57, 60–61,
133, 257
Rio, Martín del. *See* Delrio, Martín
Roa, Alonso de, 128, 154–57
Romero, Mateo (el mayor), 27, 48–49,
51, 53, 59–61, 164, 171–72, 269n29,
271n65, 275n104
Romero, Mateo (el menor), 48–49, 51,
53, 58, 116, 128, 169, 274n104, 312n10

Romo, Francisco el (ca. 1533), 53, 57–58,
60, 96, 271n61, 285n63
Romo, Francisco el (b. 1564), 101, 107,
207, 234–35, 238–39, 241, 285n63,
288n23, 308n42, 313n16, 330n51,
331n66
Romo, Juan el. *See* Mancebo, Juan
Romo, Román el, 96–97, 207, 234, 238,
241–43, 273n88, 285n63, 285n69,
330n51, 331n66
Royal Appellate Court, 16, 25–26, 95,
129, 132, 153, 192, 194, 199, 201, 203,
228, 253–54, 317n79
Royal Council, 64, 222
Rueda, Pedro de, 142, 144–45, 148–50,
156–57, 302nn50–51
Ruiz, Juan, 201, 261n11, 266n94
Ruiz de Alarcón, Juan, 165, 251–52, 254,
334n27

sacred images. *See* images, sacred
saints, 35, 36–37, 90, 211, 277n37. *See also*
Virgin Mary
Salamanca, Gerónimo de, 127–28, 135
Salazar, Count of, 5, 226, 332n85
Saleros, Leonis de, 55, 57–59
Salucio, Agustín, 248, 334n4
sanbenito, 60, 238, 250, 266n82
San Juan, Juan de, 53, *86*
Santa Clara, Gonzalo de, 28, 46, 49–50,
94, 164, 269n29, 271n56
santa hermandad, 26, 29, 207
Sanz, Ana, 15, 127, 141–50, 156, 180–81,
301n32, 309n48
scribe, 29, 50, 97, 155–57, 196, 203–4,
208, 240, 264n61
Second Revolt of the Alpujarras, 2,
23, 59, 61, 83, 85, 282n29. *See also*
Granada
sentence commutation. *See* commutation of sentence

Sepúlveda, María de, 85, *86*, 114, 319n7
sexuality, and mistresses, 87, 281n21,
326n9; women's, 24, 141, 150. *See
also* fornication
shrine, 36–37, 90, 144–45, 147, 181
shrouds, 82, 108, 111, 114, 289n33
slavery, 20, 30, 163, 173, 240, 253
Sol, Lope del, ix, 57, 59, 79, 83–84, 133,
215, 268n23, 273n88
Spain: expulsion of Moriscos from,1–3,
17, 187, 223–25, 238, 243–46, 248–49,
256–58, 316n59; fears of Mediterranean Islam in, 60, 174, 185–86, 248–
49, 301n32
Spanish Inquisition. *See* Inquisition
spirit. *See* diabolism; Liarde; Ramírez,
Román (el menor)
Supreme and General Council of the
Inquisition. *See* Inquisition
surah. See *azora*
swearing, 96, 141. *See also* cursing
(witchcraft)

Tapia Sánchez, Serafín de, 4, 284n57,
287n12
taqiyya, 77–78, 99, 174, 176, 278n58,
279n65, 279n67
Teresa of Ágreda. *See* Aunt Teresa
theater, 29, 56, 164, 306n9; *farsas*, 29,
94, 164, 170
Toledo y Dávila, Antonia de, 218–20,
221, 223, 326n7
Torrellas, 46, 49–50, 269n25, 269n42,
270n45, 271n65
towns, legal status of, 70–71, 136–38, 151,
193–95, 227–30
treason, 60–61, 174, 203, 231, 248, 253,
301n32

treasure, 124–25, 231–32, 296n40,
326nn20–21
Turks, 30, 59, 61, 77, 173, 244, 308n43.
See also Ottoman Empire

Ucedo, Ana de, 101, *121*, 153
Ucedo, Juan de, 153, 304n88
Ucedo Salazar, Antonio de, 97, 205, 228

Velada, Marquis of. *See* Dávila y de
Toledo, Gómez
Villarrubia de los Ojos, 4–5, 7, 13, 23,
217, 256, 279n70, 284–85n57, 289n33,
321n39, 332n80
Villaverde, Gerónimo de, 46, 123,
295n32
Virgin Mary, 41, 43, 90, 211, 233, 244,
268n19. *See also* saints
Viscaina, Luisa la, 56, 106, 108, 273n79

warden. See *alcaide*
wealth, 65–67, 73–74, 79, 101, 231–32,
275n14, 320n28
witches, 80, 109–11, 148, 237. *See also*
cursing (witchcraft); divination;
magic
women, 15, 24–26, 37, 101–3, 262n21,
287n8. See also *beatas*; Moriscas

Young Man of Arévalo. *See* Mancebo
de Arévalo

Zamorano, Catalina, 103–4, 202, 209,
219, 235, 287n9
Zamorano, Diego, 116, 202, 257, 282n34,
283n39, 287n9
Zapata, Jusepe, 155–58

In the Early Modern Cultural Studies series:

Courage and Grief: Women and Sweden's Thirty Years' War
By Mary Elizabeth Ailes

Travel and Travail: Early Modern Women, English Drama, and the Wider World
Edited and with an introduction by Patricia Akhimie and Bernadette Andrea

At the First Table: Food and Social Identity in Early Modern Spain
By Jodi Campbell

Separation Scenes: Domestic Drama in Early Modern England
By Ann C. Christensen

Portrait of an Island: The Architecture and Material Culture of Gorée, Sénégal, 1758–1837
By Mark Hinchman

Deza and Its Moriscos: Religion and Community in Early Modern Spain
By Patrick J. O'Banion

Producing Early Modern London: A Comedy of Urban Space, 1598–1616
By Kelly J. Stage

Words Like Daggers: Violent Female Speech in Early Modern England
By Kirilka Stavreva

Sacred Seeds: New World Plants in Early Modern English Literature
By Edward McLean Test

My First Booke of My Life
By Alice Thornton
Edited and with an introduction by Raymond A. Anselment

Age in Love: Shakespeare at the Elizabethan Court
By Jacqueline Vanhoutte

The Other Exchange: Women, Servants, and the Urban Underclass in Early Modern English Literature
By Denys Van Renen

To order or obtain more information on these or other University of Nebraska Press titles, visit nebraskapress.unl.edu.

CPSIA information can be obtained
at www.ICGtesting.com
Printed in the USA
LVHW031948160720
660876LV00008B/110